About Island Press

Island Press is the only nonprofit organization in the United States whose principal purpose is the publication of books on environmental issues and natural resource management. We provide solutions-oriented information to professionals, public officials, business and community leaders, and concerned citizens who are shaping responses to environmental problems.

In 2005, Island Press celebrates its twenty-first anniversary as the leading provider of timely and practical books that take a multidisciplinary approach to critical environmental concerns. Our growing list of titles reflects our commitment to bringing the best of an expanding body of literature to the environmental community throughout North America and the world.

Support for Island Press is provided by the Agua Fund, The Geraldine R. Dodge Foundation, Doris Duke Charitable Foundation, Ford Foundation, The George Gund Foundation, The William and Flora Hewlett Foundation, Kendeda Sustainability Fund of the Tides Foundation, The Henry Luce Foundation, The John D. and Catherine T. MacArthur Foundation, The Andrew W. Mellon Foundation, The Curtis and Edith Munson Foundation, The New-Land Foundation, The New York Community Trust, Oak Foundation, The Overbrook Foundation, The David and Lucile Packard Foundation, The Winslow Foundation, and other generous donors.

The opinions expressed in this book are those of the author(s) and do not necessarily reflect the views of these foundations.

About Wildlife Conservation Society

Founded in 1895, the Wildlife Conservation Society saves wildlife and wildlands through careful science, international conservation, education, and the management of the world's largest system of urban wildlife parks, led by the flagship Bronx Zoo in New York City. WCS scientists work in over 50 countries around the world, gathering essential information on wildlife, training scientists and working with local communities and government agencies to design and implement conservation. These activities change attitudes toward nature and help people imagine wildlife and humans living in sustainable interaction on both a local and a global scale. WCS is committed to this work because we believe it essential to the integrity of life on Earth.

The opinions expressed in this book are those of the authors and do not necessarily reflect the views of the Wildlife Conservation Society.

2006

STATE OF THE WILD

A Global Portrait of Wildlife, Wildlands, and Oceans

Wildlife Conservation Society

State of the Wild: A Global Portrait of Wildlife, Wildlands, and Oceans
Sharon Guynup, editor; Jesse Chapman-Bruschini, senior editor; Ken Kostel,
associate editor; Sandra Alcosser, poetry editor; Michael Berens,
writer/researcher; Nicolas Ruggia, researcher

Editorial Board
George Amato; Debbie Behler; Kent Redford, chair; Stephen Sautner;
Bill Weber; Dan Wharton

State of the Wild 2006: A Global Portrait of Wildlife, Wildlands, and Oceans
With a special section on *Hunting and the Wildlife Trade*

2006

STATE OF THE WILD

A Global Portrait of Wildlife, Wildlands, and Oceans

Hunting and the Wildlife Trade

EDITED BY
Sharon Guynup

Wildlife Conservation Society

ISLANDPRESS

WASHINGTON • COVELO • LONDON

Island Press, 1718 Connecticut Ave. NW, Suite 300, Washington, DC 20009.

ISLAND PRESS is a trademark of The Center for Resource Economics.

Citation: Wildlife Conservation Society. 2005. *State of the Wild 2006: A Global Portrait of Wildlife, Wildlands, and Oceans.* Washington, D.C.: Island Press.

Grateful acknowledgment is expressed for permission to include
the following previously copyrighted material:

The Essential Rumi (New York: Harper, 1995), p. 36.

"Sanctuary" © Alison Hawthorne Deming, reprinted by permission
of Louisiana State University Press from *Monarchs: A Poem Sequence*
(Baton Rouge: Louisiana State University Press, 1997)

"Bucolics," by W.H. Auden, © Edward Mendelson, William Meredith,
and Monroe K. Spears, executors of the Estate of W.H. Auden, from *Collected Poems*
(New York: Vintage Books, 1991). Used by permission of Random House, Inc.

"The Peace of Wild Things" © 1985 Wendell Berry, from *Collected Poems 1957–1982*
(New York: North Point Press, 1985)

"Place" © W.S. Merwin from *The Rain in the Trees* (New York: Alfred A. Knopf, 1988), p. 64.

ISSN 1556-0619

ISBN (paper) 1-59726-001-0

ISBN (cloth) 1-59726-000-2

Design by John Costa and Maureen Gately

Printed on recycled, acid-free paper

Manufactured in the United States of America

10 9 8 7 6 5 4 3 2 1

Let the beauty we love be what we do.

JELALUDDIN RUMI
(AFGHANISTAN, 1207–1273)
TRANSLATED BY COLEMAN BARKS

Contents

BY THE NUMBERS
Hunted, Traded, and Eaten into Extinction

SHARON GUYNUP

Increase in number of animal species classified as threatened by the World Conservation Union (IUCN) since 1996: 2,061 (from 5,205 to 7,266)[1]

Number of quarter-pound hamburgers that would equal conservative estimates of Central Africa's yearly wild meat harvest: 9 billion[2]

Number of people whose protein needs 1 square mile (2.59 km^2) of tropical forest can sustainably support with wild meat: 2.5[3]

Number of people per square mile living in remaining forests: in Latin America, 17 (46 per km^2); Central Africa, 38 (99 per km^2); Southeast Asia, 190 (502 per km^2)[4]

Percentage of hunted species in Bolivia, Sulawesi, and Central African Republic for which current hunting is believed to be unsustainable: 50, 70, and 100, respectively[5]

Number of seahorses caught yearly for traditional Asian medicine: 18 to 21.6 million[6]

Number of humans who died of Ebola in the Republic of Congo in late 2002 and early 2003: about 100[7]

Number of gorillas that died of Ebola during the same period: about 600[8]

Total number of diseases that have jumped between wildlife, domestic animals, and humans: 868[9]

Number of animals imported into the United States in 2002: over 38,000 mammals, 365,000 birds, 2 million reptiles, 49 million amphibians, and 216 million fish[10]

Approximate amount spent on hunting and fishing licenses in the United States in 2003: $1.2 billion[11]

In the United States, percentage of red drum caught in the South Atlantic, bocaccio caught in the Pacific, and red snapper caught in the US Gulf of Mexico by recreational fishermen: 93, 87, and 59 percent, respectively[12]

Number of official hunting licenses sold in Tajikistan to shoot Marco Polo sheep each year: 40 to 50[13]

Average price of a hunting license to shoot one Marco Polo sheep: $25,000[14]

Average number of items advertised on eBay per week as elephant ivory from February to May 2004: 1,000[15]

Decline from 1979 to 1989 in numbers of African elephants that were killed largely for the then legal ivory trade: between 600,000 and 1.3 million[16]

Number of African and Asian elephants that are killed each year for their ivory: more than 4,000[17]

Number of turtles confiscated in December 2001 by Hong Kong customs officials from a single trade ship arriving from Macau: about 10,000[18]

Of the 11 turtle species onboard, percent protected under the Convention on International Trade in Endangered Species: 90[19]

Estimated value this turtle shipment would have fetched in live Chinese animal markets: $3.2 million[20]

Percentage of all turtle species traded in southern China that are listed as threatened by the IUCN: 79[21]

Estimated annual worth of criminal/illegal wildlife trade: about $6 billion[22]

Number of primates legally imported into the United States as pets or research animals between 1995 and 2002: 99,939[23]

Percentage of macaque monkeys—popular as exotic pets—infected with herpes B virus or simian B, a virus harmless to monkeys but often fatal to humans: 80 to 90[24]

Percentage of tropical birds and reptiles that die during transport for the exotic pet trade: up to 80[25]

Recorded tiger bone imports between 1970 and 1993 by East Asian countries from other parts of Asia: at least 10 tons[26]

Approximate number of animals 10 tons of tiger bone represents: between 500 and 1,000[27]

Estimated number of tigers left in the wild: under 5,000[28]

Estimated number of captive tigers living in the United States: 5,000 to 7,000[29]

FOREWORD
A Brief History of *State of the Wild*

KENT H. REDFORD

As a young child I used to play in the mass of bushes running rampant in the uninhabited estate across the street. Dark and mysterious, mined with spider webs large enough to ensnare a child, it was, I thought, a wild place. Since then, I have traveled widely and have found wild places in many parts of the globe. Just recently, the Wildlife Conservation Society received a land donation from Goldman Sachs—618,000 acres (250,000 hectares) in Tierra del Fuego, Chile. Standing on a frozen peat bog in this land, whipped by wind blowing straight off the Antarctic, I understood why this land was so forbidding to the Europeans that it was known as *Finis Terra,* the end of the world. I realized then that the wild comes in many shapes and sizes.

The existence of things and places "wild" has been under a sustained cultural critique from two fronts in recent years. First, a rising tide of postmodern scholars have argued that nature is a human construct and therefore the concepts of "natural" and "wild" are human conceits and do not exist outside the human mind. On the other hand, as a recent article entitled "End of the Wild"[1] has argued, human impacts are now so strong and so pervasive that the last trace of wild has been scourged from the earth.

Many people I know don't agree with either of these positions. We believe that the wild does exist and that it is threatened by the increasing hegemony of the human race. In fact, the mission of the Wildlife Conservation Society and other like-minded organizations and individuals is to conserve wildlife and wildlands in order to preserve the biological integrity of the natural world.

State of the Wild, a product of the Wildlife Conservation Society Institute, is dedicated to the conservation of the wild. Through this volume and its successors, we hope to inform and inspire others who dream of the wild and care about its future. Our hope is to fulfill a need for a science-based publication that focuses on achievable conservation of wildlife and wildlands.

More immediately, we have four main goals in publishing *State of the Wild:* (1)

to put out in the public forum insightful, timely analyses of the most pressing global conservation issues; (2) to present global news highlights on conservation and the wild world; (3) to promote innovative, science-based solutions to conservation problems; and (4) to influence global public policy. *State of the Wild* will also explore both the successes and the shortcomings of current conservation measures, providing a self-critical voice for—and from—the field.

In order to address a range of conservation concerns, our essays call on a wide range of experts and well-known environmental authors. *State of the Wild* brings critical issues into the public discussion—and provides a forum for dialogue, investigation, and debate of larger philosophical questions in conservation.

It is increasingly difficult to find places on this earth that are completely free from the human touch, but wild places do still exist. Whether an icy, windswept bog at the end of the world, a tangled rain forest filled with the cries of gibbons, or the silent world of the open ocean, nature's last domain deserves to be protected.

Toward that end, we hope that you find *State of the Wild* both inspiring and useful.

2006

STATE OF THE WILD

A Global Portrait of Wildlife, Wildlands, and Oceans

An Introduction: Wildlife, Wildlands, and Oceans

SHARON GUYNUP

Above: A grizzly bear feasts on salmon on Russia's Kamchatka peninsula.
(Credit: Ivan Seredkin)

Two tall grizzlies play in the shallow waters along the edge of Kurilskoye Lake, located at the southern end of Russia's remote Kamchatka Peninsula—one of the planet's last truly wild places. The bears paw at each other, nipping and lunging amidst small, wind-driven waves. Occasionally they pause to grab a sockeye or pink salmon from the splashing mass schooling around them: gorging on salmon helps them gain the 200-plus pounds (90 kg) they'll need to sustain them through the long Siberian winter. Even now, in mid-August, the nights grow cold.

Somewhere between 10,000 and 16,000 grizzlies populate this peninsula, sandwiched between the Sea of Okhotsk to the west and the Bering Sea and Pacific Ocean to the east. The undulating landscape is wrapped in head-high wildflowers and luxuriant green forests, overshadowed by 200 volcanoes, towering as high as 15,000 feet (4,570 m). The bears share the peninsula with wolves, arctic foxes, wolverines, sable, sea otters, six species of salmon, caribou, spiral-horned snow sheep, and more—species that are rare in other places. Half of the world's Steller's sea eagles—the largest of all eagles—winter on the lake. In summer, it becomes the largest spawning ground for sockeye salmon in the Asian part of the Pacific.

The abundant wildlife and dramatic volcanic landscape, dotted with geysers and steaming thermal springs, prompted the creation of a nearly 13,000-square-mile (34,000 km^2) World Heritage Site in 1996. There are no permanent settlements within the site, and just over 400,000 people populate the 140,000-square-mile (363,000 km^2) peninsula, mainly clustered within the only city, Petropavlovsk. Few roads crisscross the landscape: huge, ex-military helicopters are the main form of long-distance transportation.

But even here, in this pristine wilderness, bears are not safe from humans. Trophy hunters—mostly Americans—flock to Kamchatka, paying $10,000 to shoot one of these bears. About 500 are killed each year for sport—including females, despite regulations protecting them. But the biggest threat is poaching. Bear gall bladder is a prized ingredient in traditional Asian medicine, used to treat tumors, stomachache, heart conditions, and other ailments, with gallbladders fetching $100 to $200 on the black market. The sale of other parts is also lucrative. A good quality bear

skin sells for up to $1,000 locally, and claws, skulls, teeth, and paws are sold as souvenirs. Enforcement officials can do little to stop illegal hunting, as most takes place in inaccessible areas—and Kamchatka's hunting department has neither the funds nor the staff to police poaching or trade.

But there's good news here, too. According to Alexei Maslov, who heads the Kamchatka Research Institute's salmon station on Kurilskoye Lake, pink salmon numbers are in-

> Trophy hunters—mostly Americans—flock to Kamchatka, paying $10,000 to shoot one of these bears.

creasing slightly: local seas have grown warmer, which may aid the survival of young fish.

Salmon are one of few species benefiting from a warming planet. To the northeast of here, those same warmer temperatures are melting Arctic ice. Polar bears grow thinner, with less access to prey as their icy hunting grounds disappear.

Hunting. Poaching. Illegal wildlife trade. Climate change. These are four of the many complex ecological and conservation issues addressed in this first volume of *State of the Wild*. For our inaugural issue, we've chosen to explore hunting and wildlife trade in depth through a range of essays, tracing the history of hunting in North America; quantifying the toll of commercial fishing on seabirds, marine turtles, and other marine

species; exploring the global reach of the wildlife trade for traditional Asian medicine. We've also engaged in debate on acceptable parameters for subsistence and commercial hunting—and discussed the diseases that could come along with a bush-meat dinner.

We also examine other issues, from the impacts of recent policy changes on US public lands, and why one in eight of the world's birds are endangered, to the complexity of conserving colonial and wide-ranging species—and efforts to protect a revered and vilified carnivore, the jaguar, throughout its entire range, from Arizona to Argentina.

Our closing essay, "The Relative Wild," considers what, exactly, it means for a place to be "wild," where even in the most remote corners of the planet—places like Kamchatka—there is some human impact on nature.

Lastly, you will find a poem in each section of the volume. These writings were chosen by poet Sandra Alcosser, who as poet-in-residence at the Central Park Zoo, selected these and other poems to be permanently inscribed into animal exhibits. Dan Wharton (who heads the Central Park Zoo and is a contributor to this volume) generously arranged for their use here.

We hope that *State of the Wild* will both answer and raise questions, promote discussion, and, in some way, inspire greater concern for and better stewardship of our world's remaining wildlife, wildlands, and oceans.

From "**Sanctuary**"

In the heat of the afternoon
the monarchs come down from their sleep
to huddle on the edges of streams
and meadow pools, trembling to stay warm,
and they sip, then sit, then fly off
until the air is a blizzard of orange.
The pilgrims watch quietly, lines of
school children from Mexico City,
scientists from Texas, Florida, California,
old women in rebozos on the arms
of their adult sons, tourists with
cameras and binoculars. And together
they drink in the spectacle
with the great thirst they have brought
from their cities and towns, and it is
a kind of prayer, this meeting of our kind,
so uncertain how to be
the creature we are, and theirs,
so clear in their direction.

ALISON HAWTHORNE DEMING
(UNITED STATES, 1946)

PART I

STATE OF THE WILD

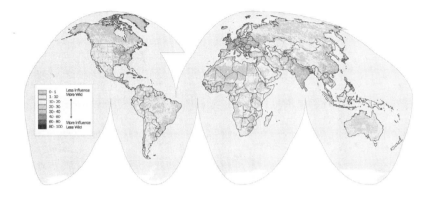

This section opens with an overview of the state of our natural world by one of the most respected conservationists of our day. George Schaller, who has spent a half-century studying mountain gorillas, giant pandas, and many other species in some of the world's last wild places, "swerves between hope and gloom" in his assessment. Landscape ecologist Eric Sanderson then quantifies the extent of human impact on the planet with his map of the "human footprint."

From this overarching perspective, we focus in on compelling facts, new legislation, and important advances in conservation methods that we've structured into short sections—sections that will repeat in each subsequent volume of *State of the Wild*. We hope that these short entries will inform and enrich the longer, more in-depth essays that come later in this book.

In "Discoveries," we describe species that are new to science. "New Conservation Methods and Technologies" catalogs some of the innovative tools being added to the conservation toolbox—unique methods, technological advances, and novel applications of existing technology that are giving researchers the ability to better track and identify animals. "Regulating the Wild" highlights recent regulations affecting the wild or impacting resource management in countries around the world. "The Rarest of the Rare" closes this section with stark examples of poor human stewardship, profiling some of the world's most endangered animals.

This section provides context for the rest of the volume, gives hope that advances are being made—and reminds us that our world is truly diminished by conservation actions not taken.

GOLD

"It is thou who,
truth to tell, art the creator,
preserver, and destroyer
of the world."

—*Tantra-tattva*

or *flowers*

ONE VIEW ON THE STATE OF THE WILD

GEORGE B. SCHALLER

When asked to write a few words abut the state of the wild, I felt rather intimidated by the request because environmental situations are so diverse, problems so immense, and solutions so complex and unpredictable. Potential topics affecting biodiversity are seemingly endless, from pesticides, deforestation, and energy conservation to the role of zoos and the dismal performance of the media in educating the public about the environment. Therefore, I will raise just a few important issues.

As was written in the Hindu *Tantra-tattva* in about 400 BC, though in a somewhat different context, "It is thou who, truth to tell, art the creator, preserver, and destroyer of the world." We all live under the same sun. It is everyone's task, each in his or her own way, to assume the role of preserver with clarity of purpose, passion, and perseverance.

After half a century of being involved in conservation, I swerve between hope and gloom. Mountain gorillas, giant pandas, and other icons of conservation that I have studied still endure, and areas I have helped to protect still persist in remote corners. Concern for the survival of species is now widespread, a love for nature encompassing everything from tigers to tiger beetles. Millions of dollars have been spent on saving the golden lion tamarin, black-footed ferret, California condor, Arabian oryx, and others in captivity and reintroducing them to the wild—even though such species now have at best a minor ecological function. This uniquely human gesture toward another form of life is based perhaps on a tinge of guilt or a vision of a better past. With species extinction estimated to be 100 to 1,000 times greater than predicted from evolutionary history, our efforts on behalf of individual species, though essential, sometimes seem little more than ambulance chasing or putting out brush fires. On a positive note, new species are described annually, among them the saola, *Pseudoryx*, a primitive bovine from the Annamites of Vietnam in 1992, and an ancient frog, *Nasikabatrachus*, discovered in the Western Ghats of India in 2003. With only about 1.7 million species described scientifically out of at least 15 million, the age of discovery is far from over.

The number of protected areas has also increased dramatically in past decades. And, as Eric Sanderson and colleagues have shown, the human footprint still remains light in many places, offering further options for protection and management.[1]

Protectionism has in recent years acquired a somewhat derogatory aura, with reserves viewed as playgrounds for social elites at the expense of local peoples. Yet the loveliest and most spectacular areas of our planet would now be degraded or destroyed had it not been for the foresight of generations past. Our ability to exterminate species increases constantly, and vigorous protection of critical areas, whether for species richness, beauty, or idealistic reasons, will become ever more important. A quarter of mammal species and one-eighth of all bird species are already threatened with extinction. Unfortunately, many protected areas are small, lack staff, and contain communities whose uses of resources progressively cause degradation.

Most protected areas cannot endure as mere islands of wilderness with nature in balance. A variety of habitats, and with them, species diversity and the functioning of basic ecological processes, cannot persist in isolation. As yet we have little idea which organism an ecosystem can do without or how many can be destroyed before the system collapses. What we know of natural species loss in such areas makes it imperative that we focus on whole landscapes, inside and outside protected areas—including integration of the needs and interests of human populations. The fact that questions such as these are being asked and efforts are being made to sustain life on Earth does offer a margin of hope or at least a phantom comfort, though neither provides solutions.

Less than 10 percent of the world's land area and little of the marine environment has a measure of protection. Drink a cup of morning coffee and rain forest somewhere falls for another plantation; use a cell phone that contains the mineral coltan, and somewhere in the eastern Congo a coltan miner kills a gorilla for food. It is disconcerting that every act of ours is also an ecological act with direct and indirect consequences.

Since I became involved in conservation during the early 1950s, the human population has doubled. More of nature has been consumed since then than in all previous history. Forty percent of the world's forest has been cut, and we are destroying the sea through ignorance, toxic refuse, and overfishing, with some fish stocks

> After half a century of being involved in conservation, I swerve between hope and gloom.

depleted by as much as 90 percent from their historical levels. Food production must increase two to three times during this century even though most arable land is already under production, and wood demand will double within 50 years.

As if such depressing statistics are not enough, issues that once were ignored or minor have become major focal points in conservation. Hunting wildlife for local consumption and sale has become intensive, with forests, markets, and guns more accessible—so much so that the larger vertebrates have been decimated or eradicated in many areas.[2] Many rain forest vertebrates are scarce and reproduce slowly, making such hunting unsustainable—to use a pervasive word in the conservation lexicon. What is the economic alternative to bushmeat for the rural poor? The trade in bushmeat, wildlife for pets, and animal products such as elephant ivory, crocodilian hides, Tibetan antelope wool, and muskdeer musk, are said to be second economically only to illegal drugs, with an annual value of well over $100 billion. Placing direct monetary value on wildlife, dead or alive, has seldom been sustainable, whether in the United States a century ago or the Amazon today. We have the power to control or solve such problems—but not the will. The United States, as the world's largest consumer of wildlife and its products,

should legislate and enforce a total ban on such imports.

Certain environmental changes will be difficult or impossible to prevent. With an increase and ease in world trade and travel, the invasions of alien species and viruses into new environments is accelerating and greatly affecting indigenous biodiversity. For example, during the past century the United States has seen its forests modified by chestnut blight, Dutch elm disease, and, most recently, sudden oak death. An estimated 50,000 alien species now exist in the wild in the United States. Cross-species transmissions of animal pathogens, especially retroviruses that can integrate their genetic material into the genome of the human host, have become a major public health and wildlife conservation concern as we come into ever-closer contact with animals. Ebola, SARS, West Nile virus, and other deadly diseases are just intimations of epidemics that could dwarf AIDS.

Global climate change is perhaps the greatest conservation issue, one that will affect all aspects of the environment. It is the kind of issue about which governments readily form a consensus: ignore it as long as possible. A prudent course would be to respond vigorously by reducing CO_2 emissions, but the politics of delay and denial continue, sanctioned by an indifferent public. The Northern

Hemisphere is warmer now than at any time in the past 2,000 years and the onset of spring in Europe and North America has moved northward by almost a week in recent decades, affecting flowering times, the appearance of insects, and the availability of sea ice on which polar bears can hunt seals, to mention just three effects with ecological consequences. We do not know how great the total impact will be. If we're lucky it will be mild. If unlucky, it will create a traumatic upheaval during which ecosystems are shredded, vegetation zones are moved, ocean currents are deflected, and sea levels rise as polar ice melts to inundate islands and coastlines. If, for instance, the warm waters of the North Atlantic current shift, it could turn Europe into an icebox. But global warming may also help some species by enabling them to expand their range northward—such as malarial mosquitoes.

Anyone can see a trend in the state of the wild as natural landscapes are converted to cropland, pastures, roads, and urban sprawl. However, the worst environmental destruction is yet to come; biotic impoverishment is inevitable as we continue to live unsustainably on the planet's natural productivity. Restoration ecology cannot re-create the integrity of ecosystems. According to a Chinese proverb, "If we do not change our course, we will end up where we are going."

I am not a professional mourner and this is not an ode to the sunset of life. But I can comprehend the reality that the passenger pigeon is absent. Saving endangered species and bits of wilderness does not, of course, address basic issues of population growth, waste, and ever-increasing consumption. We are running out of environment as the quality and even quantity of air, water, and soil are being exhausted. Often forgotten is that the complex cycle of atmosphere, water, soils, plants, and animals provides humankind with ecosystem services that are impossible to duplicate and that enable us to define our civilizations. These include producing oxygen, purifying water, decomposing organic matter, preventing erosion, regulating climate, producing food, recycling nutrients, and more.

All development, every percentage point of growth in the gross domestic product (GDP), and all aspects of our existence, are dependent on the environment. Yet development and conservation are often seen as complementary, the two existing nicely side by side and cooperating when convenient as long as the latter does not inhibit any agenda of the former. Disruption of ecosystem services, in particular the nutrient flow of living systems, leads to permanent degradation. If the environment goes wrong, nothing can go right.

A modern mantra is "use it or lose it." As conflicts between development and conservation, between short-term profit and long-term planning become more polarized, there is less talk of saving nature. Instead, evasive euphemisms such as sustainability and poverty alleviation are invoked. If we cannot find economic value for a

> "If we do not change our course, we will end up where we are going."
> — *Chinese Proverb*

species, is it valueless? Can dollar values really be assigned to ancient forests, wild rivers, and the howl of a wolf? Unless we confer intrinsic value on the life around us, it is worth nothing alive. Should we just forget about biodiversity under certain circumstances?

A few years ago a prominent conservation organization wrote that an "indigenous group has the right to decide the direction of its future, even if that future holds no place for biodiversity conservation." Aside from the fact that most people in Africa and Asia are indigenous, any society without biodiversity is doomed to poverty. Local people have, of course, always used what they needed with little concern for sustainability. Yes, if popula-

tion density was low and a community was cohesive and isolated, sustained use of resources could readily occur. However, subsistence today, even in the most remote places, means more than just finding shelter and enough food to eat, but includes purchasing power—a global cash or barter economy. When I was in the northern Congo in 2001, the local people dried elephant meat and carried it many miles to the Central African Republic to obtain aluminum pots, shoes, and other items manufactured far away. Such human needs as food, livelihood, health, and education must be addressed whether they concern rural lives or urban slums. Human welfare is basic to the policies of governments and development agencies. Yet a healthy environment is even more basic.

This being so, I am puzzled why the issue of biodiversity conservation has receded from the agendas of the World Bank, United Nations Development Program, and the rest of the development assistance community. Ideology and narrow agendas now all too often form the basis of projects, and the difference between dogma and knowledge tends to be ignored. Conservation is a highly complex endeavor in which economics, politics, culture, and social issues must be honestly addressed and integrated based on the fact that only a sustainable society has a secure lifeline into the future.

The conviction that only development will solve human problems permeates all countries. Cars and Coca-Cola buy human contentment and offer a glorious existence for everyone, everywhere. Never mind such matters as cultural pride, community, and a good quality of life, or, as the king of Bhutan phrased it, "gross domestic happiness."

Increased productivity, sustainable development, globalization, poverty reduction—the words have changed, but the aim of increasing economic growth has not. There is, of course, the laudable moral imperative of improving the human condition, which remains bleak with over a billion people living on less than $1 per day. But no matter how noble the justifications, development depends on the exploitation of resources and strives to increase consumption and satisfy consumers—not to protect the environment. Development created the biodiversity crisis, and the proposed solutions offer more of the same, year after year, as if the mindset of technocrats prevents innovation. To be sure, growth remains essential, but the amount of wealth we have matters less than how we use it.

The 1992 Earth Summit in Rio tried to meld sustainable development and conservation but offered no strategies. Then, 10 years later, at the World Summit on Sustainable Development in Johannesburg, sustainability and conservation were more or less equated even though the two concepts are distinct. Politicians no doubt went home content with the knowledge, internationally endorsed, that sustainability has one of two meanings: that everything must pay its own way, or that we must sustain a high growth rate.

There is no question that local use of resources must become sustainable, and a special section of the journal *Science*[3] discussed various criteria to make that possible, such as social bonds within a community and confidence to invest in collective activities. However, a romantic and comforting myth, still widely disseminated by some conservation consultants, holds that communities can and will harvest resources sustainably wholly on their own. I have yet to witness this. Ecologically sustainable methods of harvesting any resource—rain forests, fisheries, monkeys, or mushrooms—are complicated, requiring basic knowledge, constant monitoring, and strict enforcement of limits. This is a long-term process, often requiring at least initial outside help. Pressures to increase harvests will increase with demand. Who then makes the decisions, and who draws the line?

One problem is that the principles of sustainability have not been clearly defined, nor have we decided what the legitimate parameters are. After the United Nations General Assembly established a goal in the year 2000 of halving the number of people living in extreme poverty by 2015, Steven Sanderson and Kent Redford wrote that it "will either mark the true beginning of sustainability or the end of biodiversity. . . . Without reshaping poverty alleviation strategies, biodiversity will pay the price for development yet again."[4]

Rhetoric and promise usually far exceed implementation. Judging by the past, governments will devise various complacent programs to achieve little with politics placed above principle and moral clarity in this renewed "war on poverty." Besides, poverty statistics are famously prone to error,[5] making actual achievements difficult to assess.

Money is, of course, available in a world that spends $1 trillion a year on armaments. The United States spends just 0.1 percent of its GDP on foreign aid, less than any developed country. But sadly, foreign aid has often achieved little, especially in failing or blatantly corrupt countries, and has also turned many countries into permanent welfare states. Furthermore, development assistance has seldom benefited the rural poor, those who hunt bushmeat, destroy habitat for subsistence, and lack the experience to find jobs. Free trade is also said to raise standards of living. The principal beneficiaries have so far been certain nations, particularly the wealthier ones.

Developed countries provide over $1 billion a day in subsidies to their farmers, ranchers, and others whose overproduction drives down world commodity prices. Subsidized products such as cotton, wheat, and sugar are dumped on poor countries at prices so low that even their own products often cannot compete in the home market. Farm exports are the main escape from rural poverty and textiles from urban poverty, but import tariffs keep many of these products out of European, Japanese, and US markets. If such trade-distorting subsidies and tariffs were eliminated, much poverty would be alleviated.

In addition, the World Bank, International Monetary Fund, and others indirectly encourage countries to deplete resources. To pay off debts, countries grow crops for export rather than to feed their people. And in many countries, a few wealthy landowners have appropriated most of the fertile farmland, further creating poverty. Much knowledge of how to improve conditions for the world's poor is available but we lack implementation. Today's grand global economic schemes are likely to lead to more unbalanced

development—and more erosion of the environment. As various case studies have shown in southeast Asia,[6] Central America,[7] and elsewhere, progress in conservation cannot wait for or depend on full economic development.

At present, many leaders and government officials serve the economy rather than bringing the economy into balance with the real needs of communities to offer ecological health, jobs, justice, security, and a good life.

> Our ability to exterminate species increases constantly, and vigorous protection of critical areas, whether for species richness, beauty, or idealistic reasons, will become forever more important.

Economies must be adjusted to reflect environmental costs, which means reducing compulsive consumption and waste. We need a new paradigm, a basic change in our perceptions and values. True sustainability will require social, economic, and political transformation. Such changes must begin with the developed nations, which consume roughly two-thirds of the world's resources, plundering other countries of their future. Visionary

leaders with concern both for humanity and for life on the planet are all too rare and have little impact. "Only two things are infinite," said Albert Einstein, "the universe and human stupidity, and I'm not sure about the former."

In recent years, nongovernmental organizations (NGOs) have largely surrendered conservation agendas and policy prescriptions to political institutions and international development agencies with large budgets and programs. NGOs, with their modest budgets, have the choice of either bypassing development funds or shaping their programs to suit a donor with a different agenda.[8] Consequently NGOs have become like a flock of gulls following a fishing trawler in anticipation of a handout. This is unfortunate. With their years of active experience in the field, NGOs can add, and indeed have already added, much knowledge toward setting realistic agendas and helping modify some of the myths and misconceptions that hamper conservation efforts. The only way to address these problems is for NGOs to proceed in a spirit of cooperation with the development community. We need to jointly define issues, objectives, goals, and strategies.[9] Conservation needs more reality and less concept. Given their knowledge, NGOs have the responsibility to challenge the status quo, offer guidance, and follow the dictum of Socrates to question everything (even though Socrates was sentenced to death because of this).

Analysis of Integrated Community and Development Projects (ICDPs) offers insight into the failure and success of different conservation approaches. Initially, most were imposed top-down and were short-term, highly subsidized, and complex, giving them little chance of lasting success. Experience has shown that conservation at the community level must have clearly stated objectives, be based on solid science, have relevance to the local situation, and respond to local interests, ideas, and traditions. Local people need to help design and implement projects to ensure that they are practical and effective.[10]

Conservationists must also be flexible and constantly attuned to changes as communities confront and adapt to new conditions. The Masai in Kenya were pastoralists in the 1960s but now many are also agriculturalists by choice—a change that has had a major impact on rangeland and wildlife. Systems will inevitably change and so will sustainability. Even with the best intentions, a project may not achieve desired results. It is clear that conservation is a process, not a mission with a single goal.

Despite their name, most ICDPs are not "integrated": they overlook

family planning, do not promote jobs for those who wish to leave, fail to distribute benefits equitably, and general-

> Global warming may also help some species by enabling them to expand their range northward—such as malarial mosquitoes.

ly proceed with development goals at the expense of conservation.[11] Often, benefits are insufficient to provide incentives for conservation among the local people.

In 2000, I visited Nepal's Annapurna Conservation Area, internationally renowned as a model program. About 67,000 visitors had paid park entrance fees the previous year to trek in the spectacular mountains, and donor agencies continued to contribute much as well. Most entrance fees vanished into government coffers. Less than 10 percent of the local people in the conservation area had benefited over the years from tourism, and only 7 percent of funds spent by visitors remained there, as most profits went to external interests such as tour companies who bring their own porters, and hotel and hostel owners who live elsewhere. Conservation initiatives were modest. ICDPs do have a

valuable function, but in themselves they may not ensure the long-term preservation of an area.

Conservation must be based on solid knowledge, on science. Various large environmental problems demand coordinated research programs to answer basic questions raised by the inexorable advance of development. We still know little about the structure and function of land and marine ecosystems and of the ecological interactions of species whose fate is inextricably tied to others. The link between biodiversity and ecosystem services, a critical aspect of sustainability, remains virtually unknown. Information on resource economics, a marriage or at least cohabitation of two disciplines, is essential if the benefits of biodiversity are to be quantified. We need to be able to predict the effects of global warming on ecosystems by continuing to monitor current changes and by intensive studies of changes that occurred after the end of the Pleistocene epoch. As vegetation zones shift, only those protected areas along latitudinal or altitudinal gradients may be able to retain more or less their present assemblage of species.

Conservation NGOs must increase their valuable efforts of raising awareness, training communities to handle their own environmental issues, and collecting conservation-oriented data. Beyond that, their most important goal might be to develop distinct and clear agendas, independent of funds from development organizations, focused at field sites of conservation importance. Although relevant rural sustainability issues need to be considered, projects must never lose sight of their basic purpose, that of biodiversity protection.[11] Other important future efforts, mentioned by Steven Sanderson,[12] include surveillance of wildlife diseases, especially those with potential human impact, tracking the state of the wild, and developing a sustainability science based on monitoring and auditing the ecological health of landscapes. With conflict between wildlife and people on the increase, whether elephants destroying crops in Tanzania or snow leopards preying on domestic yak in Bhutan, such local problems need study and at least partial resolution.

International NGOs tend to cluster in cities like Nairobi and Kathmandu, virtually ignoring Dushanbe, Yangon, and dozens of other capitals in countries that deserve more foreign assistance in saving their biological heritage. To promote and support national NGOs is also an essential function of international ones. When cultural treasures are plundered in Iraq and Cambodia the countries receive worldwide publicity and immediate generous international assistance; when natural treasures are vandalized in the Congo and Indonesia any response is muted at best. How can NGOs improve such

> "Why do you seek gold when our land has such lovely flowers?"
> —Atahualpa, Incan ruler

skewed values in public perception?

I have found delight in studying little-known mammals and promoting the protection of fragments of nature to serve as repositories of species, to salvage undamaged wilderness against which changes elsewhere can be measured, and, above all, to create islands of beauty that allow future generations to glimpse the splendor that once was. Every culture has ideals that unite and inspire it and uplift the spirit. Nature is one of these. In view of the many environmental issues upon which I have touched in these pages, it may seem atavistic for me to remain simply a naturalist. Indeed, university curricula devote less and less attention to topics of natural history. Yet species must be studied in our search for the ecological patterns and principles that enable ecosystems to function—and there are still many places in the world, from the rain forests of Brazil to the steppes of Mongolia, that deserve protection or management. Old-fashioned natural history remains the cornerstone of conservation.

Once, ecological wholeness, beauty, spiritual values, and the ethics of ensuring the existence of other beings on this planet were an integral part of conservation. Protected areas were established as much for the inspiration and aesthetic experiences they provided as for any biological richness. Respect for the environment was a moral issue. There has been a waning of such spiritual content in the conservation dialogue. Instead we trample the earth under our feet with casual indifference. Nature has become mainly a natural resource to be used, a commodity to pillage. For conservation to lose its moral vision solely for an economic one would be a tragic mistake. Respect for nature remains an important part of many cultural traditions. The first principle of Buddhism is to protect all life, and this religion also encourages simplicity and frugality. For the sake of our future we should all strive to uphold such precepts within ourselves, for others, and for conservation everywhere.

When Inca ruler Atahualpa was being strangled by Pizarro's men, his last words were reported to be: "Why do you seek gold when our land has such lovely flowers?"

Congregatory bird species, such as the Caribbean flamingos pictured here, are particularly vulnerable to destruction or degradation of nesting grounds or other key habitat.

Mapping the Wild

The Human Footprint

ERIC W. SANDERSON

> What is a wild place?
> How many are left?
> What is the state
> of the wild?

AT THE BEGINNING OF THIS NEW MILLENNIUM, my colleagues and I tried to map the world's remaining wildest places.[1] It's difficult to map what's wild—the call of a loon, the integrity of a coral reef, a glimpse of an elephant in the forest. It's easier to map what's not wild. When we asked, conservationists from around the world gave us similar answers about what makes a place not wild: human population density, human access via roads and rivers, human infrastructure for agriculture and settlements, the presence of industrial power (as reflected in lights strong enough to be visible from a satellite at night). We gathered data from NASA and other space agencies, from the US government, from universities, and from other sources. Then, using a geographic information system (GIS), we added them up to generate the "human footprint" (see color plate 1).

What does the human footprint show? At its simplest, the map shows us that 83 percent of Earth's land surface is influenced by one or more of the factors above; 98 percent of the places where wheat, rice, or corn can be cultivated are influenced by people. The highest-scoring, most-influenced areas read like a list of the world's great cities: New York, London, Tokyo, Beijing, Durban, and others.

The lowest-scoring areas are the remaining wildernesses: the "last of the wild." We identified 570 such places in all the world's biomes, represented by the deepest shades of green on the map:[2] wild places in India's grasslands, the temperate forests of the United States, the mountains of South America. These wilderness areas vary in size, the largest being deserts, boreal forests, and the Amazonian rain forest. They also vary in the level of human influence and in their potential for conservation.

The human footprint was devised as a yardstick of wildness, and what it shows is that most of the world is neither wild nor not wild, which is to say, most of the world is somewhere in between. Look out your window. What most of us see are some roads, towns, croplands, lights at night, and some nature: the rain falling, plants growing, a few birds, and maybe, if you're lucky, occasionally some larger animals slipping by.

The current state of our world—and the wild—lies in the messy middle that is both wild and not wild. It's in places like the Congo forest, where a few elephants struggle to survive in the last forests that are more than 12 miles (20 km) from a road. It's in places like New York City, where little bits of salt marsh provide tiny green havens for migrating shorebirds. It's also in your neighborhood and mine. What remains wild is in daily negotiation.

Meanwhile the human footprint continues to spread, extending out from the blacks and purples on the map (the heaviest weight of our collective influence) and into the greens and yellows (the locales of elephants and loons and reefs), on the blacktop of our roads, our settlements, our factories, oil tankers, cities, and expressways. Sometimes it is "development" for the best of reasons, sometimes not. In any case, the negotiations are not going well for those who love nature.

I am a conservationist, and most of what I do is to try to blunt the color change here and there. With my colleagues, I work to keep some places a little greener, reduce the redness, the purple where I can, and protect the areas where wildlife can live in peace. I believe we can live in a world with both people and wild things. Moreover, it is our spirit of inventiveness and goodwill that will yet find a way to reverse the increasing human footprint. We can choose a new palette, reinterpret the patterns, and get to a healthier wild-not-wild place than where we are now. To that end, I hope you find this map a help.

discoveries

The *Chimaera monstrosa* was a rabbitfish identified by Linnaeus in 1758. A new rabbitfish species, *Hydrolagus matallanasi,* was recently discovered off the coast of Brazil.
(Credit: John D.M. Gordon)

BIJAL TRIVEDI

Expeditions to hidden corners of the world continue to yield surprises, including the discoveries of species that are new to science and recently explored habitats. Here are a few that caught our attention.

A TEAM OF FILIPINO AND BRITISH WILDLIFE BIOLOGISTS has discovered a new species of flightless bird tucked away in the northernmost part of the Philippine archipelago on Calayan Island. The crow-sized CALAYAN RAIL *(Gallirallus calayanensis)* is known locally as "piding," and is covered in a dark brown plumage with an orange beak and legs. Its closest relative is the Okinawa rail *(G. okinawae),* found on its namesake Japanese island, 620 miles (1,000 km) to the north.[1]

A RARE, BURROWING FROG WAS DISCOVERED in India's Western Ghats in 2003 by researchers from the Free University of Brussels in Belgium. THE PURPLE FROG *(Nasikabatrachus sahyadrensis)* represents an entirely new family; its closest relatives in the Sooglossidae family live on two islands of the Seychelles. Genetic analysis suggests that the families evolved together when Earth's continents formed a single land mass that likely split apart as a result of continental drift or rising sea level more than 100 million years ago.[2]

A NEW SPECIES OF TITI MONKEY was discovered in Madidi National Park, Bolivia, by Wildlife Conservation Society scientists. The light brown monkey has rich orange highlights on its cheeks, neck, chest, and belly; its head is topped with a golden crown, and it has a white-tipped tail. The  rare opportunity to name this new species was auctioned online at Charity Folks in February 2005, with the proceeds deposited in an endowment fund for the management of Madidi. A formal description of the species appeared in 2005 in the journal *Neotropical Primates*.[3]

ANOTHER NEW MAMMAL WAS DISCOVERED in the eastern Bolivian panhandle when molecular analysis of a brownish-gray rat revealed it to be a new species. ANDERSON'S RICE RAT (*Oryzomys andersoni*) was discovered in semideciduous savannah—a relatively unexplored area.[4]

THOUSANDS OF MILES AWAY IN MADAGASCAR, German scientists found the FAT-TAILED DWARF LEMUR (*Cheirogaleus medius*) to be the first hibernating tropical mammal. They discovered that the lemur hibernates in a tree hole for seven months of the year, even though winter temperatures can reach a balmy 86°F (30°C). The study showed that the lemur's body temperature during hibernation varies to a degree not seen in other mammals, fluctuating from as low as 49°F (9°C) to almost 97°F (36°C). For the lemur, hibernation is a strategy to cope with food shortages during the dry winter season.[5]

MARINE BIOLOGISTS HAVE ALSO FOUND NEW UNDERSEA HABITATS. Scientists from the University of Alaska Fairbanks observed a bed of RHODOLITHS near Knight Island in Alaska's Prince William Sound. Rhodoliths are marine algae that resemble colorful twigs of branched coral, and although they have been found throughout the world's oceans, this find reveals a new type of habitat in Alaskan waters. Serving as transitional habitat between rocky seabed and the sandy seafloor, rhodoliths support many species including clams, scallops, and true corals. They also store calcium carbonate within their cell walls, forming coral-like structures, but, unlike coral, rhodoliths wander like tumbleweeds across the seafloor. The discovery is likely to spur debate about protecting seafloor habitats.[7]

THERE WERE ALSO RECENT DISCOVERIES BENEATH THE SEA. Brazilian scientists discovered a new species of RABBITFISH (*Hydrolagus matallanasi*) deep in the South Atlantic Ocean, off the Brazilian coast. The fish, related to sharks and rays, is about 12 to 16 inches (30–40 cm) long, has a snub nose, winglike side fins, a spiked back fin, a stinger tail, and lives at depths of 1,300 to 2,000 feet (400–600 m). The fish was first discovered by students onboard a fishing trawler in 2001, but, unaware of its importance, they tossed it overboard after photographing it. It took two years before scientists had enough specimens to prove it was a new species.[6]

US MARINE SCIENTISTS FROM MORE THAN 20 INSTITUTIONS exploring the South Pacific's Lau Basin made another deep-sea discovery: they found a new CLUSTER OF HYDROTHERMAL VENTS along a crack in the seafloor. The basin, about 8,000 feet (2,438 m) down, is 242 miles (390 km) long and lined with volcanoes, vents, and sulfide deposits and is populated by giant snails and other animals that thrive in the hot, acidic water. The unusual geological and chemical properties of the Lau Basin are expected to harbor new life forms. The exploration is part of the Ridge 2000 program funded by the National Science Foundation.[8]

New Conservation Methods and Technologies

KEN KOSTEL

Despite remarkable advances in conservation over the past decade, many of the same scientific challenges persist. Among them are the need to more quickly and accurately track animals, identify species, and fine-tune our understanding of entire ecosystems. But unique methods, technological advances, and novel applications of existing technology are slowly transforming the way conservation biology is being conducted, both in the field and in the laboratory.

GENETICS AND GENOMICS

The genetic revolution is changing both taxonomy and forensics in conservation biology.[1] Historically, taxonomists have identified new or existing species based on painstaking assessment of often-similar physical characteristics. Now, advances in genetics have taken the process into the laboratory, allowing for greater precision in distinguishing species. In 2004, researchers at Rockefeller University used a relatively new genetic identification process—genetic "barcoding"—to suggest the existence of four new species from a sample of just 130 North American breeding birds.[2] Genetic barcoding analyzes a specific DNA sequence that highlights small differences between species. In addition to speeding up the identification process, these results suggest that analysis of other species could dramatically increase estimates of the planet's biodiversity and could one day permit identification of every species on Earth.

Genetic analysis is also proving to be an invaluable tool in enforcing wildlife laws. A simple DNA test was used in April 2004 to prosecute a suspected case of illegal fishing in Liverpool, England. Officials charged the owners and the master of a Belgian fishing vessel with misreporting a catch of highly regulated Dover sole as cheaper, nonquota sand sole. Visual identification of the fish was impossible, as the catch had already been cleaned and frozen. Using DNA evidence, the fish were correctly identified and the company and operators fined more than $17,000.[3]

Other forensic methods are also being pioneered to identify and track illegally traded species. In 2004 two separate research teams developed methods that work in tandem to determine the geographic origin of ivory. Using only small ivory samples, researchers from the University of Washington produced DNA profiles of the animals the tusks were taken from—and found that this analysis can be conducted on ivory as much as 20 years old.[4] Researchers at Harvard and the University of Washington later used genetic analysis of dung to map elephant populations in Africa.[5] Once complete, such a map could be combined with DNA profiling to track illegal ivory shipments and pinpoint the elephants' origins. This genetic mapping also provided the first evidence of hybridization between forest and savanna elephants.

Genetic analysis has also been used to identify individual species among traded animal parts. A technique developed by researchers at Florida's Nova Southeastern University can detect the presence of up to nine shark species at a time from a mixed collection of shark fins.[6] Their method has been used by enforcement officials of the National Marine Fisheries Service to test catches and has detected protected shark species in nearly half of the catches tested to date.

TRACKING AND TELEMETRY

New technology is also improving biologists' ability to track both individuals and groups of animals. Simple VHF radio collars, which identify the approximate location of a tagged animal, are slowly being replaced with more sophisticated transmitters that employ global positioning system (GPS) receivers and wireless technology. One new type of radio collar permits scientists to follow animal movements in near–real time via the Internet by transmitting data over existing cellular networks.[7]

During the first half of 2004, Save the Elephants, a Nairobi-based conservation organization, deployed these collars on 15 elephants in Kenya. The technology has already traced a new elephant corridor between the Laikipia and Samburu National Reserves, and could eventually help reduce human–elephant conflict by identifying the regions most frequented by the animals.

For animals that usually range well beyond cell phone networks, computer scientists and biologists at Princeton have collaborated to develop a radio collar that trades data with other collars over a peer-to-peer network called ZebraNet.[8] With this unique system, only one animal needs to be within range of the team's radio receiver in order to download data from all collared animals on the network.

> Unique methods, technological advances, and novel applications of existing technology are slowly transforming the way conservation biology is being conducted.

Scientists are also using various electronic tags and sensors to gather species and ocean data in the North Pacific. Scientists from seven countries are participating in the Tagging of Pacific Pelagics (TOPP) program, which plans to tag 5,000 animals from 20 taxa: albatrosses, seals, whales, shearwaters, tuna, shark, and squid, among others.[9] The instruments will record spawning sites, migratory routes, foraging locations, and species hotspots—in the context of ocean geography and chemistry. The data will not only inform fisheries management and conservation, they will also aid oceanographers studying the physical system of the oceans.

A very different data-gathering system combines traditional knowledge with advanced data collection by gathering the observations of native hunters, trackers, and local residents.[10] CyberTracker, a free software package that can be used on a small handheld computer, employs simple icons to record information and is being used to record animal signs in the African bush—and to map invasive plants in Oregon. More than 40 groups, including a geophysical expedition to the Arctic, have already used this technology.

Conservation scientists are also gaining unprecedented access to sophisticated satellite imaging systems and using them in new ways. Scientists at the US Geological Survey (USGS) and US Department of the Interior have begun experimenting with high-resolution satellite images to measure the size of walrus colonies in Alaska and penguin colonies in Antarctica.[11,12] Although the technique only currently provides population estimates of large animal congregations, researchers at the Wildlife Conservation Society are working on a method that will permit counts of individual animals on open range land.[13]

Regardless of whether these techniques permit ever-finer location of a particular animal on the savannah, ever-finer genetic distinctions among species, or better ways to understand interactions between wild animals and human societies, these innovations are providing biologists with new tools to protect the world's wildlife and wildlands.

Regulating the Wild

KEN KOSTEL

A variety of regulatory tools are being used to protect wildlife and landscapes around the world. Some recent positive (and negative) developments are highlighted here.

AUSTRALIA: In July 2004, Australia passed a re-zoning bill for the Great Barrier Reef Marine Park, creating the world's largest marine protected area. The new bill protects one-third of the 130,000-square-mile (337,000 km^2) park with a network of no-take zones that include at least 20 percent of each of the reef's 70 distinct bioregions. Previously, less than 5 percent of the reef was protected. Australia's Department for Environment and Heritage plans to compensate commercial fishers adversely affected by the re-zoning measure. An estimated 800,000 people fish recreationally in the park each year alongside approximately 2,000 commercial fishers. Another conservation measure enacted in 2003 by the Queensland government—the Reef Water Quality Protection Plan—will reduce pesticide, nutrient, and sediment runoff into the reef lagoon.[1]

In April 2004, Queensland also moved to reduce large-scale clearing of remnant bushland with passage of the Vegetation Management Amendment Act. Australia has been losing an average 1.1 million acres (445,000 ha) per year—one of the world's highest land clearing rates—making habitat destruction one of the biggest threats to endemic species. According to a 2003 report by World Wildlife Fund (WWF) Australia, Queensland alone was losing 190 million trees and more than 100 million birds, mammals, and reptiles each year. Under the new law, all threatened and "of concern" land will be protected. Clearing of less threatened regions will be capped and phased out by the end of 2006.[2]

COSTA RICA: The Ministry of Environment and Energy (MINAE) announced a new environmental tax in 2004 intending to reduce pollution in Costa Rica's rivers within six years. Heavier polluters will be taxed at a higher rate. For example, a 500-hog farm that lacks wastewater treatment would pay about $10,000 per year, while a similar farm with a treatment facility would pay about $450. The new measure is expected to raise $9.3 million annually, which will be used to fund river cleanup and restoration programs.[3]

INDIA: In 2003, the Indian Wildlife (Protection) Act of 1972 was amended to create two new types of protected areas: conservation reserves and community reserves. According to the amendment, conservation reserves can be declared on lands owned by the government in consultation with local communities. This will provide buffer zones for national parks and help link protected areas. Community reserves can be declared on public or private land if it will be used to conserve wildlife and its habitat.[4]

INDONESIA: The Indonesian government issued a *perpu* (regulation in lieu of law) in March 2004 that permits 13 companies to mine protected areas. Perpu 1/2004 amends Forestry Law 41/1999, which initially provided protection from prospecting, exploration, or exploitation of minerals without a government permit. Mining permits were invalidated by the 1999 law but will now be valid until their original expiration date. As a result, the 13 mining concerns will be permitted to extract gold, copper, nickel, and granite from the nation's protected areas.[5]

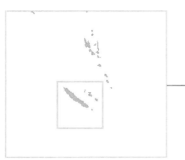

NEW CALEDONIA: The congress of New Caledonia declared the country's 200 nautical-mile exclusive economic zone as a whale sanctuary in 2003. This links Australian and Fijian reserves, creating an uninterrupted whale protection zone stretching nearly 5,000 miles (8,000 km) from western Australia to eastern French Polynesia. Whale sanctuaries created by the 11 island states now total 5 million square miles (13 million km^2)—with a goal of establishing 7.7 million square miles (20 million km^2) by 2008.[6]

PHILIPPINES: After storms swept through the Philippines in late 2004, causing massive landslides, President Gloria Arroyo suspended logging operations throughout the country and revoked logging permits in the hardest hit region of Zamboaga del Norte. Over half of the country's forests were razed during the 20th century; less than 17 million acres (7 million ha) remain, including only 2 million acres (800,000 ha) of virgin forest. Legal and illegal logging and slash-and-burn agriculture claim about 500,000 acres (200,000 ha) each year.[7]

RUSSIA: In July 2004, President Vladimir Putin altered the management structure for Russia's federal system of protected areas. Decree 400 spread responsibility for wildlands among three separate divisions within two different government departments. Previous management of Russia's protected areas fell within a single department of the Ministry of Natural Resources. Despite the bureaucratic expansion, staffing for the management of protected areas is expected to be lower than it was under the previous structure.[8]

SOUTH AFRICA: In February 2004, the Agreement on the Conservation of Albatrosses and Petrels (ACAP) was ratified by South Africa, the fifth member country within the birds' range to do so. ACAP is an international cooperative agreement that protects critical habitat, controls invasive plants and animals, and regulates commercial fishing practices detrimental to albatrosses and petrels.[9]

The South African government passed another conservation measure, the Biodiversity Act, in May 2004. The act protects threatened native species and ecosystems against development, illegal trade, alien plants or animals, and genetically modified organisms. It also contains provisions regulating the sustainable use of indigenous biological resources and the fair and equitable sharing of economic benefits generated through bioprospecting. In addition, it established the South African National Biodiversity Institute to monitor and study the country's biodiversity.[10]

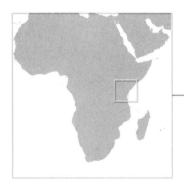

UGANDA: In 2004, Uganda created the semiautonomous National Forestry Authority (NFA) from the former Forest Department to manage the nation's forests as a moneymaking venture. The NFA will oversee 30 percent of the country's forests, including its network of protected areas. There is concern, however, that conservation priorities will be marginalized as the agency and private landowners work to profit from logging. A $14.5 million, four-year grant from donors, including the European Union and the Norwegian Agency for Development Cooperation (NORAD), will help fund the agency.[11]

UNITED STATES: The US Congress passed the Congo Basin Forest Partnership Act (HR2264) in 2004. The $18.6 million initiative supports field-based conservation activities in 13 different landscapes spread across 25 million acres (10 million h) in Cameroon, the Central African Republic, the Democratic Republic of Congo, Equatorial Guinea, Gabon, and the Republic of the Congo. According to estimates, an area the size of Rhode Island is disappearing each year. In order to muster support for the measure, the International Conservation Caucus was established in the US House of Representatives, which now boasts more than 30 members.[12]

Also in 2004, the US Congress passed the Marine Turtle Conservation Act (HR3378), providing $25 million for international sea turtle conservation measures, including protection of critical habitat. Six of the seven marine turtle species are listed as threatened or endangered species under the Endangered Species Act, and all seven are listed in Appendix I of the Convention on International Trade of Endangered Species (CITES).[13]

In December 2004, New York City became the first US municipality to make sales of all products containing or advertising ingredients from endangered species illegal. Introductory Number 367-A imposes additional fines and penalties on top of state and federal laws outlawing trade in endangered species. By specifically citing labels that advertise ingredients obtained from endangered or threatened species, the law avoids the need for DNA testing prior to enforcement.[14]

INTERNATIONAL: Three countries officially accepted the terms of the Convention on International Trade of Endangered Species (CITES) in 2004: Lao People's Democratic Republic, Palau, and Samoa—which was the 167th country to accede to the convention since it was established in 1975.

Representatives at the CITES biennial meeting in October 2004 unanimously approved tighter enforcement of the illegal wildlife trade. The new measures recommend regional law enforcement networks, cohesive national action plans to improve enforcement, improved training for wildlife law enforcement officers, and improved collaboration between national and international law enforcement agencies.[15]

The
RAREST
of the Rare

Some of the World's Most Endangered Animals

MICHAEL BERENS

By virtually any estimation, the world's biodiversity has a reached a critical point. Many scientists now believe that the rate of loss in Earth's flora and fauna is at its highest since the end of the Mesozoic era 65 million years ago. Although mass global extinctions have occurred periodically throughout history for a variety of reasons, the current trend can be traced to a single root cause: human activity. It has become widely known that species are disappearing 100 to 1,000 times faster today than before the arrival of *Homo sapiens*.

The release of the World Conservation Union's (IUCN's) 2004 update revealed some startling numbers. A total of 15,589 species of plants and animals—including one-third of all amphibians, almost half of the world's freshwater turtles, and one in four mammals—are threatened with extinction. It is already too late for the 784 plants and animals that have gone extinct on our watch. Another 60 species are currently extinct in the wild, the last individuals existing only in cultivation or captivity.

What follows are 25 of the world's most critically endangered wildlife species and descriptions of the perils that are pushing them toward extinction. Population counts are notoriously complicated; the numbers represented here are estimates based on the best available data at the time of publication.

AMERICAN BURYING BEETLE The American burying beetle *(Nicrophorus americanus)*[1] was once native to 35 states in the eastern and central United States. Today, they are found in only six states: Nebraska, Rhode Island, Oklahoma, South Dakota, Kansas, and Arkansas. The cause of their decline appears to be a combination of factors including habitat fragmentation, increased artificial lighting, and decreases in carrion, the beetle's food source.

ASIATIC CHEETAH The Asiatic cheetah *(Acinonyx jubatus venaticus)*[2] was once found from Syria and the Arabian Peninsula to Turkmenistan and the Indian subcontinent. Today it is one of the most endangered cats in the world, with just 50 to 60 believed to exist in 10 regions scattered across eastern and central Iran. Trophy hunting and hunting by herders whose livestock is preyed on by cheetahs have driven the big cats to the edge of extinction. In 2004, Indian officials began studying cloning as a way to increase the numbers of Asiatic cheetahs, with the goal of reintroducing them to parts of their former range.

BALI MYNAH The Bali mynah *(Leucopsar rothschildi)*[3] has always been rare. When it was discovered on the Indonesian island in the early 1900s, populations were thought to be between 300 and 900, though this is now believed to be an underestimate. Since then, its great popularity as a pet has sent numbers plummeting: illegal trapping, driven by a $2,000 black market price, has decimated wild populations. A captive breeding and reintroduction program was begun, but poaching remains the biggest threat. In 1999, an armed gang of poachers stole almost all of the 39 captive mynahs awaiting release into the wild. Today, only about a dozen are believed to exist in a 15-square-mile (39 km^2) protected area on Bali.

John Thorbjarnarson

David Lucas

CHINESE ALLIGATOR The Chinese alligator *(Alligator sinensis)*[4] is the world's only Asian alligator. Many of the approximately 130 wild individuals are restricted to a 270-mile (435 km) reserve on the lower Yangtze River in Anhui Province. Farmers consider them a costly nuisance, as their burrows hinder irrigation and the alligators prey on livestock. The first captive-bred reintroductions took place in 2004.

CROSS RIVER GORILLA The Cross River gorilla *(Gorilla gorilla diehli)*,[5] which was classified as a Western gorilla subspecies in 2000, is found in just five or six isolated populations scattered across Nigeria and Cameroon. Hunting is the greatest threat to the species' survival, although humans also continue to encroach on gorilla habitat. Nigeria and Cameroon's environment ministers recently agreed to protect the 150 to 200 individuals that remain.

Noel Rowe

Stuart Williams

DELACOUR'S LANGUR Fewer than 300 Delacour's langurs *(Trachypithecus delacouri)*[6] remain in a restricted belt of nonarable limestone outcroppings that stretch across northern Vietnam. Like most of the country's primates, it is threatened not only by habitat loss, but also by hunting, both as food and for use in traditional medicines.

ETHIOPIAN WOLF With about 400 remaining in the wild, the Ethiopian wolf *(Canis simensis)*[7] is the most endangered canine in the world. They are killed because of a perceived threat to livestock—and because expanding agriculture brings humans and wolves into ever-closer proximity. Domestic dogs pose another threat: they compete with wolves for food, transmit diseases including rabies and distemper, and cause hybridization by mating with wolves.

Calvin J. Hamilton

David Weller

GRAND CAYMAN ISLAND IGUANA The Grand Cayman Island rock iguana *(Cyclura nubila lewisi)*[8] survives in three partially fragmented subpopulations scattered over 3 square miles (8 km^2). Between 100 and 175 survive, stalked by domestic cats and dogs and threatened by ever-growing traffic, expanding farmlands, and development.

GRAY WHALE The gray whale *(Eschrichtius robustus)*[9] disappeared from the North Atlantic within the last 400 years and now Western Pacific stocks face a similar fate, with fewer than 100 remaining. Its principal summer feeding grounds in the Sea of Okhotsk is the site of major oil and gas exploration, and the whales must also avoid a gauntlet of fishing nets and shipping traffic along their migration route off the coasts of Japan, China, and Korea.

Iberian Lynx Ex-Situ Conservation Program

IBERIAN LYNX The Iberian lynx *(Lynx pardinus)*[10] was once common throughout the Iberian Peninsula and southern France. Today, fewer than 150 animals remain in the wild in isolated groups in Spain and Portugal. Between 1960 and 1990, the Iberian lynx lost 80 percent of its habitat, and rabbits, its main prey, have been decimated by disease.

JAVAN RHINOCEROS After "rebounding" from a low of 25 individuals in 1967, fewer than 60 Javan rhinoceros *(Rhinoceros sondaicus)*[11] survive today in two isolated locations: the Ujung Kulon National Park in Indonesia and the Cat Tien National Park in Vietnam. The rhinos, whose horn is prized for use in traditional medicines, have been poached from these small populations in recent years.

Dennis DeMello/WCS

Steve Winter/ National Geographic

KIHANSI SPRAY TOAD The tiny Kihansi spray toad *(Nectophrynoides asperginus)*[12] persists in one of the most restricted ranges on the planet—a single five-acre area below Tanzania's Kihansi Falls. A hydropower project restricted water flow by 75 percent, drying up the frog's wetland habitat. In 2003, the population plummeted from about 20,000 toads to just 40, stricken with the deadly chytrid fungus that is decimating global amphibian populations. None have been seen since February 2004, but captive breeding programs are under way in the United States at the Bronx Zoo and Toledo Zoo.

LEATHERBACK SEA TURTLE Over the past two decades, scientists have documented an alarming 97 percent decline in the total Pacific leatherback turtle *(Dermochelys coriacea)*[13] population. Globally, there were over 115,000 females of reproductive age in 1980; today, 20,000 to 30,000 remain. Longline fishing, with miles of baited fishing line, hooks many leatherbacks as bycatch, and turtle eggs are a delicacy, often consumed for their purported aphrodisiac qualities.

Matthias Schnellman

Zeb Hogan

MEDITERRANEAN MONK SEAL Like the already-extinct Caribbean monk seal *(Monachus tropicalis)*, the Mediterranean monk seal *(M. monachus)*[14] is extremely sensitive to human disturbances. It was once found throughout the Mediterranean, Marmara, and Black Seas; tourist development along the Mediterranean's 28,000 miles (45,000 km) of coastline fragmented its habitat. Now just 300 to 500 animals are split between the eastern Mediterranean and northwest Africa. Pollution poses another threat, as do fishermen who still occasionally kill seals.

MEKONG GIANT CATFISH Occasionally reaching up to 10 feet (3 m) in length and 650 pounds (295 kg), the Mekong giant catfish *(Pangasianodon gigas)*[15] is one of the world's largest freshwater fish. Once abundant in the lower Mekong River and its tributaries, the population declined 80 percent over the last 13 years. Only six were caught in 2003. The catfish is threatened by siltation caused by deforestation, dams blocking migratory routes—and overfishing: in Thailand, a 400-pound (180 kg) fish can sell for $3,000.

Australian Government
Department of
Environment and Heritage

NORTHERN HAIRY-NOSED WOMBAT Only about 100 Northern hairy-nosed wombats *(Lasiorhinus krefftii)*[16] are left in the wild, restricted to 1.2 square miles (3.1 km^2) of grassland in Central Queensland, Australia. Historically threatened by droughts and overgrazing, the population has increased from a low of 25 individuals after cattle were excluded from the region in 1982.

PALOS VERDES BLUE BUTTERFLY In 1994, the Palos Verdes blue butterfly *(Glaucopsyche lygdamus palosverdesensis)*[17] was rediscovered at a Navy fuel depot near Los Angeles, more than a decade after it was believed to be extinct; its last known habitat was destroyed to build a baseball field. It eats and lays eggs on just one plant species, locoweed *(Astragalus trichopodes* var. *lonchus).* The city has proposed a Palos Verdes Blue Butterfly Management Area to preserve the last remaining 11 acres (4.5 ha) of its habitat.

Richard A. Arnold

SAOLA Little is known about the saola *(Pseudoryx nghetinhensis),*[18] a forest-dwelling ox, which was first documented by scientists in 1992. A few hundred are believed to inhabit the steep, semideciduous river valleys between Vietnam and Lao PDR. Its scarcity has made saola meat more highly valued by locals, who prefer it over more common species.

SEYCHELLES SHEATH-TAILED BAT Fewer than 50 Seychelles sheath-tailed bats *(Coleura seychellensis)*[19] are believed to exist in the wild. Though abundant on the Seychelles Islands during the 19th century, they are now known to roost only in two caves on Silhouette Island. Among the reasons for its decline are human-induced habitat degradation and the introduction of the barn owl in 1949, which feeds on the bats.

John Thorbjarnarson

SHANGHAI SOFTSHELL TURTLE The future looks bleak for the Shanghai softshell turtle *(Rafetus swinhoei).*[20] They are thought to be extinct in the wild and only five are known to be in captivity in China and Vietnam. A growing Chinese middle class has increased demand for softshell turtles as a prized luxury food item once too expensive for all but the wealthiest few.

SPOTTED HANDFISH The spotted handfish *(Brachionichthys hirsutus)*[21] could become the first marine fish to officially go extinct in modern times. Found only in the lower Derwent River estuary in Tasmania, this unusual fish "walks" along the seafloor using its pectoral and pelvic fins. The fish were commonly sighted until the 1970s, but there have been just four confirmed sightings in the past five years. Increased siltation and heavy metal contamination have polluted waters, and the nonnative Northern Pacific seastar *(Asterias amurensis)* is out-competing the handfish for food and preying on the few eggs it produces.

SULU HORNBILL Described as "abundant" in the late 19th century, just 40 Sulu hornbills *(Anthracoceros montani)*[22] remain on one Philippine island, Tawitawi. Like all hornbills, the Sulu nests in old-growth trees and has lost much of its habitat to the spread of oil-palm plantations—and the distinctive bird makes an easy target for hunters.

VANCOUVER ISLAND MARMOT Clear-cut logging has concentrated Vancouver Island marmots *(Marmota vancouverensis)*[23] into the few remaining subalpine meadows they prefer—making them more vulnerable to predation by golden eagles, cougars, and wolves. The population collapsed from over 300 animals in the mid-1980s to 30 individuals in 2003.

Andrew A. Bryant

YANGTZE DOLPHIN The Yangtze dolphin *(Lipotes vexillifer)*,[24] or *baiji*, is the world's most endangered cetacean. It is found from the Three Gorges Dam site to the mouth of the Yangtze River in China. Entanglement in fishing gear has caused half of the reported dolphin deaths; run-ins with boat propellers also prove deadly. Numbers have fallen from 6,000 in the 1950s to 400 in 1984—to about 5 today.

Wang Ding

YELLOW-TAILED WOOLLY MONKEY The yellow-tailed woolly monkey *(Oreonax flavicauda)*[25] is found in a few locations in the montane cloud forests of the Peruvian Andes. Historically, its inaccessible habitat offered some protection. However, logging in the 1950s reduced and fragmented forests, and new roads brought in farmers, cattle ranchers, and hunters. Fewer than 250 remain in the wild.

Magic Words
after Nalungiaq

In the very earliest time,
when both people and animals lived on earth,
a person could become an animal if he wanted to
and an animal could become a human being.
Sometimes they were people
and sometimes animals
and there was no difference.
All spoke the same language.
That was the time when words were like magic.
The human mind had mysterious powers.
A word spoken by chance
might have strange consequences.
It would suddenly come alive
and what people wanted to happen could happen—
all you had to do was say it.
Nobody could explain this:
That's just the way it was.

ADAPTED BY EDWARD FIELD
FROM A NETSILIK TALE
AS TOLD TO KNUD RASMUSSEN

PART II

GLOBAL NEWS HIGHLIGHTS

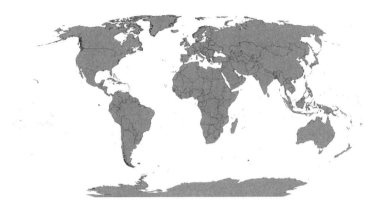

In this section, we present recent news briefs from around the world on both land and sea—some of the most important or interesting research, rulings, and events that have impacted biodiversity and conservation over the past few years. Some readers may be quite familiar with important happenings in particular regions but know little of other parts of the world. And disparate news events are rarely grouped in a way that provides a larger picture of what has happened over a period of time. Our intention in compiling this section was to create a global snapshot of recent developments that have altered—in actuality or in perception—the state of the wild.

We divided the globe into eight geographic land regions: Africa, Asia, Australia/Pacific, Central and South America, Europe, Middle East/North Africa, North America, and the poles; the ninth region covers the world's oceans. Then, we began the mammoth task of compiling information. We enlisted the aid of those who know best what's happening in the near and far corners of the world: field researchers. We sent out hundreds of questionnaires to biologists and conservationists, asking for pivotal conservation news from their regions, and enlisted the aid of Wildlife Conservation Society field staff in many parts of the world. The respondents represent environmental agencies, nonprofit organizations, research institutes, and universities; their contributions are gratefully acknowledged at the end of this section. In addition, our editorial staff scoured scientific journals, magazines, newspapers, news services, newsletters, and websites, searching for relevant news items and for more detailed information to supplement that provided in the questionnaires.

In editing the news items we gathered, our goal was not to provide an in-depth analysis of events or trends, but rather to compile a wide sampling of information. We've included short entries on everything from emerging conservation threats; the effects of disease outbreaks, pollution, and climate change on wildlife; and changes in government regulations to the creation of new protected areas—and more. In many cases, these news items provide concrete examples of issues or trends that are discussed at greater length later in the volume.

We've arranged these news briefs in chronological order—according to when the information was first published or communicated to us by field researchers—with the most recent first. Using a typical news style, we begin each entry by identifying the country or region affected, and have sourced all material.

Through these briefs we seek to broaden awareness of recent global news events that affect our wild world.

Africa

KEN KOSTEL

Conservationists in sub-Saharan Africa have been hindered by a combination of extreme poverty throughout the continent and scattered violence that often crosses borders. Despite this, scientists, policymakers, and park staff have preserved a remarkable amount of land in diverse protected areas and, by working with local residents, have also managed to protect a wide range of plant and animal biodiversity on public lands. These successes have presented their own unique challenges, however, as the needs of wildlife and landscape preservation have come into more frequent conflict with local and indigenous populations struggling to make a living. As a result, many conservation organizations are turning increasingly toward a cooperative approach, educating local residents about conservation-friendly practices and the importance of biodiversity.

Julie Maher/WCS

REPUBLIC OF THE CONGO: Congolaise Industrielle des Bois (CIB), a logging and forestry products company based in the Republic of Congo, announced in 2004 that it would permanently set aside 1.1 million acres (445,000 ha) of its 3.6-million-acre (1.5 million ha) forest concession. The preserved forest is home to a group of chimpanzees known for their complex tool use—as well as a rich array of other species. The move to preserve the region came as part of CIB's effort to obtain certification under Forest Stewardship Council principles as a sustainable harvester of tropical wood. http://www.tropicalforesttrust.com/archives/htmoldnews.htm.

Luke Hunter

SOUTH AFRICA: South African officials plan to resume culling elephant herds in Kruger National Park in 2005. Since a 1994 ban, elephant populations in Kruger have swelled from 8,000 to 12,000 animals, and officials expect the population to grow by another 1,000 animals by November 2005. Elephants are considered second only to humans in their ability to damage the environment and, aside from humans, have no natural predator. A draft plan for the cull was expected in May 2005. *Business Day* (Johannesburg), November 3, 2004; *SouthAfrica.info,* June 24, 2004.

UGANDA: A 2004 study found that the economic value of intact forest totaled nearly $350 million per year—roughly 5.2 percent of the country's gross domestic product. Unlogged forests provide a broad range of ecosystem services including soil and water remediation that have quantifiable value. Moreover, the report found that rural residents supplement their income by up to 36 percent with renewable forest products such as medicinal plants and construction materials. *The Value of Uganda's Forests* (Kampala, Uganda: Wildlife Conservation Society, 2004).

Elizabeth Bennett

WEST AFRICA: Extractive industries greatly magnify the dangers posed by bushmeat hunting, according to a 2003 study. Researchers at the World Wildlife Fund found that most regional hunting was driven by the influx of workers for oil and gas exploration in the Gamba Protected Areas Complex, which increased demand for meat in local markets. Transportation in and out of concessions also appeared to facilitate the movement of large quantities of bushmeat to regional market towns.

Other research showed that fishing subsidies in the European Union (EU) may also be influencing rising demand for bushmeat in Ghana, where fishing off the coast by a large EU fleet and others is causing a steady decline of fish stocks. Years of low catches off the Gabon coast appear to coincide with marked increases in the amount of wild meat for sale in markets. *Conservation Biology* 17(2003):1807–1813; *Science* 306(2004):1180–1183.

EAST AFRICA: A 2004 World Conservation Union (IUCN) assessment of freshwater biodiversity in East Africa found high levels of endemism as well as a wide range of threats to aquatic animals throughout the region. The assessment concluded that of the 1,600 freshwater species, 74 percent or more of all fish, mollusks, and crabs are unique to the region's lakes and rivers. More than half of those fish, one-third of amphibians, and more than one-quarter of its crab species are threatened with extinction. Pervasive threats to freshwater species include invasive plants and animals, pollution, sedimentation and eutrophication of waters, and habitat loss. W. Darwall, IUCN, pers. comm., 2004.

Nobel Foundation

KENYA: Wangari Maathai, deputy minister of the environment and one-time Kenyan presidential candidate, won the 2004 Nobel Prize for Peace for her contributions to sustainable development. The Green Belt movement that Maathai founded in Kenya in 1977 has reportedly planted more than 30 million trees to prevent soil erosion and to provide wood for cooking fires. Maathai is the first African woman and the first environmental activist to win the prize. http://nobelprize.org/peace/laureates/2004/index.html.

Doris Friedman

SWAZILAND: A request by Swaziland to permit limited hunting of the southern white rhino *(Ceratotherium simum simum)* was approved by the Convention on International Trade in Endangered Species (CITES) in October 2004. The white rhino was reestablished in Swaziland in 1965 after extinction there, and now numbers some 61 individuals. Swaziland will be allowed a limited annual harvest and live export not to exceed 7 percent of its population. *Earth Negotiations Bulletin* 21(2004):16.

TANZANIA: A gold rush in Tanzania's East Usambara Mountains threatens one of eastern Africa's most biologically diverse regions. After gold was discovered 3 miles (5 km) north of the Amani Nature Reserve in 2003, the nearby population grew from a few hundred to about 10,000 within two months. Amani park staff were initially able to keep most of the miners out of the reserve, but in September 2004 about 300 settlers moved in and began mining and clearing land for encampments. Sediment and polluted runoff from mining has already destroyed local streams and wetlands. B. Newmark, Utah Museum of Natural History, pers. comm., 2004.

Luke Hunter

SOUTHERN AFRICA: Ministers from Mozambique, South Africa, and Zimbabwe ratified a treaty establishing the Great Limpopo Transfrontier Park (GLTP) in August 2004. The 13,500-square-mile (35,000 km^2) protected area joins Limpopo National Park in Mozambique; South Africa's Kruger National Park, Makuleke region; and Gonarezhou National Park, Malipati Safari Area with Manjinji Pan Sanctuary in Zimbabwe. It also forms the core of the Greater Limpopo Transfrontier Conservation Area, nearly 40,000 square miles (104,000 km^2) of land that includes national parks, public and private game reserves, and small-scale communal farming areas. As the fences come down, scientists on the ground are focusing on ways to prevent the spread of foot and mouth disease, bovine tuberculosis, and other diseases between domesticated livestock and wildlife. *Great Limpopo: Talk of the Transfrontier* 1, no. 3(2004):8.

CENTRAL AFRICA: Naturally occurring anthrax reportedly killed nearly 2,000 wild animals in Central African parks and game reserves in 2004—including almost 200 hippos. Biologists think the infection is spread by vultures that feed on an anthrax-tainted carcass and then fly off, carrying anthrax spores on their feet. A study released in 2004 also showed that, contrary to previous belief, low doses of anthrax can prove fatal to primates. *Frontiers in Ecology and the Environment* 2(2004):456; *Nature* 430(2004):451–452.

THE DEMOCRATIC REPUBLIC OF CONGO: Attacks killed nine park guards throughout the DRC between May and July 2004. Three were killed in Virunga National Park in the first half of 2004 alone. Guards have been targeted as they try to halt poaching, which is often carried out by armed rebel groups to feed their fighters or to finance their operations with illegal ivory sales. A. Plumptre, Wildlife Conservation Society, pers. comm., 2004.

Environmental
Investigation Agency

THE DEMOCRATIC REPUBLIC OF CONGO: Poachers in Garamba National Park have turned their focus from bushmeat to rhino horn and ivory, most likely to help fund rebel groups in nearby regions. Between July 2003 and August 2004, a well-armed group of poachers on horseback entered the park from Sudan and killed an estimated 1,000 elephants and half of the remaining population of northern white rhinos *(Ceratotherium simum cottoni),* including all of the territorial adult males. Only about 15 of the rhinos now survive in the wild. http://www.rhinos-irf.org/news/african/garamba/12july04pressrelease.htm.

Alastair McNeilage

THE DEMOCRATIC REPUBLIC OF CONGO: Thousands of Rwandans crossed into the DRC in May 2004 and converted nearly 4,000 acres (1,600 ha) of forest in Virunga National Park into agricultural fields. The cleared area is known to be habitat for endangered mountain gorillas *(Gorilla beringei beringei)* and golden monkeys *(Pygathrix roxellana)* and also serves as a natural corridor for large mammals moving between the Mikeno and Nyamulagira sectors of the park. The squatters were reportedly being paid by Rwandan land developers. By July, most of the squatters had been removed from the park, but the damage remains. http://www.zgf.de/presse/hintergrund/DRCCrisis.pdf.

EAST AFRICA: Sewage discharge and runoff from agricultural land is among the most significant threats to West Indian Ocean nearshore marine habitat and biodiversity, according to a 2004 report by the Global International Waters Assessment (GIWA). The Indian Ocean contains more than one-fifth of the world's tropical inshore fish species. However, an estimated 70 percent of coral reefs in the Indian Ocean have died in recent years, due in part to algae blooms caused by sewage and fertilizer runoff. A 600-mile (965 km)-long toxic red tide off the coasts of Kenya and Somalia in 2002 killed thousands of marine animals. The Norwegian government and the Global Environment Facility pledged $11 million in 2004 to help reduce sewage, chemical, and soil runoff from five mainland African nations and five island nations. *Global International Waters Assessment* (Kalmar, Sweden: GIWA, 2004).

Julie Maher/WCS

MADAGASCAR: The World Bank awarded its single largest financing package for the environment in May 2004 to support Madagascar's National Environment Action Plan. A total of $49 million in grants will support plans to triple Madagascar's protected area by 2008. In September 2003, President Ravalomanana announced his commitment to add more than 15,000 square miles (39,000 km^2) of tropical rain forest, tropical dry forest, mangrove swamp, and coral reef to the country's protected area network. Madagascar is home to more than 200,000 species of plants and animals, three-quarters of which are found nowhere else on Earth. http://www.worldbank.org/afr/mg.

WCS

REPUBLIC OF THE CONGO: In April 2004, researchers discovered the first known baby gorilla *(Gorilla gorilla gorilla)* born in the wild from reintroduced gorillas. The newborn was with a group of five adults that were released into the Lefini Reserve in 1996 by Projet Protection des Gorilles (PPG). The mother is a 16-year-old orphan whose parents were killed by poachers. In September 2004, PPG reintroduced another group of nine young adults and juveniles to the reserve. T. King, PPG, pers. comm., 2004.

UGANDA: In 2004, Uganda created the semiautonomous National Forestry Authority (NFA) out of the former Forest Department to manage the nation's forests as a moneymaking venture. A $14.5 million, four-year grant from donors including the European Union and the Norwegian development agency NORAD will help fund the agency—which will oversee 30 percent of the country's forests, including protected areas. There is concern, however, that conservation priorities will be marginalized as the NFA and private landowners work to profit from logging. *Uganda NFP Process Learning Series* (Kampala, Uganda: Forestry Inspection Division, 2004).

Julie Maher/WCS

CAMEROON: About 1 percent of people in rural Cameroon who reported having direct contact with the blood and bodily fluids of wild primates, likely as a result of hunting and butchering bushmeat, showed evidence of being infected with simian foamy virus (SFV). Although SFV has no known human health implications and is naturally endemic in many African primates, it is a retrovirus similar to the one that causes AIDS. The 2004 findings provided the first evidence of retroviral transmission under natural conditions and suggest that the spread of nonhuman retroviruses may be far more widespread than previously thought, largely because of the bushmeat trade. *Lancet,* 363(2004):932–937.

Luke Hunter

CENTRAL AND WEST AFRICA: A review of data on African elephants *(Loxodonta africana)* found that population reports are often either out of date or inaccurate. Researchers found that much of the data scientists rely on to study population dynamics are, at best, 15 years old. Moreover, many of the numbers are based on inaccurate estimates or even guesswork. In Central Africa in particular, population estimates based on speculation were five times as large as those based on definitive data. *Conservation Biology* 18(2004):1191–1201.

REPUBLIC OF THE CONGO: In 2004 the Republic of the Congo announced plans to expand its protected area network with the Bambama-Lékana National Park. The new park will form a transboundary protected area with Bateke Plateau National Park in Gabon. The Congolese government also plans to link Conkouati-Douli National Park with Gabon's Mayumba National Park, protecting an ecologically critical network of beaches, swamps, and forests along the country's coastline, which harbor important sea turtle nesting areas. http://forests.org/articles/reader.asp?linkid=29614.

KENYA: In January 2004, 18 endangered eastern bongos *(Tragelaphus eurycerus isaaci)* were released into two enclosed semiwilderness areas on the Mount Kenya Game Ranch. They were transferred from zoos in the United States where they have been bred in captivity since the 1970s. It is hoped that their offspring will eventually help repopulate wild herds. Just one population of about 100 bongos is known to exist in Kenya's Aberdare Conservation Area. *International Zoo News* 51, no. 2(2004):103.

William Karesh

CENTRAL AFRICA: Researchers discovered that five Ebola outbreaks in humans between 2001 and 2003 were preceded by outbreaks of the highly infectious disease among several forest animals, including chimpanzees *(Pan troglodytes),* lowland gorillas *(Gorilla gorilla gorilla),* and duikers *(Bovidae).* Reports of large numbers of dead forest animals have preceded some human outbreaks, leading scientists to believe that the disease spreads from animals to humans who handle infected bushmeat. Ebola's natural host remains unknown, but most wildlife outbreaks appear to occur during the dry season in the "Ebola pocket," an area that spans parts of Gabon and Republic of the Congo. *Science* 303(2004):387–390.

Elyssa Kellerman

AFRICA: A recent survey of data on all known lion *(Panthera leo)* populations in Africa estimates that there are between 16,500 and 30,000 free-ranging animals spread across 28 countries, with just six populations of more than 1,000 individuals. Populations in southern and eastern Africa reportedly have the largest numbers, while those in central and western Africa are smaller and more isolated—and in faster decline. *Oryx* 38(2004):26–31.

Dada Gottelli

ETHIOPIA: Between late 2003 and early 2004, 38 Ethiopian wolves *(Canis simensis)* in Ethiopia's Bale Mountains died of rabies and another 36 disappeared. Members of the Ethiopian Wolf Conservation Programme immediately captured and vaccinated wolves and domesticated dogs against the highly contagious disease; by February, 69 wolves had been vaccinated. A similar outbreak in the early 1990s killed 77 percent of wolves in the region. Fewer than 500 Ethiopian wolves are believed left in the wild, half of which exist in the Bale Mountains. *Emerging Infectious Diseases* 10(2004):2214–2217.

WEST AFRICA: Three West African countries process more ivory than their individual elephant populations can produce, according to a report by TRAFFIC, a wildlife trade monitoring network. Earlier surveys of African ivory markets identified Abidjan, Côte d'Ivoire; Dakar, Senegal; and Lagos, Nigeria, as the most important ivory carving centers in West Africa, and observed more than 10 tons (9 t) of ivory on display at 294 locations. Follow-up studies found that, although the total amount of displayed ivory dropped to about 8,500 pounds (3,855 kg) in 153 locations throughout the region, Nigeria's ivory industry showed signs of being on the rise. *More Ivory than Elephants* (Cambridge, United Kingdom: TRAFFIC International, 2003).

Rebecca Cairns-Wicks

SAINT HELENA: In December 2003, the world witnessed its most recent confirmed extinction when the last remaining seedling of the St. Helena olive *(Nesiota elliptica)* succumbed to multiple fungal infections and a dry winter. The species had been extinct in the wild since 1994 as a result of habitat loss in its native range on the highest parts of St. Helena Island's eastern ridge. *2004 IUCN Red List of Threatened Species* (Gland, Switzerland, and Cambridge, UK: IUCN, 2004).

LIBERIA: Just three days before he stepped down from the Liberian presidency in 2003, Moses Blah signed three laws to protect the country's forests: the Protected Forest Area Network Law, the Sapo National Park Act, and the Nimba Nature Reserve Act. The new president, Guyde Bryant, later backed the legislation. Liberia is home to almost half of the original Upper Guinean forest, a coastal rain forest spanning six African countries from western Togo to eastern Sierra Leone. This forest contains rich biodiversity with many endemic species as well as the largest known population of the critically endangered western chimpanzee *(Pan troglodytes verus)*. Together, the three laws set aside nearly 170,000 acres (70,000 ha) of forest—a 60 percent increase in the country's protected area. http://www.naturalworldtours.co.uk/articles2003/october/oct1803h.htm.

Roger Hayman/
BirdLife

CAPE VERDE ISLANDS: Researchers on Raso Island found just 98 Raso larks *(Alauda razae)* in a 2003 census, a 25 percent decline from 2001 surveys. Males are believed to outnumber females by two to one. The bird is confined to the 1,730-acre (700 ha) island, and egg predation by giant geckos as well as drought has taken a toll on the birds in recent years. Plans to establish the larks on a larger island they once inhabited were scrapped because recent visits have shown it to be overrun with feral cats. *Bird Conservation International* 13(2003):13.

NIGERIA: The Nigerian government ceded control of Yankari National Game Reserve to the Bauchi state government in 2004. Yankari is the country's oldest protected area, but the governor of Bauchi criticized the park's dilapidated state and promised an infusion of cash to upgrade its facilities and raise it to international standards. However, conservationists are worried that the state will not provide sufficient funding over the long term and that its plans, which include a golf course and expanded tourist facilities, will pose a threat to the park environment. *Vanguard* (Lagos), January 30, 2004; *Daily Champion* (Lagos), September 1, 2004.

Asia

KEN KOSTEL

Conservation in Asia presents some unique and difficult challenges. The region's growing demand for fossil fuels, raw materials, and consumer goods is increasingly at odds with the priorities of policymakers, scientists, and local residents to preserve Asia's fast-disappearing endemic species and unique landscapes. In addition, hunting, either for subsistence or to supply the traditional Asian medicine trade, is seriously depleting many terrestrial, shallow water, and marine species throughout the region and around the world. Despite this, conservationists are making progress in efforts to conserve increasingly large tracts of critical habitat, including recent protections in Indonesia and Myanmar. Moreover, the countries of Central Asia present vast un-tapped potential for conservation in regions also being targeted by mining companies and other extractive industries.

Steve Winter

INDIA: The first genetic study of free-ranging Asian elephants, published in 2005, found that elephants of southern India are divided into two distinct populations, separated by only the 25-mile (40 km) Palghat Gap in the Western Ghats. The discovery means that conservationists must preserve the two populations separately. *Heredity* 94(2005):71–80.

Hans-Jurgen Burkard

CENTRAL ASIA: The five countries surrounding the Caspian Sea have agreed to reduce their caviar export quotas to allow sturgeon species to recover. Together, Azerbaijan, Iran, Kazakhstan, Russia, and Turkmenistan control 90 percent of the world's caviar. Their combined 2004 export quota for beluga sturgeon *(Huso huso)* caviar—the rarest and most valuable—will be set at half of the 2003 level. The quota for stellate sturgeon *(Acipenser stellatus)* was re-duced by 40 percent, and caviar exports from Russian *(A. gueldenstaedti)* and Persian *(A. persicus)* sturgeon were each cut by 10 percent. http://www.cites .org/eng/resources/quotas/sturgeon_intro.shtml.

ASIA: Fewer than half of the Asian Important Bird Areas (IBAs) designated by BirdLife International are adequately protected, according to a 2004 report, which identified 2,293 sites across Asia that are critical bird habitat or migratory stopovers. Of those, 43 percent are completely unprotected and 14 percent have only partial protection. *Important Bird Areas in Asia* (Tokyo: BirdLife International, 2004).

Pavel Sorokin/WCS

KAZAKHSTAN AND MONGOLIA: The saiga antelope *(Saiga tatarica)* population has plummeted worldwide from nearly 2 million to fewer than 30,000 in just a decade. Demand for saiga horns in traditional medicines and poaching for meat has largely driven the decline. The Kazakhstan subspecies, *(S. t. tatarica),* numbered just 21,000 animals in 2003 and has been subjected to organized poaching despite government funding of antipoaching patrols, aerial surveys, and increased powers of arrest by rangers. A recent survey of the Mongolian subspecies, *(S. t. mongolica),* found that numbers fell from 5,200 in 2000 to just 750 in 2003. As a result, the IUCN upgraded the status of the Mongolian saiga from vulnerable to endangered in April 2004. *Oryx* 38(2004):250–251.

TAIWAN: The first survey of Taiwan's nearshore coral reefs, published in 2004, found that coverage of live coral on eight major reef areas around the island has fallen below 50 percent—and in some cases, live coral covers less than 10 percent. The Chinese Coral Reef Society monitored the reefs for seven years and discovered that most nearshore reefs have suffered extensive damage from human activities such as dynamite fishing and pollution from urban runoff, as well as events such as typhoons and changing climate. At least 6 of the 15 species of once-common indicator reef fish and invertebrates that depend on live coral have also disappeared from Taiwan's waters in recent years. http://www.iucn.org/themes/marine/Word/Taiwan BleachingOCT04.doc.

VIETNAM: The government of Vietnam endorsed a comprehensive plan to control the country's wildlife trade in 2004. The National Action Plan to Strengthen the Control of Trade in Wild Fauna and Flora in Viet Nam to 2010 was approved by Deputy Prime Minister Nguyen Tan Dzung to help control the exploitation, hunting, and captive breeding, as well as transportation, confiscation, local sale, import, export, and reexport of wildlife species. The plan recommends the creation of a centralized system for wildlife enforcement authorities to share information—and recognizes the need for greater awareness among government officials of the threats facing Vietnam's wildlife. http://www.traffic.org/news/press-releases/vietnam.html.

CHINA: Chinese customs officials in the Tibet Autonomous Region seized 31 tiger skins, 581 leopard skins, 778 otter skins, and two lynx skins hidden in a truck on its way to Lhasa, reportedly en route from India, in late 2003. The tiger skins could represent as much as 1 percent of India's tiger population. *The Tiger Skin Trail* (Coventry, UK: Environmental Investigation Agency, 2004).

Dave Currey/ Environmental Investigation Agency

SOUTHEAST ASIA: In November 2004, Parties to the Convention on International Trade in Endangered Species (CITES) unanimously agreed to new controls over the trade of ramin *(Gonystylus spp.),* an endangered hardwood tree found in the peat swamp forests of Indonesia and Malaysia. One cubic yard (0.8 m^3) of the wood sells for nearly $1,000. A 2004 report by the Environmental Investigation Agency (EIA) found that 60 percent of Malaysia's reported annual production came from Indonesia, which banned the cutting and export of ramin in 2001. Ramin forests are also home to endangered species such as orangutan *(Pongo abelii)* and Sumatran tiger *(Panthera tigris sumatrae). The Ramin Racket* (Coventry, UK: EIA, 2004).

Betty Groskin

THAILAND: Outbreaks of a highly pathogenic avian influenza virus claimed new victims in 2004: tigers. More than 100 Bengal tigers *(Panthera tigris tigris)* at the Sriracha Tiger Zoo near Bangkok died or had to be culled to prevent the spread of the disease in October after they ate raw chicken apparently infected with the H5N1 virus. Laboratory experiments earlier in the year revealed that domestic cats can contract the H5N1 virus and can pass it on to other cats, but no cat-to-cat transmission was observed at the zoo where the sick tigers were isolated. An outbreak of avian flu in 2004 claimed over 30 human lives in Southeast Asia and led to the death of more than 100 million birds, mainly by culling. *Science* 306(2004):808.

I.R. DOE/CACP/WCS

IRAN: In July 2004, a local court in Jajarm, Iran, approved a 40,000-acre (16,200 ha) buffer zone around critical Asiatic cheetah *(Acinonyx jubatus venaticus)* habitat. The buffer was established to keep cattle out and minimize cheetah–human conflict. Once distributed from India to the Arabian Peninsula and Syria, between 50 and 60 cheetahs are now scattered across a handful of sites in eastern Iran—compared with about 400 animals 50 years ago. *Cat News* 40(2004):11–14; http://www.iraniancheetah.org/MiandashtBufferZone.htm.

INDONESIA: Three national parks in Sumatra—Gunung Leuser, Kerinci Seblat, and Bukit Barisan Selatan—were added to the World Heritage List in 2004 by the United Nations Educational Scientific and Cultural Organization (UNESCO). The 9,600-square-mile (25,000 km^2) Tropical Rainforest Heritage of Sumatra is home to an estimated 10,000 plant species, more than 200 mammal species, and some 580 bird species. http://whc.unesco.org/pg.cfm?cid=31&id_site=1167.

Also in 2004, the government of Indonesia announced plans to create 12 new protected areas, including the 3,300-square-mile (8,500 km^2) Muller Schwart National Park in Kalimantan and the 1,800-square-mile (4,700 km^2) Jamursba Medi National Park in Papua. At just 127 square miles (330 km^2), Tesso Nilo National Park is one of the smallest but is home to 350 Sumatran elephants and contains one of Sumatra's last tracts of lowland rain forest. Over 1,100 square miles (2,800 km^2) have been converted to agricultural plantations since 1984. http://www.panda.org/news_facts/newsroom/press_releases/news.cfm?uNewsID=11161.

Julie Maher/WCS

PAKISTAN: In July 2004, the residents of Hushey, a village in northeastern Pakistan received the Conservation Hero Award for Asia from the Disney Wildlife Conservation Fund when they caught and released a snow leopard that had been preying on their livestock. The villagers captured the leopard in January after it had killed 18 goats and sheep. They had experienced three other attacks over the past three years. The average annual household income in Hushey is between $300 and $400—the livestock were reportedly worth between $618 and $1,352. http://www.SnowLeopardConservancy.org/hushe.htm.

Alain Compost, BirdLife

EAST TIMOR: The unexpected discovery of five species of globally threatened birds in East Timor led to renewed calls in 2004 for the international community to help them establish a protected area system. Currently, East Timor contains just two pilot protected areas: a 115-square-mile (300 km^2) terrestrial and marine preserve, and a smaller, mountainous wetland that has been badly polluted and deforested. The recent survey discovered that the larger area is home to the vulnerable black cuckoo dove *(Turacoena modesta)* and Timor sparrow *(Padda fuscata)*, the endangered Timor green pigeon *(Treron psittacea)* and Timor imperial pigeon *(Ducula cinneracea)*, as well as the critically endangered yellow-crested cockatoo *(Cacatua sulphurea)*. http://www.iucn.org/themes/wcpa/newsbulletins/news_may04.html#timor.

Chris Rose, BirdLife

THE PHILIPPINES: Filipino president Gloria Macapagal Arroyo established the 800-square-mile (2,000 km²) Quirino Protected Landscape in March 2004 on Luzon Island. Together with Peñablanca Protected Landscape and Seascape, created in October 2003, the total protected area in the Sierra Madre Biodiversity Corridor totals nearly 1,500 square miles (3,900 km²) and includes habitat for the critically endangered Philippine eagle *(Pithecophaga jefferyi)*. http://www.ops.gov.ph/records/proc_no548.htm.

Dennis DeMello/WCS

MYANMAR: In March 2004, the government of Myanmar established a sprawling, 8,450-square-mile (22,000 km²) reserve for tigers *(Panthera tigris)*—the largest protected area for the endangered big cats on Earth and the only one outside of India. The Vermont-sized Hukaung Valley Tiger Reserve also contains populations of Asian elephants *(Elephas maximus)*, rare clouded leopards *(Neofelis nebulosa)*, and endangered gaur *(Bos guarus)*. Surveys in 2003 revealed that 100 to 150 tigers remain out of a population once believed to number in the thousands. When combined with three other protected areas in Myanmar that comprise the Northern Forest Complex—and a contiguous tiger preserve in India—the Hukaung forms the core of more than 11,500 square miles (30,000 km²) of mostly pristine forest habitat. *Science and Exploration* (New York: WCS, 2004).

John Goodrich

RUSSIAN FAR EAST: Russian customs officials in the Siberian state of Primorsky Krai made a record seizure of poached animal parts in 2004. A truck bound for China contained 768 bear paws thought to be from the Himalayan black bear *(Ursus thibetanus)*, 24 bear gallbladders, 280 musk glands from musk deer, 64 deer penises, 142 deer antlers, 855 pounds of sea cucumber *(Stichopus japonicus)*, 108 pounds of frog fat from an estimated 100,000 frogs—as well as more than 5,500 pelts from Siberian weasel *(Mustela sibirica)*, sable *(Martes zibellina)*, raccoon dog *(Nyctereutes procyonoides)*, red fox *(Vulpes vulpes)*, and red squirrel *(Sciurus vulgaris)*. *TRAFFIC Bulletin* 20(2004):35.

Otto Pfister

INDIA: Three species of critically endangered vulture, Oriental white-backed *(Gyps bengalensis)*, long-billed *(G. indicus)*, and slender-billed *(G. tenuirostris)*, have shown catastrophic declines in India over the past decade. In 2004, the culprit was identified as diclofenac, an anti-inflammatory drug given to cattle, that the birds ingest when they feed on dead animals; it appears to cause kidney failure and gout in vultures. Oriental white-backed vultures were once the most common raptors in the Indian subcontinent; they have declined by 95 percent since the 1990s. *Nature* 427(2004):630–633.

Dave Curry/Environmental Investigation Agency

INDONESIA: A study published in February 2004 found that the Indonesian half of Borneo has lost nearly 11,600 square miles (30,000 km^2) of forest since the last major El Niño event of 1997–1998 caused widespread forest fires. More than two-thirds of the losses were found in proposed and existing protected areas. The rate of deforestation throughout Indonesia reportedly climbed from 10 to 15 acres (4–6 ha) per minute in 2003 to 32 acres (13 ha) per minute in 2004, largely due to illegal logging. *Conservation Biology* 18(2004): 249–254; I. Khaeruddin, the Nature Conservancy, pers. comm., 2004.

CHINA: A joint Chinese–American field survey seeking evidence of South China tigers *(Panthera tigris amoyensis)* in eight reserves scattered across the animal's historic range in south central China failed to find signs of the critically endangered cat. The survey results, published in 2004, covered 180 miles (290 km) of mountain trails and nearly 400 days of infrared remote camera traps, as well as interviews with local villagers. *Oryx* 38(2004):40–47.

CHINA: According to a 2004 report, China is now the world's second largest importer of forest products; just a decade ago it ranked seventh. After devastating summer floods in 1998, China passed a logging ban in the country, causing wood imports to nearly double between 1997 and 2002. Much of the imported wood now comes from Asia, with Russia providing more than 40 percent of the country's demand. Combined imports from Malaysia and Indonesia account for another 20 percent. *China and Forest Trade in the Asia-Pacific Region: Implication for Forests and Livelihoods* (Washington, DC: Forest Trends, 2004).

Julie Maher/WCS

RUSSIAN FAR EAST: Only about 30 critically endangered Far Eastern leopards *(Panthera pardus orientalis)* currently exist in the wild, according to surveys published in 2003. Camera traps in a portion of the leopards' range support other estimates based on track distributions in snow. Genetic analyses have indicated that genetic diversity of at least one population is extremely low, but so far there are no indicators that inbreeding is a major threat. Recent surveys in China have shown that leopards cross the border, suggesting that recovery plans must include the Hunchun Tiger Leopard Reserve, which was created in China in 2002. Results of camera trap survey of Far Eastern leopard population in southwest Primoski Krai, winter 2002–2003 (WCS/ISUNR, 2003); D. Miquelle, WCS, pers. comm., 2004.

Julie Maher/WCS

AFGHANISTAN: Residents of Afghanistan's Wakhan Corridor appear to have responded to calls by the Transitional Authority to hand in their arms and stop hunting snow leopards *(Uncia uncia),* according to a 2003 report by TRAFFIC analyzing hunting and trade of the endangered cats. However, United Nations Environment Programme staff have reported that snow leopard pelts from elsewhere in Badakhshan Province were being sold in fur markets in Kabul, primarily to foreign aid workers and military personnel, for about $1,000 per pelt. *Fading Footsteps: The Killing and Trade of Snow Leopards* (Cambridge, UK: TRAFFIC International, 2003).

Ivan Seredkin

RUSSIAN FAR EAST: The United Nations Development Programme launched a five-year, $13 million initiative to promote conservation of four major rivers in Kamchatka in 2003. The grant will fund research, improve conservation strategies for the region, and help control bear and salmon poaching. Kamchatka boasts the greatest salmon diversity in the world, with six oceangoing and two freshwater species; an estimated 25 percent of all Pacific wild salmon spawn there. During the Cold War, the salmon were protected by Kamchatka's restricted military status, but since the collapse of the Soviet Union, salmon caviar poaching has become widespread, netting an estimated $1 billion annually. *Science* 301(2003):1167.

Australia, New Zealand, and the Pacific Islands

KEN KOSTEL

Virtually all of the isolated terrestrial ecosystems in the Pacific are confronting challenges particular to island biogeography—including Australia and New Zealand. These include rising human populations within a confined space, unsustainable land use, and the disastrous spread of invasive species. Very few intact forests remain on the islands and some estimates put the number of local endangered bird species at 50 times that of endemic South American birds and 100 times that of African birds. Coastal systems, too, are suffering from the effects of sediment, nutrient, and pesticide runoff. Unsustainable fishing practices, both subsistence and commercial, as well as hunting and collecting for the traditional Asian medicine market, are also taking a toll on shallow water habitat and coastal marine species. However, the immediacy of threats throughout the region has galvanized conservation action and produced some promising results for the future of these fragile ecosystems.

AUSTRALIA: Areas surrounding Darwin are preparing for an invasion of cane toads *(Bufo marinus)*. Originally released in Queensland sugar plantations in 1935 to control insects, the toads are known to crowd out, eat, or poison other animals. Populations of native wildlife have declined in areas populated by large numbers of cane toads, and potential local extinction of the northern quoll *(Dasyrus hallucatus),* a rabbit-sized marsupial, and monitor lizards *(Varanus panoptes)* in Kakadu National Park are of particular concern. *Nature* 432(2004):796–798.

Paul Baker

HAWAII: Researchers from Ohio State University and the University of Hawaii reported that coral reefs near popular cast-fishing sites in Hawaii have up to twice the damage as reefs near unfished areas. The 2004 study concluded that this was the result of discarded monofilament fishing line, which entangles and then abrades the coral as it is swept by tidal surges, killing live polyps. *Conservation Biology* 18(2004):1645–1650.

HAWAII: In November 2004, one of the last three known po'ouli *(Melamprosops phaeosoma)* died in captivity of avian malaria. The bird was captured in September in the Hanawi Natural Area Reserve and transported to the Maui Bird Conservation Center as part of what was considered a "last-ditch effort" to save the bird from extinction through captive breeding. The other two birds, believed to be a male and a female, had not been seen in several months at the time of the death. http://pacificislands.fws.gov/wnews/pooulideath.pdf.

NEW ZEALAND: The New Zealand Department of Conservation (DOC) reported in 2004 that, of the approximately 2,400 species indigenous to the country, more than one-third (847) are threatened with extinction. Of those, 77 percent are in decline and have no program specifically targeting their recovery. Species of concern include plants, ferns, and land invertebrates as well as two birds: the crested grebe *(Poliocephalus rufopectus)* and erect-crested penguin *(Eudyptes sclateri)*. *Annual Report for the Year Ended 30 June 2004* (Wellington, New Zealand: Department of Conservation, 2004).

David Ledig/US Fish and Wildlife

HAWAII: In 2004, the 'alala, or Hawaiian crow *(Corvus hawaiiensis)*, celebrated its most successful year of breeding in captivity. Already extinct in the wild, 10 'alala were born during the year at two breeding facilities, raising the total number of crows in existence to 50. A. Lieberman, Zoological Society of San Diego, pers. comm., 2004.

Lyn Wells/ BirdLife

NEW ZEALAND: Fifty Campbell Island teal *(Anas nesiotis)* were reintroduced to Campbell Island in September 2004. The release came after the world's largest rat eradication program, a three-year effort by New Zealand's Department of Conservation to rid the island of the introduced predator that originally caused the teal's demise in the wild. At one point, the population of these small ducks fell to just three known individuals. http://bibpurl.oclc.org/web/6694.

NORTHERN MARIANA ISLANDS: The US Fish and Wildlife Service downlisted the Tinian monarch *(Monarcha takatsukasae)* under the Endangered Species Act from endangered to threatened in 2004. The bird was originally listed in 1970 because habitat loss on Tinian Island threatened the small remaining population with extinction. Since then, the monarch has successfully adapted to nonnative habitat; a 1996 survey counted about 56,000 birds. http://policy.fws.gov/library/04-20700.html.

Tim Sutterfield/ US Navy

AUSTRALIA: Tasmania is clearing land faster than almost anywhere in the developed world according to a 2004 report by the Wilderness Society. An average 78 square miles (200 km^2) of native forest are clear-cut or burned annually, and 300 square miles (777 km^2) of native forest were converted for plantations in the last seven years. In 2000, the last year for which industry data are available, Tasmania produced more than 6 million tons (5.4 million t) of wood chips. The island currently retains less than 13 percent of its old-growth forest. *Protecting Forests, Growing Jobs* (Canberra: The Wilderness Society, 2004).

NEW ZEALAND: An infection that killed three highly endangered kakapos, or night parrots *(Strigops habroptilus)* in July 2004 was later found to be caused by a virulent but easily treated soil bacterium. Massey University scientists identified the bacterium as erysipelas, which had never before been seen in the kakapo. The disease outbreak claimed the lives of two juvenile females shortly after their transfer to Chalky Island, one of two islands where all known kakapo live. The remaining 23 kakapo were later inoculated against infection. http://www.doc.govt.nz/whats-new/presult.asp?prID=1519.

BirdLife International

AUSTRALIA: The Australian Koala Foundation presented the federal government with current estimates for the country's koala *(Phascolarctos cinereus)* population and requested that the animal's status be upgraded to "vulnerable." An estimated 7 to 10 million koalas inhabited Australia at the time of European settlement more than 200 years ago; today only about 100,000 remain. Their numbers were severely reduced by hunting, but today they are threatened by fragmentation and loss of their native eucalyptus forest habitat. http://www.savethekoala.com/vulnerable.html.

M. DaRocha/WCS

Jim Schultz/Chicago Zoological Society

GUAM: After a 15-year absence, the Micronesian kingfisher *(Halcyon cinnamomina cinnamomina)* returned to its home on Guam in 2003. Twenty-nine kingfishers were taken to zoos in North America in the mid-1980s to be bred after wild populations were decimated by the invasive brown tree snake, which feeds on bird eggs. The last bird was seen in the wild in 1988. Biologists are unsure why, after 20 years in captivity, their numbers have barely doubled, but they hope that by transferring the population back to Guam and feeding them a diet of endemic lizards and insects, their numbers will eventually grow to the 150 to 200 needed for reintroduction to the wild. *Draft Revised Recovery Plan for the Sihek or Guam Micronesian Kingfisher* Halcyon cinnamomina cinnamomina (Portland, Oregon: USGS, 2004).

AUSTRALIA: In April 2004, the captain and crew of the Uruguayan fishing vessel *Maya V* were fined and deported for illegal fishing in Australian waters. The ship was apprehended in January with a record 191 tons (173 t) of threatened Patagonian toothfish *(Dissostichus eleginoides)*, commonly known as Chilean sea bass, in its holds. *TRAFFIC Bulletin* 20(2004):38.

Benton Pang/US Fish and Wildlife

NORTHERN MARIANA ISLANDS: Two plant species found only on Rota Island in the Northern Mariana Islands received protection under the US Endangered Species Act in April 2004. *Nesogenes rotensis,* an herbaceous plant in the Verbena family and *Osmoxylon mariannense,* a spindly, soft-wooded tree in the Ginseng family, are threatened by habitat degradation, invasive plant and animal species, and development. Only 34 known *rotensis* and eight *mariannense* remain. http://pacificislands.fws.gov/wnews/marianaplantsfinalnr.pdf.

George Dremeaux/WCS

NEW ZEALAND: The New Zealand Department of Conservation (DOC) instituted Operation Ark in 2004, the largest predator control program the department has ever attempted. The DOC established three "arks," targeted pest control areas to protect threatened species, in the Harunui, Howdon, and Clinton valleys. Infestations of rats and stoats in the regions are threatening endangered birds such as the yellowhead *(Mohoua ochrocephala),* blue duck *(Hymenolaimus malacorhynchos),* and orange-fronted parakeet *(Cyanoramphus malherbi).* http://www.biodiversity.govt.nz/news/media/current/28apr04.html.

AUSTRALIA: A 2004 study revealed that animal pests are costing Australia an estimated $540 million per year in economic, environmental, and social damage. According to the report by the Pest Animal Control Cooperative Research Centre, rabbits cause over $85 million in economic losses, mainly due to crop destruction, and foxes cause more than $143 million in environmental degradation. The Tasmanian pademelon *(Thylogale billardierii),* also known as the rufous wallaby, and Tasmanian bettong *(Bettongia gaimardi),* a small marsupial, are now extinct on the mainland because of fox predation. *Counting the Cost: Impact of Invasive Animals in Australia* (Canberra: Pest Animal Control Cooperative Research Centre, 2004).

Ann Maben/Guam Aquatic and Wildlife Resources

NORTHERN MARIANA ISLANDS: Biologists concluded in February 2004 that two Mariana Island birds are now extinct: the Mariana mallard *(Anas platyrhynchos oustaleti)* and the Guam broadbill *(Myiagra freycineti).* The Mariana mallard, a large duck that once inhabited Guam, Tinian, Saipan, and Rota, was listed as endangered in 1977. It was last seen on Guam in 1967 and Tinian in 1974; there have been no confirmed sightings since 1979 on Saipan. The mallard's demise is linked to massive habitat loss and years of unregulated hunting. The Guam broadbill was a small flycatcher that lived only on Guam. When it was listed as endangered in 1984, fewer than 100 individuals remained. Egg predation by the brown tree snake is likely the major factor behind the broadbill's extinction. http://pacificislands.fws.gov/wnews/mallardbroadbillnr.pdf.

Shelley Clarke

GUAM: The Guam seafood company Polar International was fined $20,000 in 2003 for accepting a 3,000-pound (1,360 kg) shipment of shark fins from a Taiwanese vessel. The vessel owners were also fined $10,000. US law prohibits fishing vessels and companies from unloading shark fins without the accompanying carcasses in order to prevent fishermen from removing the fins and dumping still-living sharks back into the water to die—an effort to discourage the lucrative Asian trade in shark fins. The number of fins confiscated was estimated to represent 29,000 pounds (13,000 kg) of shark, representing thousands of individuals. http://www.nmfs.noaa.gov/ole/news/news_PID_121003.htm.

Tony Palliser

NEW ZEALAND: The New Zealand storm petrel (referred to as *Oceanites maorianus,* although the bird's taxonomy is yet to be formalized) was rediscovered in late 2003 near New Zealand's North Island. The sightings were the first records of this "extinct" species, previously known only from fossils and three 19th century specimens. Between 10 and 20 individuals were seen in November 2003 and 11 were spotted in January 2004. http://www.birdlife.net/news/news/2004/02/nz_storm-petrel.html.

NEW CALEDONIA: A study published in 2003 reported that the world's most threatened tropical dry forests are those in New Caledonia. Researchers compared data from 9 of the 11 global biodiversity hotspots containing dry tropical forests and found that in New Caledonia, only about 39 square miles (101 km^2) remain, with only 7 percent protected in just three areas: two city parks and another reserve that has been severely degraded by fire and grazing in recent years. This ecosystem holds the highest proportion of the island's endemic species. *Biodiversity & Conservation* 12(2003):1687–1697.

Central and South America

JESSE CHAPMAN-BRUSCHINI

Habitat degradation and destruction continue in Central and South America, largely driven by poorly planned economic development—which is often subsidized by natural resource extraction. Ecosystems are becoming more fragmented and are increasingly threatened by mining, oil and gas drilling, and infrastructure improvements, all of which bring new roads, dams, colonization, and an advancing agricultural frontier to once-remote areas. As a result, unsustainable hunting and illegal logging are on the rise. A few countries have resorted to military protection for their most threatened species and protected areas. In the midst of so many threats, however, there are reasons for hope. Indigenous communities are mobilizing to defend their environmental rights. Conservation organizations are building alliances with local counterparts, and there is a growing awareness of the global importance of the region's rich biodiversity.

BRAZIL: Deforestation in the Brazilian Amazon is approaching the record rates of the mid-1990s, according to the Brazilian National Institute for Space Research. Satellite images show that approximately 9,170 square miles (23,750 km^2) of forest were lost in 2003, up from 8,983 (23,266) the year before. Preliminary deforestation figures indicate that an area bigger than the state of New Jersey—between 8,920 and 9,420 square miles (23,100 and 24,400 km^2)—was razed in 2004. Along the BR-163 road that cuts through the heart of the Amazon, deforestation increased fivefold. Since 1978, an area nearly the size of Texas has been cleared—about 240,000 square miles (621,600 km^2). Much of this land has been converted to soybean farms and cattle ranches: Brazil is currently the world's largest exporter of both soybeans and beef. *Arborvitae* 23(2003):3; A. Taber, F. Marques, Wildlife Conservation Society, pers. comm., 2004.

COLOMBIA: In March 2004, the Colombian government announced that US-backed aerial fumigation of coca and poppy fields will not extend to Colombia's national parks unless manual eradication efforts fail. Colombian health officials and environmentalists claim that the herbicide damages crops and native plants and endangers animal and human health. According to Colombian antinarcotics police, more than 500 square miles (1,300 km^2) of coca and opium poppy were sprayed in 2004. Reuters, March 24, 2004; *BBC News,* December 23, 2004.

WCS

CHILE: In September 2004, Goldman Sachs Charitable Fund transferred ownership of 618,000 acres (250,000 ha) on Tierra del Fuego Island to the Wildlife Conservation Society. The parcel includes the world's southernmost stands of old growth forests, peat bogs, and 3,000-foot (914 m) mountains. It supports many guanacos *(Lama guanicoe)* that are in decline elsewhere in the region as well as threatened species, including Magellanic woodpeckers *(Campephilus magellanicus),* firecrown hummingbirds *(Sephanoides fernandensis),* and the culpeo fox *(Pseudalopex culpaeus).* http://wcs.org/353624/4556203.

Norman Arlott/ BirdLife

PANAMA: In August 2004, the US and Panamanian governments and the Nature Conservancy signed debt-for-nature agreements, reducing Panama's US debt and generating $11 million over the next 12 years for conservation of the rich lowland forests in Darien National Park. The 2,200-square-mile (5,700 km^2) park is an essential stopover for birds migrating between South and North America and is home to a number of threatened and endangered animals, including the jaguar *(Panthera onca),* harpy eagle *(Harpia harpyja),* and bush dog *(Speothos venaticus).* http://www.state.gov/r/pa/prs/ps/2004/35457.htm.

ECUADOR: Petrobras, the Brazilian national oil company, will soon begin pumping oil from Yasuní National Park, a United Nations Educational, Scientific and Cultural Organization (UNESCO) Biosphere Reserve and one of the world's megadiverse regions. In August 2004, Ecuador's Environment Ministry licensed Petrobras to build a new 23-mile (37 km) road, a pipeline, two drilling platforms, and a major processing plant within the park. Ecuadorian and international environmental groups have sued, requesting an injunction of the license. http://www.foei.org/forests/digging.html.

Graham Harris

CHILE: Conservación Patagónica purchased 270 square miles (700 km²) in the heart of Chilean Patagonia in July 2004 that it plans to donate for a national park. The parcel, Estancia Valle Chacabuco, is home to one of the largest huemul deer *(Hippocamelus bisulcus)* populations and will better connect two neighboring reserves. The huemul is one of the world's most endangered deer, with only 1,000 to 2,000 left in Chile and Argentina combined. http://www.conservacionpatagonica.org.

COLOMBIA: In April 2004, Revolutionary Armed Forces of Colombia (FARC) rebels kidnapped two field researchers and their guide near the Venezuelan border. A botanist from the University of the Atlantic in Barranquilla, an ornithologist from the University of Antioquia in Medellín, and their guide were conducting biological surveys for a potential national park at the time. After news of their abduction was broadcast, fellow biologists launched an international campaign condemning the kidnappings and held demonstrations in several countries to pressure the rebels into releasing their hostages. The botanist and guide were released on June 18; the ornithologist was held until July 15. *Science* 304(2004):1223.

ARGENTINA: Nearly 9 percent of southern right whales *(Eubalaena australis)* that reproduce off Peninsula Valdés, Argentina, are being attacked by sea gulls, particularly kelp gulls *(Larus dominicanus),* according to research by the Whale Conservation Institute. Mother/calf pairs are the primary victims. Gulls have always fed on sloughed-off whale skin, but now are pecking through intact skin to feed on whale blubber. These attacks interrupt nursing as mothers dive to escape, which endangers calf survival. Dramatic growth in local gull populations has coincided with an increase in open-air garbage dumps and fish processing plants. Provincial and municipal agencies met with regional conservation groups in July 2004 and established an action plan to protect the whales that will continue through 2008. M. Lewis, Centro Nacional Patagónico, pers. comm., 2004.

BRAZIL: The Brazilian government created two new national forests and two extractive reserves in June 2004. About 1,875 square miles (4,856 km^2) will be preserved in the Piraí do Sul National Forest in Paraná, Restinga do Cabedelo in Paraíba, and the Cururupu and Capanã Grande Extractive Reserves in Maranhao and Amazonas states. Capanã Grande is one of the areas targeted by the Amazon Region Protected Areas program, a decade-long initiative to create new protected areas in over 192,000 square miles (500,000 km^2) in the Amazon. http://www.socioambiental.org/home_html.

Julie Maher/WCS

GUATEMALA: An emergency law signed in May 2004 authorizes Guatemalan police and military to patrol Laguna del Tigre National Park, located within the Maya Biosphere Reserve. The park has been invaded by heavily armed drug traffickers, timber thieves, poachers, smugglers of illegal immigrants, and slash-and-burn cattle ranching operations. The new legislation was sparked by extensive media coverage of these illegal activities—and the threats they posed to endangered scarlet macaws (*Ara macao*). Only about 300 scarlet macaws remain in the wild in Guatemala, and all active nesting sites are located within the reserve. R. McNab, Wildlife Conservation Society, pers. comm., 2004.

BRAZIL: In May 2004, the Brazilian government doubled the size of the Grande Sertão Veredas National Park in Minas Gerais state to more than 890 square miles (2,300 km^2). The area harbors the Brazilian merganser (*Mergus octosetaceus*), an endangered duck; the entire Brazilian population totals between 200 and 300 individuals. The extension of the park's borders also creates an ecological corridor to the Serra Geral mountain range in Bahia. http://www.socioambiental.org/home_html.

CHILE: The Chilean congress formed a special committee in May 2004 to investigate the National Forestry Corporation (CONAF), Chile's Forestry and Parks Department, and legal loopholes that foster illegal logging and traffic in alerce (*Fitzroya cypressoides*) timber. A 1976 ban on alerce logging allows dead trees to be felled; since the mid-1970s thousands of acres have been deliberately burned to facilitate harvest. Alerces are one of the planet's rarest tree species, with some living 3,000 to 4,000 years and growing up to 150 feet (46 m) tall. Defensores del Bosque Chileno, a Chilean conservation group, has called for a complete ban on all commercial trade in alerce until legislation is tightened. *TRAFFIC Bulletin* 19, no. 3(2003):115.

David Fisher/Sunbird

ARGENTINA: Argentina's coastal provinces signed an agreement in April 2004 to safeguard their 2,000-mile (3,200 km)-long coastline. The Patagonia Coastal Zone Management Plan (PCZMP), fostered by Fundación Patagonia Natural, will coordinate management, limit coastal development and unregulated tourism, and better protect wildlife and marine species. Hundreds of thousands of Magellanic penguins *(Spheniscus magellanicus)* gather at Punta Tombo and the largest known colony of rockhopper penguins *(Eudyptes chrysocome)* congregate in Tierra del Fuego; large colonies of elephant seals *(Mirounga leonina)* and southern sea lions *(Otaria flavescens)* also assemble in the region, and southern right whales *(Eubalaena australis)* breed off the coast. The United Nations Development Programme (UNDP) and the Global Environmental Facility (GEF) have allocated $5.2 million over the next five years to back implementation of the agreement. *Marine Pollution Bulletin* 48, no. 11–12(2004):1013.

Sylvia Chalukian

BELIZE: An appeal to stop construction of Belize's controversial Chalillo Dam was thrown out by the Privy Council in London, the nation's highest court, in January 2004. Despite dissension by two of the five judges, the council ruled that the Belize government acted within the law in approving the dam despite conservation and safety concerns. The hydroelectric dam, to be built by the Canadian company Fortis, Inc., will flood 2,500 acres (1,000 ha) in the pristine Macal River Valley, endangering some of Central America's rarest species, including jaguars *(Panthera onca),* Morelet's crocodiles *(Crocodylus moreletii),* Baird's tapirs *(Tapirus bairdii),* and scarlet macaws *(Ara macao),* whose only known Belizean nesting sites are in the valley. *New Scientist* 181, no. 2433(2004):7.

PERU: Construction of a highway linking São Paulo, Brazil, on the Atlantic to Peru's Pacific coast is nearing the Peruvian border. The proposed route through Peru will pass near Tambopata National Reserve, which protects some of the Amazon Basin's most intact tropical forests. Areas surrounding Tambopata are being cleared for agriculture, settlements, and logging of valuable mahogany trees *(Swietenia macrophylla). Plant Talk* 33(2003):16.

BRAZIL: Sustainable wildlife management in Brazil's Mamirauá Reserve has allowed several local species to rebound. Studies by Sociedade Civil Mamirauá and the Mamirauá Institute for Sustainable Development show that a prized fish species, the giant pirarucu *(Arapaima gigas),* has increased 350 percent since 1998, and jaguar *(Panthera onca)* sightings have doubled in the last five years. Since 1994, the number of river turtle nests *(Podocnemis sextuberculata, P. unifilis,* and *P. expansa)* increased by 120 percent, and black caiman *(Melanosuchus niger)* populations have almost tripled. Healthier wildlife populations have improved the livelihoods of reserve residents who make a living from artisanal fishing, managed hunting, and forest products: household incomes have reportedly doubled since 1994. H. Lima de Queiroz, Mamirauá Institute, pers. comm., 2004.

LA PLATA RIVER BASIN: The tiny, prolific golden mussel *(Limnoperna fortunei)* that hitchhiked from Asia to Argentina in ballast water in 1991 has now reached Brazil, Paraguay, and Uruguay. These fast-spreading mussels are moving up the La Plata River and its tributaries at a rate of 150 miles (240 km) per year. They suffocate native bivalve species; smother aquatic food chains in lakes, rivers, and wetlands; and can eat enough plankton to alter entire ecosystems. http://el.erdc.usace.army.mil/ansrp/limnoperna_fortunei.htm#Distribution

BRAZIL: Critics of conservation methods in the Pantanal claim that removing cattle from privately owned protected areas increases fire risk. Without grazing cattle, "macega"—highly flammable grasses and bushes—grows uncontrolled, potentially endangering both nearby ranches and wildlife. Dense macega may also discourage marsh deer *(Blastocerus dichotomus),* capybaras *(Hydrochaeris hydrochaeris),* and peccaries from foraging, limiting prey for jaguars in the region. S. Marchini, Wildlife Conservation Society, pers. comm., 2004.

ARGENTINA: The San Juan provincial government is reportedly allowing Barrick Gold Corporation to build two large "open-sky" mines within the San Guillermo Biosphere Reserve. Additional requests for gold extraction are also under consideration, as are ways to modify the reserve's protected status. Two roads opened by mining companies in 2003 have apparently led to increased poaching of the region's wildlife. Conservationists are concerned that cyanide leaching from open-pit mines will contaminate waterways, threatening wildlife and communities living downstream. A. Novaro, Wildlife Conservation Society, pers. comm., 2004.

NICARAGUA: Poaching of critically endangered hawksbill sea turtles *(Eretmochelys imbricata)* on Nicaragua's Pearl Cays has declined by 79 percent over the past four years due to conservation efforts by the Pearl Cays Hawksbill Conservation Project, an alliance of local communities, fishing groups, and government agencies. *Marine Pollution Bulletin* 48, no. 5–6(2004):415–416.

Steve Winter/National Geographic Image Collection

BOLIVIA: More jaguars *(Panthera onca)* may live within the sprawling Kaa' Iya del Gran Chaco National Park than in any protected area in the Americas. A camera trapping study conducted in 2003 by the Capitanía del Alto y Bajo Isosog, the indigenous organization that manages the park, and the Wildlife Conservation Society, suggests that as many as 1,000 jaguars inhabit the 13,000-square-mile (33,700 km^2) park. *Journal of Zoology* 262(2004):295–304.

Europe

JESSE CHAPMAN-BRUSCHINI

European conservation is dominated by land use issues and human management of remaining wildlife and habitats. While there are some notable successes in captive breeding endeavors and reintroductions, continuing extinctions and declines in wildlife abundance and species diversity show that overall trends favor economic development over wildlife conservation—even in a place that, arguably, is better able to afford conservation than other, less developed regions. Europe's determination to address global warming by encouraging renewable energy sources is meeting opposition from bird conservation organizations concerned about the lethal effects of wind turbines on migratory bird species.

N.J. Collar/BirdLife

UNITED KINGDOM: In September 2004, a wild great bustard *(Otis tarda)* flew free in Wiltshire, England, for the first time since 1873. This large, rare bird, long extinct in the United Kingdom, is being reintroduced as part of a plan to boost Russia's bustard population and return the species to Britain. Wild bustard eggs were collected from endangered or abandoned nests on farmland in Saratov, Russia; the chicks were raised and then transported to Britain for release. The goal is to establish a population of 100 great bustards in Britain over the next 4 to 10 years. http://www.greatbustard.com/PressSept.pdf.

L. Stark/WCS

EUROPE: A 2004 report by TRAFFIC Europe revealed that wildlife trade controls in new European Union states allow the legal import of species long banned in the rest of Europe. The report warns that traders in the 10 new accession states could launder illegally obtained wildlife by mixing prohibited species with legal imports of such species as tortoises, parrots, snakes, lizards, and orchids. The report calls on EU governments to establish a Wildlife Trade Task Force to monitor illegal wildlife trade and to support enforcement officers—particularly in the 10 new member states. http://www.traffic.org/25/network4/eu/report.pdf.

UNITED KINGDOM: The most comprehensive study to date of native butterflies, birds, and plants in mainland Britain revealed that butterflies are declining faster than birds. Scientists looked at six large data sets collected over 40 years in England, Wales, and Scotland and examined 15 million records of species submitted by over 20,000 volunteers. The results showed that 71 percent of native butterfly species had decreased over the past 20 years compared to 54 percent of native birds and 28 percent of native plants. Two out of 58 butterfly species and 6 of 1,254 plants became extinct. Extrapolating the results of the study to invertebrates worldwide suggests that insects may be suffering similar extinction rates to those of larger, better-studied, and more visible animals. *Science* 303(2004):1879–1888.

EUROPE: Conservationists are concerned about possible impacts on bird species from planned wind farms in Europe. Twelve wind turbines will be erected on Bulgaria's famous Black Sea coast along Europe's second most important bird migration route. More than 200,000 birds, including 87,000 white storks *(Ciconia ciconia)* and 7,000 raptors flew through the region in 2003. A proposed 80-turbine offshore wind farm in the North Sea west of Sylt, Germany, has prompted a complaint by NABU (the German BirdLife partner) to the European Commission. The wind farm would be built at the center of the Eastern German Bight Important Bird Area, threatening key seabird populations such as red-throated and black-throated divers *(Gavia stellata* and *G. arctica),* and sandwich terns *(Sterna sandvicensis). BirdLife in Europe* 8(2003):4; *BBC Wildlife* 22(2004):22.

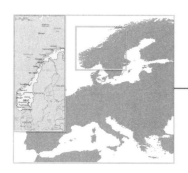

NORWAY: Europe's last remaining population of wild reindeer *(Rangifer tarandus)* is in steep decline according to a study by the United Nations Environment Programme. Half of their habitat in southern Norway has been lost in the last 50 years. The 30,000 remaining animals are fragmented into 24 isolated groups, squeezed into small areas with limited food supplies. They are threatened by construction and hydroelectric projects; infrastructure such as power lines, reservoirs, and dams act as barriers that reindeer herds are reluctant to cross. Experts have predicted that there may be just 15,000 animals left by 2020. *New Scientist* 180, no. 2416(2003):7.

M. DaRocha/WCS

EUROPE: The European Commission is developing a new large carnivore protection and management initiative. As part of this, the commission met in Spain in November 2003 to review the gray wolf's *(Canis lupus)* status across the European Union and accession countries and to discuss conservation strategies for the species. There are plans to develop similar guidelines for the Eurasian lynx *(Lynx lynx)*, Iberian lynx *(L.x pardinus)*, and brown bear *(Ursus arctos)*. *Natura* 2000 17(2004):15.

EUROPE: Europe's eel population is collapsing according to a recent study by the International Council for the Exploration of the Sea. The number of juvenile European eels *(Anguilla anguilla)* reaching rivers from their mid-Atlantic nursery grounds has fallen by 99 percent since the 1970s because of dams, pollution, and overfishing. Because the American eel population is also declining, some scientists believe that changes in ocean currents due to global warming or a parasite or virus in breeding zones may be the real problem. Eels are an important link in the food chain as prey for cormorants, herons, otters, and other wildlife. http://www.ices.dk/marineworld/eel.asp.

BirdLife International

PORTUGAL: A new colony of Europe's rarest breeding seabird, the Zino's petrel *(Pterodroma madeira),* was discovered in 2003. The critically endangered bird is found only on Madeira Island. The new colony raises the total population to 40 pairs—a 30 percent increase. Madeira National Park is negotiating with landowners to expropriate the bird's entire breeding area, and a campaign by SPEA (BirdLife Portugal) convinced the Portuguese Ministry of National Defense to relocate a planned radar station on the island to lessen its potential impact on breeding birds. *World Birdwatch* 25(2003):7.

UNITED KINGDOM: A decades-long badger culling program meant to control the transmission of tuberculosis (TB) to cattle may instead increase the spread of the disease, according to a 2003 study by the British government. Badgers *(Meles meles)* can transmit TB to cattle, and bovine tuberculosis, which has increased substantially over the past 20 years, can then be transmitted to humans. Researchers found that culling has wiped out nearly 80 percent of badger populations in areas with disease outbreaks, leaving the surviving badgers without stable social groups. This causes the badgers to wander the countryside, further spreading the disease. More than 20,000 badgers were killed between 1975 and 1997. *Nature* 426(2003):834–837.

Iberian Lynx Ex-Situ Conservation Program

SPAIN AND PORTUGAL: A 2004 study of one of the world's most endangered big cats, the Iberian lynx *(Lynx pardinus),* concluded that fewer than 150 remain in the wild on the Iberian Peninsula—just 28 breeding females exist in two separate populations. Myriad threats, from road building, farming, and forest clearing to the decline of their main prey, wild rabbits, have caused their precipitous decline. Efforts are under way in Andalucía, Spain, to develop a captive breeding population of Iberian lynx to bolster the two remnant populations. *BBC Wildlife* 22, no. 6 (2004).

UNITED KINGDOM: A shortage of food for seabirds resulted in a catastrophic breeding season in the British Isles during 2004. While overfishing may be one factor, experts now believe that climate change may be the principal reason. New research by the Sir Alistair Hardy Foundation for Ocean Science in Plymouth revealed that in the North Sea, normally abundant plankton have virtually disappeared due to warmer water temperatures. The fish that feed on these microscopic organisms, as well as the seabirds dependent on fish, are starving to death in an area that has been their natural home for thousands of years. *Nature* 430(2004):881.

Middle East and North Africa

KEN KOSTEL

The stark landscapes of North Africa and the Middle East can be surprisingly fragile. Many of the animals that rely on the delicate balance of arid ecosystems are threatened by human encroachment in the form of development and natural resource extraction, overgrazing, or water pollution. Few of the countries in the region have the environmental institutions or legal frameworks to prevent further decline. One potential bright spot in the region is the Iraqi wetlands, where so far more than $20 million has been allocated to restore the Mesopotamian marshes.

MOROCCO: An eight-year census and habitat evaluation of the Barbary macaque *(Macaca sylvanus)* in Morocco's Middle Atlas Mountains concluded that the world's largest remaining population of the monkeys is seriously threatened by human activity. The results of the census, published in 2005, found that macaques declined by between 77 and 90 percent when compared with 1994 population estimates. Much of the decline was likely caused by the loss of cedar forest due to overgrazing. *Biological Conservation* 121(2005):635.

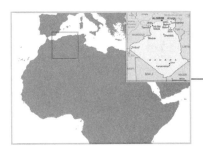

ALGERIA: Sixteen sites totaling more than 625 square miles (1,620 km^2) in Algeria were declared wetlands of international importance under the Ramsar Convention on Wetlands in December 2004. With more than 11,400 square miles (30,000 km^2), Algeria now ranks eighth in the world in total area designated under the convention. Panafrican News Agency (PANA), December 20, 2004

UNITED ARAB EMIRATES: Residents of the United Arab Emirates (UAE) have the world's largest ecological footprint, according to a 2004 World Wildlife Fund report. The footprint measures factors such as consumption of food, timber, fiber, and other natural resources; waste generated by energy production; and the amount of land used for human infrastructure. Based on these criteria, residents of the UAE have an ecological footprint of more than 4.5 times the world average. *Living Planet Report 2004* (Gland, Switzerland: WWF, 2004).

Julie Maher/WCS

SAUDI ARABIA: A 2004 study of western Arabia's hamadryas baboons *(Papio hamadryas hamadryas)* found them to be genetically distinct from those found across the Red Sea in East Africa, according to researchers at the Zoological Society of London and Saudi Arabia's National Commission for Wildlife Conservation and Development. The results suggest that the baboon—the only free-ranging nonhuman primate in Arabia—was not transported to the Arabian Peninsula by humans nor did it colonize the region from the north. These baboons likely reached Arabia via land bridges that have formed periodically in the southern Red Sea. *Molecular Ecology* 13(2004):2819.

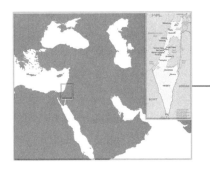

ISRAEL: Between 100 and 150 migrating storks died in the Negev Desert in August 2004 after they drank from pools containing toxic runoff from a chemical plant. The birds were on their way from Europe to their winter range in Africa earlier than usual. Officials and staff at the Rotem chemical plant in southern Israel had not yet put up bird nets and other devices they usually deploy to keep migrating birds away from the pools. Associated Press, August 24, 2004.

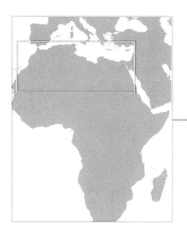

NORTH AFRICA: Satellite analysis of locust breeding areas in North Africa may have revealed one of the factors contributing to periodic regional outbreaks of the biblical pests. A study published in 2004 found that fragmentation of native vegetation, most likely caused by changing precipitation patterns, combined with increases in local food abundance, causes locusts to concentrate into small regions, which can trigger a swarm. During a swarm, billions of individuals can consume as much as 20,000 tons (18,000 t) of vegetation daily and travel up to 2,500 miles (4,000 km). North African countries spend millions of dollars to control locusts, spraying millions of gallons of pesticides on crops and native vegetation. *Ecography* 27(2004):381.

YEMEN: The Socotra Archipelago—three islands in the Indian Ocean off the coast of Yemen—was named a Biosphere Reserve under the United Nations Educational, Scientific and Cultural Organization (UNESCO) Man and Biosphere Programme in 2004. The island group also received $5 million from the United Nations Development Program and the government of Italy in 2003 to support sustainable development and conservation. The islands are reportedly among the world's richest in endemic species, with one-third of the 900 plants, 24 reptile species, and seven species of birds found only on one of the three islands. Threats to biodiversity include introduction of nonnative species such as goats, climate change, and human development. Proposals currently exist to dot the islands with five-star hotels, a casino, and a golf course. *Science* 303(2004):1753.

IRAQ: Researchers at the US Geological Survey studying satellite images of the Shatt al-Arab estuary at the confluence of the Tigris and Euphrates rivers concluded that 80 percent of the date palms in Iraq and Iran have disappeared over the past three decades. The estuary is home to the largest date palm forest in the world—in the mid-1970s there were an estimated 17 to 18 million in the region, one-fifth of the world total. War, soil salination, and pest infestations have destroyed approximately 14 million palms: 9 million in Iraq and 5 million in Iran. Many of the remaining trees are reported to be in poor condition. *Marine Pollution Bulletin* 48(2004):415.

North America

JESSE CHAPMAN-BRUSCHINI

Development, extractive industries, invasive species, and the steady march of urbanization are placing increasing pressure on North American wildlands and animals. In the United States, some existing environmental regulations are being changed or reinterpreted in ways that further threaten wilderness and wildlife. However, there is also good news, with regional and international alliances making a significant difference at local levels. New conservation areas have been established and plans for additional protection are being developed. Scientists have also made significant progress in identifying wildlife corridors that are crucial to restoring connectivity among wildlands in North America.

UNITED STATES: In January 2005, the Bush administration released new rules governing the management and planning of the nation's forests, revising the 1976 National Forest Management Act. The rules, which apply to all 298,000 square miles (770,000 km^2) of national forest and grassland, no longer require forest managers to prepare environmental impact statements when developing or revising management plans for individual national forests, and give them discretion over the methods and timing for public involvement. The new rules also drop the mandate that national forests be managed to maintain "viable populations" of fish and wildlife, a regulation that has helped regulate logging and protect endangered species since 1982. *Federal Register* 70(2005):1023; http://www.wilderness.org/NewsRoom/Release/20041222.cfm.

CANADA: In November 2004, the World Conservation Union's (IUCN) 3rd World Conservation Congress passed a recommendation calling for stronger action to protect Canada's boreal forest—one of the largest intact forests in the world. The resolution urges Canada to protect the overall health of the forest, respect the rights and interests of indigenous people in land use decisions, and consider ecosystem land use before developing further industry in the region. The 2003 Canadian Boreal Initiative aims to protect at least 50 percent of the region in interconnected protected areas and is backed by 11 companies, conservation groups, and indigenous peoples. *Taiga News* 45(2003):3; http://www.borealcanada.ca/pdf/CGR3Rec021.pdf.

UNITED STATES: Snowmobile access to Yellowstone National Park during the 2004–2005 winter season was granted after a series of legal battles dating back to 2000 were resolved. The three-year National Park Service (NPS) plan allows up to 720 guided snowmobiles per day in the park, nearly triple the number allowed the previous winter. Under the Clinton administration, the NPS banned snowmobiles in the park because of concerns over air and noise pollution and wildlife disturbance and displacement—a decision based on 14 years of scientific study. The Bush administration overturned the original ban, then appealed a court ruling reinstating the ban. http://www.nps.gov/yell/press/04121.htm; http://www.npca.org/magazine/september_october/news1.asp.

UNITED STATES: The Sierra Nevada Forest Plan Amendment was affirmed by US Department of Agriculture Forest Service Chief Dale Bosworth in November 2004. The revised management plan for 18,000 square miles (47,000 km^2) of the Sierra National Forest more than doubles logging quotas, increases the size of trees that can be cut from 20 to 30 inches (51–76 cm) in diameter, loosens protections for endangered wildlife, and opens up old-growth forest areas to tree removal projects. http://www.fs.fed.us/r5/news/2004/snfpa-upheld.html; http://www.forestsforever.org/framework2.html.

Bonnie Fischer

UNITED STATES: A November 2004 report by the Pew Center on Global Climate Change documents significant global warming impacts on wildlife and ecosystems in the United States. Some examples cited by the report include the red fox *(Vulpes vulpes),* which is moving northward and displacing the arctic fox *(Alopex lagopus).* Some plants are leafing out or flowering earlier, altering food availability for butterflies and other insects. The timing of bird migrations is also shifting: upon arrival at breeding grounds, some species are finding less food and habitat. The report warns that this century is projected to warm at 2 to 10 times the 20th century rate, potentially creating fundamental changes in US ecosystems and wildlife. http://www.pewclimate.org/document.cfm?documentID=371.

MEXICO: In November 2004, the Mexican government made the largest conservation land transaction in the country's history. The $3 million, 370,000-acre (150,000 ha) purchase of tropical forest on the Yucatán Peninsula was made in collaboration with the Nature Conservancy and Pronatura Peninsula de Yucatán. The region is in the heart of the Calakmul Biosphere Reserve and is home to a large jaguar *(Panthera onca)* population. It also serves as a stopover for 3 billion migratory birds each winter. http://nature.org/success/art14325.html.

UNITED STATES: The US Army Corps of Engineers began construction in November 2004 of a permanent electrical barrier to keep invasive Asian carp *(Cyprinus carpio)* out of the Great Lakes. The $9.1 million barrier is being installed in a Chicago canal that links the Mississippi River with the lakes via the Illinois River. Asian carp were originally imported in the 1970s to remove algae from catfish farm ponds but escaped into the Mississippi River basin during early 1990s flooding. The voracious carp grow to 150 pounds (68 kg) and can eat 40 percent of their body weight per day, outcompeting native species such as paddlefish *(Polyodon spathula),* bigmouth buffalo *(Ictiobus cyprinellus),* and freshwater mollusks. http://www.epa.gov/greatlakes/invasive/asiancarp/.

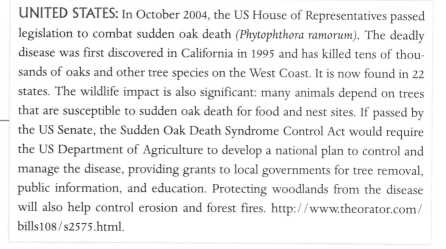

UNITED STATES: In October 2004, the US House of Representatives passed legislation to combat sudden oak death *(Phytophthora ramorum)*. The deadly disease was first discovered in California in 1995 and has killed tens of thousands of oaks and other tree species on the West Coast. It is now found in 22 states. The wildlife impact is also significant: many animals depend on trees that are susceptible to sudden oak death for food and nest sites. If passed by the US Senate, the Sudden Oak Death Syndrome Control Act would require the US Department of Agriculture to develop a national plan to control and manage the disease, providing grants to local governments for tree removal, public information, and education. Protecting woodlands from the disease will also help control erosion and forest fires. http://www.theorator.com/bills108/s2575.html.

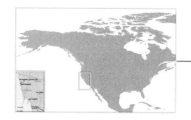

J. Maher/WCS

UNITED STATES: One-third of North America's bird species have declined significantly since 1966, according to a 2004 National Audubon Society analysis of 654 native bird species. Using national Breeding Bird Survey data, they found that declines varied by habitat. Grassland species suffered 70 percent losses, shrubland birds lost 36 percent, urban and forest birds were down 23 and 25 percent, respectively, and wetland species declined 13 percent. The report cited a range of causes, from pollution, overgrazing, and loss of grasslands to poor forest management, wetlands development, invasive species, and poor land use. http://www.audubon.org/bird/stateofthebirds.

UNITED STATES: The South Bay Salt Pond Restoration Project began converting industrial salt ponds along San Francisco Bay into marshes in July 2004. Like many other wetland restoration projects across North America, this ambitious effort seeks to restore native bird, fish, and plant species to the region and will provide stopover habitat for migratory birds. Over 80 percent of San Francisco Bay's primary tidal marshes have disappeared due to salt extraction, farming, and urban development. http://www.southbayrestoration.org/Project_Description.html.

UNITED STATES: The Center for Biological Diversity reported that the US government failed to effectively implement the Endangered Species Act (ESA) from 1973 to 1994, leading to the loss of 113 species. The May 2004 report states that 77 percent of those species were known to be endangered, but protection was repeatedly delayed—often for 10 or 20 years—until the species became extinct. The Clinton administration averaged 65 listings to the ESA per year; the Bush Sr. administration averaged 59. The current Bush administration has listed an average of 9 species per year. http://www.sw-center.org.

WCS

UNITED STATES: New York State passed legislation in May 2004 banning the sale of lead sinkers weighing one-half ounce (14 g) or less in an effort to protect ducks, swans, herons, gulls, loons, and other waterbirds from lead poisoning. Birds generally die two to three weeks after swallowing lead sinkers, which they often mistake for food or grit. Lead poisoning causes loss of balance and impairs a bird's ability to fly and to feed or care for young. New Hampshire and Maine have passed similar legislation regulating the use or sale of lead fishing tackle. http://www.adkscience.org/loons/lead.htm.

Dennis DeMello/WCS

UNITED STATES: Record numbers of endangered southern sea otters *(Enhydra lutris nereis)* washed up on the California coast in spring during 2003 and 2004. Scientists found some to be infected with parasites, *Sarcocystis neurona* or *Toxoplasma gondii,* which attack the brain and nervous system. Wildlife veterinarians believe that the otters ingested shellfish carrying the parasites, which often come from cat and opossum feces and are washed into the sea in storm water runoff.

However, studies in 2003 found that sea otter numbers grew 17 percent from the prior year to 2,505 animals—the highest count since standardized methods were established in 1983. Population analyses indicate a gradual but statistically significant population increase since 1998 of about 0.9 percent per year. *Marine Pollution Bulletin* 46(2003):799; http://www.dfg.ca.gov/news/news04/04048.html.

UNITED STATES: In February 2004, the US Department of the Interior approved BNP Petroleum Corporation's proposal to drill a second natural gas well within Padre Island National Seashore in Texas—home to 11 endangered species and primary nesting grounds for the Kemp's Ridley sea turtle *(Lepidochelys kempii).* The National Park Service approved the first well in 2003. Trucks used during drilling operations can crush turtle nests, and vibrations from rumbling trucks can kill developing embryos. In all, only about 3,000 to 5,000 adult Kemp's ridley sea turtles remain in the wild. http://www.npca.org/magazine/september_october/news2.asp; http://www.us-parks.com/padre_island/wildlife_highlights.html.

William Karesh

UNITED STATES: In the summer of 2004, 10 pronghorn antelopes *(Antilocapra americana)* were outfitted with global positioning system (GPS) collars during their 120-mile (193 km) migration from Grand Teton National Park to the Green River Basin in Wyoming. Biologists will track the pronghorns' exact routes to identify critical bottleneck areas and human activities that endanger their yearly migration—the longest of any terrestrial mammal between Argentina and central Canada. The Pronghorn Migration Corridor Initiative, an alliance of conservation nongovernmental organizations, ranchers, hunters, businesses, and federal, state, and local agencies, is seeking to protect the migration. http://www.wcs.org/pronghornmigration/.

Steve Winter / National Geographic

MEXICO: In 2004, endangered olive ridley sea turtles *(Lepidochelys olivacea)* laid eggs in record numbers along Mexico's Pacific coast largely as a result of vigorous protection of La Escobilla beach, their principal nesting site. Armed federal agents and environmental officials currently patrol the beach during nesting season. *New York Times,* October 14, 2004, p. A12.

CANADA: The Canadian government has begun implementing plans to create 10 new national parks, expand two existing national parks, and create five new national marine conservation reserves by 2008. Since August 2003, agreements have been signed to create Ukkusiksalik National Park in Nunavut and another national park in Okanagan, British Colombia, as well as marine reserves in the Straight of Georgia and Gwaii Haanas. *Nature Canada* 32(2003/4):7.

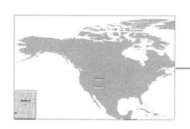

UNITED STATES: Secretary of the Interior Gale Norton announced a "no new wilderness" agreement with the state of Utah in April 2003. The agreement bars millions of acres of land in Utah from consideration as Wilderness Study Areas and protection under the National Wilderness Preservation System. Since passage of the agreement, the Bureau of Land Management (BLM) auctioned off drilling rights to 560 square miles (1,450 km^2) of land, including almost 31 square miles (80 km^2) formerly designated as wilderness-quality. Prior to the settlement, the BLM had a policy of not leasing lands that the agency agreed had wilderness potential. http://www.esa.org/pao/PolicyNewsUpdate/pn2004/09132004.php.

CANADA: The Deh Cho First Nations, 11 aboriginal communities along the upper Mackenzie River, were given temporary control over part of their traditional homelands by the Canadian government in April 2003. The new agreement removes the land from government control—and potential industrial development—for an initial five-year period while more detailed resource assessments are completed. The pristine Mackenzie River watershed covers 700,000 square miles (1,813,000 km^2), one-sixth of Canadian territory. *Arborvitae* 23(2003):5.

WCS

UNITED STATES: The red knot *(Calidris canutus rufa)*, a large beach sandpiper, could face extinction by 2010 according to a 2003 study by the International Wader Study Group. Over the last five years numbers fell from an estimated 50,000 to 31,000. The birds double their body weight on horseshoe crab eggs in Delaware Bay during a critical spring stopover on their 10,000-mile (16,000 km) migration from wintering grounds in Tierra del Fuego, Chile, to breeding grounds in the Canadian Arctic. The birds' decline is linked to two decades of heavy commercial horseshoe crab *(Limulus polyphemus)* fishing. Local and regional fisheries have banned harvesting the crabs in a designated 1,500-square-mile (3,885 km^2) Delaware Bay protected area, and all US Atlantic coastal states have reduced horseshoe crab catches by 50 percent. http://web.uct.ac.za/depts/stats/adu/wsg/pdf/the_cadiz_conclusions.pdf; http://wcs.org/sw-around_the_globe/northamerica/knotandcrab.

Oceans

BIJAL TRIVEDI

Fishermen today leave little to chance using sonar, satellite data, and global positioning systems (GPSs) to pinpoint catches with laser-like accuracy. But the industrial fishing practices they employ are not nearly as precise. Longlines and trawlers catch about 30 million tons (27 million t) of nontarget sea life annually. Bottom trawling also devastates delicate seabed habitats—like reefs and seamounts—that serve as nurseries and sanctuaries for countless species. Overfishing and habitat destruction compound the pervasive challenges posed by pollution and population growth. The result: large predatory fish populations have plummeted and many fisheries have collapsed. But there are expanding efforts to stem this decline. Many countries are establishing marine protected areas (MPAs) that restrict or ban fishing in specific areas of the sea—and results have been promising. There are new laws protecting endangered species, new research is investigating global warming impacts on ocean life, and hundreds of new life forms have been discovered.

Thomas P. Peschak

GLOBAL: The Census of Marine Life (CoML) discovered 106 new fish species and hundreds of plant and animal species in 2004. This raises the total number of ocean species to roughly 230,000—including about 15,482 marine fish. New discoveries include a goby fish found near Guam, a new genus of octopod from the deep Southern Ocean, and a minute mollusk from hydrothermal vents in the Indian Ocean. Scientists anticipate a final species count of nearly 2 million animals and plants. The decade-long count will be completed by 2010. http://www.coml.org.

GLOBAL: The great white shark *(Carcharodon carcharias)* received international protection under the Convention on International Trade in Endangered Species (CITES) in 2004. The new rules mandate that countries continuing to harvest great whites must now issue permits to ensure each specimen is caught legally and its capture did not harm the survival of the species. http://www.cites.org/eng/news/press/2004/041014_cop13final.shtml.

Steve Winter/
National Geographic

GLOBAL: Declining numbers of tuna, sharks, billfishes, and turtles have triggered a search for highly biodiverse regions where large oceanic predators and many smaller species congregate. A 2003 study discovered that these so-called hotspots tend to occur between 20° and 30° latitude, close to shore, and near coral reefs, seamounts, and islands—places like Florida's east coast, Australia's Great Barrier Reef, and southern Hawaii. Another study analyzed satellite sea surface temperatures and revealed a 48,000-square-mile (124,000 km^2) hotspot 93 miles (150 km) off the coast of Baja, California. Researchers believe that these sites are important conservation targets. *Proceedings of the National Academy of Sciences* 100(2003):9884–9888; *Oceanography* 17, no. 1 (2004): 90–101.

GLOBAL: In 2004, CITES banned international trade of the Irrawaddy dolphin *(Orcaella brevirostris)*. The small, charismatic, and easily trained dolphin numbers fewer than 1,000 animals across its Asian range. The main threat to the species, which lives in estuaries, bays, and rivers, is drowning in fishing nets. http://www.cites.org/eng/news/press/2004/041014_cop13final.shtml.

Robert Fournier/
The Wild Lensman

GLOBAL: In November 2004, 63 countries banned shark finning—cutting off their fins and throwing the animals overboard to drown—in the Atlantic Ocean. The measure was adopted unanimously by the International Commission for the Conservation of Atlantic Tunas (ICAAT)—but any country could opt out in the six months before restrictions take effect. Sharks are frequently caught by swordfish and tuna fishing operations and are finned for an escalating Asian trade. According to United Nations estimates, 100 million sharks are killed each year. Finning was prohibited in the US Atlantic in 1993. *Washington Post,* November 23, 2004, p. A21.

UNITED STATES: The US Commission on Ocean Policy delivered its final report, *An Ocean Blueprint for the 21st Century,* to Congress and the president in September 2004. It is the first comprehensive government review of US ocean policy since the 1969 Stratton report that sparked the creation of the National Oceanic and Atmospheric Administration. The "blueprint" makes over 200 recommendations, including curbs on overfishing, reduction of pollution runoff, and better fish farm regulation. The report also calls for doubled research spending and an ecosystem-based management strategy rather than a single-species approach. http://www.oceancommission.gov/.

EAST ASIA: Governments of 12 East Asian countries will create new marine protected areas and coordinate management of other regionally important sites under an accord signed in 2003. In August 2004, the group established a final plan for the Sustainable Development Strategy for the Seas of East Asia (SDS-SEA), which will integrate fisheries management, address coastal pollution, and implement sustainable use of the marine environment and resources. *MPA News 5*, no. 7 (2004).

Ron Magill

UNITED STATES: In July 2004, the United States signed the Marine Turtle Conservation Act into law. Now sea turtles are eligible for the Multinational Species Conservation Fund, which provides both a funding source for global coordination and collaboration for individual efforts in developing countries. Efforts will focus on protecting nesting sea turtles and their habitat and on thwarting illegal trade in sea turtle shell, meat, and eggs around the world. http://news.fws .gov/NewsReleases/R9/960CB35D-65B8-D6937BCC9FFE8206D4BA.html.

BirdLife International

SOUTH AFRICA: Four new nearshore marine protected areas declared in June 2004 will increase South Africa's protected coastline from 11 to 18 percent. The Ailwal Shoal, a 49-square-mile (127 km^2) subtidal coral reef, harbors many hard and soft corals and endangered endemic fish. A 502-square-mile (1,300 km^2) marine protected area (MPA) near Pondoland conserves 56 miles (90 km) of coastline near Port St. Johns, protecting part of an important sardine migration. Bird Island MPA, comprising 27 square miles (70 km^2) in Algoa Bay, was integrated into the Greater Addo Elephant National Park, a haven for the world's largest gannett colony (the Cape gannett [*Morus capensis*]), and island reefs harbor abalone *(Haliotis midae)*. Poaching was estimated to be 1,000 tons (907 t) in 2003, double allowable limits. Cape Peninsula MPA, comprising 298 square miles (771 km^2), includes the coastal waters around Table Mountain National Park and is home to a vulnerable colony of African penguins *(Spheniscus demersus)*. http://www.safrica.info/ess_info/sa_glance/ sustainable/marineprotectedareas.htm.

UNITED STATES: A new dead zone appeared off the Oregon coast in June 2004. The zone is a band of nutrient rich, oxygen-poor, North Pacific water that is several miles wide. In 2002, a similar band killed many crabs and rockfish. Human-induced dead zones occur in about 30 sites globally. A recurring dead zone could devastate local Oregon fisheries and signal changing circulation patterns in the Pacific. *Science* 305(2004):1099.

Dennis DeMello/WCS

GLOBAL: New rules governing the trade of the more than 30 recognized seahorse species took effect in May 2004. According to CITES regulations, countries must now prove that harvests are sustainable, and only seahorses 4 inches (10 cm) or larger can be caught—an effort to increase the breeding chances of adult seahorses. According to trade surveys, between 20 and 24 million seahorses are caught, dried, and sold annually for use in traditional medicines; hundreds of thousands more are captured for the aquarium trade. http://worldwildlife.org/trade/seahorse_facts.cfm.

CANADA: In May 2004 the Canadian government created a 913-square-mile (2,365 km^2) protected area around the Gully, the largest marine canyon in eastern North America. The region harbors diverse deep-sea corals and 14 species of marine mammals and is critical habitat for the Scotian Shelf population of the northern bottlenose whale *(Hyperoodon ampullatus)*. http://www.dfo-mpo.gc.ca/media/backgrou/2004/hq-ac61a_e.htm.

Robert Fournier/
The Wild Lensman

BELIZE: The world's largest fish, the elusive whale shark *(Rhincodon typus)*, was given legal protection in a 5-square-mile (13 km^2) marine protected area surrounding Little Water Caye Island in February 2004. It is the hemisphere's only known site where the vulnerable sharks congregate to feast on snapper spawn. Little Water Caye links marine reserves to the east and west. http://www.conservation.org/xp/news/press_releases/2004/021104.xml.

George R. Horn

UNITED STATES: Staghorn and elkhorn corals *(Acropora cervicornis and A. palmata)*, dominant Caribbean species, have expanded their range into the northern Gulf of Mexico, possibly in response to warmer waters, according to a recent study. Some experts predict that an increase in surface sea temperature of 1.8° to 3.6°F (1°C–2°C) could lead to richer coral species diversity in some subtropical locations. *Frontiers in Ecology and the Environment* 2, no. 6 (2004):307–314.

GLOBAL: SEAMAP, a website hosted by Duke University, now provides profiles of more than 350 marine species and houses 100 biogeographical datasets—created from almost 300,000 records spanning 1947 to 2004. SEAMAP describes the distribution and abundance of marine mammals, seabirds, and sea turtles, and includes physical oceanographic data and software tools for data analysis. The project is overseen by the Ocean Biogeographic Information System (OBIS), a worldwide consortium of academic and governmental organizations. http://seamap.env.duke.edu/.

GLOBAL: Warmer waters could trigger widespread coral bleaching and disease. About 95 percent of the Great Barrier Reef and shallow coral reefs worldwide could undergo bleaching and die by 2050 if global carbon dioxide levels are not reduced and sea surface temperatures continue to rise, according to a report compiled by the Queensland Tourism Industry Council. Higher temperatures reduce and can kill the symbiotic zooxanthellae algae that occupy and color corals. However, other research published by the Pew Center on Global Climate Change shows that some corals may recover if they become repopulated with the zooxanthellae from surrounding waters or if remaining algae survive. *Science* 304(2004):1490–1492; www.qtic.com.au/wwf.htm; http://www.pewclimate.org/global-warming-in-depth/all_reports/coral_reefs/index.cfm.

ICELAND: With declining domestic support for whaling and a waning whale meat market, the Iceland government has downsized their scientific whaling program. Iceland resumed whaling in 2003 despite global protests, catching 36 minke whales that year and scheduling a maximum take of 25 for 2004. The planned take of 500 whales, including sei and fin whales during a two-year period beginning in 2003, will instead be caught over a longer time frame. *Marine Pollution Bulletin* 49(2004):4.

NOAA

GLOBAL: Fisheries management has typically focused on maximizing a single-species catch—ignoring habitat destruction, bycatch, and the permanent evolutionary shifts resulting from this approach. But a recent policy forum suggests that ecosystem-based fisheries management (EBFM) may be a better approach. Under EBFM, the health and future of the entire ecosystem—the fate of predators and prey—is considered when deciding fishing limits. *Science* 305(2004): 346–347.

GLOBAL: Rising atmospheric carbon dioxide (CO_2) levels are changing ocean chemistry and the carbon cycle—and may seriously impact growth of aquatic life forms, according to recent research. Higher levels of atmospheric CO_2 acidify ocean water, dissolving calcium carbonate, a building block of both coral reefs and shells. In the lab, high CO_2 levels altered shell production in mollusks, plankton, and coral. *Science* 305(2004):352–353, 362–366.

GLOBAL: In February 2004, more than 1,100 scientists signed a statement to the United Nations requesting a moratorium on bottom trawling on the high seas. Bottom trawlers drag heavily weighted nets across the seafloor, damaging deep-sea coral and sponge ecosystems throughout the oceans and on seamounts where species endemism is up to 30 percent. These ecosystems are believed to be as diverse as shallower coral reefs and equally important in sustaining fisheries. http://www.mcbi.org/DSC_statement/sign.htm.

ATLANTIC AND PACIFIC OCEANS: Recent DNA analysis identified a new family of corals found only in the Atlantic, raising the total number of coral families to 19. The study also exposed flaws in the classification of Pacific and Atlantic corals, calling for major revisions in the coral family tree. This finding ups the ante for the conservation of Atlantic coral reefs, especially in the Caribbean. *Nature* 427(2004):832–835.

Yvonne Sadovy

GLOBAL: The humphead wrasse *(Cheilinus undulates)* and the dusky grouper *(Epinephelus marginatus)* were listed as endangered by the World Conservation Union (IUCN) in 2004. The wrasse, a large coral reef dweller that is a highly valued food fish in Southeast Asia, has declined by at least 50 percent over the last three decades. There is no management of this fishery, and wrasse habitat is seriously threatened by human activity throughout the Indo-Pacific region. The dusky grouper was reclassified as endangered based on an 88 percent decline in total catches for seven countries between 1990 and 2001. The grouper, which inhabits rocky reefs from 26 feet to 984 feet (8–300 m), is heavily fished across eastern Africa, Europe, and South America for food. It is particularly vulnerable because it matures slowly, with females reproducing at the age of five and males at age 12. http://www.iucnredlist.org/search/details.php?species=4592; http://www.iucnredlist.org/search/details.php?species=7859.

UNITED STATES: Recreational catches accounted for almost 25 percent of the national take of some overfished stocks, according to a new study. For some charismatic species, this far exceeds the commercial catch: the recreational catch for red drum *(Sciaenops ocellatus)* in the south Atlantic is 93 percent of the total, for bocaccio *(Sebastes paucispinis)* in the Pacific, 87 percent, and for red snapper *(Lutjanus campechanus)* in the Gulf of Mexico, 59 percent. There are more than 10 million recreational fishermen in the United States, many outfitted with sonar devices and GPSs. Current regulations address individual catches and size limits but do not control the total number of recreational fishermen. *Science* 305(2004):1958–1959.

UNITED STATES: California established a network of 12 protected areas encompassing 175 square miles (453 km^2) within the Channel Islands National Marine Sanctuary in April 2003. It is the largest string of marine reserves on the US West Coast and protects diverse life forms such as slow-producing rockfishes, abalone, lobster, and undersea forests of giant kelp. http://www.dfg.ca.gov/mrd/channel_islands/index.html.

RED SEA: Nutrient effluent released from fish farms in the Gulf of Eilat in Israel's Red Sea is killing the world's northernmost coral reef. According to Zalul, an Israeli environmental group, 70 percent of the reef has died in the last five years. The fish farm, which will likely be moved inland, produces 1,400 tons (1,270 t) of fish annually. *Marine Ecology Progress Series* 261(2003):299–303; *Jerusalem Post*, November 18, 2004, p. 5.

UNITED KINGDOM: The waters off Lundy Island are the UK's first no-take zone and its first reserve established solely for biodiversity. The 1.3-square-mile (3.4 km^2) zone guards subtidal reefs that support fragile benthic species, including solitary cup corals, sea fans, and sponges. The reserve is also expected to benefit gray seals and enhance fish and shellfish populations. Since protection in 2003, the population of commercially landable European lobster is three times higher than areas outside the no-take zone. *MPA News* 4, no.6 (2002/2003); C. Davis, English Nature, pers. comm., 2004.

Polar Regions

JESSE CHAPMAN-BRUSCHINI

Threats to the unique ecosystems of the Arctic and Antarctic have grown in recent years. These range from climate change, bioprospecting, and expanding oil extraction to the persistent organic pollutants that bioaccumulate in the food chain and undermine both human and wildlife health. Illegal, unregulated, and unreported longline fishing operations continue to threaten seabirds in the Southern Ocean, killing tens of thousands every year. Climate change is reducing the extent and persistence of winter sea ice in polar regions, threatening many species—from krill to penguins and whales. Many conservationists believe the poles are giving the rest of the world a preview of the far-reaching consequences of global warming and its cascading impacts. But there are a few hopeful notes: new protected areas, international conservation agreements, and some species showing signs of recovery.

Robert and Carolyn Buchanan

RUSSIA AND UNITED STATES: The United States and the Russian Federation signed a bilateral agreement in December 2004 to conserve the transboundary polar bears *(Ursus maritimus)* that roam between the two countries. The agreement, which creates the US–Russia Polar Bear Commission, strengthens management and research efforts for the Alaska-Chukotka polar bears and provides for active participation of indigenous people in decision making. The agreement will be forwarded to the US Senate for ratification. The Russian government has already enacted legislation to implement the agreement. http://alaska.fws.gov/fisheries/mmm/polarbear/bilateral.htm.

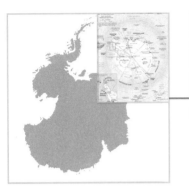

ANTARCTICA: Penguins, whales, and seals could be threatened by food shortages in the Southern Ocean according to a 2004 report by the British Antarctic Survey. Antarctic krill *(Euphausia superba)*, shrimp-like crustaceans at the heart of the region's food chain, have declined by about 80 percent since the 1970s. One factor is rapidly shrinking sea ice, which acts as a krill nursery. Krill also feed on algae found beneath the ice. The Antarctic krill population is concentrated northeast of the Antarctic Peninsula—an area that has warmed by 4°F (2.5°C) in the last 50 years. *Limnology and Oceanography* 4(2004):2152–2161.

WCS

ARCTIC: In November 2004, a four-year study by an international team of 300 scientists confirmed earlier research on Arctic climate change. The Arctic Climate Impact Assessment (ACIA) found that if current rates continue, the polar ice cap could melt completely before the end of this century, causing dramatic rises in global sea levels. Retreating sea ice also threatens some wildlife species with extinction: polar bears *(Ursus maritimus)*, walrus *(Odobenus rosmarus)*, ice-inhabiting seals, and marine birds. Shorebirds and waterfowl that breed in great numbers on the coastal plain are also at risk because of melting permafrost and rising sea levels. http://acia.uaf.edu.

Robert and Carolyn Buchanan

NORWAY: Studies conducted during 2003 and 2004 linked hormonal changes and lowered immunity in polar bears *(Ursus maritimus)* to accumulated toxic chemicals in their bodies, specifically polychlorinated biphenyls (PCBs) and pesticides. Three to four out of every 100 female bears captured on Norway's Svalbard archipelago had both female and partial male genitalia; the bears also carry up to 12 times the PCB load of Alaskan bears. PCBs, DDT, and other chemicals ride northbound winds and ocean currents and persist long-term in the environment. http://www.wwf.ca/NewsAndFacts/Features/16_09_2004.asp.

THE POLES: Large colonies of microorganisms living under rocks have been discovered in the harshest regions of the Arctic and Antarctic. A September 2004 report by scientists from the British Antarctic Survey (BAS) and Scripps Institution of Oceanography revealed that these rock-dwelling microorganisms can photosynthesize and store carbon like the plants, lichens, and mosses that live aboveground. BAS microbiologists found that opaque rocks protect these microorganisms from cold and ultraviolet radiation; during the annual freeze–thaw, cracks form, exposing the microorganisms to small amounts of light. *Nature* 431(2004):414.

Dennis DeMello/ WCS

UNITED STATES: A depleted population of beluga whales *(Delphinapterus leucas)* appears to have stabilized five years after Alaskan indigenous groups agreed to drastically reduce hunting them. A 2004 US National Marine Fisheries Service (USNMFS) census counted 187 beluga whales in Cook Inlet, compared with 174 and 192 in 2003 and 2002, respectively. At least 1,000 belugas lived in Cook Inlet until the 1980s; the population declined drastically until 1999, when an agreement was signed between local indigenous groups and USNMFS that sharply limited hunting. A year later, the agency designated the whales as "depleted"—a protected status under the Marine Mammal Protection Act. Between 2001 and 2004, hunters reported only six beluga kills. *Marine Pollution Bulletin* 48(2004):813–816.

David Weller

RUSSIA: In 2004, the United Nations Educational, Scientific and Cultural Organization (UNESCO) recognized Russia's Wrangel Island Reserve as a World Heritage Site. This region escaped glaciation during the Quarternary Ice Age, resulting in exceptional levels of biodiversity for the High Arctic. It is home to about 100,000 Pacific walrus *(Odobenus rosmarus),* the world's largest population, is the northernmost nesting ground for 100 migratory bird species, and is a vital feeding ground for endangered gray whales *(Eschrichtius robustus)* migrating from Mexico. http://whc.unesco.org/pg.cfm?cid=31&id_site=1023.

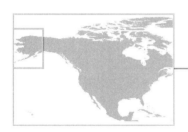

UNITED STATES: For the first time in 30 years, blue whales *(Balaenoptera musculus)* were sighted and photographed about 100 miles (160 km) southeast of Alaska's Prince William Sound. Researchers aboard a National Oceanic and Atmospheric Administration vessel got close enough to obtain skin and blubber samples for genetic testing and pollutant studies. Blue whales were hunted commercially from 1860 to 1965, killing an estimated 350,000 animals. The most recent studies estimate that about 12,000 remain worldwide. *Nature* 430(2004):496.

ARCTIC: A five-year assessment on Arctic pollution cited growing concentrations of two new persistent organic chemicals in Arctic animal and human populations. The Arctic Council found that polybrominated diphenyl ethers (PBDEs), chemicals that are widely used in the United States in flame-retardants, and perfluorooctane sulfonate (PFOS), a type of stain repellant, bioaccumulate in a pattern similar to DDT and other persistent pollutants. Research to date has shown the potential for PBDEs to disrupt human immunity, reproduction, and development. *Environmental Science and Technology* 36, no. 9(2002):1886–1892; *Science* 304(2004):1730.

UNITED STATES: Sea otters *(Enhydra lutris)* are still being poisoned 15 years after the *Exxon Valdez* coated Alaska's Prince William Sound with oil. US Geological Survey biologists studying about 70 sea otters from northern Knight Island—a region that lost 90 percent of its sea otter population after the spill—found that these otters continue to ingest oil when they eat clams and mussels in areas that remain contaminated. Sea otter life spans in the region have dropped by 10 to 40 percent, and some dead otters have been found with swollen and discolored livers. *Scientific American* 5(2004):30–31.

CANADA: Canada's largest seal cull in 50 years took place in April 2004. The Canadian government raised hunting quotas from 275,000 to 350,000 harp seals *(Phoca groenlandicus)* off the coasts of Newfoundland and Labrador. A multiyear management plan allows 975,000 seals to be taken over three years. The government maintains that harp seals are not an endangered species and that the hunt is vital to local economies trying to survive the declining cod fishing industry. *Marine Pollution Bulletin* 48(2004):1009–1169.

ANTARCTICA: Tighter regulations are needed to protect Antarctica from bioprospecting, according to a 2004 report by the UN University's Institute of Advanced Studies. Research institutions, universities, and pharmaceutical companies are seeking to claim ownership of newly discovered microscopic life forms, biological compounds, and processes. Of particular interest are "extremophiles"—organisms that have evolved unique metabolic strategies for harsh environments. One example is a protein in some fish that acts as an "antifreeze" in subzero waters. The report warned of the significant environmental consequences of a "gold-rush" mentality if sustainable bioprospecting protocols are not established. The Antarctic Treaty, which governs the southern continent, does not specify how the area's flora and fauna can be exploited, potentially opening the door to unregulated commercial research. http://www.ias.unu.edu/publications/details.cfm/ArticleID/663/search/yes.

ACKNOWLEDGMENTS

We would like to thank the many biologists and conservationists around the world who took time from their busy schedules to respond to questionnaires and provide valuable information from their region. Their insight, expertise, and advice are greatly appreciated.

Asociación Venezolana para la Conservación de Areas Naturales (ACOANA), Mariapía Bevilacqua; African Wildlife Foundation, Henry Mwima and Daniele Tedesco; Alaska Department of Fish and Wildlife, Wayne Regelin; American University of Beirut, Elsa Sattout; Animal Encounter, Mounir Abi-Said; Antarctic Research Trust, Klemens Putz; Argentine Environment and Sustainable Development Secretariat, Victoria Liechtschein; Australian Institute of Marine Science, Clive Wilkinson, Charlie Vernon; Bedford Institute of Oceanography, R. O'Boyle; Belize Audubon Society, Nellie Catzim; Birds Australia, Michael Weston; Biodiversity Preservation Center, Edem Eniang; Biodiversity Research Institute, David Evers and Wing Goodale; Biota Institute, Luis Pacheco; Bird Conservation Nepal, Hem Sagar Baral; BirdLife Cypress, Michael Miltiadou; BirdLife International, Asep Adhikerana, Ian Burfield, and A. Bennett Hennessey; Bombay Natural History Society, Asad Rahmani; Boston University, Les Kaufman; Brigham Young University, Keith Crandall; British Antarctic Survey, Paul Rodhouse; Broom Bird Observatory, Ricki Coughlan; Bureau of Oceans and International Environmental & Scientific Affairs, US Department of State, Joyce Winchel Namde; Calgary Zoo, Sandie Black; Centro Nacional de Pesquisa para Conservação de Predadores Naturais (CENAP/IBAMA), Peter Crawshaw; Centro Nacional Patagónica/Consejo de Investigaciones Científicas y Técnicas (CENPAT-CONICET), Mirtha Lewis and Mario Di Bitetti; Center for Agrarian and Environmental Studies (CEA), Andrés Muñoz-Pedreros; Centre for Evidence-Based Conservation, Andrew Pullin; Conservation International, Chistoverius Hutabarat and Joe Singh; Czech Society for Ornithology, Petr Vorisek; Dauphin Island Sea Lab, Richard Aaronson; Denver Zoological Foundation, Brian Miller; Department for Nature Conservation–Germany, Claus Mayr; Department of Primary Industries, Water and Environment–Tasmania, Stewart Blackhall; Dru Associates, R.W. Abrams; Empresa Nacional para la Protección de la Flora y la Fauna, Cuba, Juan P. Soy; Falklands Conservation, Rebecca Ingham; Fisheries UBC–Canada, Reg Watson; Flora and Fauna International, Jamison Suter, William Oliver; Forestry Department–Uruguay, Carolina Sans; Ft. Worth Zoo, Rick Hudson; Giant Otter Conservation Program, Nicole DuPlaix; Great Barrier Reef Marine Park Authority, Jon Day; Harbor Foundation for the Conservation of Natural Resources, José María Antonio Bringas; Hawk Mountain Sanctuary and Society for Conservation Biology, Christian Olivio; Hellenic Ornithological Society; Houston Museum of Natural Science, Daniel Brooks; Hungarian Natural History Museum, Andras Baldi; French Institute of Research and Exploitation of the Sea (IFREMER), Pascal Lorance; IGC, Burr Heneman and Lee Kimball; Institute of Applied Ecology, Annette Mertens; International Advisory Group for Northern Ibis, Mark Hofling; IUCN, Paolo Cavallini, Viola Clausnitzer, Will Darwall, Excellent Hachileka, Peter Kevan, Helene Jacques, Arturo Mora, Martin Schneider-Jacoby, Alvaro Velasco, and Alexey Yablokov; International Centre for Rainforest Conservation (IWOKRAMA), Graham Watkins; Jane Goodall Institute, Christina Ellis; Kalpavriksh Environmental Action Group, Ashish Kothari; Korean National University of Education (KNUE), Sooil Kim and Heon Woo Park; Kuwait Institute for Scientific Research, Ronald Loughland; Lincoln Park Zoo, Joanne Earnhardt; Mamirauá Institute, Helder Lima de Queiroz; Marine Conservation Biology Institute, Lance Morgan; Marine Conservation Unit, Danica Devery-Smith; Ministry of the Environment–

Nigeria, John Mshelbwala; Monterey Bay Aquarium, Christopher Harrold; Museum of Vertebrate Zoology, University of California Berkeley, Adam Leache; National Commission for Wildlife Conservation and Development–Saudi Arabia, Mohammed Al Toum; National Council of Protected Areas–Guatemala, María José Gonzalez and Mario Jolón; National Parks Administration–Argentina, Claudio Chehebar; National Research Institute of Far East Fisheries, Shelley Clarke; National Science Foundation, Anna Kerttula de Echave; Northern Arizona University, Paul Beir; Novosibirsk State University, Michael Sergeev; OCEANA, Karen Klenner; Oregon State University, Elise Granek; Organization for Tropical Studies, Eugenio Gonzalez; Parks Watch Guatemala, Carlos Albacete; Pew Institute for Ocean Science, Elizabeth Babcock and Christine Santora; Pontificia University, Juan Carlos Castilla; Program for the Conservation of the Bats of Bolivia, Luis Aguirre; Program for the Restoration of Sea Turtles (PRETOMA), Randall Arauz; Project Seahorse, James Hrynyshyn; Proteger Foundation, Jorge Cappato; Rainforest Alliance, Chris Willie; Rutgers University, Peter Rona; Mark Sagoff; Saharan Conservation Fund, John Newby; San Diego Zoo, Allison Alberts; Save the Environment–Afghanistan, Glulam Mohd Malikyar; Scientific Committee for Antarctic Research (SCAR) Group of Experts on Birds, Eric Woehler; Siberian Environment Center, Ilya Smelansky; Spanish Ministry of Environment, Astrid Vargas; Snow Leopard Conservancy, Rodney Jackson; Stanford University, Donald Kohrs; State University Paulista–Brazil, Marco Pizo; Taporoporoaanga Ipukarea Society, Imogen P. Ingram; The Irish Agriculture and Food Development Authority (TEAGASC), John Finn; The Nature Conservancy, Ismet Khaeruddin; The Open University, Tim Halliday; The Wilderness Society, Pamela Eaton; Tropical Science Center, Olivier Chassot and Guisselle Monge Arias; United Nations Development Programme, Donnie Ben Turtur; University of Alberta, Cheryl-Lesley Chetkiewicz; University of Basel, Peter van Eeuwijk; University of British Columbia, Daniel Pauly; University of California, Karen Stocks; University of Connecticut, Sylvain de Guise; University of Florida, James Perran Ross; University of Hong Kong, Yvonne Sadovy; University of Kent, Richard Bodmer; University of Maine, Robert Steneck; University of Newcastle, Peter Garson; University of Provence, Selma Zaiane; University of Tasmania, Keith Martin-Smith; University of Texas, Camille Parmesan; University of Venice, Giovanni Bearzi; University of Western Australia, Gerals Kuchling; University of Zagreb, Djuro Huber; University Laval, Mark Thibault; Leonard Usongo; Vidumae Nature Reserve, Tonu Talvi; Wilburforce Foundation, Gary Tabor; Wildlife Conservation Society, James Barborak, Dee Boersma, Claudio Campagna, Cathi Campbell, Archie Carr III, Kathy Conforti, Tim Davenport, William Duckworth, Keyt Fischer, Charles Foley, Janet Gibson, Michaele Glennon, John Goodrich, Craig Groves, Melvin Gumal, Jodi Hilty, Almira Hoogesteyn, Luke Hunter, Amanda Jorgenson, Leslie Karasin, Ullas Karanth, Joe Liebezeit, Andy Mack, Silvio Marchini, Fiona Maisels, Petch Manopawitr, Miriam Marmontel, Tim McClanahan, Roan Balas McNab, David Moyer, Leonard Mubalama, Andrew Noss, Andrés Novaro, John Oates, José Ochoa, Lilian Painter, Michael Painter, Graeme Patterson, Pablo Puertas, Andrew Plumtree, Justina Ray, Damián Rumiz, Jennifer Schmitz, Andrés Seijas, Chris Sheppard, Brian Smith, Sylvia Stone, Andrew Taber, John Tasirin, Alejandro Vila, Susan Walker, Rob Wallace, Joe Walston, Bill Weber, Lee White, Gillian Woolmer, Steve Zack, and Peter Zahler; World Wildlife Fund, Susan Sang; Zimbabwe Conservation Task Force, Johnny Rodrigues; Zoo Salzburg, Petra Kaczensky; Zoological Society of London, Tim Wacher; Zoological Society of San Diego, Alan Lieberman.

Grizzly bears in Kamchatka, Russia, though abundant, are pursued by mostly American trophy hunters, and are also killed for their gall bladders, skins, and claws.

(Credit: Ivan Seredkin)

Treat each bear as the last bear.
Each wolf as the last, each caribou.
Each track as the last track.
Gone spoor. Gone scat.
There are no more deertrails,
no more flyways.
Treat each animal as sacred,
each minute our last.
Ghost hooves. Ghost skulls.
Death rattles and
dry bones.
Each bear walking alone
in warm night air.

GARY LAWLESS
(AMERICA, CONTEMPORARY)

PART III

HUNTING AND THE WILDLIFE TRADE

Setting the Scene

ELIZABETH L. BENNETT AND SHARON GUYNUP

We've devoted one-third of this volume to hunting and the wildlife trade, a conservation threat that encompasses a complex range of issues and continues to grow in tandem with a burgeoning human population and growing international markets. Throughout our history, humans have hunted, collected, and fished wild species for food, clothing, decoration, and medicines. But the scale on which we do so has escalated so rapidly in recent years that human exploitation is arguably the greatest threat to wildlife worldwide. Around the globe, wild animals are being threatened by voracious and unsustainable harvesting.

In addition to hunting and fishing for our own survival, trade in wild species is now an enormous global commercial enterprise. We are overhunting and overcollecting the world's land animals and birds and overfishing its marine and freshwater species. The result is that populations of tuna, sturgeon, turtles, elephants, primates, big cats, hornbills, and countless other species are being decimated across the planet, from the highest mountains to tropical forests to the deepest oceans, threatening massive global extinctions.

At first glance, the answer seems simple—we should reduce our exploitation of wild species, whether for food, pets, clothing, or medicines, and increase instead our use of farmed animals and plants or find artificial substitutes. In our opening essay in this section, Ted Kerasote traces the history of hunting in North America, highlighting how regulations have allowed some species to recover from even devastating hunting levels once proper management was established—while remembering that these regulations came too late for others.

Unfortunately, the global story is more complex. Many people around the world depend on harvesting wild species for their livelihoods. The balance between use and sustainability is a precarious and difficult one from both practical and ethical viewpoints. Elizabeth L. Bennett, director of the Wildlife Conservation Society's (WCS's) Hunting and Wildlife Trade Program, examines the impact of hunting in the tropics, where many species' reproductive capability can't compensate for extremely effective human hunters—and where many rural people rely on hunting for survival. An essay by James Compton and Samuel K.H. Lee from TRAFFIC on the trade in plants and animals for traditional Asian medicine reminds us that, although this practice is wiping out populations of many species,

> "Around the globe, wild animals are being threatened by voracious and unsustainable harvesting."

millions of people rely on traditional medicine for health care—and the underlying medical system has a sophisticated history dating back thousands of years.

The overuse of wildlife by humans is not strictly a land-based problem. Each year, millions of sea animals are killed, caught as accidental bycatch through industrial fishing methods. In their essay, Carl Safina, Eric Gilman, and Wallace J. Nichols from Blue Ocean Institute quantify the resulting collateral damage to sea turtles, birds, and other sea life, many of which have been decimated by these wasteful fishing practices.

Hunting and wildlife trade can also spread zoonotic infectious diseases—those that jump between humans, livestock, and wildlife. WCS wildlife field veterinarians Robert A. Cook and William B. Karesh look at some of these newly emerging diseases, including Ebola, mad cow, monkeypox, and SARS, diseases that can be

contracted when handling or eating hunted wild meat, in wildlife markets, through livestock production, or via the international pet trade. The authors also note that the knowledge that some animals can transmit disease often creates a backlash against wildlife, even though history shows us that trying to wipe out "problem" wildlife usually creates more problems than it solves.

In some places, with proper stewardship, communities can successfully manage hunting. Richard Bodmer's essay details one example in the Peruvian Amazon.

Hunting and wildlife trade are two of the most crucial and complicated issues facing conservation today. Unless we can address them effectively, current overexploitation will wipe out species on a cataclysmic scale. These extinctions will bring unknown but possibly dramatic environmental consequences, as the animals and plants that maintain crucial ecological processes disappear and the critical resources that many millions of people depend on are destroyed. The following essays both outline the scope of these problems and offer some insight into ways to address them.

Many African plains animals are heavily hunted; some are still poached, particularly elephants for their valuable tusks. But a system of national parks in southern Africa has allowed many species to rebound.

(Credit: Luke Hunter)

A SHORT HISTORY OF

Hunting in North America

TED KERASOTE

Hunting in North America has been going on for a long, long time—at least 13,000 years if one believes that the spear points found near Clovis, New Mexico, represent the earliest evidence of human settlement in the New World. If one accepts the dating of artifacts found at Monte Verde, Chile, then Asian hunters, emigrating to the New World via the Bering land bridge, have affected wildlife in both North and South America for a minimum of 30,000 years.

Whether early hunters contributed to the extinction of some of the continent's ancient megafauna—mastodons, horses, giant sloths, and saber-toothed tigers—remains a hotly debated issue. Some researchers support the notion, while others claim that climate shifts began to alter North America's plant and animal communities long before people arrived on the scene.

Of one thing we can be certain: from the moment modern Europeans set foot on the Atlantic littoral with firearms, virtually all edible or commercially useful birds, beasts, and fish were swept away like leaves before the wind.

The great auk *(Pinguinus impennis)* was the first to go. A flightless seabird resembling a penguin, it inhabited the rocky islands of the North Atlantic and wintered as far south as Massachusetts Bay. Supremely adapted to its marine environment, it was an

Opposite: Theodore Roosevelt with his rifle, riding through a ranch pasture during a visit to the western United States, circa 1905.
(Credit: Boone and Crockett Club, www.booneandcrockettclub.com)

Populations of white-tail deer plummeted across the West as settlers poured in from the East, but hunters continued to shoot does and fawns. Montana, 1913. (Credit: Bronx Zoo Library)

elegant swimmer, secure from land-based predators on its lonely redoubts. But it proved easy prey for Breton fishermen exploring the Canadian coastlines in the late 1400s and early 1500s. From then on, great auks were hunted without quarter for their feathers, meat, oil, and eggs, so tame and naive that they could be driven aboard ship to their own destruction. The last great auks were a pair killed off the coast of Iceland in June 1844.[1]

That their disappearance didn't make headlines is hardly surprising. In its temperate latitudes, North America was literally spilling into the sea with an abundance of wildlife, overwhelming the senses of Europeans with the illusion of inexhaustibility.

Take Captain Arthur Barlowe, sent out by Sir Walter Raleigh to explore the New World in 1584. Making landfall south of Cape Hatteras, he was amazed to find the woods "full of Deere, Conies, Hares, and Fowle." So charmed was he by the landscape before him that he ran out of superlatives for his log and began to repeat the words "incredible" and "excellent." At last he was unable to say anything more than "I thinke in all the world the like aboundance is not to be founde."[2]

Later travelers corroborated these early impressions. They were greeted by deer and black bear (*Ursus ameri-canus*) and by species that we think of today as prototypically western and tropical. Elk (*Cervus canadensis*) and bison reportedly grazed near the coast, and there were even reports of "tygers"—jaguars—east of the Appalachians. There were turkeys, partridges, and cranes; there were curlews and gulls, gannets and pelicans, mallards and teals, geese and swans,[3] cackling, whistling, and honking. There were flocks of passenger pigeons (*Ectopistes migratorius*) that covered the sky like a hurricane.

The abundance couldn't last. In 1564—one year before the first North American city was founded in St. Augustine, Florida—the resident European population on the continent was zero. Just 80 years later, in the 1640s, there were about 28,000 people in the colonies, and white-tailed deer (*Odocoileus virginianus*) were already declining on the eastern seaboard from subsistence hunting by Native Americans and settlers alike. In 1646, Portsmouth, Rhode Island, ordered a closed season on deer from May through November.

By 1720, most of the colonies had adopted similar ordinances, and with good reason.[4] Deer were not merely a dietary mainstay; they had become a fundamental item of commerce, with Native Americans hunting to supply European merchants. Deerskin was used for clothing, windowpanes, harnesses, and book bindings. Antlers were fashioned into chandeliers, cutlery handles, and buttons. Deer hair was used for stuffing saddles, furniture, and carriage blankets. Deer tallow went into candles. In short, people owed their lives and livelihoods to deer. According to one port's records, between 1735 and 1765, Charleston, South Carolina, shipped 151,000 deer skins yearly to Europe.[5] It is from this time that the word "buck," meaning a unit of currency, was shortened from "buckskin." Turkey and passenger pigeon numbers also plummeted during the 17th century. Once a common sight in New England, both species had become respectively "rare" and "much diminished."[6]

By 1800, the European population of the 17 eastern states and eastern Canada was about 5.6 million people. As settlers moved west, the decimation of wildlife continued, abetted now by advances in firearms technology, wiping out white-tailed deer, elk, bison, and fowl, as well as grizzly bears (Ursus arctos) and mountain lions (Puma concolor). Wolves often carried a bounty on their heads. With the crisscrossing of the country by rail lines, the stage was set for emptying the forests, prairies, and marshes of wildlife to feed the continent's growing urban centers. Indeed, one might say that as settlers moved west, dead wildlife moved east.

Wagonloads of bison, passenger pigeons, and pronghorn antelope (Antilocapra americana) creaked toward the railheads, their meat kept fresh by refrigerator cars, which were introduced in 1867. By the 1890s, the cornucopia had begun to run dry, and the public abandoned the notion that North America's wildlife was inexhaustible. As an editorial in a

A buffalo hide yard in Dodge City, Kansas, in 1874. Hunters who arrived in the spring of 1874 noted the scarcity of buffalo north of the Arkansas River; vast herds had been decimated in the hunts of 1872 and '73. (Credit: Bronx Zoo Library)

Minnesota newspaper put it, "Nothing like enjoying the good things on the frontier while they last and before civilization makes the game scarce."[7]

Scarce was an understatement. By the last decades of the 1800s, white-tailed deer had nearly vanished from most of the United States, with populations reduced from between 24 and 33 million animals in the late 1500s to but half a million.[8] Bison, once numbering between 40 and 60 million in North America, were down to 1,100 animals by 1889.[9]

Elk had been the continent's most widespread ungulate, roaming from the Pacific to the Atlantic, and from northern Mexico to northern Alberta. The naturalist Ernest Thompson Seton estimated their original population at 10 million. Hunting reduced their numbers to under 41,000 animals, with most of the survivors within the Yellowstone ecosystem.[10]

Pronghorn, once as numerous as bison, had been shot back to 26,700 animals when they were surveyed in 1924.[11] By then the last passenger pigeon, a captive in the Cincinnati Zoo, had been dead for 10 years (see page 211).

In the meantime, written communication and the arts, as well as the whims of fashion, were taking their toll on birds. From AD 600, when reed pens were replaced by quills, everything from pen and ink drawings to the Declaration of Independence was executed with pens made from the primary feathers of waterfowl and raptors. North America provided a ready source of such birds: the Hudson's Bay Company exported 347,208 goose, swan, and eagle quills and wings to London in December 1828 alone.[12]

It was the fashion industry, however, that made the most profound impact on North America's bird life.

As more women entered the middle class in the 1800s, a widespread market developed for bird feathers used in haute couture, fueled by magazines such as *Harper's Bazaar*. Great and snowy egrets *(Egretta alba* and *E. thula),* with their long, feathery plumes known as "aigrettes" were most prized, but roseate spoonbills *(Ajaia ajaja)* and shore birds were also routinely killed by plume hunters, the former for their colored feathers, the latter for their long-billed carcasses, which, stuffed whole, adorned women's hats.[13]

In 1886, the American Ornithological Union put a number to the carnage. An estimated 5 million North American birds from 50 different species were being killed annually, with wagonloads coming from Florida's swampy wilderness, once a de facto sanctuary for bird life.

But impenetrable swamps, tall mountain ranges, and great distances were no longer deterrents to the relentless pursuit of wildlife by market hunters. It was the phenomenal growth of the US railroads that proved a catalyst for the slaughter: in 1830 the nation had only 23 miles (37 km) of rail, but by 1890, 220,000 miles (354,000 km) had been laid.[14] Put in the most basic economic terms, "Selling game to the railroads was so profitable that many boys and

young men abandoned jobs and school to take up its pursuit."[15]

Into this darkest chapter of North American hunting stepped, somewhat ironically, two hunters: George Bird Grinnell and Theodore Roosevelt. Both men were patrician New Yorkers, educated at Yale and Harvard Universities, respectively, Progressives who had assimilated the ideas of the leading naturalist of the day, George Perkins Marsh. In 1864, Marsh had published *Man and Nature,* a best seller that catalogued the damage civilization had wrought on the environment while putting forth the notion that "disturbed harmonies" could be restored.[16]

Both Grinnell and Roosevelt had traveled widely in the West, Grinnell as an ethnologist, Roosevelt ranching in the Dakotas. Each had shot many big game animals and had seen the pronghorn and buffalo vanish from the plains within a dozen years, leaving behind mile upon mile of bleached skeletons. Returning to the

During a three-year period, 1,350,000 pounds of buffalo bones were shipped east by railroad. The bones were sold to carbon works, used to refine sugar, or were ground up for fertilizer; horns were made into combs and buttons. (Credit: Bronx Zoo Library)

East, they vowed to remove game from the marketplace.

In 1876, Grinnell became editor of the most prominent hunting and fishing magazine of the era, *Forest and Stream*. His predecessor, Charles Hallock, was far ahead of his time, promoting game protection and the British concept of sportsmanship—an ideal that saw hunting and fishing as gentlemanly pursuits elevated above the crass philistinism and commercialism of the marketplace. Hallock railed against the "pot-hunter," "the meat hunter," and "the poacher," decrying those who shot birds on the water or the ground, and saying of the sportsman, "Quantity is not his ambition; he never slays more than he can use. . . . It is his pride to kill what he does kill elegantly, scientifically and mercifully."[17]

Grinnell took the magazine into new territory in 1886, announcing in a front-page editorial, "Very slowly the public are awakening to see that the fashion of wearing the feathers and skins of birds is abominable." He went on to propose the formation of the Audubon Society, named after his boyhood hero John James Audubon, which would "prevent, so far as possible, (1) the killing of any wild birds not used for food; (2) the destruction of nests or eggs of any wild bird; and (3) the wearing of feathers as ornaments or trimming for dress." Within two years, the new Audubon Society had 50,000 members.[18]

Roosevelt moved just as quickly. In December 1887, he and Grinnell called a meeting of friends and acquaintances, proposing the creation of the Boone and Crockett Club, an organization with a twofold mission: "to promote manly sport with the rifle," and "to work for the preservation of the large game of this country" through new legislation and by enforcing existing laws.[19]

The club's bylaws instituted the notion of "fair chase." Sport hunting could no longer be conducted at night with torches, by driving game with fire, or shooting it as it floundered in deep snow or swam across the water. Shortly, the Boone and Crockett Club

called for protection of public forests in inviolate reserves to act as cradles of wildlife production, and also for a law that would send enforcement personnel to Yellowstone National Park, where wildlife was being routinely killed by poachers. To ensure that the club's membership had the clout to back up these missions, Roosevelt and Grinnell invited the financial and political luminaries of the time to join.[20]

The ethos that Grinnell and Roosevelt instituted was an enormous sea change in how educated North Americans thought about wildlife. As Thomas A. Lund, writing in *American Wildlife Law,* points out, the two men became "exponents of the view that the chief value of wildlife was found not in the worth of its carcass but rather in its role as a source of amusement." In essence, "sporting goals" had begun to supplant "those of economic productivity."[21]

But altering how well-read aristocrats thought about wildlife was one thing, and changing the economic engine of an entire continent was another. Even though states had legislated two-month-long big game seasons by the 1890s, a significant loophole remained in the regulations: the inability to prosecute market hunters who illegally killed wildlife in one state and sold it in another.

No piece of legislation did more to close this breach than a bill drafted in 1900 by Boone and Crockett Club member John F. Lacey, an Iowa Congressman. The Lacey Act made it a federal crime to take, possess, and

transport illegally taken wildlife across state lines. To this day, wildlife cannot be bought or sold in North America. When one eats venison, bison, or pronghorn antelope in a restaurant, it has been grown on a game farm.

The Lacey Bill gave wildlife law enforcement real teeth. With this triumph behind them, a coterie of North American "sportsmen-conservationists" began a century-long campaign to expose the average hunter to the idea of fair chase while simultaneously restoring the continent's depleted wildlife.

Subsequent generations of this elite circle helped to pass the Migratory Bird Treaty Act of 1918. This ended market hunting of the continent's waterfowl and shore birds, closed the spring hunting season, and put migratory birds under the protection of the federal governments of Canada and the United States. Sportsmen-conservationists also backed the Pittman-Robertson Act of 1937, which continues to provide a way for states to purchase wildlife habitat through an 11 percent federal excise tax on sporting arms, ammunition, and archery equipment.

In the mid-20th century, no individual among these sportsmen-conservationists had more impact than Aldo Leopold. Angler, hunter, forester, wildlife biologist, and ecologist, Leopold literally invented the science of wildlife management with the publication of *Game Management* in 1933. While advocating for the sustained hunting of birds and deer,

California duck hunters prior to passage of the Migratory Bird Treaty Act of 1918.
(Credit: Bronx Zoo Library)

Leopold counseled that predators, especially wolves and grizzlies, be left unharmed.

Leopold was instrumental in preserving 574,000 acres (232,000 ha) of New Mexico's Gila National Forest in 1924 as the nation's first wilderness area. A founding member of the Wilderness Society, Leopold then made his most notable contribution in *A Sand County Almanac*. There he stated how hunting—or for that matter any human intervention in natural processes—should be judged: "A thing is right when it tends to preserve the integrity, stability and beauty of the biotic community. It is wrong when it tends otherwise."[22]

During the 20th century, the Boone and Crockett Club morphed into many organizations devoted to hunting and the welfare of wildlife: the Izaak Walton League of America, the National Wildlife Federation, Ducks Unlimited, and the Rocky Mountain Elk Foundation, to name but a few. Since the 1930s, hunters belonging to these organizations have spent $1.8 billion to set aside 112 million acres (45.3 million ha) of wildlife habitat—18 million more acres (7 million more ha) than have been protected under the National Wildlife Refuge System.[23]

Long before the Endangered Species Act was born, these hunters began to restore wildlife populations ravaged during the 19th century. By and large, conservation efforts have been successful. Today, elk number 1.2 million animals and have been reintroduced to several eastern and midwestern states. Wild turkeys *(Meleagris gallopavo)* have rebounded to 5.6 million birds across their historic range, up from 30,000 in 1890. Bighorn sheep *(Ovis canadensis),* reduced to 10,000 individuals in 1900, today stand at 230,000 animals. Pronghorn antelope number about 750,000 animals.[24] There are 80,000 free-roaming bison,[25] with another 270,000 ranched on private land.[26] Deer have increased to 36 million animals in the United States alone— more than when Columbus reached the continent[27]—and in many suburbs, they've become nuisances and hazards. It is hard to imagine how some of these wildlife populations can grow larger: much of their original habitat lies under farms, cities, and shopping malls.

These efforts by North American hunters add up to significant recompense for the excesses of subsistence and market hunting during previous centuries. Today, 14.2 million hunters continent-wide contribute $70.6 billion to the economies of Canada and the United States.[28]

However, hunters' efforts to restore America's wildlife have not been without omissions and misplaced zeal. In general, hunters have staunchly opposed the restoration of predators—wolves, grizzly bears, and birds of prey—even funding their continued persecution to increase the number of shootable ungulates, for example, supporting aerial shooting of wolves in Canada and Alaska.

BY THE NUMBERS

Number of people whose protein needs 1 square mile (2.59 km^2) of tropical forest can sustainably support with wild meat: 2.5.

Hunters have also been advocates of introducing exotic species like European wild boar (*Sus scrofa*), Persian wild goat (*Capra aegagrus aegagrus*), and Siberian ibex (*Capra ibex siberica*), all of which compete with native species. And when it has come time to promote the welfare of nongame species, hunter organizations have been silent, although their protection of habitat benefits myriad species.

Against this checkered backdrop, supporters and critics of hunters pick and choose their data, categorizing hunters either as noble conservationists or self-serving users of wildlife. The truth lies somewhere in between. Although millions of North Americans hunt for food, it's also safe to say that modern hunting retains a persistent element of machismo and competition, a legacy passed down from when Theodore Roosevelt helped to invent modern hunting, stressing the taking of large, male animals. As he wrote in *The Wilderness Hunter*, "Killing a reasonable number of bulls, bucks, or rams does no harm whatever to the species; to slay half the males of any kind of game would not stop the natural increase, and they yield the best sport, and are the legitimate objects of the chase. Cows, does, and ewes, on the contrary, should only be killed (unless barren) in case of necessity."[29]

State fish and game agencies, working hard during the last century to restore diminished North American wildlife populations, adopted this message and exported it wholeheart-edly to hunters. Since it takes only one male of a polygamous species like deer to inseminate many females, shooting bucks and sparing does was good wildlife management — in its day. Unfortunately, that policy had unforeseen consequences. Over the last century, the media has helped to transform this biological tenet into a cultural one by featuring large-antlered deer, giant-horned sheep, and enormous, threatening bears on the covers of periodicals and in TV shows. In this way, hunting's food-gathering elements have been downplayed and its so-called sporting ones enhanced.

Other trophy hunting organizations have followed suit, helping to popularize hunting as a competitive sport, with members vying against each other to see who can take the most — and largest — specimens. Indeed, the Boone and Crockett Club's mission steadily eroded from broad-based wildlife and habitat conservation to record keeping, a trend the organization is now trying to reverse by advocating the protection of roadless lands.

Despite the fact that many hunters and nonhunters alike find such trophy hunting distasteful, the activity has had little impact on the numbers of huntable wildlife in North America since the overall take is regulated. However, because trophy hunters target older males, some wildlife biologists believe that removing too many of these individuals from a population within too short a time can make both genetic diversity and behavior suffer.[30]

Some hunters have also used the public's fear of expanding carnivore populations to increase trophy-hunting opportunities. In 2003, after lobbying by members of the hunting community, New Jersey opened a black bear hunting season and parts of Wyoming increased the mountain lion quota, both moves based on questionable science.

Only recently have a few toddling steps been taken by some state agencies toward transforming hunting into a better management tool for ecosystems. Some states have begun to downplay taking antlered animals, encouraging hunters to take female elk and deer as a way to keep herds within the carrying capacity of their habitat.

Given that society will never tolerate the restoration of large carnivores like wolves into much of what is now developed North America, hunters could continue to play an important role in wildlife conservation by occupying the niche these carnivores once filled. As Joel Berger, senior scientist at the Wildlife Conservation Society, observes, if such hunting were modeled after how predators cull their prey in pristine landscapes, it could "contribute to the conservation of ecological processes and attendant biodiversity."[31] This certainly would be a welcome contribution on the part of hunters to restoring the continent's ecological integrity, which hunting itself did so much to destroy.

Consuming Wildlife in the Tropics

ELIZABETH L. BENNETT

From oceans to mountaintops, and from deserts to rain forests, people have harvested wildlife for millennia. Even in prehistoric times, hunting caused species extinctions, especially on islands. But the teeming diversity of life today shows that, for existing species, hunting must have been sustainable in the past. This is no longer the case for many species in many places. Today, anything large enough to be eaten or lucrative enough to be sold is hunted on a massive scale for its meat, skin, fur, or feathers; for the pet trade; or as an ingredient in traditional medicines. Wildlife populations are crashing, and wild areas increasingly are losing their wildlife, becoming devoid of vibrancy and life.

Humans are overharvesting all forms of life, from timber trees and ornate plants to lobsters, ocean and freshwater fish, turtles, hornbills, and big cats. This essay focuses specifically on the hunting of tropical terrestrial and arboreal vertebrates for human consumption—as unsustainable hunting for food and medicine is the most immediate threat to many of these animals. Here we also find an overlap of core concerns: conservation of some of the world's most endangered species, and nutrition and income for some of the world's poorest peoples.

Finding solutions to unsustainable hunting across the tropics is one of the greatest conservation challenges today. It is a highly complex issue because of the different agendas and different needs of those involved. Local communities are primarily concerned with their livelihoods; governments carry multiple development, political, and social agendas. For the conservation community, the focus is on species conservation. Also of importance is the fact that the tropical world is highly variable. Animals' resilience to hunting varies according to species and to the ecosystem they inhabit. Hunting levels within a given region vary according to human needs, living conditions, and aspirations. Solutions must also be sought within the highly variable cultural, socioeconomic, and political conditions of the tropical world.

In Myanmar's Hukaung Valley, the older generation of Lisu people use this type of trophy board as a sacred part of their hunting ritual, now rarely used by the younger generation who also hunt animals for sale.
(Credit: Steve Winter/National Geographic Image Collection)

Defining "Sustainable Hunting"

Defining sustainability is difficult, given the extreme complexities of biological systems and the range of relevant management goals, from species conservation to human food security. If our concern is wildlife conservation, hunting can be regarded as sustainable if hunted populations do not consistently decline in numbers over time or are not reduced to levels where they are vulnerable to extinction. Given the importance of hunted species to people, it is also important to include a third criterion for sustainability: that hunted populations are not reduced to levels where they can no longer meet human needs.

Sengi hunter in the Ituri Forest of the Democratic Republic of Congo. Some 60 million forest dwellers in Africa, Asia, and South America depend on hunting for protein and income.
(Credit: Bryan Curran)

Why Hunting Has Become a Problem

Hunting has become a much greater threat to tropical wildlife in recent years for several reasons. First, human populations have increased dramatically, up about 310 percent in Southeast Asia over the past 50 years, and up eightfold in Africa over the past century. Simultaneously, wildlife has declined as wildlands are converted for agriculture, housing, industry, and other human uses, placing increasing pressure on remaining populations.

Also, wildlands are ever more accessible to hunters and human settlers. Access to remaining wilderness has greatly increased as roads have been built, often in the rush to extract timber, oil, and other minerals.

Hunting was once predominantly a subsistence activity: most animals were hunted to feed the hunter and his family. Today, hunting has also become a large-scale business, fueled by increased buying power among urban consumers around the world. Also, hunters are now extremely well armed. Blowpipes and spears have been replaced by efficient modern weapons, most notably shotguns and wire snares. And in most places, people can hunt anything they want. The capacity and political will to manage hunting is often inadequate, even inside protected areas.

Variation in Species Vulnerability, Ecosystem Productivity, and Demand

Species Vulnerability

Some species are inherently less able to tolerate hunting than others. Species that breed slowly and naturally occur at low densities are much more susceptible than those that breed rapidly and occur at high densities. For example, up to 80 percent of the population of some fast-breeding insectivores and rodents, such as elephant shrews and agoutis, can be harvested sustainably every year, but this figure is less than 4 percent for all primates.[1]

Some species are hunted more intensively than others. These include animals that are easily killed or captured such as slow-moving pangolins or tortoises, as well as species that congregate to breed communally in accessible areas, such as seals or marine turtles. Primates, wild pigs, and other animals that live in groups also make easy targets, as do species with spectacular displays and loud calls, such as birds of paradise and hornbills. Wild cattle, pigs, and other large-bodied species are also particularly attractive to hunters because of the large quantity of meat they supply.

Ecosystem Productivity

Ecosystem productivity in terms of wild meat[2] is determined by three factors: the number of breeding animals per unit area, their size (how much meat is supplied per animal), and the average number of offspring each individual produces every year. The first two factors are captured by measuring biomass.[3] Tropical grasslands provide the most productive habitat, commonly supporting mammal biomasses of between 85,000 and 114,00 pounds per square mile (15,000–20,000 kg/km^2). Most are fast-breeding ungulates and rodents such as blue duikers (*Cephalophus monticola*) and cane rats. So in grasslands, significant amounts of wildlife can be hunted and still be sustainable.[4] In the humid tropics, human-disturbed areas such as fallow farmlands can also be very productive for rodents and ungulates.[5] In contrast, mammal biomass in intact tropical forests rarely exceeds 17,000 pounds per square mile (3,000 kg/km^2)—about one-sixth of that in tropical grasslands—and most are primates, which breed slowly.

Tropical forests can sustainably support a maximum of only one person per 0.39 square miles (one person/km^2) if that person relies solely on wild meat for a source of protein.[4] So these forests cannot support significant hunting levels without wildlife declining or disappearing.

Mandrill heads for sale. Hunting can easily impact mandrill populations, as they do not reach sexual maturity until age four, and the time between births can be up to two years.
(Credit: Paul T. Telfer)

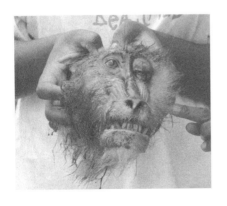

Demand

Many factors create variation in demand. The number of humans living in and around wildlife areas directly correlates with the amount of wildlife harvested there, irrespective of the continent, types of hunters, or weapons used, and even whether the land is protected. Other factors affecting demand include the types and abundance of animals present, the cultural history, hunting techniques, and the availability of affordable alternative sources of protein—as well as the incomes of both hunters and consumers and awareness of and respect for hunting regulations.

Religious beliefs and taboos are also important influences. For example, Muslims do not eat monkeys or wild pigs. Indigenous communities across the tropics have a wide variety of taboos against eating different species, or observe specific rules regulating when and how animals can be hunted. For example, the Iban peoples in parts of Borneo do not eat orangutans *(Pongo pygmaeus)* because of the belief that these animals taught humans how to give birth.

> From oceans to mountaintops, and from deserts to rain forests, people have harvested wildlife for millennia.

Hunters and Consumers of Wild Meat

Hunting of wild meat varies widely, depending on whether animals are hunted for subsistence consumption or for sale. Large markets take a huge toll, with meat sold to loggers working in forest concessions, to city dwellers, and for a growing international wild meat trade.

Rural Hunters

Although they are now relatively rare, true subsistence hunters still exist—those who depend on hunting for their livelihoods and whose sole protein sources are wild meat and fish. For example, two-thirds of the meals eaten by a remote Kelabit community in Sarawak, Malaysia, contain wild meat, and it is the main source of protein.[6] Efe pygmies in the Democratic Republic of Congo's Ituri Forest eat about 5.6 ounces (160 g) of wild meat per person per day;[7] and 10 Latin American indigenous groups consume an average of 6.5 ounces (184 g) of wild meat daily per person.[8] Some rural hunting communities eat even larger quantities of wild meat, especially if other foods are scarce. The Yanomamo in Amazonia[9] and Kalahari bushmen in southern Africa[10] eat about 9 ounces (250 g) of wild meat per person every day—more meat than many people in developed countries eat.

Even if it is not sold, wildlife can be of major economic importance to rural people. In Sarawak in the mid-1990s, each six-person family living in the interior ate an estimated 700 pounds (318 kg) of wild meat each year. The annual cost of replacing that with domestic pork would have been about $1,000 per family per year, or $75 million for all rural consumers.[6]

BY THE NUMBERS

Percentage of hunted species in Bolivia, Sulawesi, and Central African Republic for which current hunting is believed to be unsustainable: 50, 70, and 100, respectively

Brush-tailed porcupines and a blue duiker for sale at an impromptu roadside market in Cameroon. Although true subsistence hunters are rare, the United Nations has estimated that hunting to provide protein accounts for 90 percent of the bushmeat supply in Africa.

(Credit: Elizabeth Bennett)

For other rural dwellers, wildlife is an important source of cash. Many peoples across the tropics, especially in forests, are in cultural transition between a forest-dependent lifestyle and a modern cash economy. These people often sell wildlife, but also have access to weapons, agricultural tools, and markets, a combination that can be extremely destructive of natural resources unless good management is in place. For example, in communities adjacent to roads in Congo, per capita hunting rates were three to six times higher than in communities located far from roads, and up to 75 percent of the meat was sold.[11]

Logging Camp Employees

Tropical forests around the globe are being opened up by logging companies, with more than 60 percent of the land in some countries consigned to logging concessions. This brings major influxes of people into the forests—workers and their families as well as others colonizing lands along newly opened logging roads. Hunting rates rapidly increase as newcomers hunt for subsistence, sport, or trade. Company employees often buy wildlife from local hunters, a practice that is frequently encouraged by their employer as it reduces the cost of providing fresh food to staff. Workers are generally outsiders who have little regard for local hunting traditions and lack incentive to conserve resources for future use. Huge numbers of animals are hunted, often decimating the region's wildlife. In Sarawak, one logging camp of about 500 people hunted some 1,150 animals, or 19 tons (17.4 t) of dressed[12] wild meat per year.[13] And in a single logging camp in Congo-Brazzaville, 8,251 animals were hunted each year, or 137 tons (124 t) of dressed wild meat.[11]

Urban Consumers within Tropical Countries

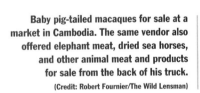

Baby pig-tailed macaques for sale at a market in Cambodia. The same vendor also offered elephant meat, dried sea horses, and other animal meat and products for sale from the back of his truck.

(Credit: Robert Fournier/The Wild Lensman)

In recent years, consumption of wild meat by urban dwellers in tropical countries has increased. The spread of road networks linking wildlife areas to towns and cities, and increased urban spending power, have fueled the trend (see color plate 3).

The trade can be enormous. In a single urban market in North Sulawesi, an estimated 3,850 wild pigs were sold every year from 1993 to 1995, along with 50 to 200 macaques, 50,000 to 70,000 forest rats, up to 15,000 bats, and occasional sales of rare cuscus and tarsiers (tree-dwelling nocturnal mammals).[14] In Gabon, more than 13,000 tons (12,000 t) of wild meat are sold annually in urban markets.[15] Domestic sale of wild meat is less of an issue in Latin America where the amount of wildlife sold is generally insignificant relative to its consumption by rural people. Even the famous large wild meat market in Iquitos, Peru, sells only 6 percent of the total amount of wild meat hunted in Loreto Province, with the other 94 percent consumed for rural subsistence.[16]

Much of the large-scale wildlife trade involves long-distance, international trade chains. Much is illegal and corrupt, sometimes using similar techniques and routes as the drugs and arms trades. The amounts of money involved are often vast, as are the quantities of meat, live animals, and animal parts that are traded. For example, in 2000, more than 27 tons (25 t) of turtles were exported from Sumatra to China every week.[17] Ho Chi Minh City is currently estimated to have around 1,500 restaurants serving wild meat, and in just four restaurants in Da Nang, more than 1 ton (1 t) of wild meat is sold each week.[18]

Wildlife trade across national borders within Africa and Latin America is generally small, but both supply other continents. Wild meat is shipped illegally from Africa to Europe and North America, and although estimates are difficult to obtain, the trade is apparently increasing. At least 13,000 tons (11,875 t) of wild meat, including monkey, rat, bat, gorilla, camel, and elephant, were smuggled into Britain in 2003, with customs seizures doubling over the previous year. Much came from western and southern Africa, as well as parts of Asia. The amount of wild meat being shipped from Africa to the United States is unknown but is thought to be considerable. An indication lies in two shipments intercepted by US Customs in 2003. One, a shipment to Boston's Logan airport, contained 26 monkeys from Guinea destined for a wedding reception in New Hampshire. The other, discovered at New York's JFK airport, carried 595 pounds (270 kg) of meat from bats, rats, squirrels, and duikers from Ghana.

Although Latin America has a major wildlife export trade, it does not include much wild meat, but mainly comprises legally exported leather and skins, and both legal and illegal trade in live animals for the pet trade, especially parrots.

> Today, anything large enough to be eaten or lucrative enough to be sold is hunted on a massive scale.

Effects of Unsustainable Hunting on Wildlife Populations

Levels of hunting in much of the tropical world so exceed sustainable levels that the effects on wildlife populations are devastating, especially in tropical forests. There are many examples. In Tangkoko Duasudara Nature Reserve in North Sulawesi, from 1978 to 1993, hunting reduced the number of crested black macaques *(Macaca nigra)* by 75 percent, anoa and maleo birds *(Macrocephalon maleo)* by 90 percent, and bear cuscus *(Ailurops ursinus)* by 95 percent.[19] In Bioko, Equatorial Guinea, hunting has reduced primate populations by 90 percent in some areas and brought local extinction in others.[20] And in 23 heavily hunted sites across Amazonia, densities of large mammals have been reduced by 81 percent.[21]

If heavy hunting and wildlife trade continue unchecked over time, whole populations disappear. In the last 40 years, 12 species of large animals, including Eld's deer *(Cervus eldii)*, batagur turtle *(Batagur baska),* and tiger *(Panthera tigris),* have become extinct or virtually extinct in Vietnam, mainly as a result of overhunting.[22]

BY THE NUMBERS

Number of African and Asian elephants that are killed each year for their ivory: more than 4,000

Effects of Unsustainable Hunting on Remote Rural Peoples

The people who immediately suffer as wildlife disappears are the millions across the tropics living at the frontier of development, those who are often the poorest and most marginalized. As their lands are opened up, wildlife declines. These people typically lack the education, skills, and cultural context to take advantage of cash-earning jobs. Without money or access to agricultural markets, they cannot readily switch to alternative livelihoods or food sources. They sometimes sell wildlife for cash, but if this is unsustainable, both their protein source and income vanish (see color plate 2).

One example of this is the Agta people in the Philippines. Between 1975 and 1985, as their land was opened up by new roads and hunting pressure increased, the proportion of successful hunts declined from 63 to 16 percent, and the number of kills per hunt declined by 86 percent. The Agta went from being hunters of abundant wildlife in primary forests to being struggling foragers with little wildlife to hunt.[23] Another example is Yuquí Indians in Bolivia. After their lands were opened up to outsiders, their daily protein intake dropped from 3.1 to 1.6 ounces (88–44 g).[24]

Many others do not depend on wildlife as a full-time source of food or income, but as a buffer to see them through times of hardship such as unemployment, crop failure, or warfare. That buffer is lost if the wildlife disappears.

Variation in Management Approaches

No "silver bullet" exists to solve the problem of unsustainable hunting in the tropics. Solutions must be tailored specifically to each region, based on detailed knowledge of local hunting patterns and dietary needs, while also considering cultural, socioeconomic, and political conditions, and the ecology of the hunted species.

The primary aim of management for an area must be clear. Is it to conserve wildlife populations? Or to provide resources for humans? In the rare cases where human populations and demand for wild meat are extremely low, the two may be compatible, but more often, different management approaches are required. If conservation is the primary objective, protected areas where hunting is strictly controlled or banned are crucial. In areas where hunting is appropriate, it must be clear who has the rights to hunt and which species can be hunted, and the management responsibilities must be both clear and legally mandated. Given that, various approaches can succeed in conserving hunted wildlife populations, if they are tailored skillfully to local conditions.

Three success stories provide a glimpse into the wide range of potential approaches. The 249-square-mile (644 km^2) Nagarahole National Park in India is home to many spectacular large mammals, including tigers, elephants *(Elephas*

> Humans are overharvesting all forms of life.

BY THE NUMBERS

Number of humans who died of Ebola in the Republic of Congo in late 2002 and early 2003: about 100

Number of gorillas that died of Ebola during the same period: about 600

maximus), gaur *(Bos gaurus,* a large wild ox), and axis deer *(Axis axis),* but potential hunting pressure for food and valuable commercial products such as tiger bones and ivory is extremely high. Numerous roads cut through the area, and more than 100,000 people live within 6 miles (10 km) of the park boundaries. However, the Indian government leads a multifaceted conservation program here, with about 250 staff engaged in the park. Management includes intensive enforcement, local education programs, and monitoring. Some communities that were originally living inside the park were voluntarily resettled outside park boundaries. As a result, over the last 30 years Nargarahole has become one of the best places in tropical Asia for viewing spectacular wildlife, even amidst such high human pressure.

At the other end of the spectrum of human population densities is a contrasting program. In the 1,245-square-mile (3,225 km^2) Reserva Comunal Tamshiyacu-Tahuayo in the Peruvian Amazon, human population pressures are low in a vast forest area, so an entirely different but equally successful program conserves hunted wildlife populations through a community-based system of management.[16]

A third success story involves the logging concessions surrounding Nouabalé Ndoki National Park in the Republic of Congo, where the government, the Wildlife Conservation Society, and a commercial logging company, Congolaise Industrielle des Bois, collaborate on wildlife management. Potential hunting pressure is vast, with a rapidly growing workforce and logging roads that provide access for the wild meat trade. But wildlife management systems are being implemented in the forestry concessions adjacent to the national park. Wildlife regulations have been written into company policy, and conservation education programs are conducted for company staff and local communities. Alternative protein supplies for these people are also being developed, including farmed fish and imported beef. Strict wildlife enforcement is carried out by locally recruited and highly trained "ecoguards," and success of the whole program is assessed through an intensive monitoring program. The abundance of large mammals throughout the concession, including gorillas *(Gorilla gorilla),* chimpanzees *(Pan troglodytes),* forest elephants *(Loxodonta africana),* and bongo *(Tragelaphus euryceros),* is testimony to the success of the project.

Successful management of hunting and the wildlife trade is not easy or cheap. Long-term, in-depth knowledge of an area is essential to determine what to do and how to do it. Access to sufficient resources is also crucial. Whether the management authorities are local communities, governments, or other agencies, adequate numbers of trained personnel are needed, along with sufficient infrastructure, equipment, and the political and legal support to do their job. Good management of hunting and wildlife trade is critical and is needed on a much greater scale than at present if we are to conserve the breathtaking magnificence of the world's wildlife and ensure the well-being of some of its most vulnerable peoples.

A boy near the Tarung River in Myanmar displays sambar deer antlers, an animal favored by both tigers and humans. Conservationists hope the recently created Hukaung Valley Tiger Reserve will curb hunting of this and other species.
(Credit: Steve Winter/National Geographic Image Collection)

BY THE NUMBERS

Total number of diseases that have jumped between wildlife, domestic animals, and humans: 868

Wildlife Trade within East Asia

Supply and Demand for Traditional Oriental Medicine

JAMES COMPTON AND SAMUEL K.H. LEE

In July 2004, a routine security patrol at the Hong Kong Zoo discovered broken locks on a cage housing several species of freshwater turtle. A quick head count revealed that only four were missing. All were Asian three-striped box turtles *(Cuora trifasciata)* — the most highly valued chelonian used in traditional Chinese medicine (TCM).

During the late 1990s, this species sold for up to $1,000 per turtle in its native China, Lao PDR, and Vietnam, highly sought after as a cancer cure. In Hong Kong, home to one of the turtle's last viable wild populations, traps have been set throughout its habitat, on both the mainland and nearby islands. As numbers decline, prices rise: the four individuals "liberated" from the Hong Kong Zoo were reportedly valued at over $6,500. No surprise then that another of the common names for *C. trifasciata* is the "golden coin turtle."

For this and many other freshwater turtles, the shell is most valuable for traditional medicine—particularly the underside, or plastron. It is prepared by grinding the shell into a powder and then boiling it into "turtle jelly," or *gui ling gao,* which is believed to detoxify the body and release excess heat. Because turtles are long-lived animals, the jelly is also consumed to increase longevity. In 2004, a 14-ounce (400 g) bowl of turtle jelly supposedly made from genuine *C. trifasciata* sold for $26 in downtown Hong Kong.[1]

Wildlife trade—the sale or exchange of wild animal and plant resources—stands at the very heart of the relationship between human societies and biodiversity conservation. The international wildlife trade, both legal and illegal, is estimated at tens of billions of dollars and involves hundreds of millions of plants and animals collected from around the globe, including chameleons from Madagascar, cockatoos from Indonesia, and American ginseng, to name a few. The demand for medicinal ingredients is one of the major drivers of wildlife harvest and trade (see color plate 4).

In East Asia, from Indonesia north to the Koreas, habitat is quickly disappearing, opening up previously remote areas. Rising human populations with growing economic power are hastening land conversion for agriculture and development, as well as mining, logging, and other resource extraction. This means more roads, which grant easier access for hunters and poachers, facilitating a largely unmanaged wildlife trade.

Because many local communities in East Asia depend on many of the same wild animal and plant species for food or medicine as those collected for the traditional medicine trade, local extinctions threaten local economies—as well as food security and health care. The World Health Organization (WHO) estimates that as many as 80 percent of people living in developing countries rely on animal- and plant-based medicines for their primary health care needs.[2] Therefore, the often-complex relationships of supply and demand for wildlife trade are of immediate concern to societies that depend on wildlife for both sustenance and income.

Consumption of wild-collected fauna and flora for medicinal benefit is a major threat to biodiversity, especially for slowly reproducing species, such as turtles. Population growth rates are naturally low for turtles because adult females produce only a few eggs per year and the young are vulnerable to predation. As a result, commercial (rather than subsistence) harvest and trade can have immediate and severe consequences for wild populations. In the case of a species with a restricted range like the golden coin turtle, intense medicinal demand has so depleted populations that it is now listed as critically endangered under the World Conservation Union (IUCN) Red List of Threatened Species. This classification indicates population losses of at least 80 percent over the past three generations.

Other species whose parts are used in traditional medicine are also in sharp decline. Tiger bones are used in anti-inflammatory preparations, rhinoceros horns are considered to be a fever reducer, and pangolin scales are used to treat various skin conditions. The musk deer is also in great demand: musk from the male's musk gland is used to treat conditions ranging from angina to delirium and paralysis. And there are many more species at risk (see color plate 5).

Because of unrelenting demand, these and other species have been listed by the Convention on International Trade in Endangered Species (CITES)—either in Appendix I, banning international commercial trade, or in Appendix II, which strictly controls commercial trade under a permit system. Despite CITES listings intended to curb supply, the persistent market demand and the high market value of certain species continue to threaten wild populations (see color plate 6).

The equation is often expressed like this: demand for wildlife in East Asia increases along with the burgeoning human population and economic growth, and unless checked, this momentum will drive more species rapidly down the road to extinction. For Japan, South Korea, and Taiwan, increased purchasing power has been a reality for the past 30 years. But China's exponential economic growth over the past 15 years, particularly in the country's southern provinces, is unprecedented in magnitude. Additionally, there is an expanding "globalization" of

The critically endangered Chinese three-striped box turtle has been heavily hunted for use in traditional Chinese medicine: it is believed to cure cancer. One turtle can fetch up to $1,000.
(Credit: John Behler)

BY THE NUMBERS

Number of animals imported into the United States in 2002: over 38,000 mammals, 365,000 birds, 2 million reptiles, 49 million amphibians, and 216 million fish

TCM among the diaspora of consumers in Chinese and other Asian communities in Europe, North America, and Australia. There is also a relatively small but growing Western consumer "vogue" for natural remedies.

For rural and coastal communities, there is great incentive to collect endangered species. Trade in wildlife can be extremely lucrative. For example, a hunter in Sumatra may net $940 from the body parts of a single tiger, more than the average annual per capita income of $710.[3]

While the overall threat to wild populations is what concerns conservationists, determining how much of this is due to traditional medicine consumption is an important consideration, particularly when considering appropriate responses to the situation. Take the case of Sumatran tiger (*Panthera tigris sumatrae*) trade in Indonesia. It was assumed that demand for tiger bone was the primary force behind tiger hunting in Sumatra because from 1975 to 1992, South Korea reported imports of 8,200 pounds (3,720 kg) of tiger bone from Indonesia. Assuming each tiger skeleton when dried weighs about 26 pounds (12 kg), this represents approximately 333 dead tigers, more than 18 per year.[4] TRAFFIC's recent report revealed that at least 50 tigers were poached from Indonesia each year between 1998 and 2002[5] from a population last estimated at between 400 and 500 animals.[6] Current trends show that a substantial domestic Indonesian market exists for tiger skins and other parts, especially claws and teeth, for trophies, charms, and souvenirs. This is not to say that demand for tiger parts used in traditional medicine is no longer a factor, but simply that this demand must be considered in context with other drivers of the wildlife trade.

Demonizing traditional medicine systems is unlikely to solve the problem—particularly given their history, which dates back thousands of years. There is also the sheer magnitude of use to consider. Even if only 50 percent of China's population uses traditional medicine, that equals approximately one-eighth of the world's population. Given this, there is an urgent need for mutual understanding between traditional medicine practitioners, consumers, and conservationists. Users need to be aware of the often-devastating effects that widespread use of these remedies has on wild populations of animals and plants. Environmentalists need to take into consideration the human need for health care, especially in places where Western medicines are not available or not accepted. Though balancing these perspectives will not be easy, it may be far more achievable than managing supply and demand on such a vast scale.

According to trade data on medicinal plants compiled by the United Nations Conference on Trade and Development (UNCTAD), East Asia is a significant exporter and importer of medicinal plant species. China and India accounted for half of the total reported global export trade in medicinal plants from 1993 to 1998; during the same period, Hong Kong, Japan, South Korea, and China accounted for 80 percent of the global import plant trade, making East Asia an in-

> The international wildlife trade, both legal and illegal, is estimated at tens of billions of dollars.

BY THE NUMBERS

Recorded tiger bone imports between 1970 and 1993 by East Asian countries from other parts of Asia: at least 10 tons

Approximate number of animals 10 tons of tiger bone represents: between 500 and 1,000

Shark fin soup is considered an Asian delicacy and has driven a lucrative global shark fin trade. Fins and other shark body parts are used in traditional medicine to treat disorders including diabetes, kidney disease, cancer, and sore throat. (Credit: Shelley Clarke)

credibly significant trade nexus for medicinal plants. There is also a huge intraregional import–export business. China's role as an exporter also includes re-exports from neighboring countries. As supplies fluctuate from wild harvesting and cultivation in China, alternative sources in Myanmar, Laos, Vietnam, and Russia have come under pressure.

The first recorded herbal traditional Chinese medicine compendium, the *Shen-long Bencao Jin,* is thought to have been written during the Han Dynasty (206 BC to AD 25). It documents 365 ingredients derived from raw or semiprocessed parts of plants, animals, and minerals in its *materia medica.* The Chinese system is also at the root of many other Asian medical traditions. Its influence in Korea began in the 6th century and Japan in the 7th century, evolving into medicinal systems known as *Hanya* (Korean) and *Kampo* (Japanese).[7] Traditional Vietnamese medicine is also derived from TCM.

Comprehending traditional Asian medicine requires its appreciation as an empirically based system—as a balance of opposing forces, known as yin and yang. Ancient Chinese tradition divides the world into five symbolic elements: wood, fire, earth, metal, and water. The relationships between these five elements and the body's vital organs (five solid, or yin, organs: heart, lungs, liver, kidney, spleen; and five hollow or yang, organs: large intestine, small intestine, gallbladder, bladder, stomach) are critical to understanding internal relationships between the body's components and how these are influenced by external factors. Traditional medicine practitioners adjust imbalances in qi (chi), or essential energy, in each patient's organs and systems.[8] The goal is to restore and maintain balance and harmony of the human body, mind, and spirit.

A doctor makes the diagnosis, then prescribes a personalized formula for the patient. In TCM as well as other traditional medical systems, ingredients are rarely prescribed in isolation. This has led some traditional medicine analysts to emphasize that no single ingredient is irreplaceable—so that a substitute can theoretically be made for any of them.

The key point here is that patients trust what doctors prescribe for their condition and are unlikely to question anything but price. Studies in Hong Kong showed that raising practitioners' awareness about the impact of traditional medicine demand on endangered species populations could greatly reduce the use of these ingredients.[9] Substantial change may also come through modification of the official curriculum taught in traditional medicine institutes.

> The demand for medicinal ingredients is one of the major drivers of wildlife harvest and trade.

Government intervention is also key, such as in China where the State Council prohibited trade in rhinoceros horn and tiger bone in 1993, specifying in the officially gazetted notice that the "pharmaceutical criteria for rhinoceros horn and tiger bone be cancelled and the pharmaceutical use of rhinoceros horn and tiger bone be prohibited."[10] This has enabled more effective law enforcement and prosecution of trade in rhinoceros and tiger parts in China, raising the deterrent against illegal activity. Penalty systems are also critical to increasing disincentives. For example, in Hong Kong anyone caught smuggling tiger parts faces fines up to $640,000 and two years in jail—but the challenges in enforcing such culturally ingrained practices are understandably large.

There have been efforts to find substitutes for some endangered animal ingredients used in traditional medicine. For example, there has been considerable research into the properties of bile extracted from bear gallbladder, which is commonly prescribed in TCM. Bear bile is believed to cool the heart and soothe the liver, thus helping to treat tumors, stomachache, jaundice, convulsions, and heart conditions. But over 50 ingredients in the TCM pharmacopoeia have similar effects and could be substituted, including coptis root *(Coptis chinensis)*, red peony root *(Paeonia lactiflora)*, scullcap *(Scutellaria* spp.), or even dandelion *(Taraxacum* spp.), depending on the health problems of the individual patient.

Bear bile has also been analyzed by Western researchers because of interest in bears' ability to hibernate for long periods without urinating, which is attributed to the presence of ursodeoxycholic acid (UDCA) in their gallbladders. Synthesized UDCA is now used to treat liver disease, hepatitis, and gallstones. Its proven efficacy has led to distribution in over 40 countries, including South Korea and Japan, where it can be used as a substitute for bear gallbladder in TCM.[11] But wild bears are still hunted for their gallbladders, and captive live bears are still farmed to extract gall by literally "tapping" their gallbladder.

Researchers are also searching for a TCM substitute with tiger bone's anti-inflammatory properties. Over the last 30 years, Chinese scientists have analyzed

These Southeast Asian box turtles awaiting export from Sumatra, Indonesia, represent an average day's trade of the species from this market; tons of live turtles are shipped daily to the major Chinese markets from around the globe.
(Credit: Chris R. Shepherd/TRAFFIC Southeast Asia)

the bones of leopard, lynx, and other cats, as well as ox, dog, pig, and bear bones, looking for the best tiger bone "match." One possible substitute was found—the sailong (*Myospalax baileyi*). The bone of this rodent, found on the Tibetan plateau, is used in Tibetan medicine to treat similar conditions: rheumatism and bone injuries. This discovery led to research and approval of patent TCM pre-scriptions for an antirheumatic wine using sailong bone.[12]

In this case, substituting a fast-reproducing rodent species for endangered tigers is great for conservation, but substitution of one species for another can have inherent risks. Tests on the horns of Central Asian saiga antelope (*Saiga tatarica*) in the 1980s found that they had similar fever-reducing properties to rhi-noceros horn, and hence could provide an alternative.[13] But with declining wild saiga antelope populations, this is not a viable choice.

If substitutes cannot be found, and demand persists for the original animal or plant ingredients specified in the *materia medica*, captive breeding and artificial propagation are seen by many as obvious solutions to make up shortfalls in sup-ply. This is currently being promoted in China and Vietnam, with the assumption that harvesting pressure on wild populations will be reduced. Since 2003, China has restricted the number of animals allowed for market sale to 54 species, partly in response to concerns raised during the severe acute respiratory syndrome (SARS) crisis that linked human health and wild animals sold in open markets. The species included on the restricted list, which includes common palm civet (*Para-doxurus hermaphroditus*), Chinese softshell turtle (*Pelodiscus sinensis*), rusa deer (*Cervus timorensis russa*), and Siamese crocodile (*Crocodylus siamensis*), are sold from farmed sources to supply food, medicinal, and "tonic food" markets.

This poses several questions—most importantly whether captive farming

Tiger bones, shown here packed in oil, are highly valued in traditional Asian medicine as an anti-inflammatory and an aphrodisiac. The illegal trade in tiger bone is still considered one of the leading threats to the tiger's survival.
(Credit: Robert Fournier/The Wild Lensman)

Cobra tonic for sale in a market in Hanoi, Vietnam. It is prescribed for a wide range of conditions by traditional Asian medicine practitioners.
(Credit: Elizabeth Bennett)

will satisfy the overall demand. One significant risk is that farming may increase the promotion of wildlife as a commodity—whether for food or medicinal use—and may even increase demand, without reducing unsustainable harvest of wild stocks. Another concern is that wild-caught animals may be "laundered" and sold as "captive bred."

Then there's simple economics. Even for a high-priced commodity like musk, traditionally sourced from wild male musk deer, the potential profit margins from farming may be low. Musk farming requires an investment of between $12,000 and $24,000 to produce 2.2 pounds (1 kg) of good quality farmed musk. When compared to the wholesale price of approximately $24,200 per pound ($11,000/kg) and the retail price of approximately $46,200 per pound ($21,000/kg) in China, the economic incentives are not very compelling for farming musk over wild harvesting, where the initial investment is relatively small and the overhead just as negligible. However, the yearly demand for musk in China ranges between 1,100 and 4,400 pounds (500–2,000 kg), killing 20,000 to 80,000 male musk deer each year. Conservation interventions to manage this ongoing wild harvest are clearly needed.[14]

We don't yet know what the conservation impacts of alternative ingredients are from captive-bred animals, substituted species, or synthetic substitutes. Even less is known about consumer preferences for naturally harvested species and their attributed properties of "wildness" over the alternatives.

Because so many people depend on traditional medicine, it may be possible to spark concern that many treatments will become unavailable without conservation management and sustainable use of key medicinal wildlife species. Unless market demand is reduced, supplies will soon run out for some species—and many more in the long term. For example, huge demand has decimated Asian freshwater turtles and tortoises, with 67 out of 90 Southeast Asian species listed as threatened under IUCN Red List criteria in 2000—double the number listed in 1996. This critical situation is being addressed at the international level through CITES and at national levels through legislation and restrictions on hunting, sale, and prescription of certain ingredients, but it is extremely difficult to police illegal hunting and trade (see color plate 6).

Smugglers go to extraordinary lengths to evade the authorities, shipping animals or animal parts via airfreight, by boat or motorcycle, hidden in the trunks of cars, under trucks, or carried in luggage on public buses. Powdered tiger bone or other portable substances are simply backpacked across one of many porous border crossings. Circuitous international trade routes are used—often the same ones used by drug smugglers. It is a huge challenge to patrol borders, airports, and seaports, and in many cases, authorities aren't capable of identifying illegally traded species. But even armed with proper information, regulatory agencies and wildlife authorities are often too understaffed to police the trade.

What is declared is usually what is inspected, so paperwork declaring country of origin or contents is routinely altered, forged, or laundered to feign compliance with CITES. Freshwater turtles become "fisheries products," animals are listed as farm-bred although they were poached from the wild, and volumes in tons become pounds on falsified permits.

The threat posed to individual species will determine the type of response needed, taking into account their life history and market demand. Innovative management approaches are needed. For example, in the case of the heavily traded Southeast Asian box turtle *(Cuora amboinensis),* government and community efforts need to be coordinated to enforce wild catch quotas. To limit the overall trade in wildlife used for traditional medicine to sustainable levels, a large-scale program of remedial action needs to be pursued concurrently at three levels: at the source (both the harvester and harvest site), at key points along the "trade chain," such as in markets, and on the demand side by working with users of traditional medicine.

Over the past 20 years, some important steps have been taken. Protected area systems have been established in countries such as Malaysia, Thailand, and Vietnam. All 10 members of the Association of South East Asian Nations (ASEAN) are now members of CITES, up from 6 a decade ago. More species are now protected by both national and international trade regulations, although efficient implementation and law enforcement remain a challenge. But the most pressing priority should be to catalyze change in market demand and patterns of consumption through education, the mass media, and government information services.

The most effective strategy may be "influencing the influential"—providing TCM doctors with sufficient information about the conservation status of heavily used or threatened animals and plants. Information on the impact of traditional medicine consumption on plants and wildlife could be disseminated with the greatest economy of effort by working with practitioners, medicine shop assistants who compile prescription ingredients, and students of traditional medicine. As a result, a symbiotic relationship between a well-managed supply and sustainable levels of demand may be a possibility for the future. This would ensure ongoing health care to a substantial portion of the world's population—while conserving flora and fauna from around the globe.

Red-eared sliders, possibly farm-raised in the United States, on sale in a market in Guangzhou, China. Farming is considered one way to reduce hunting of wildlife.
(Credit: John Behler)

Twine and the Ancient Mariners

Albatrosses, Sea Turtles, and Fishing Gear Encounters

CARL SAFINA, ERIC GILMAN,
AND WALLACE J. NICHOLS

Albatrosses and sea turtles are linked by the grace of their epic "flights" above and below the mirroring sea surface. During their wanderings in search of sustenance, albatrosses and sea turtles spend years at sea, traveling thousands of miles, crossing oceans and eventually returning to land only to breed. Along these difficult journeys, many drown.

Serious declines of these wondrous creatures indicate unseen, deeper problems in our oceans caused by modern fishing practices. Every type of fishing gear—with the possible exception of the spear—inadvertently hooks, nets, or entangles nontarget sea animals. This unintended catch, known as incidental catch, bycatch, or bykill, is a global problem along coastlines in developed and developing countries and on the high seas. It is caused by large-scale industrial fishing fleets in combination with smaller vessels and local, coastal fisheries.

The discarded animals may not be saleable species or may be too small—or there simply may not be enough room for them onboard. Roughly one in four animals caught in fishing gear around the world is thrown overboard, dead or dying. Shrimp trawlers are much deadlier: for every pound (0.45 kg) of shrimp caught, between 4 and 8 pounds (2–3.6 kg) of other marine life is discarded.

According to a United Nations report, global commercial fisheries discard 60 billion pounds (27 billion kg) of bycatch each year.[1] Among the unintended: dolphins, seabirds, sharks, seals, turtles, fish, and other marine species, many of which are caught in sufficient numbers to drive declines of some populations and threaten the recovery of others. Three major commercial fishing methods are responsible for most bycatch deaths: longlines, gillnets, and trawls. Without prompt action, many species could be fished to extinction.

But it makes little difference to sea animals whether they are targeted or caught incidentally. Fishing is the main threat to commercial species as well: catches of targeted species have declined by about 90 percent since the 1950s due to overfishing in many fisheries with high bycatch rates.[2]

An estimated 30 million tons of bycatch are netted or hooked each year by fishing fleets around the world; these animals are often discarded, dead or injured.
(Credit: OCEANA)

Bycatch was not always a problem of this magnitude. Over the last decades, the fishing industry has grown tremendously, with larger fleets and bigger, faster vessels capable of covering huge distances. The issue first captured public attention during the 1960s when thousands of dolphins were dying in tuna nets. After the 1972 passage of the Marine Mammal Protection Act in the United States and a public outcry for "dolphin-safe" tuna, deaths declined dramatically. More recently, bycatch has been recognized as one of the most serious threats to many ocean species.

Longlines

One of the most venerated of seabirds is the large, graceful albatross, the bird that inspired Samuel Taylor Coleridge's classic poem "The Rime of the Ancient Mariner." For much of their lives, albatrosses soar on their wide wings thousands of miles over the open sea, searching for food. But at least 200,000 albatrosses and other seabirds are killed each year by longline fishing fleets that crisscross the oceans. Death tolls do not include orphaned chicks that starve after their parents are killed. Accurate bykill estimates are impossible; because much fishing is illegal or undocumented, bycatch is frequently under- or unreported and numbers are based on just a few well-studied fisheries (see color plate 7).

Longline fishing probably originated during the 1500s in the Mediterranean Sea. But it was not until the end of the 19th century, when factory-made metal hooks became both widely available and affordable, that longlining began to proliferate. Foreign fishermen used longlines in Norwegian cod fisheries during the 18th century—and were condemned by locals for being too effective.[3]

Today, longlining is one of the most common fishing methods. Boats set out lines up to 60 miles (100 km) long, bearing hundreds or thousands of baited hooks to catch swordfish, tuna, cod, and other fish. Fleets from 40 countries set about 1.4 billion hooks in 2000—equivalent to about 3.8 million hooks each day.[4] Longline fishing is concentrated near the edges of continental shelves, seamounts, and other places where marine life is abundant—including both commercial species and those of conservation concern.

Longlines are particularly deadly to seabirds. As lines are set or retrieved off the rear of fishing boats, the birds dive after the free buffet of squid or fish used as bait. They swallow baited hooks or are impaled, then are dragged underwater and drown as the gear sinks.

Twenty-six of the 61 seabird species affected by longline fisheries are threatened with extinction. These include the wandering *(Diomedea exulans)* and royal albatrosses *(D. epomophora)* and other albatrosses from the family Diomedeidae, the southern and northern giant petrels *(Macronectes giganteus* and *M. halli)*, the white-chinned petrel *(Procellaria aequinoctialis)*, and gray petrel *(P. cinerea)*, to name a few.[5]

Each year in the North Pacific alone, 3,000-plus fishing vessels kill tens of thousands of seabirds on Alaskan longlines—while landing at least $300 million worth of swordfish, sablefish, halibut, and other fish. The dead include nearly 1,000 albatrosses and about 15,000 seabirds, mostly fulmars. The United States operates less than 5 percent of top-floating pelagic longlines and 15 percent of seabed-anchored "demersal" longlines in the North Pacific; the main Pacific pelagic fleets hail from Japan, China, Republic of Korea, and Taiwan, while the Canadians, Japanese, and Russians operate about 17,000 demersal vessels.[6]

Two threatened albatross species in the North Pacific are in decline: the black-

More than 100,000 albatrosses are killed every year by longline fishing boats, causing severe declines in all 21 albatross species.
(Credit: Fabio Olmos)

BY THE NUMBERS

In the United States, percentage of red drum caught in the South Atlantic, bocaccio caught in the Pacific, and red snapper caught in the US Gulf of Mexico by recreational fishermen: 93, 87, and 59 percent, respectively

footed *(Phoebastria nigripes)* and laysan *(D. immutabilis).* Population models predict further black-footed albatross declines if losses exceed 10,000 flying-age birds per year;[7] deaths in pelagic longline fisheries alone may exceed this threshold.[8] Albatrosses produce few offspring and have low natural annual mortality, long lifespans, and late sexual maturity—traits that make populations extremely vulnerable (see color plate 9).

Farther south, Hawaii's tuna- and swordfish-targeting longliners kill approximately 3,000 albatrosses annually. Seabird numbers killed by fleets from Taiwan, Japan, Russia, China, Korea, and others may total 30,000.

At the worst end of the scale are illegal fishing operations. "Pirate fishing," rampant in the Southern Ocean, lacks standards or constraints—short of gunboats. Illegal fishing for Patagonian toothfishes *(Dissostichus* spp., marketed as "Chilean seabass") kills an estimated 145,000 seabirds per year.[9]

In Mexico and other countries where turtle meat is a regional delicacy, sea turtle bycatch is often sold in regional markets.
(Credit: Jeffrey Brown/jeffreybrown.com)

Sea turtles suffer the same fate. For endangered Pacific loggerhead *(Caretta caretta gigas)* and leatherback turtles *(Dermochelys coriacea),* modern fishing methods pose the greatest threat to their continued existence. Like albatrosses and humans, turtles' natural lives span many decades and can approach the century mark. Often more than 20 years pass between the time they leave their natal beach as hatchlings and when they first breed. Their developmental and reproductive migrations take them across thousands of miles and through diverse habitats, from deep ocean basins to shallow lagoons and reefs. They spend much of their lives feeding, growing, and migrating in heavily fished temperate and tropical coastal waters. Everywhere, they are vulnerable to fishing gear (see color plate 8).

Turtles find and eat baited longline hooks and are entangled in other fishing gear—and drown. The combination takes a significant toll on sea turtle populations. In 2000, longliners worldwide were believed to have caught at least 200,000 loggerheads and 50,000 leatherback turtles.[4] Not all of these died, but the survival rates of turtles that have swallowed hooks are unknown. Swordfish longlines snare turtles at 10 times the rate of those targeting tuna, as the latter are set deeper than depths turtles frequent (see color plate 10).

All seven sea turtle species have some measure of protection under the Convention on International Trade in Endangered Species (CITES). But marine biologists at Duke University estimate that if longlining continues unabated, there is a 50 percent chance of turtle extinctions in the next 10 to 30 years, notably the leatherback turtle—and their decline is strongly linked with longline fisheries.

More than 250,000 loggerhead and leatherback sea turtles are caught each year by commercial longline fishing boats.
(Credit: Fabio Olmos)

Eastern Pacific leatherbacks, which nest on beaches in Costa Rica, Nicaragua, Panama, and Mexico, plummeted from an estimated 91,000 adult females in 1980 to only 1,690 within two decades largely because of longlines.[10]

Pelagic longlining kills many other nontarget species as well, especially sharks. The World Wildlife Fund estimated in December 2002 that 12 million sharks die each year as bycatch.

Gillnets

Gillnets also catch large quantities of unwanted marine life. These nets fish passively: they hang vertically in the sea like invisible tennis nets, set either to float or drift, or are anchored to the bottom. They are the preferred method of small-scale fishing and are used throughout the world's coastal waters.

Drift gillnets target billfishes, tunas, sharks, mackerels, dolphinfish *(Coryphaena hippurus)*, and other species, while anchored gillnets are used to catch coastal fishes such as halibut and rays. Huge driftnets have been used extensively across the high seas Pacific and parts of the Atlantic since the early 1980s. In 1993, the United Nations banned gillnets over 1.6 miles (2.6 km) in length, due in part to their nonselectivity.

Seabird bycatch in coastal gillnets is a greatly underreported conservation threat to murres and other coastal diving seabirds. The death toll can be huge: in Witless Bay, Newfoundland, fixed gillnets drowned between 20,000 and 30,000 common murres *(Uria aalge)* each year during the early 1970s—13 to 20 percent of the local breeding population.

Case studies suggest that coastal gillnet fisheries cumulatively pose a pressing threat to some sea turtle populations as well. For example, a gauntlet of drift-gillnets off the coasts of Chile and Peru have been implicated in the recent collapse of the Central American nesting population of leatherback sea turtles[11]; 80 percent of those entangled in Chilean gillnets perish.[12] In Mexico, the Magdalena Bay gillnet fishery is a major threat to the North Pacific green turtle *(Chelonia mydas)* population.[13]

One Mexican study quantified impacts. Young loggerheads congregate off the southern Baja Peninsula, where they spend two decades maturing and feeding on swarms of pelagic red crabs before crossing the Pacific to breed on their natal Japanese beaches. But many never make the trip. Near Playa San Lazaro, 394 loggerhead turtle carcasses were found washed up along a 28-mile (45 km) stretch of beach in 2003—representing just a fraction of the total killed.

Halibut fishers here reported capturing about four loggerheads each week per boat during the halibut season, which lasts four and one-half months. The local fleet numbers 50 to 70 small boats. Eighty percent perish; about 1,800 loggerhead turtles are killed each year by the Puerto López Mateos fishing fleet alone—just one of many local fishing communities. Just 20 percent of nesting females remain as compared to two decades ago, now numbering under 1,000.[14] The halibut fishery is the main reason for the precipitous decline.[15]

Trawls

Trawl nets—huge, bag-shaped nets pulled by boats directly over the seafloor or in midwater—also pick up large quantities of bycatch. Trawls target many different fishes, including cod, flounder, squid, and scallops; most shrimp vessels use trawls. The nets catch and drown many sea turtles, as they are towed for hours before being hauled to the surface.[16] Shrimp trawls are believed to kill more turtles than other gear—an estimated 150,000 each year worldwide.[17] In 1990, the US National Science Foundation's National Research Council called shrimp trawling the most lethal human activity for juvenile, subadult, and breeding sea turtles in US coastal waters.

These nets also catch many nontargeted fish species. Studies have shown that midwater trawls pose a threat to dolphins, sea lions, long-fin pilot whales *(Globicephala melaena),* and other marine mammals.

Turtle excluder devices (TEDs) have been shown to reduce bycatch of some sea turtle species by 97 percent, but their use by shrimp trawlers and others remains low.
(Credit: Carl Safina)

Gear Modifications

But there is hope, and the situation is not uniformly bleak. Modifications in commercial fishing gear can protect threatened species. Recent increases in Kemp's ridley *(Lepidochelys kempii),* green, and juvenile loggerhead turtles off the southeastern United States reflect the success of conservation actions there, including the widespread use of turtle excluder devices (TEDs).

In the late 1980s, the National Marine Fisheries Service (NMFS) began requiring use of these relatively inexpensive devices by shrimp trawlers in the United States. The TED is essentially a trap door fitted into a shrimp net that permits turtles to escape but traps shrimp. NMFS has shown that TEDs release up to 97 percent of sea turtles from nets with a minimal loss of shrimp.

But to be effective, TEDs must be large enough to allow adults to escape, their use must be legally mandated, compliance must be widespread, and enforcement must be effective. In many parts of the world, TED use is spotty or nonexistent. One example is Orissa, India, which hosts a critical olive ridley *(Lepidochelys olivacea)* rookery. The Wildlife Institute of India tallied turtle carcasses that washed up on beaches there from late 1993 to 1999. They found more than 30,000, with 13,575 in the 1997–1998 season alone.[18] In 1999, none of the roughly 3,000 trawlers operating off the coast used TEDs.

In 1989, the United States passed legislation banning shrimp imports

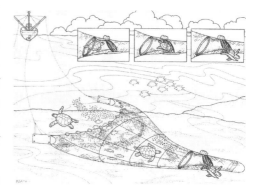

The turtle excluder device, or TED, provides an escape hatch for captured turtles from shrimp trawl nets.
(Credit: Mary Beath)

> Serious declines of these wondrous creatures indicate unseen, deeper problems in our oceans caused by modern fishing practices.

from countries that did not employ TEDs; in 1998 the World Trade Organization voted that the law violated WTO rules—and that only individual boats could be embargoed.

The United States has implemented both temporary and permanent fishery closures to protect areas where turtles congregate in response to lawsuits by environmental groups. In March 2004, California's longline swordfish fleet was banned from operating in a large swath of the Pacific. Swordfish longliners were banned from the Hawaiian Islands from 2001 to 2004, but the fishery was reopened when new turtle-friendly, G-shaped "circle" hooks were designed that cut the risk of snagging turtles. Likewise, the Grand Banks of Newfoundland were reopened to the American deepwater longline fleet last summer, also requiring use of circle hooks; the old J-shaped hooks are now banned from all Atlantic longline fisheries, including the Gulf of Mexico and the US Caribbean.

Turtles caught on circle hooks are usually hooked in the mouth, versus J hooks, which are easily swallowed, causing internal damage. However, this is beneficial only in shallow waters, as most turtles hooked in deep-sea fisheries drown regardless of how they are hooked. For deep longlines, setting gear below 328 feet (100 m) and using fish instead of squid for bait may protect turtles (see color plate 11).[19]

Over the past 15 years, national governments, regional organizations, and longline operators have developed and tested several fishing methods that nearly eliminate bird captures in longlines—and fishermen have begun using some effective low-tech, low-cost measures. Since most birds are hooked as longline gear is deployed, some fishermen are now setting longlines at night when seabirds are less active, using thawed bait that doesn't float, adding weights to lines, or dyeing bait so that birds don't recognize it as food. Birds can also be kept away from hooks by flying bright, shiny "scare lines" on fishing gear, by deploying lines through tubes that extend deeper than the birds can dive, or by setting lines off the side of the boat rather than the rear to limit birds' access to the bait.[20]

Mitigation methods must be determined according to the type of fishery, vessel design, type of fishing gear, and seabird diving abilities. Methods that increase profits by reducing bait loss and increasing efficiency—and therefore profits—have the best chance of being accepted by the fishing industry.

Bird bycatch avoidance measures are required for fleets in Alaska, British Columbia, and Hawaii as well as Australia and New Zealand, which were among the first to recognize the albatross bycatch problem and to pioneer solutions. Japan and Canada also require longliners to use bird-avoidance techniques.[21] But China, Korea, Mexico, Russia, and Taiwan lack regulations,[22] as do most of the world's longline fleets. There are many reasons for this, from inadequate management and enforcement and low industry awareness to insufficient economic incentives and habit.

Fishing and protecting marine life do not have to be mutually exclusive activities. For example, off the Pacific coast of Washington, fishermen found that putting 20 rows of visible mesh along the top of gillnets reduced common murre drownings by nearly half, yet did not significantly reduce their salmon catch. If fishing is restricted to only peak sockeye season versus fishing year-round—and is restricted to the middle of the day instead of the usual dawn to dusk hours—bird catch can be reduced by 75 percent.[23]

The authors are involved in experimental gear modifications with Baja fishermen in an attempt to reduce their gillnet bycatch by using more tautly stretched nets. Another innovative but simple solution implemented off the northeastern US coast grew from a partnership between government and the fishing industry: changing hook and bait styles reduced encounters with leatherbacks and loggerheads by roughly 65 and 90 percent, respectively.

Toward Solutions

Minimizing capture in only a few longline fleets will not sufficiently protect wide-roaming seabirds. International treaties and agreements are needed, and several have been completed.[24] But what counts is what actually happens on fishing boats.

However, agreements could mandate fishing gear design. For example, manufacturers could easily produce weighted lines made to international specifications that quickly sink hooks. Such international standards would be an important step forward, especially for fleets that currently use no mitigation methods, including illegal outfits.

The knowledge exists to reduce bird deaths from longline fisheries to insignificant levels. This reduction, however, will require raising industry awareness, widely implementing existing multilateral accords, and establishing and enforcing effective conservation measures. Motivating fishing boat captains will be crucial.

In order for other depleted species to recover, protected areas are needed, particularly in crucial spawning or nursery grounds, and will require adequate enforcement and monitoring programs to ensure compliance on behalf of fishers.

Conventions like the Inter-American Convention for the Protection and Conservation of Sea Turtles also hold promise for improved international cooperation. Enacted in May 2001, this remains the only international treaty dedicated exclusively to sea turtles, setting standards for the conservation of these endangered animals and their habitats. And last year, over 400 leading scientists and 100 organizations from around the globe petitioned the United Nations for a

To rescue marine life, we need a new sense of community that encompasses the ocean and its creatures. . . . We need a "sea ethic."

moratorium on pelagic longline and gillnet fishing in the Pacific Ocean to protect endangered sea turtles and other marine life.

There is obviously a need for a more comprehensive world strategy to reduce bycatch. Government agencies, research institutes, and nongovernmental organizations (NGOs) have begun to recognize the enormity and urgency of the problem—and the need to work collaboratively. Current initiatives include experimenting with additional fishing gear changes and working directly with fishing captains, supplying them with less deadly circle hooks, giving talks, holding workshops, and providing educational materials. Other measures include teaching fishermen turtle resuscitation and educating seafood consumers about problems with shrimp trawling to enlist them in the fight for cleaner fishing practices (see color plate 12).

Current fishing methods threaten extinction to species that have crossed oceans for millions of years. But recent innovations, which are already showing results, provide hope and impetus for sea turtle and seabird recovery, and reduction of needless slaughter of all by-caught marine species. Adoption of new policies and fishing practices can significantly lower bycatch—if we can succeed in getting their widespread use aboard fishing boats.

This will require greater effort and more funding. Haste is appropriate. The crisis is worldwide and ubiquitous throughout the seas. It goes deeper than just the gear we use. It involves the attitude of fishers and the disinterest of consumers. To rescue marine life, we need a new sense of community that encompasses the ocean and its creatures. In short, we need a "sea ethic."[25]

Ebola, SARS, and Other Diseases That Imperil People and Animals

ROBERT A. COOK AND WILLIAM B. KARESH

One morning, your six-year-old presents you with a gift that the family cat brought home from an early morning hunt—a small, dead, and bloodied prize. You quickly scrub your child's hands and admonish that such things are dirty and dangerous. Days later the symptoms begin: no appetite, a hacking cough, then he spits up a bit of blood. You take him to the local clinic and discover that others are sick—including a group of kids that were playing with a dead animal in the forest a few days before. You hear that there are hundreds of dead animals in the area, like nothing the community has seen before. The children have come in contact with many people over the last few days at school, sporting events, and family gatherings near and far, infecting many more. Will the disease spread to epidemic proportions, infecting or killing people around the globe? Or will it only continue to devastate wildlife and sicken people here in the region?

In Africa a similar scenario might involve a dog rather than a cat, or the kids could be catching small animals themselves just like children playing in the woods in North America or Europe. In other areas, adults hunting for wildlife to consume or sell provide the source of contact for diseases. The stories play out every day, everywhere in the world, moving us ever closer to possible disease outbreaks.

Increasingly, diseases are moving between people, domestic animals, and wildlife, creating concerns about food safety, public health, and wildlife conservation. Some of these diseases have been with us for millennia, while others are emerging or reemerging, gaining the ability to jump between species and overloading our traditional methods of disease surveillance and prevention. Since 1980, more than 35 new infectious diseases have emerged,[1] or about one every eight months. Acquired immune deficiency syndrome (AIDS), severe acute respiratory syndrome (SARS), bovine spongiform encephalopathy (BSE) or mad cow disease, and Ebola hemorrhagic fever are just a few of these new diseases that threaten the health and future of both animals and people.

> Of the 1,709 known pathogens that currently plague humanity . . . 49 percent are zoonotic: they spread between animals and people.

With growing globalization, people, livestock, and wildlife are coming into contact as never before, putting the health of all in danger. The threat of emerging infectious diseases spreading between people and animals is rising everywhere, fueled by human activities ranging from how we handle bushmeat and the trade in exotic pets to the destruction of wild habitat and the ways we produce livestock (see color plate 13).

This unprecedented contact fosters the spread of once-localized diseases and creates many opportunities for new diseases to be born. For example, forest animals that are trapped for the pet trade or harvested for meat are often shipped to markets in far-off cities or to other countries, where live animals from diverse environments are caged in close proximity. This widely distributes microbes from around the world, enabling these organisms to evolve, to breech the Darwinian divide, and to "jump" into new hosts that lack natural immunity to them.

Of the 1,709 known pathogens that currently plague humanity—from viruses and bacteria to fungi, protozoa, and worms—49 percent are zoonotic: they spread between animals and people. These species-jumping microbes are three times more likely to cause newly emerging diseases,[2] often deadly illnesses that can devastate whichever species happen to become the unwitting victims. Many animals carry diseases that threaten human health, from pet reptiles and birds to cows and wild buffalo.

The Forest Hunt:
How Easy Pickings in the Forest Become a Deadly Dinner

A dinner of any wild meat hunted from the forest can become the source of deadly, highly contagious diseases. But eating nonhuman primates is particularly dangerous: humans share 98 percent of their DNA with gorillas and 97 percent with chimps. We also share more than 100 infectious diseases caused by organisms that move between people and nonhuman primates with ease.

One of these organisms causes Ebola hemorrhagic fever. This disease, which first appeared in the Democratic Republic of Congo in 1976 and is named for the Ebola River, infects humans, gorillas, chimpanzees, and monkeys. It causes severe internal and external hemorrhaging and can be extremely deadly, killing up to 90 percent of its human victims. Infection spreads quickly, especially via caregivers and by those who flee to the next village or town to escape the illness. Outbreaks have been recorded in Sudan, Gabon, Republic of the Congo, Democratic Republic of Congo, Côte d'Ivoire, and Uganda—and have almost wiped out the populations of entire villages.[3]

The key to understanding how and why this disease emerges so suddenly and with such deadly force may lie in identifying the natural carrier, and though

Transmission electron micrograph (TEM) of Ebola virus 1181. Ebola can result in death rates as high as 90 percent of those infected. Its natural host remains unknown.
(Credit: CDC/C. Goldsmith)

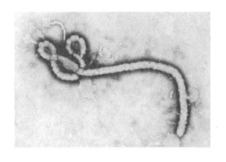

some suspect fruit bats, the actual host remains elusive.[4] But it is clear that both people and nonhuman primates suffer equally from the disease.[5]

Outbreaks have caused declines in lowland gorillas and chimpanzees in Gabon and the Republic of the Congo and chimpanzees in western equatorial Africa.[6] Other forest animals, such as duikers—small antelopes—and bush pigs may also be affected.[7] There can be great danger lurking in a bushmeat dinner of these species. When hunters discover a sick or dead animal in the forest, they usually bring it home to eat, and the Ebola virus then easily infects those handling the meat. Each of the human outbreaks in Central Africa during the last few years was traced to humans handling infected great apes.

A World Health Organization (WHO) medical team sprays the hands and feet of people attending a funeral of an Ebola victim during a 2003 outbreak of the disease in the Republic of the Congo.

(Credit: Pierre Formenty/WHO)

The Wildlife Markets:
Breeding Ground for the Next Global Pandemic?

Most hunters send some percentage of their quarry to market and for centuries wildlife markets have served as a gathering place for local trade. But now, in a globalized world, local products can be shipped around the world in a matter of days. Markets selling wild meat can be found in local villages or in major urban areas from Gangzhou, China, to New York City, with booths selling animal products to immigrants or their descendents who seek a connection with their historical traditions and tastes. Just about any animal in the world can be found in some of these markets: surveys of live wildlife in Asian markets have identified crates of masked palm civets *(Paguma larvata)*, ferret badgers, barking deer, wild boar, hedgehogs, foxes, squirrels, bamboo rats, various species of snakes, and endangered leopard cats *(Felis bengalensis)*, together with dogs, cats, rabbits, and gerbils.[8]

Typically, the animals have been through a traumatic ordeal of capture and transport and are packed together in filthy, cramped cages. This creates a perfect storm of species in poor health, unable to fight off infection, that are exposed to a plethora of microbes—and that are in intimate contact with people handling many animals as they move through the marketplace. Given these circumstances, it's not surprising that new diseases emerge in markets. Instead it is rather remarkable that it doesn't happen with greater regularity (see color plate 14).

Clearly, diseases do sometimes adapt and spread to new hosts. A recent example is SARS, which first appeared in China's Guangdong Province in late 2002. People began complaining of high fever, cough, and diarrhea, and eventually developed severe pneumonia. It was an unknown disease, and it was very contagious. Within a matter of weeks, it spread to Hong Kong, then moved across five continents, with cases reported in 25 countries.[9] By July 2003, The World Health Organization (WHO) tallied 8,437 cases, with 813 deaths.[10]

A new coronavirus (a family of viruses found in many animal species) was discovered to be the culprit,[11] and it was also detected in palm civets that were

A market in Pokola, Republic of the Congo, selling legally hunted animals, including the monkey pictured here. People share more than 100 infectious diseases with nonhuman primates, some of which can be transmitted by handling or consuming bushmeat.
(Credit: Stephen Sautner, WCS)

farmed in the region.[12] Later, it was also found in raccoon dogs *(Nyctereutes procyonoides),* Chinese ferret badgers *(Melogale moschata),* and domestic cats. A possible link between civets and SARS led to a government-ordered extermination of over 10,000 masked palm civets in the province despite the lack of hard evidence linking the animals to the outbreak[13]—and in spite of opposition from the Wildlife Conservation Society and the World Health Organization.

Two years later, questions still abound as to exactly how this organism originated and what animal host it came from. However, epidemiological studies have concluded that the first human infections did indeed come through animal contact.[14] Researchers attempting to solve this mystery are investigating two avenues: the international trade in small carnivores and venues in China that house large numbers of animals, including farms that raise them, wildlife markets that sell them, and restaurants that serve wildlife dishes. But international attention must also focus on changing traditional market practices and increasing surveillance to detect potential new threats before they result in similar tragedy.

The International Pet Trade: A Poorly Regulated Luxury Fraught with Risk

Wildlife markets in developing countries are not the only breeding grounds for disease. The allure of rare and exotic creatures from far-off lands prompts millions of people each year to purchase wildlife as house pets. The pet trade not only threatens wild populations, but these animals can also act as living disease incubators that carry foreign germs thousands of miles across continents.

Each year, an estimated 350 million plants and live animals are traded around the world, netting more than $10 billion on the legal market plus an additional $5 to $8 billion in illegal trade.[15] Of this, $826 million worth of live wildlife (mainly ornamental fish species) is sold legally as pets.[16] The volume of illegal trade is unknown, both the trafficking in endangered species and the smuggling of wildlife across borders.

Many diseases are transmitted via parasites carried by these imported animals. For example, between November 1994 and January 1995, US Department of Agriculture personnel inspected 349 reptile shipments from 22 countries containing 117,690 animals. Ticks were removed from animals in 97 shipments: infested shipments included 54,376 animals.[17] Ticks carry many diseases that threaten livestock and humans, including heartwater disease, Lyme disease, and babesiosis (a blood cell parasite).

Rodents also carry a plethora of diseases that move between people and animals. Many people know that rodents carry plague, but US doctors routinely look for many other diseases they transmit, including black jaundice, rat-bite fever, hanta virus, and lassa, to name a few. Another virus was added to the list in 2003: monkeypox. Though it was known that the illness could be spread by rodents, until then, US health professionals weren't looking for it. This rare, smallpox-like disease was first diagnosed in laboratory monkeys in 1958, hence its name. The first human cases were reported in 1970 in Africa, and a later outbreak in the Democratic Republic of Congo in 1997 infected 88 people, killing three children under the age of three.[18]

In late May 2003, the first cases of a mysterious illness were reported from hospitals in Wisconsin, Illinois, and Indiana, where people showed up with skin ulcers and fevers. Most patients had been in close contact with pet prairie dogs *(Cynomys leucurus).* These animals had been caged with imported African rodents—which had passed the monkeypox virus to them. A Milwaukee animal distributor had sold the infected prairie dogs to pet stores in Milwaukee and at an animal swap meet in northern Wisconsin. The African rodents had been legally shipped from Ghana to the United States the month before, also for the pet trade. A number of species imported at the same time carried the virus, including rope squirrels *(Funisciurus* sp.), Gambian pouched rats *(Cricetomys gambianus),* and dormice *(Muscardinus arvellanarius).*[19]

By early July, 71 human cases from six midwestern states had been reported to the Centers for Disease Control and Prevention, though no one died. At that time, any nonendangered African rodent could be legally shipped into the United States as pets. Since then, restrictions have been placed on them—but rodents from other countries and many other species continue to enter the United States and move around the world, largely exempt from oversight.

> Clearly, traditional approaches to disease management—which are currently segregated into human, livestock, and wildlife health—are no longer effective in a globalized world.

Our Fragile Food Supply: Livestock Diseases Also Threaten People

Rigorous health inspection requirements over the last decades have made us secure in the belief that our food supply is safe. For developed nations, this is more often true than not. But livestock health is under increasing attack, with rising global movements of animals and humans—and greater exposure to the many diseases that dance between them. Increased contact comes through industrial farming practices, animal markets, and agriculture: livestock is now often raised in close proximity to wildlife as forests are cleared by settlers across the tropics.

By the end of the 20th century, international demands for animal protein had transformed domesticated livestock production into an ultraintensive industry, with swine, poultry, and cattle operations packing huge numbers of animals into limited spaces. Projections indicate a doubling of livestock production in developing countries over the next 20 years. Though these practices maximize food production, such intensive management makes livestock susceptible to illness. Infection spreads quickly through these crowded factory farms, and fighting outbreaks can prove challenging because of growing antibiotic resistance. Selective

BY THE NUMBERS

Number of primates legally imported into the United States as pets or research animals between 1995 and 2002: 99,939

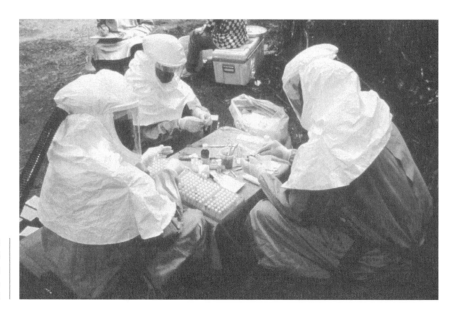

Centers for Disease Control and Prevention (CDC) and Zairian scientists collect tissue and fluid samples from animals during a 1995 Ebola outbreak near Kikwit, Zaire.
(Credit: CDC/Ethleen Lloyd)

breeding for specific traits often predisposes animals to conditions requiring repeated treatment with antibiotics, and many facilities routinely mix antibiotics with animal feed to avoid transmitted illness. Increased antibiotic use creates superbugs that can tenaciously infect both animals and humans.

High-volume food production has moved the industry toward some dangerous practices. Bovine spongiform encephalopathy (BSE), or mad cow disease, is one such example from England. Mad cow is a chronic, degenerative disorder affecting the central nervous system of cattle. It is thought to have jumped from sheep through the practice of feeding infected sheep byproducts to cows. Known as "scrapie" in sheep, the disease has existed for hundreds of years without infecting other species, but it spread rapidly through cattle herds in the United Kingdom, with 182,745 documented cases between 1988 and 2002. Cases have since been found in other European countries, Canada, and the United States.

Changes in meat processing methods exposed people to mad cow disease. These changes allowed muscle meat to be contaminated with spinal cord and spinal fluid—which is a source of the infectious prion proteins that cause the disease. (Prions are essentially defective proteins that have the ability to induce the defect in other proteins, destroying brain cells.) The disease then successfully jumped to humans as variant Creutzfeldt-Jakob disease (vCJD). The University of Edinburgh reports 132 human deaths attributed to definite or probable vCJD.

Zoonotic diseases also infect birds. Avian influenza, or bird flu, is one of these, an infectious disease that was originally diagnosed over a century ago in Italy.[20] Wild birds, most notably wild ducks and other migratory waterfowl, naturally carry various forms or strains of the virus, though it rarely causes illness in these species. But it can make chickens, turkeys, and other domestic fowl very ill. Live bird markets that sell many species provide the perfect conditions for the viral strains to mix and the flu viruses to spread among species.[21] This may be what caused the avian flu (H5N1) outbreaks in Hong Kong in 1997 and throughout Southeast Asia in 2003 and 2004.

Within months of these most recent epidemics, approximately 100 million birds—primarily poultry—had succumbed to the disease or been killed in an effort to halt its spread.[22] Asian governments have also threatened to cull wild birds—even though there has been no evidence that this strain of avian influenza came from wild populations, and recent studies suggest the outbreak was more likely caused by poor hygiene and management practices in local poultry production.[23] Rather than attempting to eradicate wild species, a better choice would be to institute sanitation and hygiene protocols in poultry operations and tighten controls on the movement of poultry.

> While the concept is centuries old, the application is new: the health of people, domestic animals, and wildlife is closely interrelated.

The threat posed by bird flu goes beyond the food supply. Thirty-four people were infected with the H5N1 strain of avian influenza virus during the most recent outbreak in Southeast Asia, causing 23 deaths—a 68 percent mortality rate. But even these startling statistics pale in comparison to the greater threat. H5N1 mutates rapidly and can acquire genes from other flu viruses infecting the same host—a mechanism known as reassortment. The fear is that genes from human influenza virus and the H5N1 bird flu virus will reassort, creating a super virus. This new bug could spread easily between people—as the human influenza virus does—and be as deadly as H5N1. There is good reason for concern: during the 20th century, there have been three global flu pandemics, and all are believed to have come from a modification of an avian flu strain. The most severe of these was the 1918 Spanish flu, which killed more than 20 million people worldwide.

Nipah virus, another recently described emerging disease, appeared in Malaysia in September 1998 with a major outbreak in pigs and humans,[24] killing 105 people. Malaysians culled over 1 million pigs to stop the spread. Five species of fruit bats were found to carry Nipah, suggesting a wide prevalence among healthy bats.[25] It seems that people acquired the virus from handling pigs infected with the disease. The pigs are thought to have been infected by bats feeding or roosting in trees above their pens.[26]

If this is indeed the chain of infection, it highlights what can happen when people and domestic animals modify previously undisturbed wild habitat. Within ecosystems, microbes and wildlife exist in balance, but the introduction of new species—like cows, pigs, dogs, or humans—may allow pathogens to jump into animals with no natural immunity or evolved resistance.

An Integrated Approach: One World, One Health

Clearly, traditional approaches to disease management—which are currently segregated into human, livestock, and wildlife health—are no longer effective in a

BY THE NUMBERS

Percentage of tropical birds and reptiles that die during transport for the exotic pet trade: up to 80

globalized world. Solving today's threats and tomorrow's problems cannot be accomplished with yesterday's approaches. Only by breaking down the barriers among agencies, individuals, specialties, and sectors can we unleash the innovation and expertise needed to meet the many serious challenges to human and animal health.

While the concept is centuries old, the application is new: the health of people, domestic animals, and wildlife is closely interrelated. We are in an era of "one world, one health" and we must devise adaptive, forward-looking, and multidisciplinary solutions to the challenges that undoubtedly lie ahead. We need proactive management to thoughtfully control the global interactions of people and animals.

Reacting to disease outbreaks costs billions that would be better spent on prevention. We also need better response to novel disease threats, quicker reaction to outbreaks, and more careful monitoring on a global scale. The Wildlife Conservation Society has been taking the lead in this initiative by convening the world's leaders in health, conservation, economics, and environmental law, and by implementing on-the-ground programs that solve and prevent critical problems that threaten the health of animals and people on this planet we share.

Hunting for Conservation in the Amazon Rain Forests

Lessons Learned from Peru

RICHARD BODMER

Deep in the Amazon, Juan Huanaquiri stalks through the murky undergrowth of the lush lowland rain forest. Toucans fly above, frogs leap off his path and the distant shrieks of howler monkeys echo through the trees. Armed with both an old shotgun and a well-used machete, he searches for prey. A Spix's guan *(Penelope jacquacu)* flushes out of a tick tree, but the bird is too small to waste a valuable cartridge on.

Soon, he hears the telltale cracking of collared peccary *(Pecari tajacu)* teeth nearby. The blast of his gun reverberates through the forest as he takes down a male. Birds scream and the remaining peccaries crash through the forest, fleeing for their lives. Before carrying his kill back to the canoe, Juan wraps it in palm leaves for fear of being attacked by a lurking jaguar *(Panthera onca)*. It will take five hours to row back to his village on the Blanco River. His family will have protein tonight, but first they must help him salt the meat and prepare the pelt. They will sell some to the *patrón* to buy soap to wash their clothes and some canned milk for their youngest child.

Juan and his family are descendants of Cocama Indians and still live in their traditional ways in a small village of 15 families. They live within the 1,245-square-mile (3,225 km^2) Tamshiyacu-Tahuayo Community Reserve in northeast Peru, an area sometimes called "the green paradise" of the Amazon rain forest. The reserve was created in 1991 by the Peruvian government to protect the range of the rare red uakari monkey *(Cacajao calvus)*. The jungle teems with life here, with one of the world's richest arrays of plants, amphibians, reptiles, and birds. There is also a greater diversity of mammals in the reserve than anywhere in the Amazon, and the 14 species of primates is the highest number found in any protected area in South America.

For both the Indian and nontribal residents of Tamshiyacu-Tahuayo, the forest is their grocery store—and they are concerned about the future. Juan's village participates in a unique approach to conservation: they and the eight other

Collared peccary is the most common peccary species that is hunted extensively for hides and meat in Latin America. It also constitutes a major source of meat for many rural and indigenous people.
(Credit: WCS)

villages near the reserve manage local hunting so that it does not deplete wildlife, and they are legally responsible for the reserve. Working closely with biologists from the Wildlife Conservation Society (WCS) and the Durrell Institute of Conservation and Ecology (DICE), they are monitoring wildlife populations and establishing hunting quotas. This reserve functions without the benefit of ecotourism dollars or patrols by park guards and is the first of its kind in Peru.

The Tamshiyacu-Tahuayo reserve is divided into strictly protected areas and hunting zones where people from local villages are allowed to hunt. Villagers must register the animals they kill after each hunt in a book held in the community. Biologists analyze hunting data and advise on quotas using sustainability models for each species. One such quota allows each family to take three hoofed animals, such as peccaries, every two months. Rules prohibit hunting of certain animals, such as tapir, giant armadillos *(Priodontes maximus),* and monkeys. Social pressure is used to enforce hunting rules (see color plate 15).

Other Amazon communities are also concerned about disappearing wildlife and have established community-based management plans to better manage resources. One such initiative by the World Wildlife Fund (WWF) is helping the Condosi and Quecha Indians of the Pastaza River develop wildlife hunting plans for their indigenous territories. This is important for wildlife conservation, since remote rain forest regions have some of the world's highest biodiversity—and also have the greatest chances for successful conservation. By helping villages establish sustainable hunting practices, conservationists protect rich wildlife communities within vast tracts of Amazon rain forest. But the most important factors in crafting a management plan are the biology and ecology of the local animals combined with the social and economic reality of the people living in the region.

The farther people live from cities and large towns, the more important animals are in their lives. Fresh produce and other food is not readily available in remote areas and many villages lack electricity and refrigeration. For rural residents living deep within the forests, animals provide a primary food source—dried, salted bushmeat, which can be stored for months.

It is unrealistic to presume that hunting for wild meat will be abolished here. Indeed, bushmeat hunting is still prevalent in countries that outlaw subsistence hunting, such as Brazil.[1] Unbridled hunting of wild meat throughout the Amazon basin has decimated some animal populations, such as manatees, tapir, and large primates, which are important sources of protein. The current bushmeat crisis will only be resolved if the solution takes into consideration the social issues of poverty and sustainable resource use. So it is imperative to find ways to convert destructive hunting practices to more sustainable ones.

Each year, hunters in Loreto kill about 113,000 mammals, or over 2,900 tons (2,630 t) of bushmeat. Local residents hunt animals both for subsistence and to sell in city markets. A recent WCS study in Peru's northeast Department of Loreto, where the Tamshiyacu-Tahuayo reserve is located, showed that most

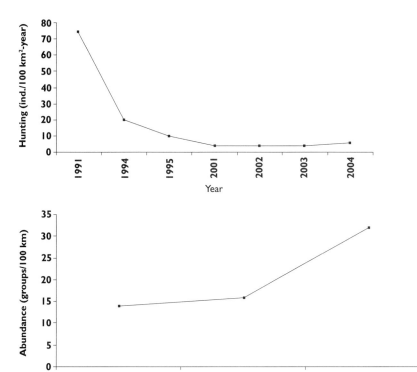

Above: Hunting pressure on large-bodied primates in the Tamshiyacu-Tahuayo Community Reserve. After implementing community-based wildlife management in 1991, hunting of these primates decreased. Below: Increase in abundance of large-bodied primates in the reserve. Data are from line transect censuses conducted within the reserve. Figures show the number of primate groups sighted per 100 kilometers.
(Courtesy Richard Bodmer)

people still hunt strictly for food. Ninety-four percent of wild meat is consumed by 600,000 inhabitants living in a rain forest area larger than the United Kingdom—over 146,700 square miles (380,000 km²). In rural villages, people eat whatever they catch.[2]

Only 6 percent of bushmeat was sold in the closest city of Iquitos, which has 400,000 residents and lies 62 miles (100 km) away with no road in between. Wild meat sold in Iquitos is mainly peccary and paca (a large burrowing rodent), which sells for under $2 per pound ($4.40/kg). Villagers use money earned from the sale of bushmeat to buy basic products such as salt, rice, soap, cooking fuel, medicines, school supplies, and other household goods.

The current situation in Loreto is mixed in terms of wildlife conservation. Some species are being overhunted, while some are stable. Others are recovering. The 6-foot (2 m)-long giant river otter *(Pteronura brasiliensis)*, the jaguar, and the black caiman *(Melanosuchus niger)* are all conservation success stories. These animals were widely hunted for their very valuable skins, beginning in the early 20th century: pelts exported from Loreto between 1946 and 1973 included 23,045 giant river otter, 17,301 jaguar, and 84,269 black caiman skins. But the pelt trade was abolished in Peru in 1973 when the Convention on International Trade in Endangered Species (CITES) placed all three species on Appendix I, prohibiting international trade.

Map of the department of Loreto, Peru.
(Courtesy Richard Bodmer)

Rebounding populations attest to the success of these efforts. Over the last decade, giant river otter sightings increased along Loreto's Yavari Miri River from zero animals per two-month survey in 1993 and two in 1997 to 18 sightings in 2001 and 40 in 2004—the data predict a peak recovery of 120 sightings.[3]

Likewise, black caiman are slowly reappearing. As black caiman were hunted out for leather shoes and handbags, the common caiman increased, filling their ecological niche. The two species compete for the same lowland flooded forest habitat, but now the black caiman is reclaiming some of its former territory.

Jaguars also are more abundant. Interviews with hunters in the Tamshiyacu-Tahuayo reserve show that the cats are sighted more frequently today than they were 10 years ago, and that the increase began after the 1973 ban on the sale of jaguar pelts.

Unfortunately, other animals are being hunted for bushmeat at dangerous levels. Not all species are equally vulnerable: animals with faster reproduction rates—that produce frequent, large numbers of offspring—have a greater chance of being hunted sustainably than slower-reproducing species.[4]

One of the first steps in developing wildlife management plans is identifying prolific species that can tolerate bushmeat hunting. Studies show that collared and white-lipped peccaries *(Tayassu pecari),* brocket deer, large rodents, and game birds are usually hunted at sustainable levels.[5] Animals that breed too slowly to withstand steady hunting pressure include tapir, otters, monkeys, and carnivores such as jaguars, pumas *(Puma concolor),* and ocelots *(Leopardus pardalis).*

> The bushmeat crisis in the Amazon is a major concern for conservation.

What hunters find and kill most are animals that reproduce the fastest, which are often not their target.[6] Surveys among hunters in the Yavari River region revealed that most prefer large mammals over smaller animals—there's more meat on bigger animals.

A species' resiliency is a consequence of being either common or uncommon natural prey. The slow-reproducing tapir and howler monkey are uncommon prey for natural predators, whereas quickly-reproducing animals such as large rodents, peccaries, and deer are more abundant common prey. When a new predator, such as a human hunter, enters an ecosystem and kills uncommon prey, these animals cannot compensate for added mortality. In contrast, common prey species can adapt to higher and variable losses from natural predators. Using "density dependent mechanisms," they are able to adjust their reproductive output, producing additional offspring to compensate for population losses. This predator–prey ecology is an important factor in determining whether animals can be sustainably hunted.

Managing resources requires a variety of strategies, including community-based conservation, establishing and regulating protected areas, and managing logging concessions. But wildlife management plans are one of the best tools available for conservation.[7] For example, when the Tamshiyacu-Tahuayo Community Reserve implemented their plan, hunting of large primates dropped by almost 70 percent. It has remained at that level for over a decade, allowing populations to rebound.

Protected area authorities also realize the benefits of managed hunting as a way to curb poaching. The Pacaya-Samiria National Reserve, also in Loreto District, enlists local, indigenous people to protect the reserve—who also benefit from sustainable hunting there. The reserve has healthy wildlife populations and is one of the last remaining refuges for Amazon manatees *(Trichechus inunguis)* in the region. Without the watchful eyes of these volunteers, poaching would destroy these fragile manatee groups as well as other wildlife communities.

Overhunting is a problem for many communities, especially when timber companies are logging in the region. These companies commonly subsidize operations by supplying their employees with shotguns and cartridges to lower food costs. On average, one timber-camp hunter can supply about 20 loggers with daily protein—and sells additional wild meat to supplement his meager income of just a few dollars a day. This intensive hunting is decimating many animal populations.

Hunting guidelines need to be established for timber concessions, especially if they are expecting Forestry Stewardship Council (FSC) approval for responsible forestry. Protected areas also need to be respected as such. In 1998, when bribes to the government resulted in nine logging concessions having access to the Tamshiyacu-Tahuayo reserve, residents protested—and the government was forced to annul the contracts.

Lessons learned in Loreto include several important strategies that need consideration when building sustainable use plans with local communities, protected areas, and forestry concessions. One of these is the establishment of "source–sink" areas—no-hunting areas adjacent to hunting zones that allow animal populations to rebuild in an undisturbed environment.

Animal populations go through natural fluctuations that are not always obvious. Nonhunted areas are necessary to protect animals against these unforeseen changes. For example, in the Yavari Valley, white-lipped peccary populations recently crashed, which has happened to peccaries in other areas across South America.[8]

In an instance like this, hunters could easily overhunt white-lipped peccaries. Nonhunted areas buffer against this, providing the safe haven needed for recovery, while protecting the entire array of rain forest biodiversity. But even more importantly, communities support and help defend these nonhunted areas because they understand that some areas should be protected for the long-term benefit of their children. This situation is often in contrast to traditional protected areas that may exclude local people from areas that were once their traditional hunting grounds.

Effective wildlife management requires accurate monitoring of what is killed. This provides information both on hunting pressure and on "catch-per-unit-

In the Tamshiyacu-Tahuayo Community Reserve hunting rules and social pressure now prohibit hunting of mammals such as tapir, giant armadillos, and monkeys.
(Credit: David Wilkie)

effort," or the effort required to find and hunt animals. Catch-per-unit-effort reflects the abundance of animals and acts as a measurement unit in hunting zones that gauges the effectiveness of management plans.

It is also important to evaluate hunting sustainability using population models. One promising model is the "unified harvest model"[9] that compiles data on hunting pressure, the density of animals in hunted and nonhunted zones, and animal reproduction rates in hunted areas. Hunters help collect hunting and wildlife data and researchers examine carcasses of female animals to gather reproduction information. Animal populations are estimated using line transects or camera traps. This method is effective for long-term conservation planning, as it takes into consideration differences in the biology of species and requires population numbers to be at healthy levels in order to be harvested safely.

Habitat conservation is another crucial component of an effective wildlife management plan. Animal populations will only survive if their food and shelter are maintained. For example, in Loreto many wildlife species, including peccaries, deer, rodents, tapir, and primates, depend on palm fruits as a major source of food. However, people living in the rain forest also eat palm fruits and palm hearts, cutting down the trees to harvest these delicacies and also using the palms for building material. Now, residents of the Tamshiyacu-Tahuayo Community Reserve conserve palm trees as an important part of the ecosystem.[9]

The regulation of animal products can also help manage bushmeat hunting. Peru is currently the only country that permits legal export of peccary pelts, which are shipped to Europe where they are made into fine gloves. But the law dictates that these skins must originate from subsistence hunters living in the Amazon.

Hunters from the Tamshiyacu-Tahuayo Community Reserve participate in a pilot certification project to see if the peccary pelt trade can help promote community-based wildlife management. Rural communities that sustainably manage local wildlife are certified to participate in the trade, which recognizes them as responsible, environmentally sensitive communities that are helping to conserve the Amazon rain forest. Thus the leather certification program brings economic benefit to rural families, improves their living standards, and helps protect wildlife at the same time.

Recent studies show that this program does provide incentive for local communities to build management plans—a "bottom-up strategy" to promote conservation at the local level. Peccary pelts are "subproducts" for rural hunters: peccary meat sells for between $18 and $30 per animal, but the skin sells for just $2 to $4. Therefore, if the peccary pelt trade were shut down tomorrow, not one peccary would be saved. Hunters are killing peccaries for their meat, not for their pelts—but pelts do provide extra income. However, since the pelt trade is regulated by government-imposed quotas and regulations, it also provides a mechanism to manage bushmeat hunting.

The conservation strategies used in Loreto can be a model for wildlife management throughout the vast rain forests of the Amazon. Management programs require the implementation of source–sink areas, catch-per-unit-effort monitoring, evaluation of hunting impact using harvest models, and habitat protection.

Lessons learned in this corner of the Peruvian Amazon clearly show that management programs should allow carefully monitored hunting of appropriate species and should protect vulnerable species. In some regions, novel incentives may be necessary, such as certification programs.

The bushmeat crisis in the Amazon is a major concern for conservation. However, with appropriate wildlife management strategies, hunting can be compatible with conservation and even be a powerful tool to save Amazonian biodiversity.

"Egrets"

Once as I travelled through a quiet evening,
I saw a pool, jet-black and mirror-still.
Beyond, the slender paperbarks stood crowding;
each on its own white image looked its fill,
and nothing moved but thirty egrets wading—
thirty egrets in a quiet evening.

Once in a lifetime, lovely past believing,
your lucky eyes may light on such a pool.
As though for many years I had been waiting,
I watched in silence, till my heart was full
of clear dark water, and white trees unmoving,
and, whiter yet, those thirty egrets wading.

JUDITH WRIGHT
(AUSTRALIA, 1915–2000)

PART IV

CONSERVATION CONTROVERSIES

One of the most complex and pressing issues facing wildlife today is hunting. A growing debate is raging in the conservation community over acceptable levels of hunting in relation to human needs—and who should be influencing policy. In order to explore a range of differing views on the topic, we invited David Brown, research fellow and program coordinator at the Overseas Development Institute, and John Robinson, senior vice president and director of International Conservation at the Wildlife Conservation Society, to respond to the following statement:

> *Harvesting of wild species has been characterized by some as a successful example of economic production by marginalized, rural people in the developing world, and by others as a shortsighted overexploitation of natural resources with significant conservation consequences.*

They were asked to comment on this statement, and to identify situations and contexts where harvests should be legally encouraged or discouraged, what institutions and organizations can provide appropriate management, and how benefits of harvesting can be maximized and costs minimized.

Each was then given the other's comments, and asked to write a short point–counterpoint rebuttal. To further broaden the debate, three additional experts were asked to respond to Brown's and Robinson's original statements: Glyn Davies, a research scientist and adviser on forest, wildlife, and biodiversity issues; Kathy MacKinnon, a biodiversity specialist at the Environment Department of the World Bank; and Ian Redmond, chief consultant with the Great Apes Survival Project (GRASP) of the United Nations Environment Programme / United Nations Educational, Scientific, and Cultural Organization.

We hope that this forum broadens the public discussion on this pivotal issue.

Let Them Eat Cake?

Some Skeptical Thoughts on Conservation Strategies in the Bushmeat Range States

DAVID BROWN

I should start by expressing certain reservations about the statements to which I am invited to respond.

As regards the first, that "harvesting of wild species is a successful example of economic production by marginalized, rural people," I have no difficulty in viewing the harvest of wild species as an *acceptable instance* of economic production by marginalized poor people, though it does not necessarily follow that it is an entirely *successful* one, at least in conservation terms. Poor people have a right to use their natural resources for their survival, and we in the West with our profligate consumption habits are not best placed to criticize them for so doing. In seeking to help them manage their resources, the starting point should certainly be a positive appreciation of their livelihood strategies. However, this does not imply that there are no issues regarding sustainability.

If we want to force people to behave differently, then we need to start by offering them better alternatives. Successes in this area have been pretty few and far between. Strict protected area designation is inappropriate in most situations and often enjoys little local support. Integrated conservation and development projects have generally not worked well and have rarely impacted very positively on the condition of the wildlife resource, particularly in Africa. The view that future ecotourism projects will provide incentive for sustainable conservation, and a justification for repressive policies in the interim, is looking increasingly overoptimistic in many areas. Only in exceptional instances does ecotourism generate sufficient benefits to divert local populations from existing patterns of consumptive behavior. Elsewhere, the lack of infrastructure, communications, and basic security often presents pretty insurmountable obstacles to attaining and maintaining the tourist volumes that would have real effects on local economies.

The second statement, that "harvesting of wild species is a shortsighted overexploitation of natural resources with significant conservation consequences," makes certain assumptions about public choice that are probably fallacious and certainly misleading. It seems to assume purposeful behavior by a social being, which would act differently—and less shortsightedly—were it to have had a superior level of awareness.

So what is the problem that we are seeking to address? Is it some colossal dereliction of duty by all categories of the population in the tropical range states, particularly the rural majority, who are not acting with a sense of global social responsibility? Possibly aided by international development partners who are foolish enough to imagine that one can solve the problems of the developing world's poor by allowing them to go on killing wild animals? Or is it something else?

> Poor people have a right to use their natural resources for their survival, and we in the West with our profligate consumption habits are not best placed to criticize them for so doing.

I would propose the latter, and suggest that we begin with a simple definition of the problem; namely: How can we help some sovereign states better manage a valuable resource, in conditions that are not propitious to good management? This may be a better way of looking for incremental improvements from an admittedly very low base.

At the outset, we need to recognize the fact that, while the outlook for many tropical wild animal species is not encouraging, the situation is usually no better—often infinitely worse, in fact—for the majority of the human beings who are living in closest contact with them. There is no necessary connection between the two, save that both are the consequence of the major failures of national and international governance that have blighted the lives of many of those who live in the bushmeat range states, particularly in West-Central Africa. These failures of governance are complex and can't be reduced to any one set of influences (for example, colonialism or neocolonialism). But neither can they be reduced to the behavior of the local people.

If the underlying issue is not one of wrongheaded cultural practices, but much more deep-seated problems of public governance, then are the strategies on offer ones that are likely to significantly improve the situation?

In fact, one finds it hard to imagine strategies that are *less* likely to solve these governance problems than the ones which have hitherto been offered in tropical Africa, both for conservation in general and for bushmeat management in particular. For, far from promoting the very standards of good governance that they demand of others, they more often undermine them.

For the most part, conservation policy is presently being generated outside of these range states, and mostly by Western nongovernmental organizations that enjoy no democratic authority of their own and are not publicly accountable. For these agencies to place heavy political, economic, and moral pressure on range state governments to arbitrarily demarcate vast tracts of land as parks and protected areas—lands that have been lived on and/or used and enjoyed for generations—does little to engender national legitimacy or even respect, and nothing to create public accountability or transparency. Starting from the primacy of species protection (rather than the long-term interests of the human populations associated with them) makes it impossible to convince local users that conservation strategies might serve their long-term interests.

Sustaining a public relations onslaught against traditional consumption habits in the name of biodiversity or disease control, pushing whatever evidence is available to its farthest limits to justify Western preservationist views, is hardly any more constructive. (Of course, animals can be associated with human diseases—if one wants evidence of that, one has only to look to the Western factory farming practices which confine animals in the most unhealthy environments.)

Attempts to impose a blanket ban on hunting not only appear futile in the extreme but also unjust, and they ultimately undermine rather than uphold the rule of law. *Ditto* the attempt to force host governments to implement repressive laws, often inherited from colonial times, which few citizens believe in and fewer still are prepared to enforce. *Ditto* encouraging logging companies to take on quasi-governmental responsibilities in their timber concession areas, not just for their own personnel but for the populations with which they come into contact. *Ditto* the promotion of local trade rules that, far from increasing the value of the forest resource and encouraging its conservation, serve only to devalue it in the eyes of policymakers.

> While the outlook for many tropical wild animal species is not encouraging, the situation is usually no better—often infinitely worse, in fact—for the majority of the human beings who are living in closest contact with them.

How, then, might the "bushmeat crisis" be solved? This is a difficult question and there are no easy answers. One of the major challenges to be confronted is that, in all probability, the volume of offtake will have to be substantially reduced in the crisis areas, so that there is little prospect of achieving a win–win situation.

Another is that, while the obvious solution is to empower the rural poor to manage the resource, the formal tenurial rights of these people are often minimal to nonexistent, and their ability to resist pressures from powerful political and economic interests no greater. Where rural social structure is complex (with large numbers of migrants in the forest, in countries like Ghana and Ivory Coast, for example), it will be doubly difficult to remedy the situation.

A third challenge is that, in seeking to make progress on one front, one could well take numerous steps backward on others. For example, control over such fugitive resources is inherently decentralized, which may be problematic in conservation terms, though it does lower barriers to entry, to the benefit of the poor. There is a need to ensure that these people are not disadvantaged by any solutions offered.

The most widely proffered solution to the problem—allowing subsistence consumption of game but banning all trade beyond the village—betrays assumptions about how poor people behave that are proving inaccurate. Recent work by de Merode et al.[1] in the Democratic Republic of Congo, for example, shows that the poor are more likely than those better off (these terms are relative) to sell their bushmeat—logically enough, as this is one of the few high-value to low-weight ratio products that come into their hands. One is anyway never going to be able to prevent farmers from killing vermin on their land, so allowing them this concession is, in reality, conceding nothing at all.

I frankly do not know what the solution is to this intractable problem, save that, in the words of a Polish proverb, "One doesn't start from here." I confess to some fairly profound doubts as to whether it is open to solution independently of broader policy reforms. It may only be solvable as a by-product of other advances on issues of governance and in relation to other debates on national and international inequality.

But to the extent that it can be addressed, my hunch is that success will be the product of strategies that do not seek directly to conserve species but, rather, to reinforce human rights. This will be done not through negative sanctions on wildlife consumption but by fostering individual and group rights and security. The aim will be to provide an acceptable framework for economic and social activity that is supportive of local cultures (and not culturally imperialistic), and which leaves decision making in the hands of local people without any opprobrium. This will include decisions about what game species to conserve and what to suppress.

It will be an approach that empowers local institutions and does not suck away their authority. One of its consequences, and one measure of its success, will be its ability to wrest the management of sovereign resources from external interests, whether these be high-cost tropical timbers that are managed as industrial concessions or the lower-cost but high-value tracts of forest lands which are presently coveted for international conservation areas. I am skeptical that this can be brought about through the kinds of external, expatriate-dominated pressures and influences that are the trademark of modern conservation.

Biting the Hand That Feeds You

The Consumption of Nature and Natural Resources in the Tropics

JOHN ROBINSON

The trade of wild animals in the tropics for human consumption (often called "bushmeat") brings into conflict two of society's most cherished ethical obligations: the stewardship of nature and the care and advancement of our fellow human beings. The wild meat trade is portrayed by advocates for nature as a rape of wild places and the shortsighted plunder of wild resources.[1] The solution proposed for this problem is often to close down the trade, ignoring the imperative that many people's lives depend on selling wildlife. In contrast, the mere existence of the trade is touted, by advocates for the world's poor, as a testament to the resilience and self-sufficiency of the poorest and most marginalized people.[2] The proposed intervention often is to promote even greater harvests, ignoring the reality that present harvests are already depleting the resources upon which people depend. Thoughtful public policy must seek to avoid such dichotomous thinking.

The concept of "sustainable development," developed in the early 1970s, attempted to do exactly that. The hope was that, by practicing sustainable use, the needs and aspirations of people could be met while not destroying people's natural resources. The World Conservation Strategy in 1980, the report of the World Commission on Environment and Development in 1987, and *Caring for the Earth* in 1991 epitomized the optimism of public policy of the time. In the case of the wild meat trade, the hope was that a managed wildlife harvest could contribute to human livelihoods while conserving valued species and ecosystems in the tropics.

The hope proved largely illusory. In the tropics, the supply of harvestable wildlife resources turns out to be lower than expected, limited by low standing biomass and low annual productivity. The rule of thumb in tropical forests, once calculated empirically, is that wildlife resources can only sustainably meet the animal protein needs of 2.5 people per square mile (one person/km^2)—a human population density exceeded in all but the most remote areas.[3] Demand for wildlife resources in tropical forests rises with human population density and as people increasingly hunt wildlife for sale and trade.

The loss of hunting sustainability generally results in the steady local extinction of large-bodied, slow-reproducing species that are often of conservation concern. As primates, ungulates, large rodents, and gallinaceous birds wink out across the landscape, the people living in the forest lose their own natural resource base. Theoretical calculations for Central Africa project, for example, that at present harvest rates the protein supply from bushmeat will drop by 81 percent over the next 50 years.[4]

Sustainable development theory posited that poor people could manage their natural resources more successfully by improving their technology use, controlling costs, removing perverse incentives, building management capacity, and developing more self-reliance. Accordingly, the response of development and conservation agencies was to strengthen the institutions that manage resources, and they poured money into social and economic interventions to transition from free access to wildlife to more managed systems (by either national governments or local communities). But most efforts to manage tropical wildlife for meat, especially in forests, are doomed by the twin pincers of low supply and high demand. Success is only achieved if other economic activities can be substituted—something exceedingly difficult to do in rural parts of the developing world.

> The trade of wild animals in the tropics for human consumption . . . brings into conflict two of society's most cherished ethical obligations: the stewardship of nature and the care and advancement of our fellow human beings.

The failure of the "win–win" scenario of sustainable development today pits advocates of wildlife against advocates of the poor. Should people be allowed to hunt in parks? Should hunting reserves be established? Should commercial trade in wild meat be allowed? The answers, in the short term, increasingly either favor wild species or the rural poor—rarely both.[5]

The way forward, I argue, is to recognize that landscapes are heterogeneous, and the use of land should be tailored accordingly. We should seek to establish areas to steward wildlife, areas for the sustainable harvest of wildlife, and areas for domestic livestock production. The choice of where to promote each land use should be determined partly by the biological importance of the area, partly by the hunting demand on the area's resources, and partly by the capacity of the area to meet that demand.

The conservation of nature and protection of wild species can be most effectively achieved by protecting areas in relatively undisturbed ecosystems. Biodiversity is generally higher in these ecosystems, and some wild species can only exist in such areas. People often live in these areas, but in parks and other reserves, conservation should take precedence. Conservationists have struggled over the last 15 years to identify areas of high priority for ecosystems and species. We should seek to protect these areas for posterity.

Human livelihoods, by contrast, are most effectively sustained in highly modified ecosystems, where humans have intensified agriculture and grazing systems. The creation of "agroscapes" largely extirpates wildlife, but local livestock production can reduce the demand for animal protein from wild species in other areas. And by redirecting primary productivity to their own use, people significantly augment their food supply. This ecosystem transformation is the most effective way to meet human needs.

It is in areas outside of these dedicated land uses where we have the most controversy. Typically these are ecosystems significantly modified by humans, containing important biodiversity, providing critical habitat for wide-ranging species, and supporting large numbers of rural, often poor, people. These people are politically disenfranchised, economically marginalized, and allocated preciously few national resources. Left largely to their own initiatives, they are encouraged to exploit wild resources that remain in these areas (except of course for the truly valuable resources like timber, minerals, and hydrocarbons, which are monopolized by the mainstream culture). Development specialists and conservationists are asked to help give them the tools to do so and to ensure that resource use is sustainable.

> The rule of thumb in tropical forests . . . is that wildlife resources can only sustainably meet the animal protein needs of 2.5 people per square mile—a human population density exceeded in all but the most remote areas.

The probability that resource use is sustainable—by definition where both conservation and livelihood goals are met—varies with ecological and social conditions. It turns out to be higher in dry forests and more mesic grasslands and lower in wet forests and xeric grasslands; higher in secondary forests and forest fallows and lower in more closed forests.[6] However, even where the probability is highest, the potential of wildlife harvesting to meet the needs of the local people is limited. Summarizing years of experience with the highly productive African savannas, John MacNab concluded: "[T]he hypothesis that game cropping would conserve wildlife and their habitats whilst providing a food source to the local people must be rejected. . . . The history of game cropping schemes in the developing countries of Africa show that almost all were uneconomical or failed the test of sustainability."

In forested ecosystems, the requirement of sustainability is just not workable once pressure on the resource rises above a certain point. Theoretically, requiring a sustainable harvest in Central Africa today, for instance, would preclude many people from meeting their minimum recommended daily amount of animal protein, and it would deny the subsistence opportunities of many others.[4]

What this means is that, whenever human livelihoods trump wildlife conservation—typically where human population density and market access increase, and where no economic alternative is provided—the conservation value of the area is lost and the resource base is eroded. With increased commercialization, harvest rates increase to many times over sustainable levels. More vulnerable wildlife species are hunted out and the wildlife resource as a whole is depleted. After depletion, harvest is restricted to those "weedy" wildlife species that can coexist in modified landscapes with humans.

This downward spiral does little for human livelihoods. Through this whole transition, the sale of wild meat does not allow rural people to accumulate enough capital to invest in alternative income-generating activities. Hunting is the occupation of the poorest members of poor communities, and hunters do not become rich. Harvests do allow rural people to augment their incomes and provide a safety net when all else fails. Those weedy wildlife species, typically rodents and invertebrates, can be quite productive and are harvested in many communities. But wildlife harvests have little potential to alleviate rural poverty, and those that promote harvests as livelihood strategies are more likely to just sustain rural people in poverty.

One concludes that in relatively undisturbed ecosystems, as long as hunting remains sustainable, then biodiversity can be conserved and people can continue to use the resources. Typically, as ecosystems are transformed by people, demand increases, sustainability is lost, and the conservation value and the resource base for people are eroded. Unfortunately, these harvests do not generate enough capital to alleviate the poverty of rural people, so that the loss for conservation is not a gain for local development but a long-term loss for both.

Once demand for natural resources is significant, then reliance on wild resources is rarely feasible. Ecosystems must be transformed to meet people's needs more directly. Wildlife species have little capacity to finance that transformation, and planners must look to other economic inputs. As more and more of our planet's surface is modified for human productivity, it becomes increasingly important to protect our remaining wild areas and maintain the heterogeneous "living landscape" that both conserves nature and supports people.

POINT–COUNTERPOINT

Response to John Robinson

Postindustrial Conservation Ideals and Real-World Politics

DAVID BROWN

This is an interesting approach, but John leaves out the central question; namely: How is all this to be achieved? He talks about "thoughtful public policy," but does not seem much interested in real policymaking by sovereign states.

We should start by recognizing that the decisions are not ours to make. Other people's landscapes cannot just be carved up according to Western conservationists. Even discounting this fundamental problem, there are massive practical difficulties. Firstly, the bushmeat trade is already a multimillion dollar industry and an important component of African economies. Secondly, most undisturbed ecosystems already have extensive and long-standing claims on them. A complicating factor is that the areas with the highest biodiversity have often experienced the highest human impacts.[1] The myth of "wild Africa" has considerable appeal to people in postindustrial societies but is a rather misleading notion.[2]

The recognition that landscapes are heterogeneous is thus a useful starting point, but only that. We can have our own notions of how much biodiversity we want to conserve—but those estimates have to be accepted by the governments and populations involved.

I agree that past attempts to integrate conservation with development have often not worked well. But this doesn't mean that we can ignore the roles that bushmeat plays in human welfare. Conservation needs the support of the affected populations. The state usually lacks the capacity, and the international conservation agencies that have the money do not have the mandate or credibility. Trade-offs will have to be made. Bushmeat may well function primarily in a safety-net role, helping poor people avoid slipping further into poverty rather than providing a means to lift them out of it, but championing the poor is an honorable aim and is preferable to worsening their plight by denying them vital access rights.

In summary, we have to think more about the incentives for conservation, not just the animals and ecosystems we would like to conserve.

Response to David Brown

The View from Versailles Contrasts with Local Reality

JOHN ROBINSON

David Brown's debating expertise ably deconstructs the false universality of this debate's first statement and the teleology of the second. Unfortunately, this armchair perspective fails to engage with the on-the-ground reality that the unsustainable wildlife harvest is affecting both people's lives and species survival, especially in the developing world.

David worries about impediments to laissez-faire capitalism, abrogation of people's rights (although he ignores people's responsibilities), the inappropriateness of land-use planning and resource regulation, the corruption of national governments (but interestingly not the corporate sector), and the heavy-handedness of multilateral and bilateral aid agencies. He perceives nongovernmental organizations (NGOs), particularly those promoting conservation, as self-serving and accountable only to themselves. This neoconservative perspective, balanced with a riff into postcolonial guilt, hides the fact that he really supports resource management and good governance. His appropriate question is: How can we help sovereign states better manage a valuable resource? But his pessimistic answer must be challenged.

I agree that there are no universal solutions of the type required by the pundits in capital cities of the developed world. But progress at the local level has been achieved by recognizing heterogeneity and managing accordingly. Zoning for various wildlife uses has supported conservation and still allowed people to harvest wildlife from the Bolivian Kaa'Iya to the forests of central Congo. Allowing harvest of certain species but not others, or harvest by some people but not others, has done the same in the flooded forests of Mamirauá in Brazil to highland forests of Sarawak. And good governance has been exhibited by a range of institutional actors, not only "sovereign" governments but also NGOs, local communities, and even the private sector.

Are the biodiversity and humanitarian crises being successfully addressed? No. But innovative efforts are being tried, incorporating scientific and indigenous perspectives, methods not straitjacketed by political orthodoxy and prejudice, but instead illuminated by local knowledge. These local solutions to wildlife management provide global inspiration.

Comments on Brown vs. Robinson

Bushmeat Trade:
Thoughts from "The Coast"

GLYN DAVIES

The essays by David Brown and John Robinson focus on the conflict between the aspirations of human development and wildlife conservation. In this brief essay I consider three points in my search for a middle ground between wildlife conservation and poverty.

The term "bushmeat" is a vernacular along the West African coast from Sierra Leone to Cameroon, describing any wildlife animal that is trapped or hunted, gifted or sold, often traded, and always eaten. One of the most obvious lessons from this region, which has numerous areas with dense human populations, is that animals trapped and hunted on farms and in farm-fallows near villages—so-called farmbush—provide a large proportion of traded and eaten bushmeat. In Ghana, for example, just under 40

> Conservation groups might profitably attempt to link with development groups that encourage fair trade in commodities as an alternative to bushmeat.

percent of the national trade comes from three farmbush species. These are often major agricultural pests, and generally not of conservation concern.

Whether we should view these species as "weedy" is not really the issue. They contribute to an important trade and have sustained this trade in some areas throughout decades of exploitation. While it is true that large-bodied species (many of which are of conservation concern) cannot withstand these levels of exploitation, bushmeat is a multispecies commodity, and the trade continues to support human livelihoods as species composition changes. Biodiversity declines as rarer species disappear, but a narrower segment of mammal species continues to support a bushmeat trade. Policy pronouncements need to make this distinction between farmbush species on one hand, such as some rodents and antelopes, and forest-dependent species on the other, including primates and ungulates.

The patchwork approach to achieving different conservation and development outcomes at different sites within a landscape is undoubtedly the way forward. But at a policy level, the underlying causes of the recent upsurge in the bushmeat trade need to be addressed if islands of good practice are not to be washed away in a sea of short-term actions that benefit few.

Bad or weak governance has repeatedly been cited by development and conservation groups as an underlying cause of both poverty and biodiversity loss. Addressing mismanagement in both arenas is a shared agenda between both conservationists and developers, and this shared agenda should be extended to include trade options.

Recurrent reports from field sites show that many farmers have turned to trading in bushmeat because of the collapse of cocoa and coffee prices. It is no longer worth their while to brush weeds from their plantations, gather the fruits, and process and transport them to trading centers. This they lament. Indeed some hunters state they would even prefer labor jobs to the tedium and hardship of hunting in forest areas. So conservation groups might profitably attempt to link with development groups that encourage fair trade in commodities as an alternative to bushmeat.

The important caveat here is that sustainable off-take of a natural resource can quickly degenerate into destruction of one resource, as trade focus shifts to another. Improved wildlife management can only be achieved through binding agreements for sustainable environment-development outcomes. Even where local arrangements encourage trade in other commodities, however, conservation voices need to join those of development lobbies in order to modify international trade agreements and national trade tariffs in favor of trade in environmentally produced goods from tropical areas.

Finally, and as a counterpoint to conservation groups taking closer account of development needs, international aid agencies need to integrate the environment into their polices, programs, and projects much more fully—the current narrow focus on poverty reduction does not amount to responsible development.

Through the Looking Glass

*The Tragedy of Depleting Wildlife Resources:
A Response to John Robinson and David Brown*

KATHY MACKINNON

These two essays reflect the breadth and complexity of the debate about the harvesting of wild species, and especially bushmeat, though neither espouses the extreme positions of the statements to which they were asked to respond. In fact they share many common sympathies for local communities and their reliance on wildlife resources. John Robinson relies on clear scientific facts and long-term research to lay out some of the challenges, and realities, of reconciling the competing goals of conservation with the welfare of some of the world's poorest and most disenfranchised peoples. David Brown is much more passionate in his arguments, staunchly pro-people and with genuine misgivings about conservation and the conservation community. As a one-time tropical biologist and conservationist now working for the World Bank, a development agency devoted to poverty alleviation, I find the arguments highly relevant to the development decisions and project investments that my agency supports.

> Even where traditional hunting is prohibited within parks, protected areas may actually enhance wildlife harvests beyond their boundaries by replenishing wild populations.

Ever since the 1980 publication of the World Conservation Strategy with its "use it or lose it" doctrine, the conservation community has wrestled to conserve the irresistible cocktail of key habitats and wildlife while providing tangible benefits to rural poor communities. Occasionally it works, but more often we fail to achieve either conservation or development objectives, as a whole generation of Integrated Conservation and Development projects attest.[1]

Brown is correct that the problems facing both local people and wildlife populations are due to poor governance. Given the less than ideal political and social landscapes within which development agencies work, however, we do have a responsibility to react to good science to direct effective action for appropriate development. There is much compelling research on hunting and the low levels of wildlife harvesting that tropical forests can sustain. By refusing to acknowledge this fact, and promoting further utilization, we may encourage "use it *and* lose it" scenarios that further impoverish marginalized communities.

Responsible national planning for biodiversity and people requires governments to identify areas for wildlife conservation, other areas for sustainable harvesting of natural resources, and lands where agriculture and other development will provide the base to address poverty. More than 170 governments, including tropical countries, adopted an ambitious protected area work plan at the seventh Conference of Parties (COP7) of the Convention on Biological Diversity in February 2004. Even where traditional hunting is prohibited within parks, protected areas may actually enhance wildlife harvests beyond their boundaries by replenishing wild populations. Around Brazil's Mamirauá Reserve, for example, wildlife populations as well as human nutrition and income are increasing.[2] Outside park boundaries, responsible conservationists are not advocating blanket bans on hunting nor reliance on ecotourism, but are using practical and adaptive resource management based on biological realities and opportunities. The challenge for all of us is to find the win–win solutions that benefit wildlife conservation and local communities.

As development practitioners, we may not like the message, nor even, sometimes, the messengers, but the harsh reality is that wildlife in tropical forests can only be harvested sustainably at very low levels. Ignoring the biological realities of Robinson's "twin pincers of low supply and high demand" and encouraging continued exploitation of limited resources does a disservice to the very people that we most want to protect—the indigenous and marginalized communities whose survival and well-being are dependent on tropical forests and the wildlife within them.

Let Them Eat LSD Bushmeat

Thoughts Arising from Brown vs. Robinson

IAN REDMOND

Bushmeat, game, bush-tucker—call it what you will, the issue of meat from wild animals is suddenly on everyone's lips. These two thoughtful essays jolt us with a double reality check: one cannot fault John Robinson's observation that biological systems are finite and will disintegrate if overexploited, nor David Brown's that people will seize any means available to survive and improve their family's situation in life—especially if they are parents. But is it really beyond human wit to devise a system that serves both goals? Is there anywhere on Earth where hunting wild animals is successfully regulated and poaching a thing of the past? Yes and no, respectively.

Ghana, for example, like most countries in Europe and North America, has a system of legal hunting that, with better enforcement, could provide a model for other developing countries. But let's face it, poaching has been with us ever since one group of humans claimed exclusive rights to some land or animals and another group of humans went ahead and hunted anyway. So if rules limiting or banning hunting are going to be broken

> . . . if hunting is not the only source of food, a hunter might show self-restraint today if he can be convinced that by doing so, he and his children could continue to hunt tomorrow.

by anyone who thinks they can get away with it, what might dissuade a potential poacher? Social, legal, and religious pressures, for starters: if your family or community will disapprove, you might think twice; if there is any effective law enforcement that might lead to arrest and punishment, you might be put off; and if your religion forbids killing or eating certain species, or a certain patch of forest is considered sacred, fear of divine retribution is a powerful curb on behavior.

There are other disincentives too. Hunting primates carries the risk of infection by viruses such as Ebola or Marburg. For many cultures, hunting primates—

especially great apes—raises ethical questions that influence some hunters, and even traditional ape hunters have been known to think again when given evidence of apes' cognitive abilities.[1] Finally, if hunting is not the only source of food, a hunter might show self-restraint today if he can be convinced that by doing so, he and his children could continue to hunt tomorrow.

Sadly, the human species' record for self-restraint is pretty poor—especially when the person showing restraint is surrounded by others who do not. One only has to look at another open-access resource that, like bushmeat, is difficult to monitor—marine fisheries. Each year, European fishermen fight European Union quotas even though evidence of overfishing is all around them.

Personally, I've always enjoyed eating wild meat, as long as it is LSD (and ideally, H): Legal (not a protected species, nor from a protected area), Sustainable (hunting levels are below the reproductive capacity of hunted species), Disease-free (bushmeat should be subjected to the same meat inspections as domestic stock in the interests of public health), and finally, if at all possible, Humanely killed (with a clean shot, and not the result of a slow, painful death in a leghold trap).

> Personally, I've always enjoyed eating wild meat, as long as it is LSD (and ideally, H): Legal . . . Sustainable . . . Disease-free . . . and finally, if at all possible, Humanely killed.

Most African countries facing a bushmeat crisis are a long way from these standards, but it is surely best to set our targets high. Enlightened self-interest is the best way of influencing someone's decision about which species to kill or how many—and only with the use of both positive and negative reinforcement will bushmeat regulations work. Working with hunters and traders to meet LSD and H guidelines could achieve conservation benefits, secure livelihoods and protein supplies, provide public health benefits—and maybe even animal welfare benefits.

One thing is certain—bushmeat hunters *will* stop hunting large mammals, and bushmeat consumers *will* stop eating them within our lifetime. The only question is whether they can be persuaded to stop now, while there are still some left to play their ecological role in their respective ecosystems, or whether they will stop in 10 or 20 or 30 years when they are all gone. We are the generation that must decide.

Red-eyed tree frog, Costa Rica. Frogs around the globe are in sharp decline, decimated by loss of habitat, climate change, pollution—and a deadly fungus.

"Birdfoot's Grandpa"

The old man
must have stopped our car
two dozen times to climb out
and gather into his hands
the small toads blinded
by our lights and leaping
like live drops of rain.

The rain was falling,
a mist around his white hair,
and I kept saying,
"You can't save them all,
accept it, get in,
we've got places to go."

But, leathery hands full
of wet brown life,
knee deep in the summer
roadside grass,
he just smiled and said,
"They have places to go too."

JOSEPH BRUCHAC
(ABENAKI, CONTEMPORARY)

PART V

WILDLIFE

In this section, we examine a broad spectrum of wildlife conservation challenges—and some of the thorniest. We look closely at what is needed to conserve a single species within its habitat, and then step back to consider what it takes to preserve birds, fish, or other animals that migrate over large distances, sometimes en masse. Then we take an overarching view of global impacts on wildlife from human-induced climate change and on some of the most exploited ocean species. In each case, human activities are the driving force behind wildlife declines.

To explore the many reasons why one in every eight bird species faces extinction, we enlisted Joseph Tobias, Leon Bennun, and Alison Stattersfield, experts from BirdLife International. These authors detail the status of the world's birds and the threats they face, as well as what is being done to stem their downward trajectory.

We chose jaguars as our "Species in Focus" for this volume. Alan Rabinowitz was the obvious choice to write on the elusive cat: his fieldwork helped establish the world's first jaguar reserve, and he discusses landmark efforts not only to save jaguars but to protect them throughout their entire range from Mexico to Argentina.

Environmental writer Glenn Scherer has written on climate change for many years. In his essay, he catalogs the many current and potential impacts of climate change on ecosystems and wildlife, discussing both current research and possible mitigations.

In conservation, many groups tend to focus either on animals of the air and the land or on those that dwell in the sea. We prefer a planetwide approach, as wildlife is under siege everywhere. Recent research has revealed the devastating impacts that commercial fishing and habitat destruction have had on ocean dwellers. Ellen K. Pikitch, who heads the Pew Institute of Ocean Science, describes the first possible victims of a modern wave of ocean extinctions.

The section closes with thoughts by one of the world's preeminent conservationists, William Conway, on the complexities of protecting birds, wildebeest, seals, walruses, and other animals that congregate to mate, nest, or migrate. Although these animals may mass in large numbers, they may rely on just one or two crucial places to winter or bear young—and are exposed to many dangers in their often long journeys to arrive at these locations.

Future volumes will use these same focused and wide views to look at other individual species and groups of animals and to examine wider issues that threaten wildlife. We hope you enjoy this varied perspective.

THE HUMAN FOOTPRINT

Color plate 1: The Human Footprint. This map shows the extent of human influence across the globe. Of the land's surface, 83 percent is influenced directly by human activities, 42 percent is wild, and 26 percent is in areas defined as the "Last of the Wild."

(Credit: Wildlife Conservation Society and CIESIN-Columbia University)

Color plate 2: A Tibetan hunter in northern Myanmar carries a red goral he brought down with a crossbow and poison arrow.

(Credit: Steve Winter/National Geographic Image Collection)

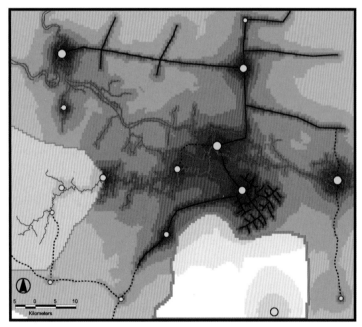

Hunting Pressure Index

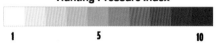

1   5   10

Legend

Population Density
- ○ 60 - 100
- ○ 101 - 200
- ○ 201 - 300
- ○ 301 - 500
- ○ 501 - 600

- Rivers
- Roads
- Trails

Protected Areas Effectiveness
- Higher
- Lower

Color plate 3: Hunting in the tropics depends directly on access and population. This map shows hunting pressure in a hypothetical region of the tropics. Large villages and towns stimulate the most hunting. Hunting is also concentrated around roads near villages and in logging concessions. Protected areas should reduce hunting pressure and provide a refuge for wildlife, but their effectiveness depends on the degree of enforcement provided. In the best case, parks may prevent hunting and restrict forest access; in many places, they exist only on paper.

(Credit: Gosia Bryja and Eric W. Sanderson)

Color plate 4: *(left)* Hunters in Myanmar killed a bear to sell its paws, worth $8, which are made into soup and used as an ingredient in traditional Asian medicine.
(Credit: Steve Winter/National Geographic Image Collection)

Color plate 5: *(below)* A market in Myitkyina, Myanmar, offers macaque and gibbon skulls, tiger bone, elephant skin, and other animal parts used in traditional Asian medicine.
(Credit: Steve Winter/National Geographic Image Collection)

Color plate 6: Dried shark fin can fetch as much as $20,000 per pound; shark fin soup is an Asian delicacy and is used as a medicinal tonic. The annual number of sharks killed for the fin trade is estimated at 26 to 46 million.
(Credit: Shelley Clarke)

Color plate 7: *(left)* A drowned wandering albatross hooked off eastern Australia on a longline set by a Japanese tuna fishing vessel.
(Credit: Graham Robertson)

Color plate 8: *(below)* Researchers are tagging and tracking sea turtles to measure the impact of longline and gill net fishing off the Pacific coast of Costa Rica.
(Credit: Steve Winter/National Geographic Image Collection)

Color plate 9: As a result of bycatch mortality, breeding populations of laysan albatross declined by one-third on Midway and Laysan islands, where over 90 percent of the world's population nests.
(Credit: James Orr)

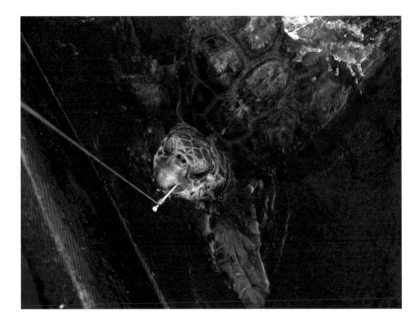

Color plate 10: Changing from traditional J-shaped to circle-hooks on longlines could reduce unintentional hooking or snagging of sea turtles by 90 percent, although turtles can still swallow these hooks.
(Credit: OCEANA)

Color plate 11: Longline fishing boats kill more than 300,000 seabirds unintentionally every year. Birds gather to feed on bait, like these following a longline fishing boat off the coast of Brazil.
(Credit: Fabio Olmos)

Color plate 12: According to the United Nations, fisheries around the world discard some 30 million tons of bycatch each year—dead or dying animals that were caught accidentally and are often dumped into the sea.
(Credit: NOAA)

Color plate 13: Just as wildlife diseases can jump to humans, wild animals are susceptible to human diseases. Even the common cold can be deadly to endangered mountain gorillas.
(Credit: Alastair McNeilage)

Color plate 14: *(above)* A slow loris for sale at a market in Hanoi, Vietnam. Although there are cultural taboos against eating lorises, they are believed to have magical powers, and their body parts are often sold as good luck charms.
(Credit: Elizabeth Bennett)

Color plate 15: *(left)* Hunter with a red brocket deer in the Tamshiyacu-Tahuayo Community Reserve in northeast Peru. The reserve regulates hunting, and as a result, many animal populations have rebounded.
(Credit: Mark Bowler/www.markbowler.com)

Color plate 16: Fires in tropical forests are rare, except where human disturbance is high. Researchers have found that rhinoceros hornbill and other hornbill species in Indonesia face declines of up to 63 percent in fire-damaged forest due to canopy loss and scarce food supplies.
(Credit: Dr. Chan Ah Lak)

Color plate 17: Jaguars have been hunted for their skins, feared and revered by humans, and vilified and exterminated by ranchers. Now, efforts are being made to protect jaguars across their historic range, from Mexico to Argentina.

(Credit: Steve Winter/National Geographic Image Collection)

Color plate 18: This "problem" jaguar was shot by local ranchers in the Brazilian Pantanal for killing cattle. An exaggerated perception of the cat as both dangerous adversary and persistent cattle killer is one of the greatest threats to the jaguar's survival.

(Credit: Steve Winter/National Geographic Image Collection)

Color plate 19a: *(top)* Satellite photo of minimum sea ice concentrations over the Arctic Circle in 1979.
Color plate 19b: *(bottom)* Satellite photo of minimum sea ice concentrations over the Arctic Circle in 2003. A NASA study found that Arctic perennial sea ice has been decreasing at a rate of 9 percent per decade since the 1970s. Globally, the largest temperature increases have occurred over North America.
(Courtesy NASA)

Color plate 20: *(left)* Global warming is affecting some cool mountain regions, like Costa Rica's cloud forests. The resplendent quetzal, pictured here, is now threatened by predators that have moved up from lower altitude rain forest regions.
(Credit: Steve Winter/National Geographic Image Collection)

Color plate 21: *(below)* Climate change is reducing the extent and persistence of winter sea ice in polar regions, threatening many species—from krill and whales to polar bears and penguins.
(Credit: Doris Friedman)

Color plate 22: An oceanic whitetip shark with a group of pilot fish. Once one of the most common sharks in the ocean, oceanic whitetips are now endangered because of their highly sought after fins.

(Credit: Neil Hammerschlag/PEW Institute for Ocean Science)

Color plate 23: *(above)* Conservationists are unsure how declines of one of the ocean's top predators, the great white shark (shown here feeding on a Cape fur seal off South Africa), will affect the marine food chain.

(Credit: Neil Hammerschlag/
PEW Institute for Ocean Science)

Color plate 24: *(left)* Over the past decade, even midsize beluga sturgeon like these have become a rare sight in Russia's Volga River because of the highly lucrative caviar trade.

(Credit: Hans-Jurgen Burkard/Bilderberg,
courtesy Caviar Emptor)

Color plate 25: *(above)* On the plains of Africa, vast migrating herds of wildebeest form during the dry season, following the rains in search of fresh grass. Moving in such large numbers offers some protection from predators.

(Credit: Doris Friedman)

Color plate 26: *(right)* Local communities along Argentina's Patagonian coast value the area's penguin colonies and sea lion rookeries as tourist attractions and are working to preserve these wildlife spectacles.

(Credit: Claudio Campagna)

Color plate 27: The protected coral reef habitat in St. Lucia's marine reserve provides food and shelter for many reef fish, allowing once-depleted populations to rebound. Pictured here, a parrotfish and a pipefish.
(Credit: Tim McClanahan)

Color plate 28: Leopard pelt for sale in Kabul. Western military personnel and aid workers in Afghanistan are a ready market for skins of the endangered cats.
(Credit: UNEP/PCAU)

Listening to the Birds

JOSEPH TOBIAS, LEON BENNUN,
AND ALISON STATTERSFIELD

The history of humankind is part fact and part fable and is strewn with iconic references to birds throughout. When the Gauls crept up the moonlit slopes of Capitoline Hill back in the first century BC, the sentries and their dogs slept, blissfully unaware of the danger. It was the geese that woke and raised the alarm, according to Titus Livius, just in time to save the garrison. The tale echoes, in romantic fashion, the theme of this essay. All around us, the clamor of birds is signaling danger: will we wake from our complacent sleep in time?

It is increasingly clear that biodiversity, the bedrock of life, is eroding away. We can only hope to reverse this process through vigilance and sound science—by assessing the risks biodiversity faces and setting priorities for its protection. Aside from our Roman geese, there are a number of reasons to consider birds as the most reliable early warning system at our disposal: birds are highly visible, familiar, and responsive to environmental fluctuations.

Avian diversity—around 10,000 species by current reckoning—is broad enough to show subtle shifts and patterns, and yet not so broad as to strain recording and analysis. Birds are widespread from poles to equator, from midocean to mountaintop. They are also better understood than all other vertebrates in terms of taxonomy, biogeography, and ecology. An active global network of expert and amateur ornithologists constantly generates a huge supply of data, allowing a glimpse of global population trends over recent decades. Birds provide a valuable starting point for mapping the richness and uniqueness of species in an area, as well as threats and conservation priorities. Therefore, until we are equipped with the time and resources for rigorous interdisciplinary exploration and analysis, we can, and should, use birds to judge and monitor the state of the wild.

A great deal of information on the status and distribution of birds has been compiled and analyzed by BirdLife International[1] and synthesized in the *State of the World's Birds*.[2] This document can serve as a progress report for global biodiversity, assessing its health, why it is being lost, and how we should conserve it;

the document can also play a role on a global scale similar to that of the canary carried down into the shaft of coal mines to test the quality of the air. What noxious fumes are lurking there?

More than 150 bird species are known or suspected to have disappeared since 1500,[3] almost entirely because of human activity, and the process continues today: wild populations of at least 17 species were lost in the last quarter of the 20th century. There is no road back for the Guam flycatcher *(Myiagra freycineti)*, devoured by alien tree snakes, and no second chance for the Colombian grebe *(Podiceps andinus)*, a victim of wetland loss, pollution, overhunting, and predation by introduced trout.

Extinction officially threatens 1,211 species—roughly one in eight of all birds. Of these globally threatened birds (GTBs), 179 are critically endangered. They stand at the brink of oblivion because of rapid declines or dismally small populations or ranges. An estimated 77 species are represented by less than 50 individuals, rendering them very vulnerable to environmental fluctuations and catastrophes, to demographic vagaries (one year, perhaps, most offspring might be male), and to a variety of social and genetic disruptions. At last count, there were 10 pairs of Tahiti monarch *(Pomarea nigra)* in French Polynesia and 12 wild Bali starlings *(Leucopsar rothschildi)*. Time may have run out on Hawaii's po'ouli *(Melamprosops phaeosoma)* when the last individual in captivity died late last year and the last two in the wild had not been seen for some months. Taking into account this overcrowded emergency ward of ailing species, and given the time lag between habitat loss and extinction,[4] a sizeable proportion of the world's birds may be living on borrowed time.

White-rumped vulture.
(Credit: Otto Pfister)

But extinction is only part of the story. Even if extinction is averted, a world full of rare birds, clinging to existence in captive-breeding facilities and pockets of protected habitat isolated in an overpopulated, intensively cultivated, industrialized landscape, is hardly cause for celebration. Unfortunately, there are plenty of signs that such a world looms before us. The Red List Index—a score based on extinction risk documented in the IUCN Red List of Threatened Species—shows that birds overall are sinking deeper into danger.[5] Other analyses agree, documenting population declines and shrinking ranges. In South America, most threatened birds have disappeared from at least 30 percent of their range; in particularly hard-hit areas such as southeast Brazil, ranges have contracted by up to 99 percent.

Even common birds are feeling the pinch. The skylark *(Alauda arvensis)* and the red-winged blackbird *(Agelaius phoenicius)* have long been among the most familiar species in Europe and North America, respectively. However, European farmland birds, including the skylark, have declined by over a third since the 1960s.[6] Meanwhile, across much of the United States, blackbird numbers dropped at least 1 percent each year between 1980 and 1999.[7]

Waterbirds and seabirds are also struggling. Reliable population data are available for roughly half of all wetland species, including ducks, herons, storks, and others: 41 percent are declining and 15 percent are considered globally threatened.[8] News from the high seas is even more alarming. Long-term studies have revealed yearly declines of up to 4 percent for albatross species breeding at Bird Island in the South Atlantic over the last three decades.[9] Data from other breeding sites show similar trends, indicating rangewide declines of these spectacular seabirds.

Wandering albatross.
(Credit: Tony Palliser)

The caged canary has long since stopped singing, and agitated geese are cackling nervously in the citadel. In concert, birds by the millions are telling us we are in danger: biodiversity, the world's self-regulating life-support mechanism, is at risk.

But birds are giving us much more than a warning. They are telling us which threats are most serious, and which responses are needed. For example, a link is easily drawn between declining albatross numbers and the longline fisheries that claim the lives of tens of thousands of seabirds each year.[10] But, recently, a staggering 95 percent decline in certain Indian vultures was harder to explain. The finger of suspicion pointed first at a viral disease, but the culprit is now known to be a veterinary drug, diclofenac, an anti-inflammatory routinely administered to livestock. Vultures ingest diclofenac when they feed on cattle carcasses, with lethal results. In these cases, the pathway of cause and effect can be traced, and the solution is readily identified, though not always easy to implement. To save albatrosses, we need to control unregulated fisheries and modify the way we fish; to save vultures we must substitute other, safer drugs for diclofenac and protect the remaining population.

In general, causal pathways are less straightforward, though the culprits may be more familiar. On a global scale, habitat destruction, degradation, and fragmentation is by far the most pressing problem, affecting 86 percent of threatened birds. Unsustainable forestry undermines 64 percent, and some forests are fast disappearing. In Indonesia, where three-quarters of logging is now illegal, 40 percent of existing forests were logged between 1950 and 2000. Elsewhere, intensifying agriculture threatens many open-country species. Even in the world's great wildernesses, habitat is being eroded by the inexorable spread of urbanization, cultivation, industry, and infrastructure. These changes bring other problems along with them—disturbance, fire, pollution, hunting, invasive species—all of which decimate birds and other wildlife (see color plate 16).

Whether threats are direct or indirect, there is no escaping the fact that we are the problem: 99 percent of endangered birds are at risk from human activities. Hunting impacts 345 bird species (nearly 30 percent of all at-risk birds), with 262 species overhunted for food and 117 species trapped for the pet trade.

Some birds are particular hunting targets: waterfowl, birds of prey, galliforms (pheasants, quails, and francolins), pigeons and doves, curassows and guans, and an alarming 47 percent of cranes. Harvesting wild birds provides a vital source of both protein and income for many rural communities, but expanding markets, increased demand, and modern guns and traps have pushed the exploitation of many species beyond sustainable levels.

Among parrots, no less than 52 species are threatened by the caged-bird trade. They form a significant chunk of the estimated 4 million wild birds that are traded internationally each year,[11] valued at about $60 million. Although the United States and Canada no longer import wild birds as pets, the European Union remains a major market. In the United Kingdom alone, 88 percent of parrots imported between 1995 and 2000 were caught in the wild—about 24,000 birds, and at least as many will have died during capture and transportation.

Southeast Asia is a notable hub of trade in live birds. This biodiverse region includes some of the world's poorest and most rapidly developing countries. Increased spending power in some places, and continued poverty in others, fuel an intensive wildlife trade. Birds that were once widespread are disappearing fast, such as the straw-headed bulbul *(Pycnonotus zeylanicus)* and the Philippine cockatoo *(Cacatua haematuropygia),* which are in high demand as caged birds.

Both national laws and the Convention on International Trade in Endangered Species (CITES) provide some controls on the trapping and sale of birds. Unfortunately, these are not always effective. Of the birds traded internationally each year, some 1.5 million are protected under CITES. But there is great demand for many species. Wild birds are still often cheaper to buy than captive-bred ones, driving a widespread illegal trade—the size of which can only be guessed at. The rarer the bird and the more restricted the trade, the higher the prices that specimens command in illegal markets. For example, Lear's macaw *(Anodorhynchus leari),* a big, blue, critically endangered parrot from Brazil, is reportedly worth more than $45,000 on the black market.

Where people have not hunted birds into extinction, the animals accompanying us often have. Invasive species have wiped out at least 65 unique bird species since 1500, and currently affect two-thirds of imperiled birds on oceanic islands. On most of these islands, the native fauna has suffered from the arrival of humans and their tendency to introduce—inadvertently or otherwise—cats, rats, snakes, mongooses, pigs, and dogs, among other scavengers and predators. Lacking defenses against these unfamiliar animals, many island birds (and their eggs and chicks) have proved easy pickings. On the Hawaiian Islands, additional pressure is imposed by novel pathogens.

The Blyth's tragopan is considered vulnerable because of deforestation of its restricted Himalayan range.
(Credit: Jean Howman/WPA)

Two introduced diseases, avian pox and malaria, carried by mosquitoes (themselves introduced), have contributed to the extermination of over 50 bird species.

Looming behind these immediate pressures is the specter of climate change. We can already see its effects on bird distribution and behavior. To give just a few examples: in Costa Rica, lowland and foothill species such as the keel-billed toucan *(Ramphastos sulfuratus)* have extended their ranges up mountain slopes, as the level of the cloud-base rises. In the United Kingdom, many birds are breeding significantly earlier than they used to. Others, like the great tit *(Parus major)* are not, though food supply for this species' nestlings now peaks earlier and is out of synchrony with their breeding timing. In Europe, birds that spend the winter south of the Sahara are setting off earlier, possibly so that they can cross the Sahel before the seasonal dry period, while those wintering north of the Sahara are migrating later. In the northeastern United States, many migrants are arriving substantially earlier from their wintering grounds.

It may seem surprising that climate change is a major threat to birds. Can't they just fly off to where the climate suits them? Unfortunately, many will have nowhere to fly as climate shifts. Some bird species will be pushed off the top of mountains or the edge of continents, others will find their islands under water or their little remnant patches of habitat simply disappearing. Climate change brings in its wake new pressures from competitors, predators, parasites, diseases, and powerful disturbances such as drought-induced fires or storms that may act in synergy with other threats. How many species we may lose, and how far we can manage and mitigate the effects, depend crucially on how far and fast temperatures rise. Models suggest that a rise of more than 3.6°F (2.2°C) in the next century will be catastrophic for birds, biodiversity, and people.

If we look at the ranges of threatened birds, we find that most of them are distributed in the tropics, with four-fifths restricted to developing countries. Three quarters of these are essentially forest dwellers, many of which require pristine or lightly modified habitat to thrive. Indonesia has the dubious distinction of supporting the most at-risk bird species of any country, 119 to be exact—barely beating out Brazil's 117. Meanwhile, roughly a quarter of all Asian birds are of conservation concern, a testament to the region's high and ever-growing human population and consequent scramble for resources. Islands are having a tough time too: while only 17 percent of the world's avifauna is restricted to islands, half of all threatened birds are island dwellers. Tropics, forests, islands, densely populated developing countries with high

The bristle-thighed curlew, a bird that nests on the Alaskan tundra and winters on tropical Pacific islands, is flightless during its winter molting season—making it vulnerable to cats, dogs, and other introduced predators.
(Credit: John Clarkson)

The extinction rate of endemic island birds remains high. A series of protected areas in Cuba has helped preserve populations of native birds, including Cuban screech owls, pictured here.
(Credit: Steve Winter/National Geographic Image Collection)

species uniqueness: these are the primary foci where conservation attention must urgently be trained.

We might think that efforts should already be under way to protect these key areas, but it requires financial commitment. Each year, the pitifully small global expenditure for protected areas totals $7 billion—about one-third the estimated need—and only $1 billion is spent in developing countries.[12] In fact, correcting for the preponderance of threatened birds in developing countries, conservation investment is almost 20 times lower there than in the developed world. To counteract this skew, investment in biodiversity needs to be much greater and more strategic. This might sound unreasonable, but conservation is affordable. We can safeguard the bulk of global biodiversity for much less than is spent on soft drinks in the United States each year.

Many birds concentrate in small, often overlapping, ranges, or in a few specific locations. These are the sites most deserving of conservation attention. Identifying these critical sites produces a global conservation strategy coded into a vast but conservable network known as Important Bird Areas (IBAs). If properly and effectively managed, IBAs will help ensure the survival of a large proportion of the world's birds as well as much other biodiversity.[13]

But saving IBAs is no mean feat. Tackling deforestation, curbing agricultural expansion, regulating the burning of grassland or drainage of wetlands: these objectives are easy to recommend but difficult to achieve because the issues involved are so complex, and the vested interests often so powerful. Human populations continue to grow, along with our demands on natural resources. Consumption

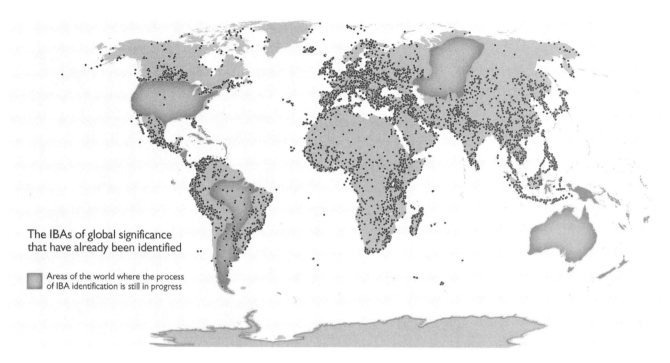

The IBAs of global significance that have already been identified

Areas of the world where the process of IBA identification is still in progress

and expectations of material wealth are rising in richer nations, driving agricultural intensification, habitat destruction, and overexploitation elsewhere.

According to our feathered indicators, we are using land unsustainably, and biodiversity is suffering as a result. Of course, our destruction of nature is driven by deeper problems based on a subtle interplay of greed, unfair trade, asymmetrical power, and distorted value systems. Above all, the state of the world's birds is symptomatic of a deep-rooted flaw in the way we value nature.

In developed societies, nature is increasingly popular as an aesthetic refuge, but the services that ecosystems provide are little understood or appreciated. Wild nature provides us with raw materials, medicines, and food—and stabilizes our climate, cleans our waste, consolidates our soils, and produces the oxygen we breathe. Biologists and economists recently attempted to hang a price tag on these ecosystem services, arriving at a figure of $33 trillion per year—not far short of the annual gross global product. And yet, we harvest nature's spectacular bounty as if it were limitless. Why do we destroy a natural heritage that is not only beautiful, but fantastically valuable?

The answer has something to do with ignorance, arrogance, and hefty short-term profits for a privileged few. It has little to do with sustainable economics. In monetary terms, the long-term benefits of conserving our planet's natural habitat are estimated to exceed the costs by at least 100 to 1.[14] These facts must be driven home if policymakers are to shift their stance toward more sustainable forms of development and ensure that biodiversity conservation achieves the legal and financial backing it so badly needs.

More than 6,400 Important Bird Areas of global significance have been identified in 167 countries and territories worldwide. (Credit: BirdLife International)

The Eurasian spoonbill migrates between western Europe, northeast Africa, and China, exposing it to a broad range of human threats.
(Credit: BirdLife International)

There is international consensus that biodiversity is worth preserving, and commitment to slow its loss before 2010, a target confirmed at the World Summit at Johannesburg in 2002.[15] But if the planet's disappearing birds are any indicator, we are patently failing in our task. Policies are weak, vague, and riddled with loopholes. Options are narrowing. Time is running out.

Given the value of biodiversity, and the irreversible nature of extinction, our failure seems likely to affect all of humanity, permanently, and therefore constitutes a much more terrifying threat—with further-reaching consequences—than terrorism. Our freedom, security, and quality of life are endangered by our mismanagement of nature, and yet there is no government-touted, corporate-driven, prime time "War on Extinction."

There is, however, a war on extinction of a different kind—a lower-case war, with lower profile and lower outlay—being fought by an army of motivated individuals, enlightened politicians, and conservation organizations. In the face of collective apathy and a shortage of political will, this army is managing to get things done.

In 2000, BirdLife compiled a list of 5,500 key actions for 1,186 globally threatened birds. By 2004, some of these actions had been implemented for an impressive 67 percent of targeted species, and at least some benefit was evident for one-quarter. However, the full suite of conservation measures is under way for a mere 5 percent. Plenty of challenges remain, not least of which are protections for the rarest of the rare—the 28 critically endangered bird species for which no actions are currently in place.

While we should not flinch from the central sobering message—that the state of the world's birds is deteriorating fast—it is important to appreciate that many crucial steps have been taken toward reversing that trend. For conservationists, the emphasis must now switch from analyzing data and establishing priorities to active conservation. International treaties and paper commitments must be turned into positive action, and working relationships must be fostered among governments, corporations, nongovernmental organizations (NGOs), and communities to seek new ways of protecting biodiversity.

Therein lies our only chance of ensuring that birds will be protected worldwide. Birds are not only excellent ecosystem indicators but provide a gateway into environmental awareness. If we can use birds to engage the true support of governments and civil society, and if we can bring about a real change in values and behavior, there might yet be a song of hope.

This would be fitting because hope, after all, is the one virtue birds have symbolized for millennia. Perhaps the most famous of all is the white dove freed by Noah that returned seven days later with an olive leaf clasped in its beak, proof that the flood had abated (according to the author of the Book of Genesis). Birds, seemingly among the most fragile of animals, may have brought us a vital clue, and may yet help us steer the ark—harboring all the world's biodiversity, ourselves included—toward a brighter future. Whether this remains a myth or becomes a reality depends squarely on us.

Species in Focus

Saving Jaguars throughout Their Range: From Theory to Practice

ALAN RABINOWITZ

When God created man, the jaguar already existed, having ruled the earth since the beginning. But God also gave men guns to keep the jaguar in his place and dogs to help man hunt for food. The jaguar was non-plussed, claiming that he would catch the bullets man shot at him, then eat the dogs. On God's instructions, man shot at the jaguar, wounding him in the paw, then sent the dogs to chase him up a tree.

"Now you have learned your lesson," God told the jaguar. "You must not eat man or dog. The other animals are yours to eat. Now go away and live in the bush."

This was the story told to the famed anthropologist J. Eric S. Thompson by the Mayan Indians of southern Belize in the 1920s. Five decades later, the next generation of Belizean Mayans had appended the tale.

"There is no place for the jaguar to live in peace," my Mayan assistant said to me as I kneeled in the dirt measuring the footprint of a large male jaguar. "All the land is needed by people, and the people will not live with jaguars."

The jaguar *(Panthera onca)*—the third largest cat in the world and the largest cat in the Western Hemisphere—has been one of the most powerful and recurring motifs in Central and South American religions and cultures. Yet, until recently, much of what was known about this species was anecdotal. The beauty, power, and mystery of the jaguar, and the fear and respect that it inspired in pre-Columbian people, created a world of two jaguars—the real and the imaginary, the natural and the supernatural.[1] The desire to dominate and possess both of these jaguars fed into a tradition of hunting the animal that continues to this day.

The earliest and most serious threat to peaceful coexistence between jaguars and humans began in the 1500s with the introduction of domestic livestock to the New World. God clearly never told jaguars not to take cattle, a readily available food source that was placed in the forest right in the face of these powerful predators. Naturally, jaguars sometimes killed cattle, but often under circumstances that could be easily changed by better cattle husbandry. The fact that livestock often died in the field from many other causes—everything from parasites to starvation—seemed lost on many ranchers, who simply blamed jaguars for any and all livestock losses. Many instituted a "shoot on sight" policy for jaguars.

By the 1960s, when fur coats again became fashionable in the Western world, jaguar killings skyrocketed. Tens of thousands of jaguar and other spotted cat skins were shipped out from countries in South America. Jaguars declined sharply from areas where they'd once been abundant. In 1969 alone, 108,000 pounds (49,000 kg) of jaguar skins valued at $5 million were exported from Brazil—mostly to the United States and Europe.[2]

Finally, in 1973, the Convention on International Trade in Endangered Species (CITES) made it illegal to trade jaguar skins or parts across national borders. Most countries that were home to the cat also banned jaguar hunting, and killings immediately tapered off. But the damage had been done: The jaguar's historic range, once extending from the southwest United States to central Argentina, had been reduced by more than 50 percent. However, there was some good news: large contiguous areas of jaguar habitat still remained intact throughout Mexico, Central America, and South America.

I began the first systematic field research on jaguar ecology, behavior, and their relation to livestock in the 1980s. Studies over the next two decades disproved many preconceived notions about jaguar predation on livestock and even helped to create the world's first jaguar preserve in the Cockscomb Basin of Belize.[3] But by the end of the 20th century, jaguars remained one of nature's mysteries. No one had any idea how many there still might be out there in the wild—and they continued to be vilified and hunted as pests (see color plate 17).

It was with this in mind that in 1999, the Wildlife Conservation Society (WCS) initiated a rangewide assessment of the status of the jaguar. Our plan was to design a conservation blueprint for a sustainable, contiguous landscape where jaguars and people could coexist. It was an innovative approach intended to conserve jaguars across their entire biological range.[4]

Thirty-five of the world's jaguar experts from 18 countries convened in Mexico to amass existing knowledge regarding jaguar status throughout Latin America, identify threats relating to jaguar survival, and prioritize research and conservation needs for the species. Using this workshop as a foundation, WCS then created the Jaguar Conservation Program (JCP) to save the jaguar in perpetuity.

The consensus among the jaguar experts was that there were six critical issues that needed to be addressed if a rangewide jaguar conservation strategy was to succeed. One of the highest priorities was collecting good data on jaguar

The jaguar was revered among Meso-american cultures. For the Olmec and the Maya, the cat became a symbol of authority and hunting prowess and was a spirit companion for shamans.
(Credit: Steve Winter/National Geographic Image Collection)

Radio tracking a jaguar along the Paraguay River in the Brazilian Pantanal.
(Credit: George B. Schaller)

populations, distribution, habitat fragmentation—and hunting losses. Long-term ecological and behavioral research at important jaguar sites was also necessary. And contact with ranchers was desperately needed to better understand and mitigate jaguar–livestock conflicts. Other priorities included health and genetic studies, conservation education, and national policy initiatives to better protect jaguars.[5]

Long-term, sustainable conservation must have good science at its core—using methodologies that are accurate, repeatable, and comparable, which is then published and made available to others. Jaguar conservation has been hampered by a lack of available, high quality data. This is due, in part, to the difficulty of conducting research on a species that easily blends into its surroundings—and travels widely, often covering 10 to 20 miles (16–32 km) in a single night. But there has also been a serious lack of training, publishing, and communication among researchers. As a result, many jaguar studies have been poorly planned and executed.

Much of our early data on jaguars came from radiotelemetry studies.[6,7] As I learned early in the jungles of Belize, safely catching and radio collaring a jaguar is difficult. Yet the hardest part comes later, when trying to follow the beeping radio signal from the collared animal as it moves through the miles and miles of thick undergrowth that jaguars call home. When I couldn't "find" my collared jaguars on foot or by truck, I would use a small airplane, flying low over the jungle until I located the animal's signal. Much time, effort, and expense were devoted to tracking jaguars and plotting their locations on a map. This produced crucial baseline data on the size of jaguars' home ranges and their movement and activity patterns.

Many field researchers rely on indirect evidence, such as feces and pugmarks

(footprints), to make inferences about jaguar numbers and behavior. Fecal matter can provide important information about the presence, movement patterns, and diet of jaguars. But the assumption is that a researcher can properly differentiate between jaguar, ocelot *(Leopardis pardalis),* puma *(Puma concolor),* and other carnivore feces. However, this is often not the case, especially if the researcher lacks experience with the many species that share the forest with jaguars.

Even when feces are properly attributed to the right donor, it is another skill entirely to properly identify prey remains. Many researchers never take the time and trouble to create a reference collection of prey parts before beginning their study, and thus often report only what they can identify. Additional bias is introduced when a researcher uses the identified prey parts to estimate numbers of different prey consumed and their relative importance in a jaguar's diet. Few researchers consider that small animals with many indigestible parts, such as a turtle or an armadillo, appear more readily and more often than a large, meaty animal such as a 50-pound (23 kg) peccary.

Likewise, sometimes it is difficult to differentiate between the pugmarks of large cats like jaguar and puma, as perfect footprints are rarely left behind in nice soft mud. And while tracks can be valuable in identifying an animal's presence, travel routes, and activity patterns, they cannot be reliably used to estimate jaguar abundance. One jaguar can make lots of different-looking tracks when moving at different speeds over different terrain.

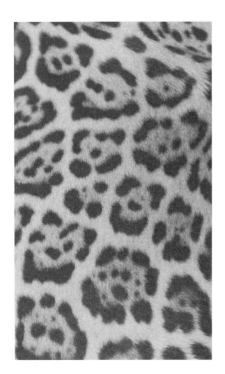

Since no two jaguars have exactly the same coat pattern, researchers use the rosette patterns to identify individuals—much like human fingerprints.

(Credit: Steve Winter/National Geographic Image Collection)

By the 1990s, new, more reliable techniques became available, methods that moved some jaguar research from the field into the laboratory. With breakthroughs in molecular biology, newly developed DNA analysis allowed us to identify individual animals and to track their genealogy using feces and hair samples.

It also became possible to more easily and accurately track jaguars using satellite collars—downloading the cat's movements directly to a laptop computer. Camera traps also came into use: small cameras attached to a tree or bush that use an infrared beam to trigger the shutter. When jaguars or other animals walk by, they break the beam, taking their own pictures. Camera traps were initially developed for hunters to trace the travel routes of target species, but within the last decade they were adapted by biologists for regular use in field surveys. The fact that no two jaguars have exactly the same coat pattern allows us to identify individuals by the rosette patterns on their coats, which are much akin to a human fingerprint. The problem remained, however, that many researchers were either unaware of these new tools or lacked the training and funds to use these relatively costly new techniques.

Since you must walk before you run, the jaguar program's first endeavor was to design standardized protocols for conducting research, from how to use camera traps to estimate jaguar numbers to the proper collection and handling of hair and scat samples for analysis. We developed a manual for the immobilization and handling of jaguars in the field in order to decrease trauma or even death of captured animals. We even developed a manual detailing how to engage and work with ranchers on the issue of jaguar–livestock conflicts. These protocols have been disseminated in workshops and publications and are now posted in English, Spanish, and Portuguese on a jaguar conservation website (www.savethejaguar.com). This site is maintained by the JCP so that researchers and others can share new methods and technologies and explore issues relating to jaguar conservation.

Jaguar Distribution Surveys, Population Status and Long-Term Research

Establishing the presence of jaguars in an area is not difficult. But without the ability to accurately estimate populations, we couldn't quantify or analyze threats to their survival. This has now changed. In the first accurate jaguar count ever conducted, biologists in the Cockscomb Basin estimated a density of about nine jaguars per 39 square miles (100 km^2) in 2002.[8] Camera traps were placed along a grid system in the jungle, then statistical programs compared jaguar "captures" on film with numbers of "recaptures," providing a population estimate for the camera-trapped area. Similar jaguar surveys are currently under way in Brazil, Bolivia, and Panama.

Commitment to a particular site over time is the most efficient and cost effective way to carry out detailed research on a species. Study sites must be carefully chosen, as long-term research is costly and labor intensive, requiring researchers to capture and handle jaguars, collect blood and other bodily fluids for health assessment, and track the animals over long distances. These long-term studies yield information on reproduction, demographic trends, and responses to environmental changes. Initial research sites include the Brazilian Pantanal, with its vast expanse of privately owned jaguar habitat, the lowland forests of Madidi National Park in Boliva, and the coastal forest of Costa Rica's Corcovado National Park.

Jaguar—Livestock Research and Rancher Outreach

Most jaguars live on private lands, where people fear the cat and perceive it to be a dangerous adversary and a persistent cattle killer. This is the greatest imminent threat to the jaguar's survival. One of the jaguar program's most intensive initiatives is a rancher outreach program, pioneered in the Brazilian Pantanal—home to both the world's largest jaguars and some of the most serious jaguar–livestock conflicts. The goal of this program is sustainable coexistence between jaguars and cattle ranchers, addressing both the needs of jaguars and the social, economic, and cultural needs of humans that share the land with them (see color plate 18).

Jaguars are frequently blamed for the loss of livestock, something we now know is more often caused by a host of factors, including disease, malnutrition, flooding, and puma predation.[9,10] During one study in the Pantanal, the examination of 10 dead cattle implicated a jaguar in only one death.[11] Ironically, however, while many ranchers continue to blame and even kill jaguars for all livestock losses, these same ranchers insist that jaguars should not be completely exterminated from the land. The cats are viewed as part of the heritage of the Pantanal.

The rancher outreach program provides information and engages ranchers through workshops and private visits. During our first workshop, we learned the importance of listening to ranchers' ideas and perceptions, empathizing with their problems—and encouraging their suggestions on how to move forward. This helped build relationships and allowed us to integrate jaguar research data with sound cattle husbandry and veterinary practices in a manner that was acceptable to—and ultimately requested by—the ranchers themselves.

Health and Genetics Research and Education Activities

As habitats become more fragmented and jaguar prey such as peccaries, deer, and paca decline, jaguars come into more frequent contact with humans and domestic animals. This could create a new problem: disease. Researchers are trying to learn more about the dynamics of diseases that could readily pass between jaguars, livestock, and humans. Research is currently under way in Bolivia to compare diseases and parasites in jaguars and domestic dogs. The jaguar

Researchers collaring a jaguar in Brazil's Pantanal region. Global positioning system (GPS) collars are now being used to track jaguar movements: ranchers readily blame jaguars for any livestock loss, and biologists are collecting data to quantify the true extent of jaguar predation.
(Credit: Steve Winter/National Geographic Image Collection)

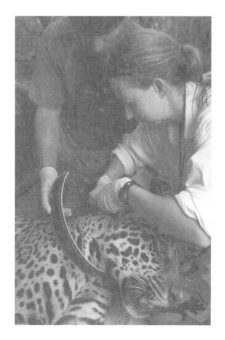

program is also collecting baseline data on blood parameters and parasite loads in jaguars, information needed for long-term monitoring of health issues.

Education is also an important component of the jaguar program. In conjunction with the WCS Education Program, we are currently designing a jaguar ecology and conservation curriculum. This program, "Teachers for Jaguars: An Educator's Toolbox," is targeted at children in grades 4 through 12 and is being translated into Spanish and Portuguese for use in schools throughout the jaguar's range. A web-based curriculum, "Wild Explorations," includes modules for high school students on jaguar ecology and behavior, jaguar conservation, jaguar–human conflict—as well as the jaguar's cultural significance to indigenous peoples.

Policy

At the local level, we conduct research and protect jaguars. But we must also act at the national policy level to work toward rangewide conservation and the overall objective of creating a contiguous jaguar landscape from Mexico to Argentina. As a first step, we are examining data obtained since the 1999 Mexico meeting and taking a closer look at the gaps in our knowledge about jaguar distribution.

Using available data, we are mapping a rangewide jaguar corridor that delineates a theoretical path of travel for a jaguar walking from southern Mexico to northern Argentina. Of course, individual jaguars would never walk that far, but a connected landscape, linking up public and private lands, will allow jaguars to maintain contact with their immediate neighbors and will ensure the future genetic diversity of the species. With such an objective in mind, we are working on a country-by-country basis to keep the spotlight on jaguar conservation and to promote the idea of national jaguar corridors. Popular publications by WCS researchers and a recent National Geographic documentary, *In Search of the Jaguar,* have helped us get our ideas out to the public.

> In 1969 alone, 108,000 pounds of jaguar skins valued at $5 million were exported from Brazil.

Most species-based conservation efforts don't take into account the entire geographic range of the animal from the very beginning. The coordination of research and conservation efforts across broad geographic landscapes is difficult and is often stymied by cultural and linguistic differences, legal inconsistencies, varying political climates across borders, available funding opportunities, or differences in the knowledge and skills of researchers. It is for these reasons that most biological conservation plans respect political boundaries more than ecological ones.

While this seems expedient for managing research and conservation activities on a local or national scale, it is not strategic in the long run if the goal is to save a species from extinction. What often occurs is that some populations of animals are saved, while other potentially important representative populations of the species are lost. The conservation model presented here is based on the assumption that sustainable conservation of a species throughout its range can be accomplished only through a priori strategic planning, followed by a systematic and coordinated effort by an organization committed to the survival of that species.

Conserving large mammals, and carnivores in particular, is increasingly difficult in a landscape dominated by humans who are themselves dealing with issues of poverty, landlessness, and population growth. But most people claim to understand that we must find a way to live with wildlife because balanced ecological systems create a healthier world—and because animals are part of our natural legacy. However, while many conservation organizations use endangered large carnivores as part of their logos and raise funds on the backs of such species, there is a dearth of commitment and action once the talking is finished, the meetings are adjourned, and the reports are written.

Saving large, wide-ranging species like the jaguar is not easy. Beyond the initial investment of time, money, and staffing, eternal vigilance is needed to conserve these species. As governments change and new political issues arise, protection of the natural world is continually weighed against improving human livelihoods. But people and governments must be made to understand that wildlife conservation and the betterment of people's lives are closely related. And it is up to the international conservation community to carry the banner on this issue and commit to species conservation regardless of the obstacles.

> The true measure of success will be when jaguars and other wildlife have a secure home and a secure future.

There is no quick fix to conserving jaguars or any other species. Our efforts will always be hampered by funding, political considerations, and a dearth of committed individuals, but such limitations are not an excuse for inaction. There is always work that can be done to conserve wildlife. While still far from achieving our ultimate goal, WCS's Jaguar Conservation Program is making significant strides and represents a model for species conservation that can be applied almost anywhere in the world. This is no small accomplishment. But the true measure of success will be when jaguars and other wildlife have a secure home and a secure future. That goal is within our grasp. And our reward for reaching it will be a richer, healthier world.

Climate Change and the Wild

Into the Great Unknown

GLENN SCHERER

The world changed profoundly 3.5 billion years ago when microscopic blue-green algae first evolved photosynthesis and "exhaled" waste oxygen into the atmosphere as a by-product. That oxygen became Promethean fire, super-charging newly evolving microorganisms that could use it. But it was deadly poison for those that could not, bringing cataclysm and extinction for most species of anaerobic bacteria—the previous masters of the planet. The addition of oxygen to the atmosphere unbalanced a chemical and biological equation that had endured for eons, altering Earth's ecosystems forever.

Today another organism is altering atmospheric chemistry: in less than 100 years, the oil, coal, and wood fires lit by billions of *Homo sapiens* could double preindustrial atmospheric carbon dioxide levels from 280 to 560 parts per million. Various models predict that the resulting greenhouse effect could rapidly raise average planetary temperatures by anywhere from 2.5° to 10.4°F (1.4°–5.8°C), which would alter global climate and potentially affect every organism on Earth, for good or ill.[1]

As climatologist Wallace Broecker warned of humanity's uncontrolled global warming experiment: Climate is "an angry beast, and we are poking it with sticks."[2] The "beast" may already be lashing out with record heat waves, drought, and deluge. And from pole to pole, deepest ocean to highest peak, some species and ecosystems are experiencing impacts that could ultimately remake the world's biological playing field (see color plates 19a and b).

Just as in the Precambrian era, the destabilization of atmospheric chemistry could be catastrophic for some species and a boon to others. Precisely how these changes will affect Earth's organisms, no one knows; the factors are too complex to predict accurately. However, civilization in the 21st century could experience dramatic global change: we are crossing a climactic threshold into an unforeseeable brave new biological world.

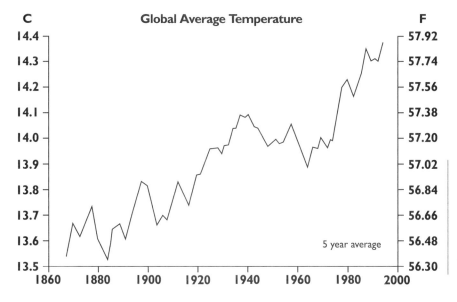

Global Average Temperature

C / F

5 year average

Global average temperature chart. The Intergovernmental Panel on Climate Change (IPCC) reports that the average surface temperature of Earth has warmed during the last century by as much as 1.5°F (0.8°C)—to a warmer level than at any time during the past 1,000 years, with the warmest years recorded during the past decade. (Credit: IPCC)

A Heat-Driven Exodus

While politicians haggle over the reality of global warming, some of Earth's plants and animals are already responding to it. In 2003, two studies found clear signals that a warming planet is forcing some species to move toward the poles and mountain summits, and causing others to alter lifecycle rhythms. One study looked at 1,473 plant and animal species that have recently undergone biological change. It found that 81 percent—species ranging from tree swallows *(Tachycineta bicolor)* and marmots to wild geraniums *(Geranium maculatum)*—are responding to rising temperatures.[3] A second study looked at 1,700 species. Half exhibited changes matching climate change predictions—after a warming of just 1°F in the past 100 years (see color plate 20).[4]

In 2004, the most extensive study ever of global warming impacts on biodiversity examined more than 1,100 plants, mammals, birds, reptiles, frogs, butterflies, and invertebrates from six diversity-rich regions covering about 20 percent of the planet's land surface. Researchers concluded that a global temperature rise of 1.5° to 3.6°F (0.8°–2°C) would put between 15 and 37 percent of those species on the road to extinction by 2050. Extrapolated to include all life, that could put over a million species, from insects and birds to mammals, on the fast track to oblivion by midcentury.[5]

These approximations could be conservative, however, since the study only identified extinctions caused by reduction in a species' range. But impacts could extend far beyond range contractions. As the world warms and climate zones shift, entire biomes—including the taiga, boreal, and temperate forests—may need to move geographically. Individual species will likely initiate these movements at different times and at dissimilar rates in a piecemeal manner that could disrupt or even rip wild communities apart.

The resplendent quetzal, pictured here in Guatemala's Biotopo del Quetzal cloud forest is losing numbers to a new predator. As temperatures warm, lowland keel-billed toucans are expanding their habitat, predating quetzal chicks.

(Credit: Steve Winter/National Geographic Image Collection)

Indeed, such asynchronous rearranging of ecosystems appears to be under way. In 2003, scientists found the North Sea ecosystem undergoing rapid change. As the sea has warmed, cold-water microscopic plankton—the lowest rung on the food chain—has shifted northward. As a result, small fish such as sandeel that survive on plankton are disappearing. This may be the cause behind a recent, abrupt sea bird population crash: in just four years, a half million guillemots, terns, and skuas have vanished from the northern British Isles. Simultaneously, cold-water-loving cod stocks have crashed, and the first warm-water fish such as tuna, red mullet, and squid have appeared in the North Sea.[6]

For species that have to move to adapt to changing temperatures, arrival in cooler climes will not assure survival. Local conditions other than temperature—terrain, precipitation, competition, disease, and human interference—could conjoin to make a new home inhospitable. Human infrastructure—such as highways, croplands, and cities—could pose deadly barriers to climate change-induced shifts in range. The collision of previously isolated ecosystems will also breed surprises. In Costa Rica, for example, resplendent quetzal chicks *(Pharomachrus moccino)* in high altitude cloud forests are now succumbing to new predators: lowland keel-billed toucans *(Ramphastos sulfuratus)* that are expanding their habitat into the warming mountains.

Flight, even if successful, will have limits. Polar bears, for example, depend on year-round sea ice as a platform for seal hunting. But melting Arctic ice could put them among the first of climate change–induced extinctions.

Threats to Slow-Moving and "Stranded" Species

Climate change episodes in Earth's remote past have caused vast movements of species, with some species hybridizing and adapting to new habitat. Adaptation could help some organisms survive, and even thrive, in a new, hotter regime in the future. But models suggest that 21st century warming will happen faster than some species can respond—especially plants and trees. A 6°F (3.3°C) rise could, for example, shift the range of sugar maple trees northward, out of the United States, within 100 years. But such a shift, carried out only by seed dispersal, could take far longer. Unless forests have some as yet unknown means of adapting, the ecosystems that they support will be at risk.[7] A die-off of sugar maples, for example, could harm species reliant on them—such as white-breasted nuthatches *(Sitta carolinensis),* various mice, and white-tailed deer *(Odocoileus virginianus).*

In some situations, wildlife will be stranded with no place to go. A 2003 study found that Africa's Lake Tanganyika—Earth's second most biologically diverse

Warming Arctic climate has caused a 7 percent reduction in ice cover in 25 years. This impacts polar bears like those pictured here near Cape Churchill, Canada; earlier spring melts have been correlated with lowerered hunting and reproductive success.

(Credit: Robert and Carolyn Buchanan)

lake, boasting 350 fish species—has lost 20 percent of its productivity. Hotter air has meant less wind to stir vital nutrients from the depths to feed surface algae and aquatic plants, leaving less food for starving fish, potentially leading to the demise of some species.[8]

Coral reefs could be the first biome to suffer a similar fate. The hottest year on record, 1998, brought planetwide coral bleaching: 16 percent of the world's reefs died, with massive coral mortality in Bahrain, the Maldives, Sri Lanka, Singapore, and Tanzania. Some models suggest that remaining reefs, harboring 25 percent of all marine species, could disappear in a century—though there are signs that some corals could survive by forming new bonds with heat-tolerant algae.[9]

With fossil fuel emissions still on the upswing, the reshuffling of global habitats could last for centuries. When ecosystems do restabilize, they may look very different, probably less diverse—with survivors determined much by chance.

Disrupting Nature's Timing

Researchers planetwide are finding examples of a natural world "growing out of sync with itself." Some animals and plants that share precisely orchestrated seasonal interactions are altering lifecycle rhythms in response to changing climate.

One 2003 study found that springtime events—blooming, egg laying, and the end of hibernation—now occur an average of 5.1 days earlier per decade.[10] Another study counted 172 plants, birds, butterflies, and amphibians that have advanced spring lifecycle events by an average of 2.3 days per decade.[11]

Some species may benefit from such temporal shifts. Longer summers, for example, offer a longer growing season for plants and could allow some birds to lay two clutches of eggs instead of one. But, as with spatial migrations, temporal shifts can pose their own threats. In Europe, for example, an earlier spring has thrown the winter moth out of sync with its major food source, oak trees.

Temperature triggers their spring awakening differently, so caterpillars now hatch up to three weeks before oaks leaf out, and the insects starve.[12]

Rising Oceans

In its 2001 report, the United Nations Intergovernmental Panel on Climate Change (IPCC) projected that seawater's thermal expansion, combined with glacial melt, could cause ocean levels to rise 3.5 to 34.6 inches (8.9–88.0 cm) between 1990 and 2100, with a midrange estimate of 18.9 inches (48.0 cm).[13]

Such an increase could flood many Pacific atolls and engulf coastal estuaries and mangrove forests—some of the world's richest ecosystems. It could also flood beaches, putting seal rookeries, nesting sea turtles, and sea birds at risk, squeezing them between deepening water and inhospitable habitats such as coastal roads, sea walls, and other human structures. Rising oceans could also cause salt intrusion far up freshwater rivers, altering habitat and species makeup.

Extreme and Subtle Weather

According to the IPCC report, global warming has triggered more frequent and extreme weather events. Increased radiant energy trapped at the Earth's surface has intensified storms and droughts since the 1990s.

Consider 2003, the third warmest year on record: Europe endured the worst heat wave in 500 years, which took 35,000 lives. In India, harsh cold killed 1,900 people, then premonsoon temperatures soared to 120°F (48.9°C), killing 1,500 more. In the United States, 562 tornadoes ripped across the nation in a single month—the prior record was 399 in 1992. Sixteen named Atlantic hurricanes formed the same year, compared to the 11-storm average seen between 1944 and 1996.[14] The following year, a hurricane hit Brazil for the first time on record.

> Climate is "an angry beast, and we are poking it with sticks."
> —climatologist Wallace Broecker

While the human toll from extreme weather is well known, wildlife casualties go mostly undocumented. We do know that local extinctions of butterflies have been traced to severe drought or record precipitation, and many animals, such as migrating birds, die in intense storms. But extreme weather impacts can cascade through a food web to affect many species. For example, widely variable rain has caused dramatic changes in seed production by plants on the Galapagos Islands, impacting the foraging success of Darwin's finches.

Even subtle changes can prove catastrophic. In the Antarctic, shifting snowfall patterns have forced Adelies penguins (Pygoscelis adeliae), which once laid eggs on bare stone, to now lay them in snow. Waterlogged eggs fail to hatch, and penguin numbers have dropped precipitously.[15]

Another little-considered impact of global warming is its possible effect on the

New Zealand's tuatara, an ancient reptile, could be at risk from warming climate. Gender is determined by nest temperature, and a 1.8°F (1°C) rise can change developing young from all female to all male.
(Credit: Wildlife Conservation Society)

sex ratio of some animals. For many reptiles, including New Zealand's tuatara *(Sphenodon punctatus)*—a creature more ancient than the dinosaurs—the sex of hatchlings is determined by nest temperature. A 1.8°F (1°C) rise can change developing young from all female to all male. Without quick adaptation to rising temperatures, the tuatara and other reptiles could face extinction.

Pests and Wildfire

In 1827, a British ship emptied casks of stagnant water into a Hawaiian stream, introducing mosquitoes to the island chain. The warmth-loving insects carried avian malaria that devastated endemic lowland honeycreepers. Now, even mountain-dwelling birds are becoming infected, as their high refuges grow warmer and mosquitoes expand their range. Malaria and other mosquito-borne diseases are similarly spreading into the once-cool highlands of Asia, East Africa, and Latin America.

Rising temperatures are increasing both the geographical range and the virulence of some animal and plant diseases. As viruses, bacteria, fungi, and parasites spread, they come into contact with species that lack resistance to them. Adding to this problem, many pathogens and their vectors (mosquitoes, ticks, and rodents) thrive under warmer conditions. In one study, recent climate-driven disease outbreaks were identified in oysters, oaks, birds, butterflies, lions, and corals.[16] In Florida, the number of coral diseases jumped from 5 to 13 during the 1990s, the warmest decade on record.

Fire is another problem aggravated by global warming. In some areas, severe droughts, hotter summers, milder winters, and expanding insect populations combine to create tinder for wildfires. Bark beetles that survive warmer winters are killing trees at unprecedented rates from California to Alaska, providing fuel for record wildfires. By 2002, these beetles had infested over 9 million acres (3.6

million ha) in British Columbia and 4 million (1.6 million ha) more on Alaska's Kenai Peninsula, where officials say that average warming of 5°F (2.8°C) in summer and 10°F (5.5°C) in winter since 1970 has helped the insects reproduce at twice past rates.[17] During a typical Alaskan summer, between 500,000 and 1.5 million acres (200,000–600,000 ha) used to burn; in 2004, over 5 million acres (2 million ha) were destroyed by fire.

Carbon Dioxide and Its Effects

One of the least-understood aspects of CO_2 is its direct impact on plants and animals. Though many past studies have shown that a doubling of atmospheric CO_2 will accelerate plant growth—seemingly beneficial to crops and natural systems—more recent studies hint that additional CO_2 could radically alter ecosystems.

In the Amazon, for example, increased carbon levels are already shifting the competitive balance between tree species. A 15-year study there found two tall, fast-growing canopy species becoming significantly more common, while 14 slower-growing, smaller trees, were becoming rare.[18] And in the United States, experiments have shown that some weedy invasive plants—among the most damaging to the nation's forests—thrive in CO_2-rich environments.[19]

A growing body of research has also recognized another disturbing CO_2-induced phenomenon: "hidden hunger." As atmospheric CO_2 levels rise, the chemical composition of some plants changes, lowering their nutritional value. Nitrogen and protein levels decrease, as do vital micronutrients such as iron and zinc.[20]

> While politicians haggle over the reality of global warming, some of Earth's plants and animals are already responding to it.

Scientists have found that cabbage white butterfly caterpillars (Pieris rapae) living in a chamber with doubled CO_2 levels—as they might exist by 2100—required up to 40 percent more plant matter to survive than controls living under current atmospheric conditions. Other research found that leaf miners living in CO_2-enriched environments, while forced to eat more to survive, were twice as likely to starve to death as those feeding on plants grown in our current atmosphere.[21] Hidden hunger would likely ripple up the food chain, eventually impacting wildlife and people. But far more study is needed to determine if the effect occurs throughout the plant world, and to see if plants can develop adaptive strategies to increase nutrient levels in the face of rising CO_2.

Researchers are also concerned that higher CO_2 levels will also impact sea life. Oceans absorbed 476 billion tons (432 billion t) of CO_2 from 1800 to 1994, nearly half the total released by humans, which acidifies seawater. Further seawater acidification could dissolve calcium carbonate—the building block of calcifying organisms—melting away corals and clam, oyster, and plankton shells, potentially altering the marine food web.[22]

The Interplay of Climate Change with Other Human Stressors

One of the greatest unanswered questions regarding climate change is how it will synergize with other human environmental disturbances to impact the wild.

Global warming may already be worsening air pollution. Longer, hotter summers increase smog, which is created when intense solar heat combines with car and factory emissions to make ozone. Smog bleaches and burns plant cells and the lungs of animals, and is known to harm 30 tree species in US national parks.[23]

More frequent extreme weather events could also intensify water pollution. Flooding from Hurricane Floyd in 1999, for example, flushed millions of gallons of untreated industrial hog farm waste into North Carolina waterways, poisoning aquatic ecosystems. Likewise, extreme drought can turn a polluted world more toxic: as waterways dry up, pesticides and sewage become more concentrated, killing fish.

Global warming could also decrease some agricultural yields due to coastal flooding, storms, drought, and increased plant pests. But with human population expected to grow to about 9 billion this century, heightened competition for scarce food resources could put extraordinary human pressure on existing wildlands and wildlife.

A 2003 report from an unlikely source adds food for thought. The US Pentagon examined the national security implications of an unlikely but possible abrupt climate change scenario—a global warming–induced stalling of deep-sea ocean currents, precipitating a sudden new ice age. Such an event could result in global war in a grab for sparse resources that would spell serious endangerment for the wild.

> Researchers planetwide are finding examples of a natural world "growing out of sync with itself."

What's to Be Done?

In the face of such huge and potentially catastrophic impacts, the only sane choice is to immediately curb fossil fuel use. Some energy experts propose a new Manhattan Project, mobilizing the world's technological, economic, and political muscle to end fossil fuel dependence and convert to wind, solar, and hydrogen power. But even if we cut CO_2 emissions to zero today, we could still endure major climate shocks caused by already-released greenhouse gases. A massive infusion of money and global cooperation is needed now for research into climate change and its ecosystem impacts—and for the creation of better forecasting tools.

Capital may be needed to relocate species in a warmer world. In order to keep pace with changing climate zones, emergency programs to replant temperate forests may be needed to keep pace with shifting climate zones. New wildlife corridors—natural byways that lead through the maze of human infrastructure—

could also be needed. Such corridors exist on a small scale in places such as British Columbia and Florida, where green bridges and tunnels provide passage for bears and panthers over and under roadways. There are also large-scale examples: the Paseo Pantera project, launched in 1990, is creating a green corridor from Panama to Guatemala. Such models could be duplicated around the world.

Zoos and so-called "frozen zoos" could continue to act as arks, preserving live animals and cryogenically frozen genetic material. But they will become especially important if climate change accelerates, preserving diversity and serving as breeding pens for species that might be reintroduced later to restored ecosystems.

However, the best solutions to these complex problems are probably yet to be discovered. We have barely begun to understand the mechanisms of climate change and their impacts on living things (see color plate 21).

Toward the Unknown

During the Precambrian era, anaerobic bacteria, poisoned by a rush of atmospheric oxygen, were incapable of avoiding extinction. Now humanity has a chance to show that our intelligence gives us an adaptive edge that those lowly microorganisms lacked. We must heed climatologists' warnings to redirect technology and take steps to protect ecosystems.

But can we act in time and with unity? Can we focus the will and wisdom of the world's people on curbing planetwide climate change? Our past record of devastation—wrought on ecosystems and our own kind—doesn't bode well.

There is one certainty: no species in Earth's history has ever been capable of standing at a pivotal moment in its evolution, analyzing its destructive behaviors, and then deciding to change course with the intent of saving itself and its fellow creatures.

Perhaps humans will be the first to make the right choice for all. We shall see.

The Gathering Wave
of Ocean Extinctions

ELLEN K. PIKITCH

The myth of resource inexhaustibility has plagued human civilizations for centuries, but this myth has been held more tenaciously for the sea than for any other place on Earth. The ocean was believed to be so vast, impenetrable, and filled with riches that its bounty was considered endless. During the past century we have witnessed a massive diminution of ocean wildlife, including the loss of 90 percent of top ocean predators[1] and the collapse of some of the sea's greatest and longest-reigning fisheries. Our understanding has been revised: economic and ecological extinction have been recognized as real possibilities. Yet the prospect of irreversible loss in the sea continues to be incomprehensible to many.

But there have been ocean extinctions, some occurring centuries ago, others within the last 50 years. Among these were sea mammals, including the Steller's sea cow *(Hydrodamalis gigas),* the largest animal in the manatee/dugong family. This giant creature was highly prized for its meat, which supposedly tasted like veal. The last known animal was killed in 1768, just 27 years after it was discovered by the naturalist Georg Wilhelm Steller off the coast of Kamchatka. The sea mink *(Mustela macrodon),* believed to have ranged from New England to southern Canada's rocky shores, was exterminated for its silky coat by 1894. And during the 1600s, aggressive hunting of the Caribbean monk seal *(Monachus tropicalis)* for its oil and skin caused its numbers to plummet, though some survivors held on. The last confirmed sighting of the seal was in Serranilla Bank, halfway between Jamaica and Nicaragua, in 1952.

In the ensuing years, other marine life has joined their ranks. By 2003, the local, regional, and global marine extinction toll stood at 133 species, including birds, fishes, corals, and even algae.[2] But total extinctions are probably underestimated. They occur silently in the sea, are difficult to detect, and many ocean species remain yet undiscovered. The pace of extinctions has quickened, especially during the past 40 years—but even more alarming is the possibility that known extinctions could merely be the forerunners of a gathering wave.

Bycatch mortality has resulted in an 89 percent decline of hammerhead sharks in the Northeast Atlantic in less than 20 years.
(Credit: Steve Winter/National Geographic Image Collection)

The belief that fish are extinction-proof may be the most enduring myth of all, possibly because of the relatively few global fish extinctions that have been observed during our current geological timeframe. Thus far, none of them has been attributed to exploitation,[3] but that could change by the time this essay appears in print. A number of species teeter on the brink.

We are only now beginning to observe fish extinctions attributed to fishing: large-scale, industrial fishing is a relatively recent phenomenon that began after World War II. The typical lag time between the last sighting of a species and documented extinction is about half a century.

Fishing is the leading cause of all extinction in the sea, accounting for just over half, while habitat destruction weighs in at a close second, at over one-third. The past 50 years have seen an enormous increase in the quantity, efficiency, depth, and extent of fishing. Marine fish catches rose 300 percent between 1950 and 1992,[4] spurred by rapid technological innovation. The first factory processor was a converted whaling ship, reworked in Scotland and launched in 1954. It immediately headed for Newfoundland cod fishing grounds, and within two years, the Soviets launched two dozen factory ships. But industrial fishing really took off as World War II and Cold War technology filtered to the private sector, with diesel engines that could haul in huge nets with mechanical winches and surveillance technology such as sonar and radar that left no place for fish to hide.

Some of these industrial fishing methods also decimate habitat. Bottom trawling, huge nets dragged along the ocean floor, rips up reefs and sea plants as nets engulf everything in their path, literally emptying the sea of life. It is widely regarded as one of the most destructive of all contemporary fishing methods.[5] Bottom trawling now occurs across about half of the world's continental shelves, an area 150 times greater than the amount of forestland clear-cut each year.[6,7]

Another source of the belief that fish are extinction-proof stems from the idea that their reproductive output is, in many cases, enormous. It is not uncommon for fishes to produce hundreds, thousands, or even millions of eggs at one time. But sheer quantity is not sufficient to ensure survival, and scientific evidence is mounting that the reproductive output of fish does not guarantee their resilience.[8] It is because the odds of survival are so overwhelmingly small that so many eggs are produced: most of the eggs produced by so-called broadcast spawners are small, provisioned with minimal nutrients, and as a rule, although these young hatchlings have limited mobility, they must fend for themselves without the benefit of parental care.

The World's Most Imperiled Fishes

Which fishes do we have the greatest risk of losing first? Many factors influence the likelihood of extinction, but it is clear that we should take a close look at uniquely valuable species, those that are highly sought after by humans, and those that are particularly vulnerable to the ravages of fishing and other human-induced disturbances. This discussion will focus on a few concrete examples of species groups that meet each of these broad criteria: the sturgeons, sharks, and croakers.

Sturgeons

Sturgeons and their close relatives, the paddlefish, are ancient fish that are the highly prized sources of black caviar. According to the *Guinness Book of World Records,* the beluga sturgeon *(Huso huso)* holds the record as the most valuable fish in the world.[9] A beluga caught in Russia's Tikhaya Sosna River in 1924 yielded 540 pounds (245 kg) of the best-quality caviar—which would have fetched $289,000 then—but today, at an estimated market value of $130 per ounce (28 g), that fish would fetch a whopping $1,123,200.

The beluga sturgeon is the world's largest freshwater fish species, reaching lengths of nearly 20 feet (6 m), weighing over 6,600 pounds (3,000 kg)—and can live a century or more. But intense fishing pressure, fueled by the extremely lucrative international caviar market, has caused steep population declines in belugas as well as other sturgeon and paddlefish (see color plate 24).

This group of fishes has a whole suite of life history characteristics that makes them especially vulnerable. While sturgeons spend most of their lives at sea, adults migrate at predictable times of year to spawn in freshwater. There, they fall easy prey to fishing as they enter the human lair through river mouths and into the relatively shallow waters of their natal rivers. This makes them susceptible to human impacts in a diversity of terrestrial and aquatic realms.

> [Extinctions] occur silently in the sea, are difficult to detect, and many ocean species remain yet undiscovered.

Trawl surveys in 2002 revealed a 39 percent decline of beluga sturgeon in the Caspian Sea over the previous year.
(Credit: Hans-Jurgen Burkard/ Bilderberg, courtesy Caviar Emptor)

Logging, dam-building, dredging, pollution, and water extraction have each taken their toll on sturgeon.

They are relatively long-lived fish that grow, mature, and reproduce slowly. About half these species first spawn at the age of 15, and most species spawn only every three or four years thereafter.[10] Late maturity and periodic spawning make recovery of depleted sturgeon populations a slow and precarious proposition. Although they release huge numbers of eggs, this does not confer immunity against extinction. Beluga sturgeon, for example, release anywhere from 360,000 to 7 million eggs in one year, but the species declined by 90 percent over the last two decades.

Sturgeon and paddlefish are listed as endangered or threatened, depending upon the species, and some protection is afforded by national and international management authorities. But current conservation measures do not address the full range of threats faced by these fish, nor do they ensure their long-term survival. Although the unsustainable nature of sturgeon fisheries has been recognized for decades, a burgeoning illegal harvest and trade continues, further driving major caviar fisheries to the brink of collapse. Illegal Russian caviar exports have been estimated at close to $400 million, with the illegal catch estimated at 6 to 11 times greater than the legal catch.[11–13] The total legal international trade halved from 1995 to 2003, from 326 tons (296 t) to a global quota of 160 tons (145 t).

The caviar trade in combination with overfishing, habitat destruction, and pollution has led to ever-shrinking geographic ranges and has caused local extinctions of 19 out of the 27 sturgeon and paddlefish species. The ship sturgeon *(Acipenser nudiventris)* is believed to be locally extinct in the Aral Sea. The beluga sturgeon is gone from the Adriatic Sea, and the shovelnose sturgeon *(Scaphirhynchus platorynchus)* is extinct in three US states (New Mexico, North Carolina, and

Pennsylvania). The American paddlefish *(Polyodon spathula)* is no longer found in Ontario and four US states, (Maryland, North Carolina, Pennsylvania, and New York), and the lake sturgeon *(Acipenser fulvescens)* is thought to be extinct in four states (Alabama, Arkansas, Mississippi, and West Virginia). The Syr Dar shovel-nose sturgeon *(Pseudoscaphirhynchincus fedtschenkoi)* may have disappeared altogether: intense water diversion has eliminated the connection between the Aral Sea and the Syr Dar River in Kazakhstan, the fish's only known spawning habitat.

Preventing further sturgeon extinctions will take a concerted effort to reduce or eliminate key threats combined with a comprehensive recovery program. For many species, a long-term moratorium on fishing is needed to avert irreversible loss. Such an approach was adopted for Atlantic sturgeon, which collapsed at the turn of the 20th century. They are now on a path toward recovery, with catches prohibited under a moratorium declared in 1998 that is expected to last 41 years.

Croakers

Another group of seriously threatened fishes are scianids, commonly referred to as croakers or drums. One of these, the totoaba *(Totoaba macdonaldi)* has the dubious distinction of being the first marine fish to come under the protection of the Convention on International Trade in Endangered Species (CITES). This massive fish—up to 6.5 feet long (2 m) and weighing up to 220 pounds (100 kg)—is threatened in both its Colorado River nursery grounds and the northern Gulf of California where it spends its adult life. As water has been diverted from the Colorado, the brackish waters near the river mouth have continued to shrink—and with it, the fish's nursery ground. While at sea, the totoaba has been heavily overfished. Despite 30 years at the highest level of CITES protection (Appendix I), the species has not recovered.[14]

In the early 1930s, another giant croaker species, the Chinese bahaba *(Bahaba taipingensis)* was discovered in Chinese fish markets, and later found to exclusively inhabit the Chinese coast. It was heavily fished, and by 1988, it was listed as a State Protected Species in China—and was commercially extinct in Hong Kong by 1997.

Both the bahaba and the totoaba can produce millions of eggs each year but share characteristics that make them highly vulnerable to extinction: extremely limited geographic range and a tendency to amass close to shore at predictable times. They also alert fishermen to their whereabouts when making a unique "drumming" sound, which is produced by muscles vibrated against their swim bladders. Fishermen used to find them by placing an ear to the ship's hull before sonar came along.

Those swim bladders could cause the ultimate demise of this fish, as they are highly prized ingredients in traditional Asian medicine, and their value has sky-rocketed with the bahaba's growing scarcity. Among fishermen, the Chinese bahaba swim bladder is known as "soft gold." In 2001, it was literally worth about

The totoaba currently faces extinction. A 1953 sportfishing catch in Baja California, Mexico, is pictured here; poaching of the critically endangered croaker continues in the Sea of Cortez.

(Credit: Tony Reyes Baca, Tony Reyes Fishing Tours, San Felipe, B.C., Mexico)

seven times its weight in gold and individual bladders have sold for as much as $64,000.[14]

Overfishing, lack of management, escalating value, and heavily exploited coastal habitats together have severely diminished the numbers of these giant croakers. The only hope for their future lies in severe cutbacks in fishing and protection within their geographic range.

Sharks, Skates, and Rays

The first recorded local marine fish extinction was the so-called common skate *(Raia batis)* from the Irish Sea,[15] which was last sighted in the early 1980s. It was an innocent bystander, a bycatch victim of bottom trawling. Disappearances of other skate species, the long-nose skate *(Dipturus oxyrhinchus)* and the white skate *(Rostroraja alba),* as well as an angel shark *(Squatina squatina),* have since been noted in the same location.

Other huge declines of sharks, rays, and skates have been observed. Just 1 percent of oceanic whitetip sharks *(Carcharhinus longimanus)* remain in the Gulf of Mexico.[16] This shark was once thought to be the most abundant vertebrate in the entire Gulf, so common it was considered a nuisance by fishermen who unavoidably encountered whitetips in their pursuit of tuna (see color plate 22).

A recent shark assessment in Australasia found that 34 of the 175 species studied were threatened with global extinction, with 12 more species regionally threatened in Australia or Southeast Asia.[17] Deepwater sharks were disproportionately represented in the most critically endangered category, despite the relatively recent expansion of fishing into deepwater. Given the exemplary reputation of Australia and New Zealand in shark research and management, these statistics do not bode well for sharks in less protected portions of the globe.

> Fishing is the leading cause of all extinction in the sea, accounting for just over half, while habitat destruction weighs in at a close second, at over one-third.

Sharks, skates, and rays are particularly slow to recover once depleted. Like the sturgeon, they mature late and grow slowly, but unlike most other fish, they bear relatively few live young or lay few eggs—which is a major liability. This set of traits served them well for more than 400 million years but now places sharks and their close relatives in jeopardy, as humans have replaced sharks as the foremost predator of ocean life. Some shark species may have already gone extinct. Among them is the Pondicherry shark *(Carcharhinus hemiodon),* which has not been seen for two decades despite surveys throughout much of its range in the Indo-Pacific.

Great white sharks outfitted with satellite transmitters have been tracked across thousands of miles of open ocean. But they are in danger everywhere they go; they are globally threatened with extinction in such far-flung places as South Africa, both coasts of North America, the Adriatic Sea, and Australia, where they are known as "white death." They are often killed, as they are greatly

A 13-foot great white shark investigates a research boat near Seal Island, South Africa. In 2004, the great white was listed as "vulnerable" by CITES.
(Credit: Neil Hammerschlag/PEW Institute for Ocean Science)

feared as man-eaters. They are also accidentally caught in nets, drowned on fishing lines, and trophy-hunted for their impressive jaws that command up to $50,000, with a single tooth netting hundreds of dollars. The great white shark is also a victim of the accelerating, unregulated, and highly lucrative trade in shark fins: shark fin soup is a delicacy that sells in Asia for more than $100 per bowl (see color plate 6).

Recent studies have documented great white population declines ranging from 60 to 95 percent in various areas of the ocean over the past half century. This behemoth, up to 20 feet long (6 m) and weighing well over a ton, takes about 15 years to sexually mature; after that, females produce only a handful of pups every two or three years. In October 2004, the great white shark was given international protection. It was listed on Appendix II of CITES, which may help stem further declines of this important species through the control of trade in rare jaws, teeth, and fins (see color plate 23).

It is time to replace the old myth of the sea's inexhaustibility with understanding of the fragile and limited nature of ocean dwellers. Already, dozens of marine animals have been pushed beyond the point of no return, gone for all time. Still more are critically endangered. We are pushing against the boundaries of the sea's resilience, testing its limits, and if we don't pull back hard and fast we may soon see a great wave of ocean extinctions rushing in (see color plate 24).

There is still time to conserve the largest and most biologically rich place on Earth, but we cannot afford to wait for further clarification of the oceanic crisis before taking action. Today we can hear the sounding of the alarm by the simple act of placing an ear to the hull, but if we forgo action now, even the sonar will read silent after the great wave has passed.

Conservation Strategies for Colonial and Social Species

WILLIAM CONWAY

There is majesty in great wildlife congregations, a grandeur in their profusion. A wildebeest migration on the Serengeti, a great seal rookery in Alaska, an albatross city in the Falklands, or even a horseshoe crab congregation on a Maryland beach can call forth feelings of awe and a sense of life's primal significance apart from humanity. These gatherings have astonished and inspired us since we were first capable of inspiration. Their decline or disappearance diminishes our world ecologically as well as aesthetically.

Some colonial and highly social species are still common and a few, such as most seals and sea lions, have recovered from uncontrolled slaughter. But some are considered pests: Argentina's threatened burrowing parrots (Cyanoliseus patagonus), Africa's bush pigs (Potamochoerus porcus), and even gorillas are among the many animals that eat cultivated crops and are hated by farmers.

Whether admired or hated, most assemblages of large wild animals are disappearing because of overhunting and exploitation, conflict with invasive species, and habitat destruction. Conservation efforts focusing on their plight are rare, despite the fact that they are almost always of exceptional ecological and conservation importance because they affect the lives of innumerable other species. Except for birds, even the status of most congregatory species is unclear. This essay addresses their significance, the reasons why they exist, and some of the conservation strategies necessary to their survival. But first, what or who are they?

Colonial and congregating species are distinguished by regular gatherings when a large part of their populations converge, and usually by the constancy of their use of particular places. While birds and mammals make up only a minority of such species, their size and lifestyles make them both exceptionally familiar and vulnerable. Hence, they provide some general insights and strategies for congregatory species conservation.

Among birds, wood storks, egrets, penguins, gannets and terns, oilbirds, some parrots, some Asiatic vultures, most weaverbirds, and all flamingos are colonial.

For flamingos and other congregatory birds, the number of successful breeding colonies is almost as important as the number of individual birds. Cuba's Maximo River Faunal Refuge protects important nesting grounds for Caribbean flamingoes, pictured here.
(Credit: Steve Winter/National Geographic Image Collection)

Colonial mammal species include prairie dogs, fur seals, sea lions, and many bats, among others. These animals breed almost exclusively in groups and rear their young in more or less isolated rookeries and colonies. Although wildebeest, mandrills, geladas, macaws, cranes, caribou, zebras, buffaloes, river hippos, marine iguanas, and peccaries are not colonial, at some stage in their life cycles, they assemble in large groups to breed, feed, or travel. They associate in herds, flocks, or extended families and usually in particular places, if not in fixed colonies. Moreover, the birthing or hatching of their young is often synchronized, although parenting may be accomplished on-the-walk, if not on-the-run, or left to chance (see color plate 25).

Over half of the world's 24,000 marine and freshwater fishes, such as grunion and groupers, also show some kind of congregating behavior, as do many frogs, toads, and salamanders—as well as thousands of invertebrates, from horseshoe crabs (Limulus polyphemus) to monarch butterflies (Danaus plexippus).

Large associations of such species occur at rich sources of food, often on migration routes, as in the case of many antelope, geese, shorebirds, and some whales and dolphins. Congregations also occur in places that are especially favorable for depositing eggs or giving birth, such as some of the laying sites of megapodes—pheasants or turkey-like birds—and sea turtles. The majority of the larger megapodes and six of the seven sea turtle species are endangered.

Most conservationists are focused upon those areas of the world inhabited by a high diversity of species. These "hotspots" are, at one and the same time, crucibles of evolution and cenotaphs to life's history. However, sizeable congregations of birds and mammals are likely to be elsewhere. Although variety may be the "spice of life," it is not always its essence. Their spice has more to do with biomass than biodiversity and, since humans appeared, congregating has become a

Black-browed albatross breeding colonies in the Falkland Islands host over 85 percent of the global population. For this and other congregatory species, habit protection is crucial.
(Credit: William Karesh)

dangerous behavior,—as the passing of 9 billion passenger pigeons *(Ectopistes migratorius),* 50 million bison *(Bison bison),* the great auks *(Pinguinus impennis),* vast numbers of springbok *(Antidorcas marsupialis),* and, recently, the decline of the majority of commercially hunted schooling fishes—attests. The nature and history of these intensely social species provokes three questions:

- Why should such animal assemblages be a high priority for conservationists?
- Why do they exist, anyway?
- How can we assure that they will persist?

Why Should the Fate of Colonies and Other Gatherings of Larger Species Be a Priority for Conservationists?

Despite the Lilliputian scale of their terrestrial sites, great cities of penguins, albatrosses, cormorants, and flamingos, as well as the big rookeries of terns, ibises, seals, and sea lions are the nurseries of wildlife populations that range over vast regions. These colonial creatures, along with the great congregatory herds of mammals such as caribou and antelopes, the migratory flocks of geese, even the breeding associations of frogs and salamanders, of fishes and invertebrates, impact both their individual niches and their ecosystems in ways that less concentrated species cannot.

For animals that breed only in colonies, the number of effectively breeding colonies is nearly as important as the number of breeding pairs.

Imagine the impact of, say, 400,000 Serengeti wildebeest *(Connochaetes taurinus),* weighing a total of perhaps 80,000 tons (72,600 t), as they maintain the savanna free of trees like a vast mowing machine, providing fertilizer as they go. Consider the 45,000 to 50,000 southern elephant seals *(Mirounga leonina)* of Argentine Patagonia, which consume over 330,000 tons (300,000 t) of invertebrates and fishes each year, or the 1.5 million lesser flamingos *(Phoenicopterus minor),* which periodically descend upon Kenya's Lake Nakuru, straining about 113 tons (103 t) of blue-green algae and invertebrates from its poisonous waters daily. While the numbers of such creatures may hold us spellbound, their concentrated foraging determines the nature of entire communities of other animals and plants.

For animals that breed only in colonies, the number of effectively breeding colonies is nearly as important as the number of breeding pairs, and for species that form regular breeding assemblages, the number of secure congregations is the unit of safety.

Because they concentrate in small areas, most colonial species and many breeding and feeding associations of social species are easily destroyed. They are evolutionary and ecological contradictions: dangerously vulnerable wildlife superpowers. But how can species that number thousands of individuals in a single colony be considered threatened?

Entire populations of congregating species are now dependent on a very few locations for breeding, feeding, or migration. Consequently, to preserve them, we must identify and prioritize congregations. For example, 90 percent of all lesser flamingos now breed in one Tanzanian lake and 85 percent of all James' flamingos (P. jamesi) breed at one Bolivian lake.

The most detailed attempt to classify critical colonial and social bird species sites is the work of BirdLife International and its Important Bird Area (IBA) program. BirdLife uses four criteria, one or more of which must apply. The site must:

- Hold, on a regular basis, 1 percent or more of a congregatory water bird species that is restricted to a particular zoogeographic region
- Hold 1 percent or more of a species' global population
- Hold at least 20,000 water birds or 10,000 pairs of seabirds
- Be a bottleneck site where at least 20,000 birds pass regularly on migration

BirdLife adds that the site should also be different in character from the surrounding area and exist as an actual or potential protected area. Many critically important sites where threatened species other than birds congregate will not fit these criteria, but they clearly set forth the nature of the selection challenge. More than 2,000 IBAs have already been designated and BirdLife International has now published *State of the World's Birds 2004*.

Conservation International, in dealing with the entire zoological realm and its relative scarcity of population information, has offered a simplified criterion: individual sites holding more than 1 percent of a particular species' global population in a particular place at a particular time. The Ramsar Convention on Wetlands, the American Bird Conservancy, and other conservation programs use comparable criteria.

Why Do Wild Animal Congregations Exist?

To explain congregations, we have to believe that the advantages of intensely social behavior are more compelling than the disadvantages of crowds. After all, colony members, herds, and flocks face greater competition for food and more exposure to disease. Large numbers also create rivalry over nesting space for birds, roosting space for bats, and harem space for sea lions. Worse yet, colonies and congregations provide an overflowing buffet for the predators that can reach them. Additionally, the constancy of colony locations and the routes of migratory animals make them regularly accessible to experienced predators, especially human beings. There are few more depressing chapters in natural history than that of the human slaughter of wildlife congregations. Nevertheless, when humans are absent, colonies and social assemblages clearly work.

Southern sea lions at Peninsula Valdés, Argentina. Sea lions mate and breed synchronously with hundreds of others; pups are somewhat protected from predators by sheer numbers. This simultaneous birthing system also promotes group bonding among pups. (Credit: Claudio Campagna)

Colony sites are only partly determined by proximity to food. Although food attracts animal concentrations, proximity is a relative term. Penguins can make foraging trips within a radius of 35 miles (56 km) or more from their colonies and still get back in time to feed their young. Sea lions can cover more than 90 miles (145 km), and albatrosses can soar over thousands of miles. However, breeding groups (not colonies) of nonflyers such as grazing antelopes and caribou need food immediately at hand, and for mammal herds, this usually means that they must keep moving. At breeding time, their herds can almost be viewed as walking rookeries.

Animals acquire a great deal of information about the availability of food by monitoring the actions of others, and there is no better place to do so than in a group. Social cues reveal the location and even the quality of food to many species. By watching, smelling, tasting, and even listening, they make use of what animal behaviorists call "public information"—information not purposefully conveyed but there to be observed. The tendency to imitate even affects habitat choice; thus the formation of colonies—and of breeding and foraging groups. This has been demonstrated in animals as different as lekking antelope (*Kobus* spp.) in Africa and gull-like kittiwakes *(Rissa tridactyla)* in the Northern Hemisphere. Imitation has been shown to affect mate choice and response to predation as well.

Much of what we know about colonial species has an avian slant. Ninety-eight percent of all seabirds nest in colonies. In theory, a colony divides the predator's attention: the larger the colony, the smaller the risk of being eaten. Crudely, the concept is also applicable to herds of zebras, wildebeest, and caribou; schools of fishes; and even big troops of baboons—although some predators can pick out a herd's most vulnerable members no matter what its numbers are. Still, the pro-

tective effects of crowd confusion, as with plains zebras *(Equus quagga)*, or group-reinforced belligerence, as with African buffalo *(Syncerus caffer)* and Arctic musk ox *(Ovibos moschatus)*, are clear.

If herds and colonies confer protection by dividing predation threats, being near their center rather than their edges ought to be safest, and it usually is. The average numbers of Patagonian imperial cormorant *(Phalacrocorax atriceps)*, royal tern *(Sterna maxima)*, and cayenne tern *(S. eurygnatha)* eggs and chicks that survive in the central parts of their colonies are much higher than those in nests on the periphery. Can you picture a single pair of terns, penguins, or flamingos raising its young alone in a world of foxes, skunks, wild cats, hawks, skuas, gulls, and other predators? Colonies enhance vigilance, and colonial birds often are effective mobbers and bombers. Even sea lion pups survive better in colonies.

In addition, colonies and social assemblages bring the sexes together, enhancing the process of mate choice while the "social facilitation" of massed courtship activity helps put everyone's reproductive hormones on the same schedule, thus providing the peculiar benefits of birthing, hatching, and rearing all at the same time.

Because of such synchronization, the hungry fox in the bird colony or lioness in the wildebeest herd is suddenly flooded with chicks or calves—more than it can possibly eat—so some will survive. But such costly predator satiation is most successful as a long-term defense when followed by predator starvation. Suppose you are a fox raising your cubs near a nesting seabird colony. Masses of chicks, easy pickings, are available all at once. You gorge. So do your cubs. Soon, however, your supermarket flies or swims away as the colony completes its breeding season. Suitable prey living nearby is rare. You starve. Most of your cubs die.

Reproductive synchronization, combined with alternating cycles of predator satiation and starvation, can minimize the number of predators awaiting the colony next season. Even oak trees use this sacrificial strategy. Some years, oaks produce only a few acorns, minimizing the number of squirrels that can survive the winter. Then, in a subsequent year, the trees produce a flood of acorns, so many that at least a few are sure to survive the depredations of the minimized squirrel population and get a chance to sprout. However, neither the benefits of mate choice, colony defense, nor reproductive synchronization will sustain colonial species in the absence of a suitable breeding site.

Colonial species must find areas where ground predators are rare or nonexistent: cliffs, steep banks, and islands at sea or amidst impassably muddy *lagunas,* remote stands of trees in swamps, isolated beaches, and headlands, often far from covering vegetation and fresh water. Such places are usually widely separated and, consequently, so are colonies, making distances between predation opportunities forbidding. Thus, beyond feeding and migratory congregations, the main reasons for colonies and social breeding assemblages are defense, the availability of public information, reproduction, and the tendency to gather in sites that may be near food and are relatively free from disturbance. None work in the absence of that last qualification.

How Can We Assure That Great Wildlife Colonies and Congregations Persist?

Over 90 percent of gray-headed albatrosses *(Diomedea chrysostoma)* nest within about 800 feet (244 m) of where they hatch. On Midway Island, albatrosses *(Diomedea immutabilis)* nest within 72 feet (22 m) of the nest where they were born, even though they do not nest at all until they are eight or nine years old. Green turtles *(Chelonia mydas),* which do not nest until over the age of 20, return to the same sandy beaches where they hatched to lay their own eggs. Southern sea lion *(Otaria flavescens)* bulls choose that familiar stretch of featureless beach where they have established their harems before, and penguins nest where they themselves were raised. The vast majority of congregating birds and mammals, of reptiles and amphibians, and of many invertebrates are tied to the places where they were born and the migratory routes that they, their parents, and even their great-great-grandparents have long followed. And they are often attached to each other.

Thus, for colonial and social species, protection of traditional breeding and congregating sites is conservation's first strategy. Second is the use of their presence as a major criterion of conservation priority, focusing efforts and establishing protected areas and zones responsive to them. Third is ensuring that the social or colonial species' own protective strategies are not disabled, especially their reproductive, synchronization, and predator satiation/starvation behaviors, within an overall strategy.

Lasting conservation strategies require not only the determination and analysis of the threats to each species of concern—within the context of its landscape—but also ongoing monitoring and responsive action, particularly in the ever-lengthening shadows of the unexpected.

Zebra herds often graze with other species, such as wildebeests, which helps protect individual zebras from becoming easy targets for predators.
(Credit: Joshua Ginsberg)

Global increases in human activity have made the long arm of unexpected consequences a serious threat to wildlife of every kind, especially to species that congregate—and their effects are damnably difficult to anticipate. Invasive species, disease, habitat destruction, and overhunting are challenging enough. But humans also feed some predators of congregatory species all year with a constant stream of both tasty garbage and badly protected domestic animals, thus rupturing colony site selection and predator starvation strategies. Foxes, gulls, hyenas, feral dogs, cats, and other enemies multiply. In Patagonia, for example, excessive numbers of gulls *(Larus dominicanus)* now not only kill more penguin and cormorant chicks but have also begun to seriously harass southern right whales *(Eubalaena australis),* landing on their backs and biting out chunks of skin and blubber. Response requires public education, distasteful predator control, waste management, and long-term conservation commitments.

Although no species is ever more secure than its current state of protection, many colonial and congregatory species have made heartening comebacks. For example, North America's northern elephant seal *(Mirounga angustirostris),* American bison, and great egret *(Ardea alba)* have all recovered from near disappearance thanks to successful conservation efforts. The Serengeti wildebeest, the South African blesbok *(Damaliscus dorcas),* the Costa Rican population of the green turtle, and the South American sea lion are growing in numbers. And there is now evidence that the great blue whale—which at 200 tons (180 t) is the largest animal that has ever lived—is beginning to recover too (see color plate 26).

Fortunately, many wildlife colonies and social species provide fascinating and beautiful spectacles. They attract tourism and stimulate local supporters. Moreover, the present-day conservationist's task of addressing wildlife protection by bringing together appropriate stakeholders with whom wildlife shares resources in a science-based process of consensus building and analytic deliberation is increasingly better equipped. Penetrating scientific studies and the developing technologies of landscape ecology and geographic information system mapping have brought powerful tools to the conservation table.

Ultimately, however, success in saving wildlife's marvelous colonies and congregations depends upon making their stories known and making their wonder and beauty a matter of human pride and appreciation—and, as with all wildlife conservation, reaching the human heart.

Passenger pigeons once migrated across the eastern United States in flocks so vast that their numbers darkened the sky. In 1808, a single flock in Kentucky was estimated at 2 billion birds. By 1914, the species had been hunted to extinction in the wild.

(Credit: BirdLife International)

From "Inversnaid"

What would the world be, once bereft
Of wet and of wildness? Let them be left,
O let them be left, wildness and wet;
Long live the weeds and the wilderness yet.

G. M. HOPKINS
(ENGLAND, 1844–1889)

PART VI

WILDLANDS AND OCEANS

The essays in this section take on vastly different conservation issues, but have many threads in common. Each of these authors writes about places they know well, love, and have fought for years to protect, in one case, a rich valley in the western United States, and in the other, a Caribbean reef. These locations act as a microcosm: they are endangered by many of the same things that threaten other US wilderness areas and similar seascapes. On land, the constant quest for resources is driving destruction of pristine forests, grasslands, and mountain regions, and development brings ever-more roads and humans. Undersea life is under siege ocean-wide from overfishing.

Environmental author Rick Bass uses his home in the Yaak Valley of Montana as a basis for examining changing US management policies that are impacting wildlife and wildlands. Marine biologist Callum Roberts describes how fish populations around St. Lucia's reefs have rebounded since a bold new management plan created marine protected areas there in 1995. He also describes unprecedented moves towards ocean protection around the globe in response to alarming fish declines.

These two essays illuminate how changes in land management and overharvesting the sea impact all the creatures that inhabit or use these places—for better or worse.

The Land the Wilderness Act Forgot

RICK BASS

I've always been leery of the world-in-a-grain-of-sand idea—the provincial notion that by understanding, say, the Yaak Valley in extreme northwestern Montana, you can understand national or international issues. And yet, in these days of steadily increasing antiwilderness policies cascading out of Washington, D.C., you'll have to forgive me, if only to make the entire subject more manageable, for considering that my own tiny square of the world contains nearly every contemporary environmental woe that might somehow conspire against wilderness.

My postage stamp of a valley is somewhat unique. Though it's wild and vibrant, the Yaak still doesn't have a single acre of protected wilderness. But like other wild places around the country, that wildness is under attack. Both the Yaak, and the American wilderness—eons in the making—are being disassembled, piece-by-piece, by the people who should be protecting it.

In many ways, our country faces the worst of both worlds. The vitality is being drained from our remaining wilderness—we don't have enough wildlands left untouched—and we still haven't adequately protected that which most needs preserving.

Scientists around the world largely agree that in order to maintain the character and content of wild and native landscapes in a viable, sustaining fashion, a well-planned minimum of 12 percent of that landscape needs protection. Excluding Alaska, only 2 percent of the United States—in theory, the world leader in such matters—is protected under the gold standard of US land management classifications: wilderness.

The million-acre island of the Yaak, with its soft, low, verdant hills, at the lowest elevation in Montana (1,880 feet or 573 meters), represents the kinds of land that the Wilderness Act forgot, or overlooked, 40-plus years ago.

The Yaak Valley is 97 percent public land, a beguiling mix of richness and diversity: Montana's only rain forest, home to giant Ponderosa and other pines, cedar, hemlock, spruce, aspen, cottonwood, and many more tree species. It was hard-logged in the past, though roughly one-third of the landscape remains pristine. It's believed that nothing's gone extinct here since the Pleistocene, that we still have a full array of predators and prey, from grizzly and black bears *(Ursus arctos, U. americanus),* lynx *(Lynx canadensis),* wolverine *(Gulo gulo),* and marten *(Martes americana),* to bald and golden eagles *(Haliaeetus leucocephalus, Aquila chrysaetos),* bull and westslope cutthroat trout *(Salvelinus confluentus, Oncorhynchus clarkia lewisi),* bighorn sheep *(Ovis canadensis),* and gray wolves *(Canis lupus).*

However, many of these populations have dipped to double- or even single-digit numbers, and it's been over 15 years since there was a verified sighting of a woodland caribou *(Rangifer tarandus).* Once-abundant porcupines *(Erethizon dorsatum)* are also apparently absent. Only one has been seen in many years; some Native American tribes describe their absence as a harbinger of ecological ill health. No amount of money can completely restore these intricate and sophisticated, interlocked species, once they are gone from so complex and rich an ecosystem.

Still, it is all here, even if in bits and pieces, like a reverse kind of Noah's Ark; the tail end of a miracle.

Perhaps the greatest chance the Yaak had of securing a protected wild core, a wild heart, existed in the Roadless Area Conservation Rule, developed over three years by the Clinton administration with public comments from almost 2 million respondents. Over 95 percent of them favored permanent protection for the last remaining roadless areas in unbroken wildlands 1,000 acres (405 ha) or larger on national forest lands administered by the US Forest Service. The Roadless Rule, which protected 58.5 million acres (23.7 million ha) of such lands, was later disassembled by the Bush administration.

In his confirmation hearings, former attorney general John Ashcroft vowed to uphold the rule, then failed to defend it against various lawsuits brought by extractive industries such as Boise-Cascade Timber, which claimed, among other things, that there had been no public participation in the rulemaking process. The administration then proposed turning the decision-making process for these lands over to individual governors, making them vulnerable to the volatilities of local politics. As a result, the nation runs the risk of losing its most forward-looking and commonsense conservation measure. At press time, the public comment period had just finished.

Research has shown that roadless areas possess great biological diversity and ecological function, and that these areas are of particular importance to grizzlies, mature bull elk *(Cervus elaphus),* and westslope cutthroat and bull trout. In addition, many biologists are convinced that the seemingly limited act of cutting a

> The vitality is being drained from our remaining wilderness—we don't have enough wildlands left untouched—and we still haven't adequately protected that which most needs preserving.

narrow swath through a large, forested region is one of the most degrading things that humans can do to the wilderness—worse even than logging or running heavy metal smog-belching machinery up and down those roads. Currently, the Forest Service maintains more than 400,000 miles (644,000 km) of roads in the United States—almost 10 times the length of the interstate highway system.

Nearly 10,000 miles (16,000 km) of road cut through the Kootenai National Forest, where the Yaak resides. As elsewhere, many of these roads act as both source and conduit for sediment that flows into nearby waterways, raising the temperature of creeks and rivers, reducing fish spawning success, and killing native coldwater fish, like trout. These forest roads act as vectors for human-caused fires and noxious weeds, and channel water out of and away from forests, which is particularly damaging during drought years in the arid West.

How much water can the system lose before amphibians, vegetation, and the whole house-of-cards system begins to falter and fall? No one knows for sure, but a group of distinguished independent scientists sent a letter in 2004 to the White House, calling on the government to reinstate the Roadless Area Conservation Rule. They expressed the generally accepted position within the scientific community that "a strong roadless conservation rule is one of the cornerstones to sustainable public lands management, biodiversity conservation, and ecosystem health of the national forests."

If the Yaak is the Land the Wilderness Act Forgot, then Alaska is the land the Wilderness Act was dreaming of when it was enacted. Yet here, too, robust wildlands are under attack. The centerpiece of US energy policy for the next century involves securing another six months' supply of oil by drilling in the Arctic National Wildlife Refuge—despite the fact that 95 percent of the Alaskan coastal plain is already open to oil and gas development.

The government has trumpeted its Arctic plan as imposing minimal impact on the sprawling 19-million-acre refuge, with only 2,000 acres (800 ha) slated for development under current drilling plans. That is, say some, like claiming land the size of the Charlotte airport from an area the size of South Carolina. The only trouble is that the 2,000 acres is scattered throughout the refuge and only counts things like the concrete pads beneath pipeline supports—not the pipelines themselves, nor the gravel pits or roads that will crisscross the entire reserve.

> The new so-called Healthy Forest Initiative (HFI) represents a truly Orwellian strike against viable American wilderness.

Alaska's majestic old growth Tongass National Forest is also suffering from the lost Roadless Rule, with six logging projects approved for roadless lands, and over 40 on the drawing boards. Further south, in Oregon, the proposed Biscuit sale—a post-wildfire "salvage" timber sale—calls for logging 30 square miles (78 km^2) in roadless forests that are already rebounding naturally from the 2002 fire season.

The new so-called Healthy Forest Initiative (HFI) represents a truly Orwellian strike against viable American wilderness. HFI calls for an aggressive logging program to reduce a build-up of "fuels"—*trees*—in our national forests after decades of unnatural fire suppression. This sounds fine in theory, but the models for "healthy forests" are based largely on dry Ponderosa pine sites, not moist forest types like those in the Yaak and the Pacific Northwest. Further, much of the logging industry prefers the larger-diameter trees that typically survive fire rather than the small-diameter "fuels" that feed fires in the first place. Only with last minute lobbying were provisions for citizen participation and protection of old growth trees tacked onto the bill.

> Ten thousand elements of the wilderness, or 10 million, are being bartered away under our watch, with future generations paying the price, mourning the loss, the absence.

Other legislation may put human and wildlife health at risk. The new "Clear Skies" initiative raises allowable limits of mercury pollution from coal-fired power plants from 5 tons (4.5 t) per year proscribed under the Clean Air Act by 2008 to 26 tons (23.6 t) per year by 2010. Mercury is a toxin that impairs the health of people and animals and has been shown to effect behavioral changes in waterfowl such as loons.

Even places that would seem safe from smog are not. Yelowstone National Park is overrun by snowmobiles in winter, bringing air pollution and noise, forcing the park's bison, elk, and other wildlife to flee the machines, wheezing their way through winters that were once pristine reminders of a time before internal combustion. The Clinton administration banned snowmobiles from the park; the Bush administration overturned the ban—and then appealed a court ruling reinstating the ban. In the end, 720 snowmobiles per day will be allowed in the park.

Back east, the Clean Water Act and the National Environmental Protection Act, those hallmarks of the early 1970s, are also in question. Across the Appalachians, whole mountain ranges are at risk of being blasted away by coal mining operations that the Bush administration seems content to let police themselves. The rubble from these so-called mountaintop removal mines is dumped into surrounding ravines, turning rivers into poisoned, mud-choked trickles. By the government's own reckoning, over 1,200 miles (1,900 km) of free-running Appalachian streams were buried between 1985 and 2001—and current plans for mountaintop removals would decimate an area the size of Delaware over the next decade.

Our nation's on-the-ground management of wilderness is failing us. We are losing the nuts-and-bolts vital components of the American wilderness: clean air and water; wild, self-regulating forests that are free to grow old, rot, or burn, begin anew, and grow old again at their own pace, and under their own rhythms, not man's; grizzlies, lynx, trout, wolverine; solitude. Ten thousand elements of the wilderness, or 10 million, are being bartered away under our watch, with future generations paying the price, mourning the loss, the absence.

Other, stealthier wilderness changes are accelerating. Executive orders have directed government agencies to expedite energy projects, requiring a written explanation of any decision that hindered energy production—such as protecting wildlife. The *Washington Post* reported that the Bureau of Land Management (BLM) and Interior officials began rewarding employees who rushed through new drilling permits on public lands. In January 2004, Secretary of the Interior Gale Norton challenged Wyoming BLM workers to triple the number of drilling permit approvals in the state's natural gas fields from 1,000 to 3,000 a year.

In the Utah redrock desert, Secretary Norton ruled that BLM no longer had the authority to describe public lands as having wilderness characteristics, nor to manage them in such a way as to preserve and protect those qualities. Secretary Norton and the Department of Interior did not, however, impugn the agency's ability to identify, describe, and manage public lands for oil and gas production, cattle and sheep grazing, hydroelectric production, timber, coal, gold, silver, copper, uranium, nor even, it would seem, the storage and retention of spent nuclear fuel rods.

> The epitome of the American wilderness is perhaps the grizzly bear; some current measures regarding this species appear to stand in stark opposition to the survival of the country's wild heart.

The government also sought to define old wagon train trails, and it seemed, any bent blade of grass or wheel-rut (the markings of which can assume a kind of near-geological permanence in the desert) of an illegal motorcycle or all-terrain vehicle incursion as a "road," and to take jurisdiction of that "road" away from the federal government and to transfer it to local counties.

The epitome of the American wilderness is perhaps the grizzly bear; some current measures regarding this species appear to stand in stark opposition to the survival of the country's wild heart. Our local grizzly population, the Cabinet-Yaak grizzlies, is the most endangered in the Lower 48. When I came here almost 20 years ago, there were about three dozen bears. There have been 21 known human-caused grizzly mortalities in the last five years alone, and grizzly bear expert Louisa Willcox has called the Cabinet-Yaak grizzlies "the walking dead." Another five years of failure to protect their habitat and the entire population will be extinct.

In addition to eroding roadless areas, the grizzlies are threatened by exploding private land developments in riparian areas and by the proposal of one of the world's largest copper and silver mines in the narrowest, most vital link of their range. The proposed mine would effectively cut off the bears' migration from the Purcell Mountains in Canada, across the US border to the Yaak, down into the slender Cabinet Mountains and then south, toward the Greater Yellowstone and Bitterroot country—creating a new kind of bear-trap.

What few bears remain, should they prove adventurous enough to colonize, or recolonize, their ancestral lands, would encounter mines, highways, and logging roads ever closer on both sides—until they reach the tip of the point, the place through which they cannot pass: the Rock Creek mine. As almost always happens, when grizzly bears—the uncompromising spirit of the wilderness—encounter humans and human communities, the bears lose, wilderness loses, and, ultimately, we lose.

Despite the fact that the Cabinet-Yaak grizzlies are in free-fall, a few state and federal biologists claim that grizzlies are fully recovered elsewhere in the United States, largely due to anecdotal observations of bears in places where they haven't been seen in 20 years, and that these populations could be used as reservoirs to restock the Cabinets. These officials have proposed capturing young female grizzlies near Glacier National Park, tranquilizing them, caging them, and transferring them into the knifey spine of the Cabinets. This would be a near-certain death sentence, given the present rate of human-caused bear mortalities and the marginalized habitat there. The officials argue that since the same game management technique is used for deer and bighorn sheep, it will work for the bears, despite the fact that grizzlies are one of the widest ranging land animals in the world, with a home range as much as one hundred times that of deer and bighorns. Twenty years ago, four grizzlies captured in British Columbia were relocated to the Cabinets. In under a year, one was dead and the others had disappeared. Nonetheless, proponents of relocation are now calling this relocation a success.

> "We need as much wilderness as can be saved."
> —Wallace Stegner

Such an approach fails to consider that many biologists believe grizzlies to be one of the most sentient and social species in the American wilderness, matched perhaps only by wolves and humans. They also possess a deeply maternal culture where mothers spend three years teaching the young where to go in each season, where to find certain foods at certain times of year, and where to hide, and when, and how. Seemingly unconsidered is the ethics of removing an intelligent wild creature from its native landscape and potentially putting it in harm's way.

How much more robust, elegant, and enduring it would be to establish a system of corridors, bands of greater connectivity, between Glacier and the Cabinets. How much more biological integrity such a system would possess—rather than helicoptering bears in, as if on a business shuttle. How much more crafted and fitted through the elegant teeth of natural selection such transfer would be when accomplished the old-fashioned way, with one careful paw in front of another. Yes, it might take 5 or 10 or even 20 years to be effective, but it would be more durable, more enduring.

"We need as much wilderness as can be saved," Wallace Stegner once said, arguing also for as many types as possible, not just rock and ice spines—"recreational wildernesses"—but deep woods, low-elevation "biological wildernesses" such as the Yaak. And we need them connected in a planned and functioning manner that is dedicated to their ongoing survival and health. If we take care of the wilderness, the wilderness will take care of us, serving as a reservoir for the cherished species the American continent has sculpted over the last 100 millennia.

We also need wilderness to continue serving as the great and irreplaceable filtration systems for what little clean air and clean water we still possess in the continental United States. We need wilderness areas as wellsprings for spiritual renewal as well, and artistic inspiration, and as the echo of the original (and ongoing) creation, against which to measure much scientific inquiry.

The wilderness is, and always has been, larger and more powerful than we are. We can harm it, certainly, and we can dishonor it, diminish it, even destroy and eradicate it. But what a wonderful, rare idea to pay homage and respect, and to treat with reverence, something so vastly more powerful than we are, and to allow it to continue to exist untouched for the sake of its own identity, and under its own dignity. This, I believe, is nothing less than an opportunity for us to participate in the divine, and to grow beyond ourselves.

> We must stop ravaging the last of the wild.

Whether operating by instinct or reason, by science or religion, we must change our legislative direction, while we still can. We must stop ravaging the last of the wild with mines and roads cutting into the wilderness, must stop pushing to drill the last 5 percent of the Arctic coastal plain, must not roll back air and water protections in which we have already invested decades of commitment—and in which the earth itself has already invested an eternity, creating the American wilderness before which we still, by grace, stand, awed and amazed.

Marine Protected Areas

Can We Rebuild Marine Ecosystems
by Closing Areas to Fishing?

CALLUM M. ROBERTS

Soufrière, home to 10,000 people on the West Indian island of St. Lucia, lies cupped within a protecting crescent of forested mountains. From the sea it is guarded by the Piton Mountains, bleached granite monoliths that tower 2,500 feet (762 m) over the Caribbean. The breeze wafts scents of jasmine across the bay from vines that cling to their sheer slopes, sharpened by sulphur fumes from the volcano hidden in the hills behind. It appears to be a vision of paradise, but when I first visited in 1994 the fishermen who lived there were far from happy. Beneath the water that lapped the Pitons, the fish they depended on had nearly disappeared.

Diving for the first time in Soufrière Bay, I understood their concern. Schools of damselfish shimmered among the corals and delicate wrasse picked among seaweeds, but there were few animals larger than the size of my hand. Although I searched hard, I saw no big groupers haunting the ledges and caves and no large snappers stalking prey among the sea fans. Nor were there the dense crowds of grunts familiar to me from Belizean reefs. The reef was eerily devoid of large predatory fish. The reason for their absence was straightforward, if unexpected. Armed only with the simplest of fishing methods—wooden canoes, hook and line, spear and trap—local fishermen had severely overexploited their quarry. Sought-after food fish like black grouper and triggerfish were now just memories. Small fish, used only for bait in the past, were all that was left to feed families and make a little money. But this would soon change, they hoped.

I went to St. Lucia to witness the beginning of a bold new management effort. The fishermen of Soufrière were about to set aside a third of their fishing grounds in a network of marine reserves interspersed with areas where they could continue to fish. This agreement was the culmination of years of effort by the local community in partnership with the government. The marine reserves would, they hoped, provide refuges in which fish could live longer and grow larger and more numerous. The idea was that fish would have a safe place to grow and their young could repopulate the reef. If the idea worked, those reserves

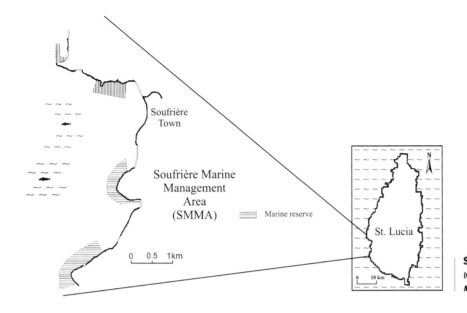

Soufrière Marine Management Area.
(Credit: Roberts, C.M. and J.P. Hawkins (2000). *Fully Protected Marine Reserves: A Guide.* WWF-US, Washington DC)

would one day help to restore the fishers' livelihoods. A dedicated park manager and his enthusiastic crew of rangers would protect the reef.

Over the next eight years, I returned each summer with a team of marine biologists to record progress. We were surprised by the speed of the reef's recovery. Within a year, we detected a significant increase in the numbers of commercially important fish. Those gains continued year upon year, surviving initial local protests by trap fishermen who felt that cuts in fishing area fell mostly upon them. Their goodwill was secured with a year of compensation payments from the government to help them through the period until reserves began to work, and fish multiplied (see color plate 27).

In addition to the pleasure we gained as scientists from proving that our theories about reserves were correct, it was a joy to see the reefs coming alive with fish again. Predatory eyes once again peered from the dark recesses of the reef, and schools of snappers coalesced around promontories. After four or five years, herds of grazing parrotfish and surgeonfish once again grazed across reef slopes. Rare animals became common, common animals abundant, and small fish grew large.

It was also deeply pleasing to watch the sacrifice made by poor local fishermen repaid with steadily growing catches. Five years after establishing the protected areas, trap catches were up by between 46 and 90 percent,[1] and fishing profits had grown by a similar amount.[2]

Since then, life for both fish and those who pursue them has continued to improve. By 2002, after seven years of protection, stocks of commercial fish rose by five times in reserves and more than doubled in nearby fishing grounds—and there is little sign as yet of this growth leveling off. Experiences from other parts of the world suggest that benefits from protection will continue to grow for

View of the Piton Mountains surrounding Soufrière on the West Indian island of St. Lucia. A network of marine reserves established here has replenished previously depleted fish stocks.
(Credit: Callum Roberts)

After seven years of protection, lobsters became more plentiful and reef fish populations rose by five times in St. Lucia reserves and more than doubled in nearby fishing grounds. (Credit: Callum Roberts)

decades, as large and long-lived species recolonize and grow and as habitats continue to recover from the effects of fishing.

There are very few places in the Caribbean where we can see what the full potential of protection might be because most of the region has been intensively exploited for hundreds of years. Early writings suggest that reefs can support a far greater abundance of life than we know. For example, in John Esquemeling's 1678 account of the bloody exploits of pirates, *The Buccaneers of America*,[3] he makes this observation on fishing: "[At the Isla de los Pinos] some went about that work of careening the ship, while others betook themselves to fishing. In this last we were so successful as to take in six or seven hours as much fish as would abun-

The Soufrière Marine Management Area is now a success story that illustrates how an integrated approach to fisheries management can both protect sea life and improve human livelihoods.
(Credit: Callum Roberts)

dantly suffice to feed a thousand persons." Back then, giant groupers and snappers were hauled in from these waters almost as fast as lines were let over the side. The same cannot be found today, but the marine reserves proliferating across the Caribbean give us hope that before too long, they may be.

Developing countries like St. Lucia have pioneered marine reserves. They had few other tools to manage their fisheries: the expensive technoscience fixes beloved by developed countries were not an option. In countries like Britain, where I live, there are almost no marine reserves and fish only find protection from

Local St. Lucia fishermen set wicker drop and lift traps baited with bread, fish, or coconut on the reef. Catches with these traps increased by 46 to 90 percent after five years of marine reserve protection.
(Credit: Callum Roberts)

fishing in military test ranges or munitions dump sites—hardly the best places to seek nature in the raw. Protection of the sea still desperately lags behind that on land. But a growing movement is building on successes like that in St. Lucia to create a system of marine protected areas that circles the globe. At the 2002 World Summit on Sustainable Development, coastal nations committed to creating national networks of marine protected areas by 2012. We are seeing unprecedented new commitment to ocean protection. However, to take full advantage of the opportunity, it is essential that marine protected areas offer the right kind of protection.

Twenty years ago I made my first dive in the Firth of Clyde on the west coast of Scotland. It was a gray day and a low swell washed the shore. The visibility was awful as I struggled through the seaweed and suspended muck into deeper water. As my eyes adjusted to the gloom, the particles around me came into focus, revealing themselves as the more resilient markers of sewage pollution: crumbly remains of ancient condoms, colorful flecks of toilet tissue and sanitary towels. If there were any fish, I didn't see them.

Since then, Britain and other European nations have made progress in cleaning up the sea. European laws enacted in the 1990s now ensure that sewage is treated to higher standards before release, sewage sludge is no longer dumped at sea, and industrial wastes are more closely regulated. But while this investment has made the waters of the Clyde more pleasant to swim in, less smelly, and a fetching shade of blue rather than brown, fishermen have continued overfishing. There is almost nothing left to see in the newly refreshed water. Gone are the herring, gone the cod, the haddock, and the plaice. The only animals that are thriving are prawns that scuttle muddy trails across the seabed—and fishers have now turned their nets upon them. This mirrors ecosystem changes across the Atlantic along the northern US and Canadian coastlines, where a crustacean renaissance has followed the crash of cod populations.

This year I returned to the Clyde to attend a meeting of fishermen who wanted to know whether protected areas could help bring back the region's fish. Although they seemed quite happy with their new prawn fishery, as prawns bring good money, they were also concerned. Clyde fisheries have become monocultures: other than prawns, there is nothing else.

This is a dangerous situation. Monocultures attract pests, and Clyde prawns are no exception. Fishermen are reporting an alarming prevalence of a nasty parasite called *Hematodinium* that renders prawns unsaleable; in some places the infection rate is as high as 80 or 90 percent. *Hematodinium* is a single-celled microbe that invades the bodies of crustaceans and multiplies in the organs until one day the animal can no longer move. When an infected prawn is immobilized the microbes make a spectacular exit, streaming forth in such dense clouds that the animal appears to be on fire. Parasitized prawns slow down as the infection develops and spend more time outside the safety of their burrows. When cod were common, these prawns were picked off early on and infection rates kept to a few percent or less. Today, no such control exists.

Healthy marine ecosystems support numerous species arrayed across many levels of the food chain. Over the last century, fisheries have been reducing the complexity of these systems to the point of instability. Sustainable fisheries depend on maintaining a rich and complex marine food web. Clyde fishers—like many others around the world—have yet to understand this connection. A local community group on the Isle of Arran has proposed creating a marine reserve in Lamlash Bay where anglers used to hold an annual two-day fishing festival. Until the 1960s, as many as 5,000 fish were landed during one festival, weighing about 16,000 pounds (7,300 kg). By the 1980s, the catch was less than one-tenth of this, and by 1994—the last year that the festival was held—it was under 200 pounds.

Although the community group's modest proposal seeks to protect an area smaller than the average shopping mall, it is strongly opposed by the local commercial fishing association. Apparently, two of their members would be inconvenienced by this fishing restriction. But the future of their industry depends on the creation of far larger marine reserves. Without adequate protection, the fish-

Marine biologist assessing growth of fish populations after coral reef habitat within the Soufrière reserve was protected from fishing.
(Credit: Callum Roberts)

ermen will remain on their destructive path that will only lead to the final disappearance of their quarry and the extinction of their way of life.

Marine protected areas that afford significant protection from fishing are strikingly effective in rebuilding marine ecosystems. A growing body of data from around the world shows that exploited fish stocks typically increase by two to three times within two to five years of protection. Some species increase by more than an order of magnitude. In Florida, for example, yellowtail snapper *(Ocyurus chrysurus)* populations increased 15 times in Sanctuary Protection Zones after a four-year fishing ban.[4] In three New Zealand reserves, which have been protected for up to 20 years, densities of large snapper *(Pagrus auratus)* were 14 times greater than in fished areas.[5] Catches of four shorefish species in South African protected areas were 5 to 21 times greater than those in fishing grounds.[6]

Wherever real protection from fishing has been established, reserves have worked well. The benefits have been documented from tropical to cool temperate habitats and from shallow waters to deep seas, on reefs, seagrass beds, and muddy continental shelves—and improvements have been noted by both local and industrial-scale fishing operations.[7]

But not all animals benefit equally. Less mobile species, such as scallops or snappers, gain greater protection from reserves than more wide-ranging animals such as cod or tuna, because they spend more time within the safety of reserves. Complex habitats built by organisms like corals and sponges benefit more than shallow wave-swept sediments; reefs suffer more harm from destructive fishing gear than habitats that are naturally disturbed on a regular basis. But reserves provide the necessary conditions for any exploited ecosystem to recover from fishing impacts. They are the most powerful tool we have for conservation of the sea.

However, there is widespread misunderstanding about the role marine protected areas play, even within conservation organizations. In developed countries in particular, talk of protection from fishing is seen as dangerous. Commercial and recreational fishing lobbies are so powerful, and their opposition to protection can be so entrenched, that creating protected areas that exclude fishing is often viewed as too difficult. As a result, government agencies and some nongovernmental organizations are planning and implementing reserves that offer little real protection from fishing.

> The time for apology is over: returning large tracts of the oceans to the wild is a necessity. . . . This global system of marine protected areas will need to protect around one-third of the sea from fishing to keep ocean ecosystems healthy.

Prior to a recent trip to Canada, I browsed the Parks Canada website entry on a proposed marine park off the south coast of Nova Scotia. The intention, they were at pains to make clear, was not to stop fishing in this park but to achieve sustainable fisheries. Marine reserves can only support fisheries when they act as refuges where fish stocks can rebuild and ecosystems can recover. Without a high level of protection, neither fish nor fisheries will see gains. If we are not to seek protection from fishing in marine protected areas, then where on Earth—in the sea—are we going to protect? If protection of sea creatures and their ecosystems from hunting is not the goal, then what is a marine protected area?

I came across a telling image in a seaside shop selling tourist trinkets in Nova Scotia. On the wall was a picture of a sinking ship with a headline above that read: *The Lunenburg Marine Park*. I have never understood scuba divers' enthusiasm for junk, yet junk is so often associated with marine parks and recreation. A burned-out hot dog van would be an eyesore on land, but the same van underwater would exert some magical appeal. Perhaps our enthusiasm for sinking ships stems from the fact that we can find nothing else to look at beneath the waves. Our expectations underwater have been so badly let down by the disappearance of fish that we must fill the void with something. Imagine that instead of waterfalls, side trails in Yosemite led to wrecked trucks or coils of rusting steel cable. Standards for wildlands and oceans are vastly different.

We have a wonderful opportunity in the run-up to 2012 to build a global network of marine protected areas that could end the long, slow death of marine life. But as we go about the task, it is essential to remember that real conservation and protection from fishing are indivisible. The machinery of extraction has been too successful over the last century to have it otherwise—and our success in regulating the fishing industry has been slight. Even in Europe, a place with quality science and a predisposition toward conservation, highly developed regulatory structures, and sophisticated surveillance, we have failed. The proud record of Europe's fishery managers has been to preside over a rise in the number of fish stocks in danger of collapse from 7 percent in 1970 to 48 percent in 2000.[8] If sustainable fisheries are the goal, then large-scale networks of marine reserves that remain off limits to fishing are essential.

The time for apology is over: returning large tracts of the oceans to the wild is a necessity. The best available science suggests that this global system of marine protected areas will need to protect around one-third of the sea from fishing to keep ocean ecosystems healthy—and to keep the world's fishing industry in business.[9] One estimate puts the cost at somewhere between $12 and $14 billion per year,[10] less than the $15 to $30 billion the world currently spends subsidizing harmful fishing levels and practices—and less than half the amount Americans and Europeans spend on ice cream. Future generations will never forgive us if we fail to take this opportunity to save our fish and fisheries.

To answer the question posed in the title of this essay, yes, we can rebuild marine ecosystems by closing areas to fishing. But protected areas that fail to greatly restrain fishing will not permit recovery. Without refuges from fishing, healthy undersea ecosystems and sustainable fisheries will remain just as elusive as they are today.

From "Woods"

A small grove massacred to the last ash
An oak with heart-rot, give away the show:
This great society is going smash;
They cannot fool us with how fast they go,
How much they cost each other and the gods.
A culture is no better than its woods.

W. H. AUDEN
(ENGLAND, 1907 – 1973)

PART VII

PEOPLE AND CULTURE

Our cultural values influence all we do, including the way we treat or use the other creatures we share the planet with. For example, Muslims do not eat pigs—wild or domesticated. In New York, rats are considered filthy creatures that would never be eaten, but in West Africa, the rodents are a common source of protein. Most people in the Western world recoil at the idea of eating cats, dogs, or other animals that we keep as beloved pets; in some parts of Asia, these animals are readily consumed. And among people living in the Ituri forest of the Democratic Republic of Congo, pregnant or lactating women (and sometimes their spouses) are very careful about eating certain animals, as they believe their offspring can acquire the creature's traits—such as an elephant's long, floppy nose. In each volume of *State of the Wild,* we will explore the impact of cultural values and practices on wildlife, wilderness, and resources in a different corner of the world.

In this volume, we analyze the cultural values here in our own back yard. Bill Weber, director of the Wildlife Conservation Society's North America program, shares his ideas on a pervasive cultural attitude in the United States toward conservation. He calls this perspective the "designer ark," characterized by a desire to maintain an array of wildlife that lacks certain "inconvenient" or "dangerous" large animals and predators, regardless of their importance to a healthy ecosystem. This designer ark stocks volumes of desirable fish in our rivers for anglers while culling black bears that encroach on rural neighborhoods.

This essay provokes reflection on how we decide what species should be conserved: what belongs on the world's "ark"?

Culturally Determined Wildlife Populations

The Problem of the Designer Ark

BILL WEBER

On a brisk September morning, Yellowstone's Lamar Valley offers one of Earth's great wildlife spectacles. Coyotes and ravens glean choice leftovers from an elk carcass, while full-bellied wolves digest their feast within sight. Hundreds of elk graze nearby, seemingly unmoved by the fate of their former herd mate and unconcerned by the satiated wolves. In the distance, a grizzly sow with two cubs browses just below the golden line of aspens at the valley's edge. It is easy to imagine a natural order unchanged for thousands of years.

But however wild and wonderful, the Lamar spectacle is neither natural nor unchanged. Across the vast Greater Yellowstone Ecosystem in northwestern Wyoming, southwestern Montana, and eastern Idaho, wildlife populations are in a chronic state of disturbance due to a head-spinning array of human interventions. And farther afield, in much of our country, the natural disequilibrium is complete. It's not that Americans don't like wildlife, it's just that we want a "designer ark." We want a landscape in which our cultural values determine strict limits for dangerous and inconvenient species, a certain amount of shared space for "good" animals, and by far the greatest room for ourselves—our homes, our towns, our roads, and our beloved machines. The problems caused by this desire for a more orderly ark extend beyond our times and national boundaries.

The United States, or at least the Lower 48, is home to the world's most notable collection of culturally determined wildlife populations. The shaping began long before modern times, with the arrival of the first human hunters and their terribly efficient role in eliminating the mammoths and other megafauna of the last postglacial era. As the descendants of these early bands spread to occupy almost all of North America, they used fire, too, to shape local habitats and the wildlife within them to their likes and needs.

European Americans most forcefully imposed their will on the landscape. Beaver and bison, perhaps the two best examples of North American plentitude, were hunted to the very brink of extinction. The passenger pigeon was shot-gunned into the abyss. Industrial-scale logging left scars across New England that have taken a century to not-quite-heal, while the ravages of Appalachian mining continue and may never heal. We created cities and industries that spewed waste in such quantities that death and disease were borne by the very air and water needed to sustain us. And when those cities became unattractive, we created leapfrogging suburbs and a spreading web of roads to connect them.

> It's not that Americans don't like wildlife, it's just that we want a "designer ark."

At points along the way, visionaries have appeared to diagnose our ills and prescribe environmental cures, including healthy doses of wilderness. But even our most committed efforts to save the wild have fallen short. John Muir helped preserve the High Sierras and other spectacular western landscapes. In the process, we gained a spiritual salve for our battered souls. But while saving high-elevation "rocks and ice," we acted too late to protect the valleys in between and other lowlands needed by wildlife in harsh winter climes.

In 1872, the notion of the national park was born in the United States with the creation of Yellowstone. There, protection was given not only to rugged highlands and fantastic geothermal formations but also to at least the summer habitat for a full array of western wildlife. Yet, no sooner had the world's first national park been established than its stewards—the US cavalry—initiated a policy of lethal predator control in favor of more desirable species. One hundred years later, we recognized the error of our ways. But by that time, the wolf and cougar were long gone, and the grizzly bear was reduced to a garbage-feeding clown.

There is progress in the United States, especially in wildlife recovery and reintroduction. The cougar reestablished itself in Yellowstone in 1987. Barely seven years later, the wolf was brought back in a highly successful—if not fully appreciated—reintroduction. Meanwhile, the grizzly continued a slow recovery from its earlier decline and from its lethal addiction to Dumpsters. Today in the Lamar Valley, all three of these charismatic predators compete for market share of the overabundance of elk that developed in their absence. As their populations expand to the south, the first large predator colonists are just reaching the "promised land" of Jackson, Wyoming: the home of the National Elk Refuge.

In the early 1900s, my organization—the Wildlife Conservation Society—supported the creation of the refuge and the winter-feeding of elk to save the species from extinction. A century later, the feeding continues despite what is widely recognized as an excessive population of more than 10,000 elk on the winter range. This biological equivalent of elk-on-welfare is sustained by a powerful hunting lobby that deeply resents the idea of wolves sharing in this subsidized bounty, fearing that the returned predators will prove to be too much competition. As of press time, Wyoming was considering a zero-tolerance, shoot-on-sight policy for wolves outside of the Yellowstone and Grand Teton parks once the species is delisted as a federal endangered species. This free-fire zone would effectively preclude wolves from reaching the National Elk Refuge.

It is illustrative to look at the interpretation and application of the US Endangered Species Act. The act itself contains no definition of "recovery." So-called recovery plans were a later addition, and they vary considerably in their objectives. For grizzly bears, the core criterion for "recovery" was set at 40 breeding females across their entire northern Rockies range: a threshold estimated to assure the population's genetic diversity over a minimum 30-year period. For wolves, the target was 30 breeding females documented for three consecutive years. Interestingly, a far more ambitious standard of recovery was used for bald eagles across most of their former range. Thus, while science contributes to recovery targets, cultural values clearly play a central role. For wolves and grizzly bears, we set minimal standards for population and/or genetic viability: a few hundred large predators in our midst will suffice. For our less threatening national symbol, it took thousands of breeding bald eagles to trigger delisting.

The same species can elicit quite different cultural responses across different areas of the United States. Over the last 30 years, wolves in the western Great Lakes region have spread from a small enclave along Lake Superior, recolonizing much of their former range in Minnesota, Wisconsin, and the Upper Peninsula of Michigan. At the end of 2003, Minnesota was home to more than 2,500 wolves, while Wisconsin and Michigan each supported roughly 350.

This natural recovery has engendered far less public outcry and resistance than the federally imposed reintroduction in Yellowstone. Perhaps accordingly, the states' current wolf targets far exceed federal criteria for delisting. Whereas the original federal plan called for a minimum of 1,000 wolves in Minnesota and 100 in Wisconsin and Michigan combined, these states' management plans now call for minimum populations of 1,600 in Minnesota, 350 in Wisconsin, and 200 in Michigan. None of the states has established a maximum, implying that these numbers will be determined by a combination of biological data and cultural criteria. In the Rocky Mountains, where wolf populations have also surpassed federal recovery criteria, the states of Montana, Idaho, and especially Wyoming continue to grapple with much lower minimal standards that are acceptable to local popular and political interests.

The effect of cultural values can be seen in our management of many nonendangered species as well. Black bears have reclaimed large areas of their former range and are viewed by many as a nonthreatening curiosity when they first appear. As they begin to feed and breed in suburban and exurban settings from Reno to northern New Jersey, our tolerance gives way to calls for removal, lethal control, and renewed hunting seasons. To an almost total degree, these calls are based on perceived threats and cultural fears, rather than any real evidence of danger. In New York's Adirondack Park, bears accosted six humans with scratches, cuffs, and licks in 2000—the same year that more than 2,100 domestic dog attacks were reported in the 11-county Adirondack region. Yet no one is calling for a hunting season on dogs.

Back in Yellowstone, harsh winters drive many browsers to seek food at lower elevations. For bison, following this ancient urge can be fatal if their movements take them outside the park's boundary with Montana, where sharpshooters await their arrival. The official rationale for this is fear that bison will transmit brucellosis to Montana cattle. Abortion-inducing brucellosis is a real threat to the livestock industry, even if evidence of transmission outside of captive situations is seriously lacking. However, elk making the same trek—and with a comparable risk of disease transmission—are allowed to pass untouched into Montana's aptly named Paradise Valley. As in neighboring Wyoming, elk are given value as hunting targets; bison are not.

For some other species, values change with time and locale. The decline in populations of white-tailed deer and especially Canada geese at different points in the last century provoked concerted recovery efforts. These efforts were led by state and federal wildlife agencies, responding to their primary constituencies of hunters and outfitters. With time, the geese and deer numbers rose and constituencies changed: as hunting declined in popularity, the emerging suburban culture embraced deer and geese as symbols of the wild within their increasingly domesticated landscapes. But when the deer consumed too many planted hedgerows and flowerbeds, and the geese left green streaks across suburban soccer fields and uniforms, suburbia rang with calls for control. With killing an unpopular option—and untenable in suburban settings—no viable solution is in sight. For the time being, we must live with our management "success."

The massive replacement of native American fish faunas with introduced species more attractive to anglers is another hugely important example of culturally determined wildlife values. From New England to the Sierras, native trout varieties have been almost entirely replaced by introduced brook and brown trout. Even in our first national park, introduced trout species are outcompeting the endemic Yellowstone cutthroat trout. In California's Davis Lake, state authorities have poisoned the lake several times in a thus far unsuccessful effort to eliminate the introduced pike that are threatening downstream native trout.

No discussion of how cultural values affect attitudes toward wildlife would be complete without mention of the spotted owl. Throughout the 1980s and early 1990s, the spotted owl was at the center of a highly contentious public and political debate. At issue was the owl's endangered status and the impact its protection would have on the logging industry in the Pacific Northwest. The best biological evidence indicated that the owl was almost certainly endangered, but the highly polarized attitudes that surrounded this fact had little to do with public concern for, or even awareness of, the creature itself. In fact, the owl flew below the radar of all but the most devoted bird watchers until it was caught in the endangered species spotlight.

A denizen of the deep forest, the spotted owl prefers the structure of old-growth forests, where it is adapted to prey on the small mammals that scurry about the relatively open understory. Logging tends to radically alter this environment, thus limiting the owl's hunting—and survival—prospects. Logging activities also engender strong attitudes, both pro and con.

The projection of these attitudes turned the once-anonymous spotted owl into an icon for both sides in a pitched battle that raged for years. Its iconic values were, of course, positive for those who wished to protect old-growth forests, negative for those who saw economic decline and job losses in such protection. Spotted owl barbecues and "save a logger, eat an owl" T-shirts may not be as popular as a decade ago, but the controversy continues to simmer.

It is clear that American cultural attitudes—preference, tolerance, antipathy—play a central role in determining the species that get attention, the size to which their populations can grow, and the space allocated to support their existence. So, what's wrong with this designer ark?

First, like all designer items, carefully tailored wildlife populations are expensive. The Yellowstone wolf recovery has cost more than $3 million in its first nine years; much more if several secondary costs are considered. Even assuming that the success of this effort will result in delisting, federal monitoring of the wolves and direct state management will cost millions more in coming years.

> Like all designer items, carefully tailored wildlife populations are expensive.

The US Fish and Wildlife Service currently is in charge of 1,024 species recovery plans—plans that require an estimated $10 to $20 million per year to implement. That doesn't include the backlog of listed species still lacking plans, nor the growing number of candidate species awaiting formal listing. Though estimates vary widely, it is certain that further significant costs are borne by the private sector—timber companies, residential developers, some ranchers—as a result of land-use restrictions under the "critical habitat" requirements of many recovery plans. In the case of the spotted owl, the species' need for old-growth forest led to contentious limits on logging. If nothing else, the cost of species recovery should teach us that an ounce of preservation is worth a pound of restoration.

But we pay for abundance, too. The annual bill for the winter-feeding program at the National Elk Refuge exceeds $400,000, while total refuge management costs exceed $1 million per year. The cost to control overabundant deer in eastern suburbs ranges from $200 to $400 per deer using sharpshooters, $300 to $600 per deer for live capture and relocation, and up to $700 for each sterilized deer. At densities that commonly approach 40 per square mile in suburban environments (versus no more than four deer per forested square mile in presettlement times), this represents a budget-breaking cost of $7,700 to $27,000 per square mile (2.6 km^2). A nonlethal proposal to control the deer in New Jersey's leafy Princeton township has been budgeted at $250,000 in its first year.

The second problem with our designer ark is the extent to which culture trumps science in the management arena. Sound research may determine whether a species is threatened or endangered, but public opinion certainly seems to influence recovery actions. Birds and butterflies may have fewer or less vocal advocates than do wolves, but they have virtually no opponents—with the notable exception of the spotted owl. Thus recovery thresholds for "good" animals and plants have no limits. But for large, dangerous species, those targets tend to reflect a minimal standard. Often this is a genetic standard derived from some calculation of the minimum viable population required to avoid problems of inbreeding. This can be a flat total or, more commonly, the number of successfully breeding females over a period of time.

The public generally understands and accepts this approach, especially if the number is low for inconvenient species. Increasingly, however, population geneticists and biologists are calling for much higher numbers to buffer species from periodic catastrophes, disease, and quirks of fate. Only at these higher levels, they argue, can we expect to sustain population levels over much longer periods of time.

Growing numbers of ecologists suggest that our targets should be "ecologically functional" populations: a combination of numbers and densities that permits the animal to play its original role within a given ecosystem and in relation to other species. In this view, wolves and grizzly bears would only be considered "recovered" in the Greater Yellowstone Ecosystem when they effectively control prey populations of overabundant elk or moose, which in turn would reduce overgrazing. By all accounts, this functional threshold is far beyond the federal mandate of a few dozen breeding females of either species. It also is far beyond the current tolerance levels of Greater Yellowstone ranchers and many other local residents.

On the abundance side of the equation, our likes and dislikes also weigh more heavily than scientific criteria in the wildlife management arena. This is especially true where cultural values translate most directly into political and economic influence—as in the case of elk. And nowhere is it more evident than in the world of fish, where anglers spend billions annually on their sport. When it comes to abundance, repeated experience shows that we have management skills like those of the sorcerer's apprentice: we can create much better than we can control.

Finally, we have made important progress in recent years in public awareness of the twin problems of biological loss and ecological degradation. If we want fu-

> Perhaps most troubling is the perception that we are asking the world's poorest people to do the heavy lifting in conservation, while we in the world's wealthiest nation resist any comparable level of engagement.

ture generations to benefit from and build on that awareness, then we must find a way for emerging majority values that favor wildlife to overcome the tightening grip of powerful business and political interests on the remaining natural world. If we fail, then our children will inherit a more impoverished planet.

We also need to address conservation inequities in our own society. The sometimes very real costs of wildlife recovery and protection disproportionately affect rural Americans, most of whom are not wealthy. Nor is biological abundance readily converted into more appreciable benefits for most people living around parks and protected areas. We must face these bioeconomic facts of life to avoid the damaging—and unfounded—perception that conservation is little more than a luxury pursuit of the distant well-to-do.

Perhaps most troubling is the perception that we are asking the world's poorest people to do the heavy lifting in conservation, while we in the world's wealthiest nation resist any comparable level of engagement. We ask Asians to live with tigers, Latin Americans with jaguars, and Africans with an entire array of potentially dangerous predators, from leopards and lions to crocodiles and wild dogs. Yet we resist all but the most limited coexistence with wolves, cougars, and bears in our tidy American back yard. We ask those in other lands to protect functional wildlife populations in large, interconnected reserves, but too often aim for minimal populations within isolated islands of nature at home.

The problem here is not the sincerity of American conservation efforts abroad, as there are very sound reasons to protect more and bigger. Rather, it is the appearance of hypocrisy. We are fortunate that so many of the world's less developed nations have embraced the conservation cause and taken steps to protect significant wild areas and the rich array of species and ecosystems they sustain. But the conservation tide may be turning. As poverty concerns take prominence on the global agenda, we should not be surprised if those in other, wilder nations cast increasingly envious looks at our more orderly vessel—and then seek to rid their nation-arks of big and dangerous troublemakers, while making more room for human passengers and their economic aspirations.

From *Memoirs*

The saws cutting the huge logs ground out their shrill lament all day long. First you heard the deep underground thud of the felled tree. Every five or ten minutes the ground shuddered like a drum in the dark at the hard impact . . . giant work of nature, seeded there by the wind a thousand years before. . . . The forest was dying. I heard its lamentation with a heavy heart, as if I had come there to listen to the oldest voices anyone had ever heard.

PABLO NERUDA
(CHILE, 1904–1973)
TRANSLATED BY HARDIE ST. MARTIN

From "Place"

On the last day of the world
I would want to plant a tree

W. S. MERWIN
(UNITED STATES, 1927)

PART VIII

THE ART AND PRACTICE
OF CONSERVATION

In this section, we attempt to tease out solutions to wider philosophical questions in conservation and take on some of the more difficult questions within the field. In some cases, the web of issues and threats is so interwoven and complex that innovative, creative solutions are required—a type of artistry combined with practical, science-based solutions. Here, individuals from across the conservation community offer insightful, timely analyses of some of these larger global issues: looming extinction, mitigating the often catastrophic effects of both war and logging, and the successes and shortcomings of current conservation measures.

A team of experts offer their insights into protecting wildlife conservation amidst armed conflict. Peter Zahler, who led the United Nations Environment Programme (UNEP) post-conflict assessment team in Afghanistan, presents an overview. David Jensen, Hassan Partow, and Chizuru Aoki, also with UNEP, detail the restoration of the Iraqi marshlands. John Hart, a senior scientist with the Wildlife Conservation Society who has worked in the Democratic Republic of Congo since 1973, shares lessons learned by those working there before, during, and after the country's bloody civil war.

Dan Wharton writes on the controversial topic of captive breeding—heralded by some as a crucial conservation tool for the animals that teeter on the brink of extinction, and criticized by others as a distraction from the "real" work of conservation. Francis E. Putz proposes ways to promote wildlife and ecosystem conservation in and around forests that are "managed for timber," in contrast to those that are razed using destructive logging practices.

Finally, for "What Falls through the Cracks in Conservation Strategies"—a section that will repeat in future volumes—Sharon Guynup interviewed two preeminent conservationists, marine biologist Sylvia Earle and conservation biologist Thomas Lovejoy. Here, they share their thoughts on what needs to be done—or done differently—in conservation, both on land and in the "blue heart of the ocean."

Conservation and Conflict

The Importance of Continuing Conservation Work during Political Upheaval and Armed Conflict

PETER ZAHLER

Warfare has always had deep political, social, and economic repercussions that often extended far beyond the battlefield and even beyond the states engaged in conflict. However, this knowledge has had little effect on the frequency of new outbreaks: the dawn of the new millennium has seen a threefold increase in documented conflicts compared to just 50 years ago.[1] The cost of war in human life, livelihoods, and social dislocation has been well documented. But only recently has the international community realized the cost of the resulting environmental degradation—and the long-lasting consequences for whole ecosystems and people who rely on natural resources to stay alive.

Over the past few years, conservation biologists have begun to describe their experiences working in war-torn regions, documenting the often devastating effects on endangered species, biodiversity, and ecosystem function.[2] This new information dramatically broadens the total cost of war and better defines the threat that modern-day warfare brings to biodiversity conservation, worldwide security—and even to human survival.

The Environmental Consequences of Armed Conflict

Although conservation has often been left out of the conflict and post-conflict equation, conservation in wartime is not a luxury, nor is it "just" about wildlife preservation. It relates directly to human health, cultural survival, and long-term regional stability.

Most modern-day conflicts are fought in developing countries where most people live off the land in rural regions, with powerful local impact. In Afghanistan, for example, where approximately 80 percent of the population is directly dependent upon the country's natural resources, the environment has been ravaged by three decades of conflict: devastated by bombs, troop movements, and the movements of more than 6 million refugees. Without resource management,

Destroyed tank in Afghanistan near Jalalabad. Three decades of conflict have left the country littered with debris and environmental scars that impact wildlife and ecosystems.
(Credit: UNEP/PCAU)

forests have been razed, lakes and rivers have dried up, clouds of eroding soil swirl on the wind, wildlife is vanishing, and several million landmines litter the landscape.

This is a stark example of war's devastating effects on environment, which can trigger additional civil unrest and insurrection as people scramble for limited food and clean water. Even small, internal conflicts can spark global problems, including dramatic and often long-term ecological damage.

Modern, media-driven images of warfare focus on firefights and bombing runs, which are not the greatest threats to wildlife, but can still have powerful repercussions. Large-scale bombing, ground battles, and hungry soldiers kill wildlife, destroy and pollute habitat, and otherwise damage local ecosystems. A longer-term and more insidious danger comes from landmines, which have killed threatened species such as elephants and tigers—and remain in place for decades after a conflict is resolved, stopping conservation dead in its tracks—sometimes literally.[3]

More dramatic damage can come from what is now termed "scorched earth policy" or "ecocide." This strategic destruction of the environment has a history perhaps as long as war itself: the ancient Romans used salt to destroy the agricultural fields of their enemies. A more modern example is the 19 million gallons (72 million l) of defoliants that were sprayed on Vietnamese forests by U.S. forces to expose enemy troops, which, combined with bombing, decimated an estimated 7,700 square miles (20,000 km^2) of habitat.[4] Burning oilfields and refineries during the Gulf War ruined huge stretches of Iraqi coastline, killing seabirds and disrupting the marine ecosystem by damaging sea grass beds, coral reefs, and sea turtle breeding grounds. Draining the Mesopotamian marshlands effectively destroyed perhaps the single most important wetland for wildlife in western Asia (see page 254). In Colombia, guerrilla attacks on pipelines spilled 2.5 million barrels of crude oil—nearly seven times that of the *Exxon Valdez* spill in Alaska.[5]

A flamingo killed by oil released during the 1991 Persian Gulf War. An estimated 6 to 8 million barrels were intentionally spilled into the Gulf, contaminating more than 400 miles of coastline.

(Credit: Colin Wells)

While the immediate effects of war are often sudden and dramatic, we now know that much of the long-lasting environmental damage comes from the corollary effects of conflict. A big problem is the proliferation of accurate, rapid-fire weapons: war dramatically increases the number of available guns, which are often turned to use in hunting. Local people, commercial hunters, and even people in countries bordering war zones can quickly decimate local wildlife populations with AK-47s, M-16s, or worse. For example, after 25 years of conflict in Afghanistan, much of Pakistan is now awash in modern weapons. The giant markhor goat *(Capra falconeri)* and other big game was once the bailiwick of a few local hunters using single-shot rifles. Today, almost any man or boy hunts wildlife with modern automatic weapons.

But the movement of people during conflict, and their subsequent ravage of resources, is probably the greatest threat to the environment and to wildlife. The combatants themselves create especially pernicious problems. Since guerrilla factions rarely have the means to feed and shelter fighters, soldiers must hunt and forage for survival. Another threat involves factions that extract and sell natural resources to finance long-term insurgencies—or to protect against them. Uncontrolled logging and mining can devastate wildlands and protected areas, as well as the wildlife they support.[6]

But the displacement of people from cities, villages, and traditional farming or grazing lands takes the biggest toll. In many cases, thousands or even hundreds of thousands of people are forced to relocate without access to food, water, or shelter. People fleeing conflict naturally seek a safe haven, so it is no surprise that they often target wildlands and protected areas, where they hunt for food, cut trees and bushes for shelter and firewood, and lay waste to large stretches of land simply through clearing for encampments and the waste these camps create.[7]

Field staff trying to protect wildlands may become unintended or even deliberate casualties of war. Around the world, numerous park personnel have been

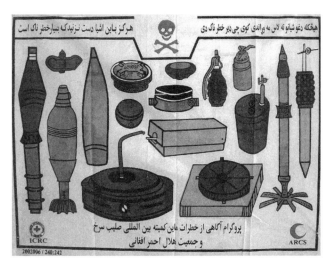

Poster describing mines and other explosives found in Afghanistan. Unexploded munitions pose a threat to residents, conservationists, and wildlife for years after a conflict ends.
(Credit: UNEP/PCAU)

threatened or killed. In Colombia, combatants have seized and held field researchers,[8] and in the Democratic Republic of Congo, about 100 of Virunga National Park's staff have been killed in battle since 1996 (see page 252). Unfortunately, when field staff or park personnel leave, the loss of this on-the-ground presence opens wildlands to increased poaching, logging, and other unsustainable use by local communities, refugees, and the warring factions themselves.

When conservation projects pull out because of insurrection, momentum toward conservation goals is lost, often abrogating agreements with local communities or ending direct protection, such as park management or antipoaching patrols. Important records are often destroyed, including data representing decades of research in areas of conservation importance—information that is crucial to inform post-conflict reconstruction efforts within both the environmental and the development sectors.

The idea that conflict can have positive effects on wildlife and habitat has recently become an issue of some contention. Some have argued that regular tribal conflicts in precolonial North America created "no-man's" zones between territories that served as havens for big game. More recently, the same case was made regarding parts of New Guinea and the demilitarized zone between North and South Korea, among others.[9]

However, it appears that in those few cases where conflict has improved conditions for wildlife, the situation usually has been short-lived. Returnees or refugees may flood back into the area once fighting stops or moves on, dramatically increasing impacts on wildlife and habitat. In a postwar period, a state's shattered infrastructure and depleted funds—coupled with international efforts directed largely toward economic and social reconstruction—means that little attention is given to environmental protection or reconstruction. The destruction can continue unabated for years.

Conservation during Conflict

Although there are dramatic environmental consequences of war and immediate conservation needs, the inherent dangers of armed conflict may leave the conservation community feeling impotent. While the dangers are real, organizations can and should act to avert as much of the damage as possible.

Probably the single most important action that can be taken during conflict is maintaining personnel in and around protected areas if at all possible.[10] One of the highest priorities is to engage local community members as field staff, as they have a personal commitment to remaining in the area during fighting and a greater likelihood of realizing the importance of project goals.

Designing a project security plan and training staff to implement it are also critical tasks. A plan should include response during invasion as well as evacuation procedures for both personnel and for important data and records. Maintaining close communication is essential to assist staff in managing and adapting to changing situations, to assist in evacuation if necessary, and simply to provide a connection to the outside world and a belief that their work continues to matter.[11]

Even if fieldwork and patrols must be curtailed, they remain important to conservation activities in war-torn countries. Organizations can shift to longer-term goals such as wider landscape-level monitoring and analysis, as in Colombia, where remote sensing of increased forest fragmentation and coca farming is being combined with databases on existing protected areas and the distribution of threatened species.[12] In this way, staff can continue to monitor conditions, prepare intervention and policy recommendations for postwar reconstruction, and simply keep the region's conservation needs before the international community.

Finally, in today's interconnected, media-driven world, warring factions are often strongly motivated to gain the upper hand in public opinion worldwide. When active conflict makes on-the-ground conservation too dangerous, organizations can still pursue conservation goals by lobbying those involved to minimize environmental damage.[13]

Because there is always the risk of appearing to support one side over another—an especially dangerous perception if the lobbying effort focuses on the eventual loser—the appearance of neutrality through equal communication with both sides in the cause of conservation is critical. Additionally, the international community can help limit the damage through environmental monitoring activities or by banning trade in threatened resources from countries at war to mitigate unsustainable extraction used to fund military activities.

> Conservation is possible during and after war and is a critical element in global biodiversity conservation.

The Post-Conflict Setting

Ironically, peace can have an equally devastating effect on wildlife and the environment. In a post-conflict setting, governments and donor agencies immediately turn to economic development for recovery. In poor countries with a war-ravaged infrastructure, natural resources are often viewed as a means to jump-start humanitarian efforts and economic growth. Unfortunately, in these countries a large proportion of people directly depend on natural resources for survival. The sudden increase in state and internationally sponsored resource extraction frequently limits local availability of timber for firewood or building materials, native wildlife and plants for food and traditional medicines, and even fresh water. These shortages threaten long-term

Afghani hunters with the horns of a Marco Polo sheep. The proliferation of weapons in conflict and post-conflict regions often creates serious, long-term conservation problems.
(Credit: UNEP/PCAU)

humanitarian efforts and sustainable development and can increase the potential for renewed civil unrest (see color plate 28).

However, this post-conflict period also presents an enormous opportunity to improve a nation's capacity to preserve its natural landscape and native species. Post-conflict governments are actively searching for recovery assistance and are generally receptive to advice on sensible restructuring and improvement of their environment. Conservation organizations that take advantage of this opportunity stand to make significant gains that could last for generations and help protect an often-fragile peace.

Guidance during this critical period can spur changes in high-level ministerial mandates and duties, creating improved data collection, analysis, and environmental impact assessment protocols—and, ultimately, better-protected parks and wilderness. This is also an opportune time to encourage participation in international environmental treaties as well as public participation through environmental education and the formation or reformation and support of local nongovernmental organizations (NGOs).

If conservation organizations have maintained monitoring efforts during the conflict, they are well positioned to present recommendations to improve or expand protected areas. In some circumstances, linkages can be made between governments that strengthen transboundary collaboration or between government and local communities to improve resource management, with the added benefit that such activities may help reduce still-simmering hostilities.

All of these interventions involve coordination with the wider international community, including donors and relief and development agencies. This can be extremely difficult, as the usual focus is on humanitarian and economic recovery. However, without conservation considerations, energy is often directed toward unsustainable or environmentally destructive initiatives that only jeopardize further recovery.

Both conservation personnel working in a country at war and the greater conservation community must maintain a dialogue with these agencies during and after a conflict to ensure that environmental issues are not ignored to the point that irreparable damage is done. Environmental coordination or training can prove especially helpful in refugee camps by reintegrating displaced populations, rebuilding infrastructure, and designing development projects.[14] This can be combined with media-driven efforts to keep wildlife conservation in the public eye and to maintain pressure on state agencies to include the environment in their policies and plans.

Conservation in a conflict setting is not an impossible proposition. Long-term conservation efforts in war-torn regions of Africa, coupled with more recent experiences in Iraq and elsewhere, have shown that conservation is possible during and after war and is a critical element in global biodiversity conservation. Pre-conflict training and coordination with local staff, communities, and NGOs; maintaining a presence on the ground during war (or at least continuing to monitor the situation from afar); and ensuring that conservation is included in the post-conflict rehabilitation process are the keys to successful conservation in conflict-torn regions.

If recent experience is any indicator, war is not going away any time soon. While there is an understandable focus on the human and economic costs of conflict, it is essential that the conservation community make a concerted and coordinated effort to ensure that conflict-related environmental damage does not continue to rise in the ranks of major threats to global biodiversity.

Neither War nor Peace

Protected Areas Still at Risk in DR Congo, 2005

JOHN HART

The Democratic Republic of Congo (DRC) is Africa's most biologically diverse country with the continent's oldest protected area network—home to okapi *(Okapia johnstoni),* white rhino *(Ceratotherium simum cottoni),* bonobo *(Pan paniscus),* and an array of species found nowhere else on Earth.

During DRC's civil war that began in 1996, the country's protected areas came under attack. Illegal mines and logging operations appeared inside parks, squatters seized land, poachers hunted elephants and gorillas, and armed fighters occupied protected areas. Since the beginning of the conflict, over 100 park staff have been killed, park buildings destroyed, and equipment looted.[1]

Looking back over eight years of war, we learned that the single most important factor in protecting imperiled reserves is the continuous presence of well-trained national staff—especially when expatriate conservationists are forced to leave and communication with the national parks headquarters is cut. In the Congo, brave and committed individuals confronted miners and squatters, collected data on poaching and incursions—and provided up-to-date information on what was happening in the national parks throughout the conflict.

This information was used to pressure the occupying military to control some of the most egregious abuses: commercial elephant hunting, illegal land allocation, and occupation of park infrastructure. Timely reports from the field prompted the World Heritage Commission to declare five of the Congo protected areas World Heritage Sites in Danger, making them eligible to receive emergency United Nations Foundation Funds.

DRC's Protected Areas: Nexus of a Resource War

The use of armed force to acquire and control valuable natural resources was the fundamental cause of DRC's war.[2] Although a unified transition government was established when hostilities ended in 2003, the country's parks remain under siege. Parks are seen as readily available land and as a rich supply of bush-meat and other natural products that have been overexploited elsewhere. Large, impoverished rural populations—including landless, displaced peasants—use the parks' resources for basic subsistence: food, firewood, building materials, and rattan. There has been a new wave of illegal logging and mining operations, often conducted with the support of Congolese military and militia.

The Congolese National Parks Institute's (ICCN) ability to administer protected areas was inadequate before the war, but was further weakened by the conflict. Arms and munitions, widely available after eight years of conflict, have made wildlife poaching and intimidation of park guards common. Armed gangs, renegade militias, and pockets of recalcitrant rebels continue to use some sites as bases and strategic outposts. The location of some of Congo's parks near international borders with southern Sudan, Rwanda, Burundi, and Uganda exposes them to other regional conflicts and international smuggling.

Many of those involved in illegal exploitation and land grabs find that the parks provide easy takings. ICCN's control is weak, and state and traditional authorities do not have mandates in protected areas. There is a very real danger that ICCN control of protected areas, once lost, will not be totally recovered, and that preserves will be fragmented and ultimately degraded.

Members of a rebel militia group encamped in the Democratic Republic of Congo's Maiko Park display an AK-47. Automatic weapons used during armed conflicts in the DRC are now being used to hunt wildlife.
(Credit: John Hart)

Hold What Can Be Held

The future of Congo's parks will be determined by the infrastructure, staff, fauna, and flora that can be protected and maintained today. It is imperative that key habitats and corridors are preserved to ensure that depleted wildlife populations can recover once poaching is controlled.

In order to control illegal activities, local negotiations and arrangements are needed, as well as national and international lobbying and diplomacy. A comprehensive antipoaching effort is needed, and the sites must be cleared of militias and armed bandits before major progress is possible.

Well-managed operations with park guards supported by Congolese military have proven successful, but international support may also be required. One way to achieve

> Looking back over eight years of war, we learned that the single most important factor in protecting imperiled reserves is the continuous presence of well-trained national staff.

this might be to broaden the UN peacekeeping mission in DRC to include securing the country's World Heritage sites and other protected areas.

During the period of conflict, three crucial factors mitigated the effects of conflict: on-the-ground field staff, continuous information flow, and secure funding. They are as essential now as they were during the war if the parks are to survive the transition from conflict to peace.

Five World Heritage Sites in the Democratic Republic of Congo received continuous support throughout the country's recent conflicts. These sites, among the best monitored and documented, represent the range of threats currently affecting all of DRC's protected areas.
(Courtesy John Hart)

	Garamba	*Virunga*
ILLEGAL EXPLOITATION		
Poaching flagship species	Elephant, rhino *Fewer than 20 rhino remain*	Elephant, hippo
Mining		Gold
Forest Products		Charcoal
ILLEGAL SETTLEMENT		
Cattle and agriculture		Widespread
Fisheries		Illegal fisheries threaten international resource
INSECURITY		
Staff killed	Yes	Yes
Occupation by armed groups	Periodic incursions, Sudanese rebels	National military and rebels, Rwandan military and rebels
Socio-economic and political context	Borders civil wars zone in southern Sudan	Central location in Great Lakes regional conflict. High population densities. Displaced peoples.

Kahuzi-Biega	Okapi	Salonga
Elephant, gorilla *100 of 240 pre-war gorillas in upland sector remain*	Elephant, okapi *Over 300 elephants killed in 2003–04. Over four tons of ivory removed 2002.*	Elephant, Congo peacock *Probably fewer than 2,000 elephant remain.*
Coltan, casserite, gold. >106 mining sites >10,000 miners	Gold, coltan, diamonds. At least 15 major mining sites	Diamonds
Charcoal, saw logs, bamboo	Charcoal, saw logs	Saw logs
Widespread	High potential for immigration	
		Confrontations with local populations over fishing rights
Yes	Attempted	Attempted
National miliary and rebels, Rwandan rebels.	National military	
Central location in Great Lakes regional conflict. High population densities. Displaced peoples.	Exploitations by competing militias. Demographic frontier for neighboring regions.	Poaching supported by Congolese military.

The Destruction of Iraq's Wetlands and Impacts on Biodiversity

DAVID JENSEN, HASSAN PARTOW,
AND CHIZURU AOKI

Since 1970, there has been widespread destruction of the once-vast Mesopotamian marshlands. The United Nations Environment Programme (UNEP) documents the exceptional scale and speed at which the wetlands have disappeared in two UNEP reports, The Mesopotamian Marshlands: Demise of an Ecosystem (2001)[1] and Desk Study on the Environment in Iraq (2003).[2] Based on historical records and satellite imagery, the reports show that the Middle East's most extensive wetland system had shrunk by 90 percent, from 7,700 square miles to 770 square miles (20,000–2,000 km^2).

Construction of more than 30 large dams on the Tigris and Euphrates rivers began the precipitous decline. But extensive drainage works built from 1991 to 1997, in the wake of the Gulf War, caused the fast, wholesale disappearance of the marshlands. By 2000, the landscape had been largely transformed into desert and salt flats.

In a dry region such as the Middle East, Iraq's wetlands are of immense ecological importance. The marshes once comprised a complex of tall reeds, seasonal marshes, and lagoons, dominated by desert shrub and grasses, shallow and deep-water lakes, and regularly inundated mudflats—and according to incomplete ornithological surveys, were home to at least 134 bird species.

The draining of these marshes has affected global biodiversity from Siberia to southern Africa, particularly migratory birds. Mammal and fish species that existed only in these marshlands that now may be extinct include the endemic smooth-coated otter *(Lutra perspicillata maxwellii)*, the bandicoot rat *(Nesokia bunni)*, and the long-fingered bat *(Myotis capaccinii)*. Critically threatened waterbirds include the African darter *(Anhinga rufa)*, sacred ibis *(Threskiornis aethiopica)*, and goliath heron *(Ardea goliath)*; 66 additional bird species are at risk.

Migratory aquatic species also have been affected, including penaeid shrimp *(Metapenaeus affinis)* and Hilsa shad *(Tenualosa ilisha)*, which move between the Persian Gulf and nursery grounds in the marsh. Increasing salinity in the Shatt al-Arab estuary has damaged the breeding grounds of another fish, the silver pomfret *(Pampus argenteus)*.

The destruction of the vast Mesopotamian marshlands will go down in history along with other human-engineered changes such as the desiccation of the Aral Sea and Amazon deforestation as one of Earth's major and most thoughtless environmental disasters.

However, all is not lost. Signs of an environmental upturn in Iraq emerged after the end of major combat in May 2003, as desiccated land was reflooded. Plentiful rainfall marked an end to a four-year drought (1999–2002), and local communities modified earthworks and drainage structures, reintroducing water into the marshlands. Monitoring efforts to analyze water quality and biodiversity have also resumed since 2003. Preliminary monitoring results, reported by the Iraqi Ministry of Environment, show signs of biodiversity recovery in some areas.[3]

Institutional frameworks for environmental management are being established and reinforced. The Ministry of Water Resources established the Center for the Restoration of the Iraqi Marshlands in September 2003 to guide rehabilitation planning. The ministries of Environment, Municipalities, and Public Works and others have begun discussing coordinated response for sustainable marshland management.

The interim government of Iraq and major donors, including the governments of Japan, Italy, Canada, and the United States, are supporting efforts to protect remaining marshlands and to restore other areas. Of priority concern is conservation of the shared Al-Hawizeh/Al-Azim marshes, straddling the Iran–Iraq border, which are the only intact remains of the original Mesopotamian wetland complex—an important refuge for endangered and endemic wildlife.

UNEP has launched a major project within the UN Iraq Trust Fund to support environmental management of the Iraqi marshlands, with funding from the government of Japan. Pilot projects on wetland management techniques and provision of water and sanitation options to area residents are being developed, using environmentally sound technologies. As part of the project's data collection and analysis efforts, UNEP is monitoring ongoing reflooding through satellite remote sensing and associated changes in vegetation cover. Over the past two years since May 2003, an estimated 20 to 30 percent of the original marshland area has been reflooded. Reflooding, however, is not synonymous with restoration, hence the importance of continuously surveying ongoing changes.[4]

> Historical records and satellite imagery . . . show that the Middle East's most extensive wetland system had shrunk by 90 percent, from 7,700 square miles to 770 square miles.

Captive Breeding

Miracle Under Fire

DAN WHARTON

The literature of human progress is rife with examples of naysayers. And so it is that the relatively new world of wildlife conservation should inch along with the fits and starts and political wrangling that mark all innovation. The very concept fluctuates in importance from one day to the next, while humanity ponders in relative confusion whether wildlife truly is a critical component of a sustainable planet. One thing is certain: no nation has placed wildlife conservation among its highest priorities. If wildlife is indeed critical to human health, education, and welfare—decided priorities in human affairs—the convincing argument that wildlife should be a priority has yet to be made.

During this last century of uncertainty about conservation, captive or conservation breeding has emerged as a proactive strategy—a hopeful strategy that attempts to stop the clock on the downward trajectory of an endangered species. It is a kind of time-out where a species can be plucked from a failing habitat, temporarily removed from the race between thoughtless destruction and the dawning forces of effective protection. However, there has been perpetual misunderstanding about captive breeding, about what it is, what it accomplishes, and, very importantly, what it is not. Is it conservation? Or is it merely another form of human exploitation, giving false purpose to the drama of endangered species exhibition by zoos?

From the Hay Barn: A Miracle and a Mission

In the early 20th century, biologists and zoo curators began to notice that collecting and exhibiting certain animals had had a potentially profound effect: species that had vanished from nature could be found in relative abundance in zoos. The Pere David deer *(Elaphurus davidianus),* the Mongolian wild horse *(Equus przewalskii),* and the European bison *(Bison bonasus)* were shining examples of this early and largely accidental conservation success. These hardy, social-herding species thrived and multiplied on zoo diets and health care protocols copied from those used to raise domestic cattle and horses.

But zoos also ignored opportunities to safeguard other seriously endangered animals in their early collections, including the now-extinct Carolina parakeet *(Conuropsis carolinensis)*, passenger pigeon *(Ectopistes migratorius)*, pink-headed duck *(Rhodonessa caryophyllacea)*, Tasmanian wolf *(Thylacinus cynocephalus)*, and quagga zebra *(Equus quagga)*. However, it was the conservation failures as much as the successes that led to a modern revolution: today, zoos routinely orchestrate animal sciences, from nutrition to genetics, with the singular goal of maintaining a wide range of species in captivity, and with dozens of zoos focusing on the same species concurrently. The zoo mission has become one of good science, perpetuating captive populations, including endangered species, and, of course, animal welfare. The accidental successes of the early 20th century are now the highly organized miracles of the 21st.

Some other animals owing their current survival to captive breeding include the American bison *(Bison bison)*, Arabian oryx *(Oryx leucoryx)*, California condor *(Gymnogyps californianus)*, black-footed ferret *(Mustela nigripes)*, Guam rail *(Gallirallus owstoni)*, Micronesian kingfisher *(Halcyon cinnamomina)*, Mauritius pink pigeon *(Columba mayeri)*, several Lake Victoria cichlid fish species, and the Wyoming toad *(Bufo baxteri)*. For many other species, animals bred in captivity represent a significant percentage of the entire existing population, animals such as the Cuban crocodile *(Crocodylus rhombifer)*, Chinese alligator *(Alligator sinensis)*, thick-billed parrot *(Rhynchopsitta pachrhyncha)*, snow leopard *(Panthera uncia)*, Siberian tiger *(Panthera tigris altaica)*, and Puerto Rican crested toad *(Peltophryne lemur)*.[1]

One thing is certain: no nation has placed wildlife conservation among its highest priorities.

Unfortunately, humanity is still learning to appreciate—and concomitantly regret—the loss of individual components of a highly complex natural landscape. To many, the day after the death of the very last passenger pigeon looked very much like the day before. That we might have done something to change the outcome is even further removed from the vocabulary of regret.

Meanwhile, wildlife conservation moves along as a self-described "crisis discipline,"[2] whereby the call to action addresses the fact that every single day without adequate support means a planet with fewer and fewer species. Some outstanding results have been achieved by protecting habitat, by implementing recovery plans for both individual species and entire ecosystems, and by passing conservation legislation. But the cause of the wildlife crisis is left to other disciplines—to sociology, education, sometimes religion, and, inevitably, to politics.

Given that nature is literally losing ground by the day, one might expect a fair degree of respect and admiration for heroic strategies that rescue and protect some of the most vulnerable and charismatic animals on Earth. However, the drama and publicity around captive breeding have often created suspicion, with critics damning captive breeding for what it is not, instead of embracing it as a unique option—and as a less-than-perfect emergency kit for the inadequate world of conservation action.

The Insurmountable Opportunity

Even some of the most notable captive breeding successes were accomplished amidst opposition and misunderstanding. In the dramatic cases of the black-footed ferret and California condor, political opposition led to a very late, nearly fatal start in breeding efforts.

As condor numbers dwindled during the 20th century, some condor advocates argued a "death with dignity" position to "protect" the species from the ignominy of captive breeding. The debates continued into the 1980s,[3,4] but opposition lost momentum when it became clear that this position advocated extinction. "Death with dignity" was rapidly being accomplished by unrelenting persecution from pest and trophy hunters, food shortages resulting from the urbanization of their Southern California habitat, and damage to eggs from ingesting DDT.

Field conservation had become a process of documenting declining condor numbers, from a high of 60 birds down to under 10. The captive program was finally begun in 1983 by a consortium of zoos and conservation organizations. Biologists used a "double clutching" method, removing one egg from a female's first clutch, which was then hatched in captivity. This stimulated the bird to lay a second egg, which hatched in the wild.[5] By 1987, the last few wild birds were captured and integrated into an already established captive population. Today, there are 147 captive California condors; 100 have been reintroduced into former habitat in California, Arizona, and Utah.

The black-footed ferret was considered extinct until the rediscovery of one small group in Meeteetse, Wyoming, in 1981. However, this did not prompt quick action to breed them.[6] Then disaster struck: in 1984–1985, canine distemper, a disease that is lethal to ferrets, reduced the remaining colony to just 18 animals.

But captive breeding proved effective. Now about 240 animals are housed among several zoos and a US Fish and Wildlife Service (USFWS) facility in Wyoming. Approximately 220 ferrets have been reintroduced each year since 1991 among locations in Wyoming, Arizona, Utah, Montana, South Dakota, Colorado, and Mexico. The Conata Basin population in South Dakota is the most securely established, with 60-plus wild-born litters observed every year.[7]

In both of these cases, the captive breeding profession was handed a tall order: guard the last few specimens on Earth, use them to work out all the details of nutritional, behavioral, and reproductive management—and save the species from extinction at the same time. Biologists have long offered conciliatory recognition of captive breeding as a method of "last resort," but this implication of desperation has all too often been translated to mean "last minute" as well.

In response to the critical issue of timing, the World Conservation Union (IUCN) issued a policy statement prepared by its Captive Breeding Specialist Group (CBSG) in 1987:

> Management to best reduce the risk of extinction requires the establishment of supporting captive populations [early], preferably when the wild population is still in the thousands. Vertebrate taxa with a current census below one thousand individuals in the wild require close and swift cooperation between field conservationists and captive breeding specialists, to make their efforts complementary and to minimize the likelihood of the extinction of these taxa.[8]

Nearly two decades later, this recommendation is rarely considered when constructing conservation strategies for declining species. It is still considered politically incorrect to both zoo and field biologists to suggest that captive breeding might have an important role in preserving such species as the nearly extinct Simien jackal *(Canis simiensis)* or the mountain gorilla *(Gorilla gorilla beringei),* numbering only a few hundred. Since both jackals and gorillas tend to do well in captivity, the likelihood of breeding success is better than that of the condor or ferret. But it remains that neither success in captivity nor failure in the field are yet capable of informing objective discussion on best courses of action regarding breeding efforts.

Myth versus Fact in Captive Breeding

There are five basic misunderstandings that continue to undermine the role of captive breeding in the world of wildlife conservation:

1. Captive breeding is insignificant because it does not save habitats.
2. Captive-bred wildlife will become more like domesticated animals than wild animals.
3. Captive efforts are a drain on wild populations.
4. There will be no end to the need for individual specimens of a wild species.
5. Captive breeding is expensive and captive reintroductions tend to fail, anyway.

Myth #1: Captive breeding is insignificant because it does not save habitats.

Captive breeding is often erroneously perceived as an unworthy objective that competes with conservation in the wild. Although captive breeding does not save habitats, neither do other components of multifaceted conservation strategies aimed at creating stable wildlife populations within sustainable habitats. However, among such species conservation strategies as food and nesting box provisioning, disease control, exotic pest removal, and poaching reduction, only captive breeding is thought to represent an end in itself. Perhaps because animals are

> Captive breeding is often erroneously perceived as an unworthy objective that competes with conservation in the wild.

removed from their habitat and years pass before there are visible results, it becomes easy to confuse conservation's captive breeding with commercial utilization of wildlife, such as raising chinchilla (*Chinchilla lanigera*) for their fur and budgerigars (*Melopsittacus undulates*) for pets.

Meanwhile, species management per se continues to have a prominent place in securing the integrity of wild places. Certain "flagship" species, animals like the Siberian tiger (*Pathera tigris altaica*) or the whooping crane (*Grus Americana*), can be the linchpin in the political will to save large tracts of land from development. However, the classic study published by William Newmark in 1987[9] found that local extinctions of many species occur in protected areas—making it clear that habitat preservation alone, without species management, is not necessarily the universal antidote to extinction. The simple conclusion is that habitat preservation, species management, and species rescue or captive breeding require separate consideration even as they become intertwined for good conservation results.

Myth #2: Captive-bred wildlife will become more like domesticated animals than wild animals.

Critics fail to recognize that zoo biologists understand the profound differences between domestic animal "sculpting"—breeding to enhance certain favorable characteristics—and breeding wildlife for conservation purposes.[10] The conservation breeding objective is to save all the genes, all the behaviors, and all the variation of each species being managed. This is completely opposite of domestic animal breeding, which retains only those traits that enhance physical type or production—characteristics such as phenomenal milk production or weight gain in cows, egg production in hens, or tracking skill in dogs.

For some wildlife species, cryogenically frozen sperm and embryos offer a way to preserve the genes of many generations of captive animals.[11,12] The "frozen zoo" concept continues to develop slowly, as more collections are established and new "individuals" added. But even this is a complex process. Sperm and embryo freezing techniques must be pioneered for each species—and some defy successful freezing. However, the concept is scientifically sound and will continue to grow and play an important role in maintaining genetically viable populations of endangered species.

Myth #3: Captive efforts are a drain on wild populations.

Some argue that endangered populations, which by definition are already handicapped, cannot bear further depletion for any reason. The underlying assumption is that even a radically destabilized habitat always offers a better survival opportunity than captive breeding.

This view underestimates zoo and captive breeding specialist expertise in managing captive animals. It also fails to recognize that field and captive conservation efforts are not mutually exclusive. But most importantly, it ignores basic population biology. In assaulted habitats, animal deaths often exceed births, creating a downward spiral toward extinction.[13] Judicious removal of several animals, especially the injured or orphaned, has virtually no impact on the population whether it is stable at 10 million—or in tragic and inevitable decline to zero.

Myth #4: There will be no end to the need for individual specimens of a wild species.

The number of wild-caught progenitors, or "founder" animals, needed to establish a captive breeding program is relatively small and, once established, very few new individuals are required to maintain it. The ideal number of founders is actually under 30 unrelated animals[14]; rarely do additional wild-caught animals possess genes not already represented in the first 25.[15] Founders can be recruited over many years if the process is initiated early. When multiplied by the offspring they produce, this minimal number of wild-caught animals not only can affect the long-term genetic health of a captive population but can also ensure the future of reintroduced populations. These animals act as an insurance policy against extinction and offer conservation education and conservation ethics-building experiences for millions of zoo visitors annually.

Myth #5: Captive breeding is expensive and captive reintroductions tend to fail, anyway.

As an intensive care method, captive breeding is expensive since it requires skilled professionals plus specialized facilities. However, several variables are not always considered when calculating the cost. Where zoo partnerships are possible, many expenses are absorbed by the zoo, which is funded by cultural institution dollars generated by the communities that those zoos serve. Endangered species breeding and exhibition can also be designed to generate revenue for conservation, providing support for other efforts to save a species and its habitat. Most importantly, cost/benefit analyses do not factor in the risk of species extinction—nor the equity of multiple and complementary conservation strategies.

Some of the misconception that reintroduction does not work stems from a 1994 paper by Benjamin Beck and colleagues[16] describing the failure of attempted reintroductions when they were conducted inappropriately. Reintroduction of captive-bred animals is a new science. Although it may seem deceptively simple, successful reintroduction requires complex analyses to identify proper reintroduction sites, preparation or training of appropriate-age animals, seasonal timing of release, and follow-up studies. As with reproduction or "natural introduction," success is in the numbers: if enough introduced animals and their offspring survive, then the population will grow and stabilize. As long as the captive population is stable, then failed reintroduction efforts become more a point of information about the reintroduction site and/or methodology than an end result. Though complex, there are numerous wildlife reintroductions making good progress from golden lion tamarins *(Leontopithecus rosalia)* to gray wolves *(Canis lupus)* and trumpeter swans *(Cygnus buccinator)*. The difficulty of the process should not be an appropriate justification for extinction when captive breeding emerges as the single viable option for survival.

Obstacles and Critics in Every Corner

In the United States, an unlikely obstacle to captive program development has been the US Fish and Wildlife Service (USFWS) Federal Permit Office. Zoos and breeding facilities can be denied permits to transport captive-bred animals across international borders for breeding purposes even when they are recommended by the American Zoo and Aquarium Association's (AZA) Species Survival Plans. Under the Convention on International Trade in Endangered Species (CITES) and the US Endangered Species Act, importing regulated species must be on a "nondetrimental" basis that does no harm to wild populations—a criterion that zoos emphatically support but is open to unreasonable interpretation. Ever-stricter interpretation now requires that zoos seeking import or export permits demonstrate "enhancement" or commitment to support the same species in the wild—requirements that deny that captive breeding has legitimate conservation value in its own right. Meanwhile, a US District Court judge recently twisted the issue even further by assigning inappropriately inflated value to captive breeding, once again confusing strategy with objective. It was ruled that Oregon coast coho salmon *(Oncorhynchus kisutch)* were no longer eligible for listing under the Endangered Species Act since salmon hatchery fish of the same species could be included in a count of the wild population. By declaring breed-and-release as equal to species recovery, the court not only ignored past failures of the technique but leveled an unprecedented insult to the scientific principles of captive breeding, reintroduction, habitat protection, and wildlife conservation in general.[17]

The zoo profession has been unprepared to defend captive breeding as one of its most unique accomplishments, often bowing to criticism: the AZA and Conservation Breeding Specialist Group (CBSG) have deemphasized captive breeding while promoting the undisputed value of direct field conservation.[18,19]

Reinvention of self in the image of one's critics remains a poor fit for most zoos, institutions whose major strengths are in the areas of exotic animal husbandry, exhibition, and public education. The time has come for a reexamination of what captive breeding is, and what it does—and to reposition it as the important centerpiece of zoo conservation action that it is.

Making Changes

Certain changes in US and international endangered species policy would greatly improve the development and success of captive breeding programs. Streamlining the animal import/export permit process would allow accredited, participating zoos to use a preapproved process. To inform this process, individual AZA Species Survival Plans should detail the needs of endangered species breeding programs, listing foreign and domestic collaborators. More timely permitting would allow international efforts benefiting endangered or CITES-listed species to move ahead relatively unimpeded, allowing greater and quicker response to the international wildlife crisis.

To facilitate this, the AZA should continue its recent analysis of Species Survival Plan effectiveness. Likewise, AZA's full commitment to professional population management would be an important step in giving captive conservation breeding greater credibility within the conservation world.

It is slowly being recognized that captive wildlife population management is at least as technical as wildlife veterinary medicine. The AZA is currently training population management professionals through its Population Management Center at Chicago's Lincoln Park and Brookfield Zoos; additional population management centers and associated advisory boards are needed.

There are changes within the zoo profession, primarily within the world's zoo associations and the CBSG, that would help the conservation community better evaluate what captive breeding accomplishes. The AZA and international counterparts such as the European Breeding Program (EEP) need to develop a more precise, articulate, and unapologetic policy on the role of captive breeding in conservation. This new voice should both inform the public and facilitate discussion and interaction with other conservation organizations.

Lastly, as a respected part of the IUCN, the CBSG should encourage the use of captive breeding as a legitimate conservation strategy. The CBSG has the ability to objectively assess the potential for breeding success and to determine where it will be economical and synchronous with other conservation efforts. Although it should not be employed in all cases, conservation breeding has miraculous potential in select cases involving mammals, birds, reptiles, and amphibians. The CBSG is the ideal bridge between the larger conservation community and captive breeding facilities.

The power of captive breeding as a conservation strategy has been greatly underestimated, perhaps because diligent science and implementation efforts are just two decades old. The zoo profession has largely developed these methods,

> The so-called strategy of "last resort" still promises many miracles of survival where extinction might otherwise occur.

but has purposely slowed progress while entertaining the opinions of those who debate its value.

We can already predict that 21st century conservation efforts will preserve fragmented habitats and that conservationists will need to be creative with broken systems. Species survival will emerge as a clearly separate agenda from habitat preservation, a global experiment in biospheric rescue where the lines between nature and captivity will become increasingly blurred. The so-called strategy of "last resort" still promises many miracles of survival where extinction might otherwise occur. But amidst the promise, captive breeding is also a grim reminder of the needless, ongoing destruction of nature and a conspicuous target for those who would deny that an era of last resort is upon us.

Can Tropical Forests Be Managed for Timber Production and Wildlife Protection?

FRANCIS E. PUTZ

During the heyday of logging in North America, the giant lumberjack Paul Bunyan was a cultural icon. Back then, forests were generally viewed as sources of raw materials—and as impediments to farming and other more profitable land uses. Now, a century later, loggers are often vilified and forests are increasingly valued for their beauty, biodiversity, and other nonuse values. Growing global urbanization will continue to diminish acceptance of logging as people are less frequently exposed to "working forests."[1] The sound of chainsaws and the sight of tree stumps will become more disturbing as the connection between logging and the forest products we enjoy becomes increasingly vague.[2] And while the alarming rate of tropical deforestation is very much in the public eye and most school children are taught concern over deforestation in the Amazon, per capita consumption of wood, paper, and other forest products is steadily increasing in wealthy countries.

Although many conservationists are concerned about the fate of the world's forests, the topic is complicated, and easy solutions are proving to be elusive. Forests are being destroyed and degraded around the world, but threats and management practices vary widely. For example, principal threats to US and European forests are fragmentation by encroaching suburbs and invasion by exotic species. But in the tropics, remaining forests are mostly damaged by wildfires and unsustainable logging practices. This raises a question: To what extent are forest management activities compatible with wildlife protection and other conservation goals?[3] More specifically, under what conditions and with what sort of management practices can forests satisfy the growing demand for forest products while also protecting wildlife and maintaining vital ecosystem services?

It will help to restrict this discussion to the species-rich tropical forests that are of such concern to the conservation community—focusing specifically on the impacts of logging and timber stand management on forests and wildlife, putting aside the issue of deforestation for agricultural purposes such as soybean fields, oil palm plantations, and cattle ranches.

Logs cut from the forests of Sarawak, Malaysia, are trucked to yards like this before being floated downriver to the coast and shipped overseas. (Credit: Elizabeth Bennett)

Before considering the status of wildlife populations in "managed" tropical forests, it may help to define "management" within a broader conservation context. Many forests are logged, but few are "silviculturally managed." Silviculture is the science of forest stand management, whereas logging is the felling and extraction of timber. While logging can be a silvicultural intervention that promotes the growth and regeneration of commercial species (without compromising other forest functions), all too often it is a destructive process in which timber is torn from forests without concern for sustainability.

It is even difficult to generalize about the environmental impacts of logging, as timber harvesting ranges from clear-cutting that razes entire forests to the selective removal of only a tree or two per acre. Clear-cutting is still common in low-diversity forests in the temperate and boreal zones: places like Canada and Russia. Selective logging occurs in more species-rich tropical forests throughout Asia, Africa, and Latin America, where few tree species produce marketable timber. In Amazonian forests, for example, rarely is more than 1 out of 10 trees harvested.

Images of massive clear-cuts on steep slopes haunt the imaginations of many environmentalists, who are justifiably concerned when this type of forestry is proposed. Nevertheless, where light-demanding canopy trees such as most pines and mahoganies are being harvested, silviculturalists can sometimes defend intensive harvesting as appropriate for stand management. In fact, where these light-demanding species are targeted, gentle selective logging opens gaps in the canopy too small for many commercial species to regrow, so these trees become increasingly scarce with each round of harvesting. Familiar examples of this phenomenon include the mining of mahogany trees from the forests of Latin America and the ongoing removal of red oak from the forests of New England. Unfortunately for the future of timber production and, to a lesser extent, the

Recent studies indicate that cloud forests, home to some of the world's most endangered species, may be especially vulnerable to damage from even selective logging.
(Credit: Steve Winter/National Geographic Image Collection)

maintenance of biodiversity, many environmentally concerned policymakers equate increases in logging intensity with increases in environmental abuse, which is not always the case.

The observation that intensive silvicultural interventions are often needed to regenerate commercially valuable species is a clue that the forests where these species grow may have suffered intensive disturbances in the past. European settlers razed New England forests for farmland, but when these farms were abandoned in the late 19th century, forests regrew. Now, foresters are having great

Congolaise Industrielle des Bois, which operates a 3.6 million acre forest concession in the Republic of the Congo, has set aside nearly one-third of the area to pursue sustainable logging certification.
(Credit: Stephen Sautner, WCS)

difficulty regenerating recently harvested red oaks. Similarly, in the Amazon Basin, archaeologists have uncovered evidence of forest-clearing agricultural activities by pre-Columbian farmers. There is also evidence of tree species that failed to regenerate when those lands were abandoned: 90 percent of the Amerindian population died soon after European colonization.[4]

It is critical to note that even low-intensity selective logging can be extremely destructive if carried out by untrained crews. Often, loggers are paid for each tree they fell, much like factory piecework, and as a result, they work without concern for sustaining timber yields or minimizing ecosystem damage. But stand damage can be minimized if reduced-impact logging (RIL) techniques are used in all phases of the extraction process.[5] These techniques are not new, but they are seldom used in the tropics where loggers seek short-term profits at the expense of long-term sustainability. For example, if forest workers are trained in directional felling, damage to nearby trees can often be avoided. Cutting woody vines connecting canopy trees well in advance of logging can further reduce harvesting damage and also lower the risk of developing vine tangles that can impede tree regeneration for decades.

There is little resemblance between a forest harvested using RIL techniques and one logged by untrained, unsupervised workers—even if the same number of trees were harvested. Some logging companies are now adopting RIL practices out of enlightened self-interest, as they are more efficient, safer for forest workers, and, hence, more profitable.[6]

To return to our central question of whether forest management activities are compatible with biodiversity maintenance, it is no surprise that the answer is "it depends," given the wide range of extraction methods used—in both legal and illegal logging—as well as the diversity of wildlife species affected by these activities.[3] For example, populations of some tropical birds, such as hummingbirds and other flower-visiting species, typically increase in logged areas, while others, such as antbirds and other terrestrial, insect-eating birds, typically suffer. Even within the same species, such as long-tailed macaques and other forest primates, there are conflicting reports of populations increasing, decreasing, or remaining steady after loggers leave. Some of these apparent conflicts may be due to differences in the type and intensity of logging, but it does appear that many species are tolerant of selective logging or can recover quickly after harvesting activities cease.

But even where forest management is carried out with care, the importance of maintaining unlogged areas within management units cannot be underestimated. Protecting bands of forest along streams and around other wetlands is particularly important for many animal populations, but other patches of unlogged forest should also be retained as refuges for animals and as sources of seed for reforestation. Particularly where logging intensities are high, it is important to retain clusters of live as well as dead trees to serve as dens and roosting sites.

There are substantial ecological impacts from silvicultural activities such as conducting controlled burns and liberating future crop trees from smothering blankets of vines. This is not surprising, given that these treatments are intended to promote some tree species at the expense of others. While these constitute the direct impacts of forest management, environmentalists should really be paying more attention to the indirect impacts, many of which are consequences of logging road construction. Roads bring an influx of hunters and slash-and-burn colonists into once-remote areas, which then spark widespread wildlife poaching, wildfires, and rampant illegal logging. Even during logging operations, overhunting is rife if laws protecting wildlife are not enforced and logging crews are not provided with other protein sources by the companies they work for.

Logging roads in tropical forests provide access for farmers and other settlers who continue to clear and burn the logged areas once the heavy machinery is gone—and opens the forest to poachers and illegal loggers.
(Credit: Stephen Sautner, WCS)

Access provided by roads increases the financial profitability of activities ranging from poaching to forest clearing for agriculture. Where there are ready markets for bushmeat, as in many African countries, huge swaths of forest are quickly emptied of wildlife by hunters—some of whom are well armed and others of whom employ simple wire snares.[7,8] Similarly, logging roads inadvertently promote the activities of pirate loggers who strip the forest of remaining timber. Illegal logging in the tropics nets billions of dollars each year,[9] so this pressure on forest resources cannot be disregarded from either conservation or development perspectives.

Widespread illegal logging is a symptom of the larger failure of governance in frontier forests in much of the tropics. It is also the failure, at the global level, to realize the true value of tropical forests. As cash-strapped tropical governments allow their forests to be degraded or cleared for agricultural uses, they argue that the revenue is needed for development. Malaysia is such an example.

Loggers who operate within the law argue that if they do not quickly extract the economically valuable timber rapidly, someone else surely will—or the forest will be cleared by unregulated agricultural colonists. Illegal loggers argue that their traditional forest harvesting activities have been criminalized by governments acting on behalf of national elites, not local people. Meanwhile, consumers in the United States pay less for a door made from a 100-year-old tropical forest tree harvested without regard for sustainability than they do for one made from a 20-year-old pine grown on worn-out cotton land in Georgia.

Even people who loathe the idea of logging tropical forests—or logging local forests—agree that most wildlife species are better off in logged forests than in cattle pastures, crop fields, oil palm plantations, or suburban subdivisions.

Well-managed national parks and other nature preserves can save some forests, and the full complement of species they contain, but conservation goals are better served if "working forests" are included in a diverse conservation portfolio.

Unfortunately, with agricultural subsidies and the high prices of land, beef, soybeans, and palm oil relative to the price paid for timber, it is often difficult to financially justify preserving intact forests. What is needed, therefore, are mechanisms for capturing the true value of tropical forests, which takes into account their species diversity, the carbon they store, the water they filter, and the imaginations that they inspire. One concrete way that consumers can support good forestry in the tropics is by purchasing products from forests certified as well-managed by the Forest Stewardship Council (FSC). But more profound policy changes are needed to ensure that our planet's renewable natural resources are managed appropriately. For example, international efforts to compensate forest owners for their conservation efforts, through carbon offset and other programs, should reward sustainable forest management as well as outright forest protection. But such rewards are only likely if people recognize the importance of good forestry practices in maintaining wildlife populations and other biodiversity.

What Falls Through the Cracks in Conservation Strategies?

Interviews with Sylvia Earle and Thomas Lovejoy

SHARON GUYNUP

In recent interviews with marine biologist Sylvia Earle and conservationist and biologist Thomas Lovejoy, I asked each of them to talk about what they feel is not being adequately addressed in conservation—and what needs to be done or thought about differently, both now and in the near future. Here are their thoughts.

Sylvia Earle, *executive director of Conservation International's Global Marine Program, program director for the Harte Research Institute, and Explorer-in-Residence at the National Geographic Society:*

The good news is that the marine conservation community is moving forward in new ways. There is a deliberate trend toward finding solutions to many problems. There is also an increasing focus on the connection between people and the environment, on recognizing that we're a part of nature—not apart from it.

Many think that the ocean has been fully explored, but less than 5 percent has been seen, let alone subjected to scientific scrutiny. The two big discoveries of the 20th century about the ocean are (1) that all life on Earth is dependent on the ocean, and (2) that we are risking our very ability to prosper on this planet because of what we're doing to the cornerstone of Earth's life support system. The obvious issues relate to what we're putting into the ocean and what we're taking out of the ocean.

One of the most important issues concerns lack of public awareness. The world needs to know the real cost of their seafood dinner. We need both global and regional communication plans that educate the general public worldwide to ocean problems; in developing nations, we need to use information networks such as tribal elders and to build local ability to disseminate the message.

For example, people don't understand the damage caused by trawling the deep oceans. They might be upset to learn that the price of their shrimp or orange roughy *(Hoplostethus atlanticus)* translates into the loss of ancient deep-sea coral ecosystems—similar to old growth forests—that may never repair. These undersea treasures are sacrificed for a few pounds of fish; it's like leveling a forest for songbirds or squirrels. And it has nothing to do with food security, but it has everything to do with disproportionate economic gains for a handful of individual companies.

We, who are the market, are the cause, and people need to know that. If nobody ate orange roughy or if nobody consumed deep-sea prawns, these coral gardens would remain untouched. Or if people simply said "no" to eating Chilean sea bass *(Dissostichus eleginoides),* swordfish *(Xiphias gladius),* or tuna, about 300,000 albatrosses, petrels, and other ocean birds that die each year as incidental bycatch in those fisheries would be saved. And those fish would rebound from unprecedented declines. Where in all of history have swordfish, tuna, or other big fish known a predator that can reduce their numbers by 90 percent in less than 50 years? As fish numbers have declined, our techniques for finding and capturing them have greatly improved. Fishermen can find every last one with the same technologies that were used to find enemy submarines during the Cold War.

These are code-red alarms that the ocean is in trouble and therefore our future is in jeopardy. In 50 years, we have done as much damage to the ocean as it has taken humankind 10,000 years to do on the land.

> People don't understand the damage caused by trawling the deep oceans. . . . It's like leveling a forest for songbirds or squirrels.

We need to use whatever means possible to educate people about human impact on the ocean—and to help them make the connections between human health and the degradation of coastal ecosystems and the open ocean.

From the scientists' point of view, it's not only *doing* the science but getting it out there. If scientists discover something and keep the news to themselves, it doesn't do any good. And environmental organizations need to work together and better recognize ocean issues. We also need to develop an expanded, applied research program focused on priority marine environments, areas with high biodiversity and large numbers of endemic species including undersea mountains (seamounts), shallow- and deepwater reefs, continental slopes, and caves.

Our goal should be to do what my mom and dad advised me as a kid: to leave the place at least as good as we found it, and if we really do our job, we'll leave it better off. We need to manage ourselves. We don't manage anything in terms of natural systems; we manage ourselves relative to them. That means restoring some of the damage that we've already caused, and drawing inspiration from our predecessors, such as those that developed national parks. This desire inspired what Aldo Leopold referred to as the "land ethic" during the 20th century, but now an "ocean ethic" is urgently needed. We have a once-and-nevermore opportunity to protect the sea; all future generations either will look at us and say thanks for being so smart, or will rage at us for squandering—for extremely short-term interests—those things that are vital for human survival, for damaging and chopping up our life support system.

We need to establish marine protected areas within wider management regimes, or "seascapes," that protect broad ocean systems. Seascapes are interconnected regions of plant and animal life that are leashed together by common currents—places like the Gulf of Mexico, the eastern tropical Pacific that runs from northern Peru to Columbia, including the Galapagos, or the Galleass current that goes from Kenya to Cape Town and includes Madagascar. We need to increase the area embraced for protection from the present level (less than 1 percent of the ocean) to at least 10 percent within a decade—and adequately protect these areas.

It doesn't mean that we have to stop fishing. What keeps the ocean stable is having intact wedges of life, the predator–prey relationships, the food webs, and the ecosystems. We must protect breeding areas, feeding areas, life cycles, and the ability of a population to tolerate some fishing level while maintaining the integrity of the natural systems of which they are a vital part. We also must create corridors between reserves that protect a suite of migratory species: turtles, sharks, whales.

Then there is the blue heart of the ocean, the 60 to 64 percent that lies beyond any national jurisdiction, that needs global governance. We need to treat these parts of the world ocean that lie outside of national exclusive economic zones as a World Ocean Public Trust, and establish legal and implementation approaches concerning use of the high seas—including fisheries—under coordinated, international, multiuse zoning regimes.

We need overarching policies that protect localized species as well as the whole range of migratory sea species. Along some seamounts, for example, 30 to 50 percent of resident species exist nowhere else on Earth. They are like thousands of individual Galapagos Islands.

> The world needs to know the real cost of their seafood dinner.

Another big thing that we need to do is to reform fisheries across the board. Using market-based mechanisms and subsidy changes, we can reform fisheries through development of sustainable fishing programs and the establishment of a global fund to provide incentives for the adoption of sustainable practices. We must tackle and redirect fishing subsidies; the world's $50 billion dollar annual subsidy equals just about the total net worth of global fisheries. If subsidies were eliminated, commercial fishing would collapse.

Also, destructive fishing practices must be revealed to the public at large for what they are. Trawling, longlining, and drift netting are not acceptable approaches. We're not talking about a small boat with hooks and lines, but rather fishing on an industrial scale with factory trawlers using millions of pounds of bait to catch thousands of pounds of fish.

Another huge problem is that we're taking predators like swordfish, shark, and tuna, carnivores that are often 10 or 30 or 50 years old. Decades of investment is consumed in 20 minutes when we eat top predator fish. These animals are the top of the food chain, representing tens of thousands of pounds of plants for every pound that reaches our plate, compared with two pounds of plants for every pound of farmed catfish or tilapia that we eat. The fish that we farm are all herbivorous. We don't account for the cost of eating carnivores. We don't raise 10-year-old beef cows—it would be too costly to feed them—and we don't eat animals that sit at the top of the food chain, animals like lions and tigers. Moreover, there is a profound disruption when whole categories of creatures are removed from an ecosystem, such as the selective extraction of large carnivores—the top predators.

We need to look seriously toward responsible aquaculture. That's not a blanket endorsement of aquaculture, but if we are to consume aquatic creatures we need to learn how to grow them, just as we did on the land.

Also, fishermen currently have a disproportionate voice in terms of US national policies. There is this attitude that the fish in the ocean belong to the fishermen. But if they belong to anybody, they belong to everybody, and some of us would really prefer that those fish stay alive, recognizing that fish alive in the ocean are as important as birds are in the air and on the land. People are starting to acknowledge the importance of having fish swimming alive in the ocean—instead of just swimming on a plate amongst lemon slices and butter.

There are many things that individuals can do. First of all is to recognize that no one is powerless. Anything that has ever happened throughout human history started with somebody who had an idea or a conviction, somebody who was willing to stand up and do something—and often that has meant that other somebodies came and stood with them. That's what is required now, individuals first of all becoming informed and, secondly, recognizing their power. Use that power to touch others and realize that the goal is a better life for all of us, not just in the next quarter or in the next year but for all time.[1]

Thomas Lovejoy, *president of the H. John Heinz III Center for Science, Economics and the Environment:*

First of all, we're falling way short in fostering public concern about conservation, so these issues get pushed way down on the agenda by other things that seem more urgent. In this way, short-term human needs trump the longer-term ones such as environment and biodiversity conservation, undercutting conservation opportunities and pushing them off into the future. We need to continually think about creative new ways to make people feel part of the natural world and concerned about what's happening to it.

We also need to be good at explaining the importance of conservation to people without allowing ourselves to be co-opted by other agendas. Just look what's happened in the last few years: the big international conservation discussions are now mostly about poverty—which is hugely important—but the poverty problem can't be solved if there is no biodiversity left. We have to get people off the notion that these agendas have to be addressed linearly while the environment is put on hold. There are multiple tasks in front of society, and one of the biggest is protecting our ecological underpinnings. Pitting poverty alleviation against conservation creates a false dichotomy.

However, it is impossible to succeed in conservation without taking indigenous and local people into account. All of us, including indigenous people, need a planet that is biologically healthy, functional, and diverse. This is essential for sustainable development or long-term poverty alleviation. Sustainable development must include protected areas where people are essentially absent as well as vast inhabited areas that are managed and used with a gentle imprint. The science-based approach of the major nongovernmental organizations should be lauded and not portrayed as opposing the interests of indigenous and local people. The only sensible way to set priorities is to use science to maximize conservation and to avoid missing important elements. Such priorities must then be integrated with the socioeconomic matrix to achieve successful programs. We really need to be seen as being on everybody's side.

> We're falling way short in fostering public concern about conservation.

I also think we're still struggling to act on the scale of the problem. You can look back at what the conservation community has done collectively in the last 20 years and see definite improvements in that direction, but we still are obviously falling short. We need to set our sights higher.

Originally conservation was focused on particular species. The focus broadened to encompass particular habitats: there was almost an illusion then that you could save nature by putting fences around it—and although that's very important, it doesn't do it all. Now we must begin to think on a regional scale. Protecting only parts of an ecosystem is not sufficient. Conservationists must find ways to preserve the vitality of entire natural systems. We must protect what George Woodwell of the Woods Hole Research Center calls the "functional integrity of landscapes."

We are now trying to approach conservation on a regional scale with corridors, such as Brazil's Ecological Corridor Project, but even that is still not focused on the whole system. One larger-scale project is the Congo Basin Initiative, which is trying to protect the region's moist tropical forests at the system level.

The pace of deforestation is such that conservationists must implement these huge initiatives without complete knowledge of exactly what they are trying to save. What is needed are plans that are comprehensive enough to provide wall-to-wall coverage of entire systems, such as the Amazon.

Also, we really must address climate change. Nature is already responding to the changes that have already taken place. Those who understand biodiversity have to be the ones articulating where the line should be drawn limiting greenhouse gas concentrations. Ecosystems are the most sensitive of the three elements included in the United Nations Framework Convention on Climate Change: agriculture, economics, and ecosystems. If we don't address climate change vigorously and right now it will be "curtains" for a lot of biodiversity, starting with coral reefs.

We also need to be much smarter about sustainable development. One of the ways to measure whether development is sustainable is by looking at what is happening to a region's biodiversity. This approach is based on work done 50 years ago by Ruth Patrick, the honorary chair of the Academy of Natural Sciences in Philadelphia. In the late 1940s, she figured out that she could read what was being done to a watershed in the biology of its river. I think that this "Patrick Principle" applies everywhere, not just in freshwater. What you often see are many, mostly isolated, individual efforts—each very much in the right direction—that nonetheless must ultimately add up to something that's significant for a region. I think these efforts are best measured by this Patrick Principle.

> A great poem can make as much difference as three volumes of scientific analysis or a piece of legislation.

Consider a region like South Florida, from north of Lake Okeechobee down through the Everglades and Florida Bay to the Keys and the reef beyond. This is essentially one region, dependant on sheet flow of water through the "river of grass." Over a century or more, individual decisions—which seemed fairly reasonable in their context and their time—have cumulatively led to a reduction in freshwater flow of one-quarter to one-half of normal. The consequences include all kinds of problems with South Florida species. Viewed through the lens of the Patrick Principle, alarm bells clearly are ringing: human impact is affecting South Florida unsustainably.

The base biodiversity of a region should therefore be the standard by which to measure sustainability from an environmental point of view. That works because everything we call an environmental problem affects living systems: so biodiversity integrates everything we do, from habitat destruction and local pollution to acid rain and climate change.

Ecosystem management and adaptive management must be applied at the scale of a region. In South Florida, this means fixing the "plumbing," which is being attempted, however imperfectly. It also means protecting wildlands. County coordinating councils are also needed. The biggest gap in conservation is often at this level, where government is small, resources are few—and where many land use decisions are made.

The good news is that most people do not deliberately set out to destroy the environment. If there are alternative ways for people to meet their aspirations, they are usually quite willing to do so. The most important thing is to engage people *early* in the process before vested interests are built up and before resources have been invested in something that shouldn't happen. We need to find more effective ways to find our natural allies within communities and work with them. It is a big job, but that shouldn't be surprising. Saving life on Earth is a 24-hour job forever.

Another issue is that, too often, the conservation community spends more time criticizing and competing with each other than moving forward together. There has to be a division of labor: some organizations should buy land, others are better at diagnosing the problems and doing scientific analysis. Others are real advocates. Some people need to be watching animals with binoculars and figuring out what they need, while others have to be doing applied social primate behavior on Capitol Hill in Washington.

Lastly, eager young people who want to make a difference often ask, "What should I do? Should I study science?" My answer is: do what you feel you do best. Follow your heart. A great poem can make as much difference as three volumes of scientific analysis or a piece of legislation. I believe that all human beings are capable of feeling wonder and awe in the face of the natural world if they would just open up to it. That human potential is our biggest resource.

From "The Peace of Wild Things"

When despair for the world grows in me
and I wake in the night at the least sound
in fear of what my life and my children's lives may be,
I go and lie down where the wood drake
rests in his beauty on the water, and the great heron feeds.
I come into the peace of wild things

WENDELL BERRY
(UNITED STATES, 1934)

The Relative Wild

BILL MCKIBBEN

The first few miles in the morning are often the sweetest part of a day's hike, and so it was this summer day, as we headed up Giant Mountain. A thunderstorm had washed a little of the humidity out of the air, and the trail climbed gently upwards through a lovely Adirondack forest, with some big stands of old shaggy yellow birch. I was hiking with an old friend, and by ten we'd reached the morning's first objective, a granite knob called Owl's Head.

Owl's Head sticks up from the middle of this Adirondack Mountain wilderness like . . . an owl's head. We rested atop a boulder and took in the 360-degree view: high mountains, rocky slides, green ridges, and infinite trees. With the single exception of a fire tower visible on Hurricane Mountain to our north, there was no human mark on the scene before us. "It's hard to match the wildness of the view from an Adirondack mountaintop. Out West you can almost always see a clear-cut," my friend said, quoting the outdoors writer George Wuerthner.

Which is true. I remember climbing Mt. Rainier maybe a decade ago. We set out for the summit under a full moon just after midnight: The view was sublime, with endless peaks in every direction. But as the sun came up, I could suddenly see with sad precision the boundaries of the national park that had been hidden in the darkness—where the checkerboard of clear-cuts stopped. It always rouses us Adirondack chauvinists to hear any comparison between our homeland and the West. We want it recognized that we're in country just as tough and rugged as those North Dakota Badlands or those Montana High Plains or those Idaho river canyons. That we're the West, just back East. All in all, then, it was a wild morning. By myself, except for a companion, in a wild setting, with a wildly heavy pack on my back, with thoughts of wildness on my mind.

But the very idea of being out by yourself in capital W Wilderness in the early 21st century raises a whole set of philosophical questions. Questions like: What is wilderness? And is trying to protect our shrinking wilderness a pointless delusion in an increasingly human-dominated world?

When you walk through the wilderness, then, you walk through an idea, the roots of which lie partly in the Adirondacks. Five or six days' hike to the south of Giant Mountain, hard against the Siamese Ponds Wilderness, lies the cabin where a man named Howard Zahniser spent his summers, enjoying the Adirondack scenery and drafting the federal Wilderness Act. It stated that "A wilderness, in contrast with those areas where man and his works dominate the landscape, is hereby recognized as an area where the earth and its community of life are untrammeled by man, where man himself is a visitor who does not remain."

Passed by Congress in 1964, that language may represent the single most philosophical stand our legislators have taken since the birth of our nation—and those words have had powerful impact. They have allowed protection of tens of millions of acres, land free from cattle grazing, mining, tree-cutting, road-building, dirt-bike riding, and pretty much every other intrusion except wandering around on your own two feet. For most of the next three decades, the battle over wilderness was pretty much between those people who wanted more of it, and those who wanted to graze, mine, cut, build, and roar around in it.

"A wilderness . . . is hereby recognized as an area where the earth and its community of life are untrammeled by man, where man himself is a visitor who does not remain."
—The Wilderness Act, 1964

In many ways the Wilderness Act was modeled on the older Adirondack wilderness law—an 1894 amendment to the state constitution that declared that the 2.7 million acres (1.1 million ha) through which I was now hiking would be "forever wild"—its trees never to be cut or leased or sold. Much of 20th century environmentalism involved setting aside land to preserve the country's dwindling expanses of untouched wilderness. It was articulated best by another Adirondack denizen, Bob Marshall, who conceived the idea for the Wilderness Society on top of one of the neighboring High Peaks. The wilderness idea was eventually, thanks to Zahniser, enshrined in the federal statute; perhaps its greatest triumph is the Alaska Lands Act of the Carter administration. Since then, it has spread around the world.

But of course that progress was not so steady. A conservative reaction set in with Ronald Reagan in the early 1980s—during his presidency, the Sagebrush Rebellion came to Washington, led by antiwilderness zealots like then Secretary of the Interior James Watt, who argued that the federal government should have far less to say about the management of western lands.

Then, in the mid-'90s, a new critique began to emerge from the Left. Its most prominent advocate was an environmental historian named William Cronon, who had by that time already written several books destined to become classics—most notably, *Changes in the Land,* the story of how both the Indians and the settlers had thoroughly and permanently reshaped the landscape of New England. Instead of imagining that Native Americans had inhabited a primeval eastern paradise which colonists corrupted, Cronon said his objective was "to locate a nature which is within rather than without history."

So it was understandable for him to argue, in a paper he published in 1995 called "The Trouble with Wilderness," that land truly "untrammeled by man" was unlikely to be found. Indeed, he maintained, the insistence on a kind of wilderness purity was doing the environmental movement harm by leading to a neglect of more ordinary (and much larger) landscapes. By worshipping wilderness, said Cronon, "We reproduce the dualism that sets humanity and nature at opposite poles. We thereby leave ourselves little hope of discovering what an ethical, sustainable, honorably human place in nature might actually look like."

Talk like this excited a number of academics, because it fit reasonably well with the deconstructionist agenda of the time. A generation of thinkers had become used to looking at a book and saying it was, in and of itself, nothing more than a reflection of its author's subjectivities, something to be "read" with an eye not to plot or character or language but to gender, class, and other such categories. To them, Cronon seemed to be saying that wilderness too was not exactly real, that it was a mere construct, simply another category to be ascribed to the internal, subjective definition of who we are as individuals. You could therefore argue that I was hiking not through the Giant Mountain Wilderness, but through an abstraction—and perhaps even a dangerous abstraction, one that kept me from dealing with much more serious environmental problems that exist in the "real" world—one of toxic waste dumps, polluted skies, and the disenfranchised poor.

These are not the only questions about wilderness that keep rising. Just as Cronon was concerned about its past and how human hands had shaped the land, I was taken with questions about its present and future. In the late 1980s I wrote a book called *The End of Nature* that grew in part from my years in the Adirondacks, the first book for a general audience about global warming. Half of it was straight science reporting: here's how much the temperature is going to go up, here's how we might rein it in a little. But the other half explored the reasons that the prospect of massive climate change made me so sad—because it threatened my newfound love affair with the wild world. I had found the place I belonged, but suddenly that place was in jeopardy.

Say people, in their carelessness, pushed the world's average temperature up 4° or 5°F (2.2°–2.7°C) during this century, which is the current middle-of-the-road, consensus prediction. In that case, Owl's Head might never look out over another real winter, just one long mud season. In the fall, instead of the birch and beech turning yellow and orange in this vast wood, those trees would be dead, replaced if at all by the drab brown of oak and hickory. In the first warm days of March, there'd be no maples left to bleed their sweet sap. Many of the very things that make these mountains the Adirondacks and not, say, the Rockies or the Great Plains, would fade.

Since it's already started getting warmer, is this still the Adirondacks, still the

Champlain Valley? Is this place wild, or natural, anymore? For that matter, was *any* place? Humans have always changed the places they lived and farmed, building roads, clearing fields, clear-cutting forests. But always before, our impact has had a clearly defined limit. Air pollution, acid rain, and other problems began to indicate that our impact was expanding mightily; with global warming we seem to be *everywhere*. The physics of global warming mean, in fact, that the North and South Poles will be hardest hit—the places that are most free of human imprint, that really are wild if any place is wild—might just as well be in the middle of the eastern megalopolis or the Southern California suburbs. With the temperature rising and flora and fauna utterly changed, no place seems wild anymore.

And of course you could go beyond climate change to other examples of unthinkable environmental disaster. There are also our conscious attempts to take control of what once were "wild" processes. Genetic engineering is the best example. We've begun, quickly and systematically, to cross things that until, say, 1990, could never have mated: pine trees and peas, jellyfish and rabbits. A few years earlier, a feminist academic named Donna Haraway wrote that humans were, happily in her view, on the verge of finally becoming totally unnatural: cyborgs, connected to computers, soon to be genetically engineered, and thus liberated from the idea that we were "men" or "women" or even "human beings"—and hence liberated from the idea that we had to act in certain ways. In a world such control imagines, it's not easy to see what the idea of something apart from man, something untrammeled, would be.

For me, though, the idea that there's no such thing as pure wilderness has made the *relative wild* all the more precious. Yes, Cronon's right, and so was I—there's no place that isn't touched by humanity. I have a friend, Curt Stager, who teaches biology at Paul Smith's College, who spent years out with his students looking for a pristine Adirondack Lake—one that hadn't been sterilized by acid rain, one whose sediment cores didn't show telltale signs of logging or road-building in the watershed. He never found one, and he had 3,000 to choose from. Today it rains or snows or doesn't on those lakes in some small measure because of the kind of cars we drive or the ways we heat our homes. In 2003, scientists compiled studies of leaf-out in the spring, of migration dates, of hibernation patterns—and concluded that, due to global warming, spring was coming an average seven days earlier at this latitude than just a few decades before.

But it's precisely *because* of such things that we badly need more wild, not less. If plants and animals are going to need to move north against the rising temperature, we have to give them as much room, and as many corridors, as we can carve out. But beyond that, we need more wild for *human* reasons: we need to set aside land simply to prove to ourselves that we can do it, that we don't need to be in control of everything around us. The deepest cause of all our environmental woes is the idea—embedded deep in consumer society—that each of us as individuals is at the center of the world, that our desires are the most important fact of the world, and that we are very, very big.

Disproving that fallacy and replacing our hyperindividualism with something a little humbler will be the work of decades, but it is one of the important functions of wilderness. When you're in it you feel small, a part of something larger; and by protecting it you pledge yourself publicly to the idea that at least in this place humans should be a little smaller.

We are guests, not remodelers. The battle for the future is precisely between those who are willing to engineer every organism and every natural process for our convenience, who will countenance the radical change of our climate rather than risk any damage to our cosseted and swaddled economy—and those who are willing to say there is something other than us that counts. The concepts of wilderness and Gandhian nonviolence were the two most potentially revolutionary ideas of the 20th century because they were the two most humble. They imagine a whole different possibility for people and for the planet.

There's another, less stern, reason we need the wild too, of course, and that's for sheer comfort. For me, stepping out the door into the wild world is the best way by far to deal with the despair that can come from thinking about and working on the deep problems, environmental and otherwise, now afflicting the planet. Despair is not an irrational mood for our moment, but it is a useless one. So to be in this recovered wild of the Adirondacks, and to see that where humans have taken a step back, nature retains the vitality to resurge—well, that's hope enough for me. I see the endless check dams of the beavers, and stumble across moose scat on the trail, and follow the claw marks of bears up beech trees, knowing that beaver and moose and bear were all absent here a century ago. A world without Giant Mountain, or a Giant Mountain with a toll road on it, or a cable car, or an ATV mosh pit, seems more worth fighting against than ever. In some ways, these wildernesses are the highest monuments of our civilization. "Forever wild," as the New York constitution puts it, even if "wild" means a little less than it used to, and if "forever" seems somewhat shorter.

It is also important to realize that places can grow more wild, not just less. With Eden and its downfall as our mental template, we imagine a one-way arrow. But here's where the Adirondacks are particularly comforting. People came late to these mountains—Mt. Marcy, the highest peak in New York, wasn't climbed by a European until 1834, a generation after Lewis and Clark stumbled home from the West. But once people came, they came with a vengeance. They came mostly to log, damming the lakes and streams to float the timber down to mills at the margins of the park. They worked mostly with axe and crosscut saw, and

> The battle for the future is precisely between those who are willing to engineer every organism and every natural process for our convenience, who will countenance the radical change of our climate . . . and those who are willing to say there is something other than us that counts.

yet they accomplished truly impressive feats of deforestation—there are pictures from some of these mountaintops showing not a tree still standing. The piles of slash were set afire by the trains hauling the logs away. During some years at the turn of the century, hundreds of thousands of acres burned.

But then, humans took a step back. Much of it was accidental—having timbered off their land, many owners didn't want to pay taxes on it while the trees regrew. And so the state inherited the land, setting it aside as part of the forest reserve. Those millions of "forever wild" acres were the core of a sweet biological resurgence—in many places now you need to be a decent forester to tell you're not in old-growth forest. Many of the creatures that belonged here returned—beaver, then bear, then moose, everything but the top predators. (And depending on whom you listen to, the coyotes may have adapted to fill that niche, hunting in packs and killing deer.) All in all, it is a place of renascent glory. Not impregnable—acid rain threatens, as I have said, and climate change, and other woes. But for the moment, the Adirondacks stand as a monument to what can still happen when people decide to take that step back, to leave some room for something else.

So this day on Giant Mountain we could sense two possibilities: either a resurgence of green—or a steady, growing tide of brown. Human influence growing larger yet, which is certainly the trend, or people deciding to make themselves a little smaller. That would take technology (the hybrid engine and the windmill) and political will (for compromise, for cooperation, for sharing) and most of all it would take a kind of individual redefinition: a willingness, a desire, to find satisfaction in human and natural communities, not in possessions and in power. The question might be: Who will be the true giants, people or mountains? On that hinges much.

ACKNOWLEDGMENTS

We would like to thank the many people who contributed time, energy, and ideas to this effort—those who helped conceive *State of the Wild;* provided information, contacts, and other support; facilitated production; and reviewed content.

Rodolfo Arauz, Felicity Arengo, Elizabeth Babcock, Andre Baumgarten, John Behler, BirdLife International, Sharon Blessum, Ramon Bonfil, Jackie Bonnano, Orietta Brewer, John Bruschini, Gosia Bryja, John Calvelli, Archie Carr III, Nancy Celini, Rebecca Cerroni, Avecita Chicchón, Peter Clyne, Chad Cohen, Lori Cohen, Kathy Conforti, Pete Coppolillo, John Croxall, James Deutsch, Karl Didier, Gail Dole, Environmental Investigation Agency, Eva Fearn, Joshua Ginsberg, Nancy Green, Dawn Greene, Donna Marie Grieco, Catherine Grippo, Craig Groves, Jefferson Hall, Susan Hannah, Graham Harris, Pamela Hassell, Matthew Hatchwell, Cathy Higgins, Jodi Hilty, Joanne Hoersch, Julie Holdom, Luke Hunter, David Jensen, Arlyne Johnson, Steve Johnson, Jan Kaderly, Beth Karpowic, Laura Klein, Linda Krueger, Danielle LaBruna, Richard Lattis, Liz Lauck, Rob Lee, Helder Lima de Queiroz, Andrew Mack, Julie Maher, Julia Mair, Silvio Marchini, Sarah Marinello, Fernanda Marques, Sarah McGranahan, Seamus McGraw, Roan McNab, Mary Mester, Carolina Murcia, Than Myint, Tom Nangle, Andrés Novaro, Matt O'Brien, Shannon O'Brien, David Olson, Todd Olson, Steve Osofsky, Michael Painter, Tracey Paradiso, Graeme Patterson, Meade Love Penn, Gina Pfaff, Karen Phillips, Colin Poole, Nick Raitelu, Angela Resch, Alexandra Rojas, Howard Rosenbaum, Anne-Marie Runfola, Eric Sanderson, Stephen Sanderson, Christine Santora, Glenn Scherer, Martha Schwartz, Diane Shapiro, Christine Sheppard, Samantha Strindberg, Andrew Taber, Yemi Tessema, Pat Thomas, John Thorbjarnarson, Karen Tormey-Lettieri, Adrian Treves, Maria Elena Urriste, Tim Wachter, Dale Walker, Lynne Warberg-Nations, Amy Weinberg, Gillian Woolmer, World Conservation Union, Pablo Yorio, Steve Zack, and Peter Zahler.

. . . and special thanks to Sandra Alcosser, George Amato, Debbie Behler, Elizabeth L. Bennett, Michael Berens, William Conway, Robert A. Cook, William B. Karesh, Ellen Pikitch, Alan Rabinowitz, Kent Redford, John Robinson, Nicolas Ruggia, Carl Safina, Stephen Sautner, George B. Schaller, Bijal Trivedi, Amy Vedder, Bill Weber, Dan Wharton, David Wilkie, Steve Winter, and lastly, to our wise and wonderful editor, Barbara Dean, and our impeccable assistant editor, Laura Carrithers.

Thank you all. This book could not have been produced without your help.

The poems in this collection are part of a permanent installation in the Central Park Zoo sponsored by Poets House, New York, and the Wildlife Conservation Society, with a grant from the Institute of Museum and Library Services.

Notes

By the Numbers: Hunted, Traded, and Eaten into Extinction, by Sharon Guynup

1. http://www.iucn.org/themes/ssc/red_list_2004/summarytables_EN.htm.

2. D. Wilkie and J. Carpenter, "Bushmeat hunting in the Congo Basin: an assessment of impacts and options for mitigation," *Biodiversity and Conservation* 8(1999):927–955.

3. J. Robinson and E. Bennett, "Carrying capacity limits to sustainable hunting in tropical forests," in J. Robinson and E. Bennett, eds., *Hunting for Sustainability in Tropical Forests* (New York: Columbia University Press, 2000).

4. E. Bennett, "Is there a link between wild meat and food security?" *Conservation Biology* 16(3)(2002):590–592.

5. E. Bennett and J. Robinson, "Hunting of wildlife in tropical forest: implications for biodiversity and forest peoples," *Biodiversity Series—Impact Studies* (Washington, DC: World Bank, 2000).

6. A. Vincent, "International Trade in Seahorses," TRAFFIC International 1996; Project Seahorse, 2005, unpublished data.

7. W. Karesh, Wildlife Conservation Society, pers. comm.

8. W. Karesh, Wildlife Conservation Society, pers. comm.

9. L. Taylor, S. Latham, and M. Woolhouse, "Risk factors for human disease emergence," *Philosophical Transactions of the Royal Society London B* 356(2001):983–989.

10. *New Scientist* 183(2459)(2004):8.

11. http://federalaid.fws.gov/license%20holders/Hunting%20License%20Data.pdf.

12. *Science* 305(2004):1958–1959.

13. G. Schaller, Wildlife Conservation Society, pers. comm., 2004.

14. G. Schaller, Wildlife Conservation Society, pers. comm., 2004.

15. D. Williamson, *Tackling the Ivories: The Status of the U.S. Trade in Elephant and Hippo Ivory* (Washington, DC: TRAFFIC North America, 2004).

16. http://www.hsus.org/wildlife/issues_facing_wildlife/wildlife_trade/elephant_trade_fact_sheet/.

17. T. Milliken, *Monitoring of Illegal Hunting in Elephant Range States* (Cambridge, UK: TRAFFIC, 2004).

18. www.eaza.net/turtle/download/EN38_p18_19.pdf.

19. http://news.bbc.co.uk/1/hi/world/asia-pacific/1732508.stm.

20. http://news.bbc.co.uk/1/hi/world/asia-pacific/1732508.stm.

21. *Wild Animal Trade Monitoring at Selected Markets in Guangzhou and Shenzhen, South China, 2000–2003.* KFBG Technical Report #2, June 2004.

22. C. Seabrook, "Scientists Urge Curbs on Trade in Wildlife," *Atlanta Journal-Constitution,* January 15, 2004, p. A3.

23. http://www.hsus.org/legislation_laws/wayne_pacelle_the_animal_advocate/the_us_should_tighten_its_borders_to_imported_exotic_animals.html.

24. http://www.hsus.org/legislation_laws/wayne_pacelle_the_animal_advocate/the_us_should_tighten_its_borders_to_imported_exotic_animals.html.

25. http://www.hsus.org/legislation_laws/wayne_pacelle_the_animal_advocate/the_us_should_tighten_its_borders_to_imported_exotic_animals.html.

26. Anon., *Killed for a Cure: A Review of the Worldwide Trade in Tiger Bone* (Cambridge, UK: TRAFFIC International, 2004).

27. *Killed for a Cure.*

28. *The Tiger Skin Trail* (Coventry, UK: Environmental Investigation Agency, 2004), p.10.

29. http://hsus.org/wildlife/issues_facing_wildlife/captive_exotics_and_wild_animals_as_pets/the_whims_and_dangers_of_the_exotic_pet_market.html.

Foreword

A Brief History of State of the Wild, *by Kent H. Redford*

1. S. Meyer, "End of the wild," *Boston Review* 29(2004).

I: State of the Wild

Gold or Flowers: One View on the State of the Wild, by George B. Schaller

1. E. Sanderson et al., "The human footprint and the last of the wild," *Bioscience* 52(2002):891–904.

2. J. Robinson and E. Bennett, eds., *Hunting for Sustainability in Tropical Forests* (New York: Columbia University Press, 2000).

3. "Tragedy of the commons?" *Science* 302(2003):1907–1929.

4. S. Sanderson and K. Redford, "Contested relationship between biodiversity conservation and poverty alleviation," *Oryx* 37(2003):389–390.

5. Anon., "More or less equal?" *Economist* 370(2004):69–71.

6. T. Li, "Engaging simplifications: community-based resource management, market processes and state agendas in upland Southeast Asia," *World Development* 30(2002):265–283.

7. A. Carr, "Utopian bubbles," *Wild Earth* 14(2004):34–39.

8. S. Sanderson, "The future of conservation," *Foreign Affairs* 81(5)(2002):162–173.

9. J. Caldecott, *Designing Conservation Projects* (Cambridge, UK: Cambridge University Press, 1996).

10. J. Sayer and B. Campbell, *The Science of Sustainable Development* (Cambridge, UK: Cambridge University Press, 2004).

11. S. Kellert, J. Mehta, and L. Lichtenfeld, "Community resource management: promise, rhetoric, and reality," *Society and Natural Resources* 13(2000):705–715.

12. S. Sanderson, "The future of conservation."

Mapping the Wild: The Human Footprint, by Eric W. Sanderson

1. E. Sanderson et al., "The human footprint and the last of the wild," *BioScience* 52(2002):891–904.

2. A complete listing can be found at: www.wcs.org/humanfootprint.

Discoveries, by Bijal Trivedi

1. D. Allen et al., "A new species of *Gallirallus* from Calayan Island, Philippines," *Forktail* 20(2004):1–7.

2. S. Biju and F. Bossuyt, "New frog family from India reveals an ancient biogeographical link with the Seychelles," *Nature* 425(2003):711.

3. R. Wallace, Wildlife Conservation Society, pers. comm., 2004.

4. D. Brooks et al., "A new species of *Oryzomys* (Rodentia: Muridae) from an isolated pocket of cerrado in eastern Bolivia," *Occasional Papers, Museum of Texas Tech University* 241(2004):1–12.

5. K. Dausmann et al., "Hibernation in a tropical primate," *Nature* 429(2004):825–826.

6. J. Soto and C. Vooren, "*Hydrolagus matallanasi* sp. Nov. (Holocephali, Chimaeridae) a new species of rabbitfish from southern Brazil," *Zootaxa* 687(2004):1–10.

7. http://www.eurekalert.org/pub_releases/2004-09/uoaf-usd092104.php.

8. http://www.eurekalert.org/pub_releases/2004-09/ps-nhv092304.php.

New Conservation Methods and Technologies, by Ken Kostel

1. R. DeSalle and G. Amato, "The expansion of conservation genetics," *Nature Reviews Genetics* 5(2004):702–712.

2. P. Herbert et al., "Identification of birds through DNA barcodes," *Public Library of Science Biology* 2(2004):1657.

3. Anon., "DNA tests reveal fish culprits," *Marine Pollution Bulletin* 48(2004):1012.

4. K. Comstock et al., "Amplifying nuclear and mitochondrial DNA from African elephant ivory," *Conservation Biology* 17(2003):1840.

5. S. Wasser et al., "Assigning African elephant DNA to geographic region of origin," *Proceedings of the National Academy of Sciences* 101(2004):14847.

6. Anon., "Shark protection," *Promise of Marine Biotechnology in Florida* 2004:10–11.

7. D. Gachuche et al., "GPS-GSM Animal Tracking Project," (2004), http://www.save-the-elephants.org/PDF%20Files/gsm-june04-web.pdf.

8. M. Martonisi et al., "The ZebraNet wildlife tracker," (2004), http://www.princeton.edu/~mrm/zebranet.html; pers. comm., 2004.

9. B. Block et al., "Revealing pelagic habitat use: the tagging of Pacific pelagics program," *Oceanologica Acta* 25(2003):255.

10. N. Bazilchuk, "Backward compatible," *Conservation in Practice*, 5(4)(2004):37.

11. R. Sanchez and G. Kooyman, "Advanced systems data for mapping emperor penguin habitats in Antarctica," *USGS Open File Report 2004–1379* (2004), http://erg.usgs.gov/isb/pubs/ofrs/2004–1379/OFR2004-1379.pdf.

12. B. Woods, "A window on walrus," *Imaging Notes* (2002), http://www.imagingnotes.com/janfeb02/woods.htm.

13. E. Sanderson, Wildlife Conservation Society, pers. comm., 2004.

Regulating the Wild, by Ken Kostel

1. http://www.gbrmpa.gov.au/corp_site/management/zoning/.

2. http://www.legislation.qld.gov.au/LEGISLTN/SLS/2004/04SL190.pdf; http://www.wwf.org.au/News_and_information/Publications/PDF/Report/qld_landclearing.pdf.

3. http://aol.countrywatch.com/aol_printwire.asp?vCOUNTRY=42&UID= 1071635.

4. http://envfor.nic.in/legis/wildlife/wild_act_02.pdf.

5. http://dte.gn.apc.org/cper04.htm; http://dte.gn.apc.org/61MIN.HTM.

6. Australian Department of Environment and Heritage, 2003, http://www.deh.gov.au/minister/env/2003/mr19aug03.html.

7. http://www.senate.gov.ph/press_rel/pimentel1_dec3.htm.

8. http://www.wild-russia.org/archives/oct2004.htm.

9. http://www.cms.int/species/acap/acap_bkrd.htm.

10. http://www.internationalwildlifelaw.org/BioBill_B30D_03.pdf.

11. http://www.nemaug.org/nfa.htm.

12. http://frwebgate.access.gpo.gov/cgi-bin/getdoc.cgi?dbname=108_cong_bills &docid=f:h2264enr.txt.pdf.

13. http://frwebgate.access.gpo.gov/cgi-bin/getdoc.cgi?dbname=108_cong_bills&docid=f:h3378enr.txt.pdf.

14. http://www.nyc.gov/cgi-bin/misc/pfprinter.cgi?action=print&sitename=OM.

15. http://www.cites.org/.

The Rarest of the Rare: Some of the World's Most Endangered Animals, by Michael Berens

1. University of Nebraska State Museum, "Endangered American burying beetle update," http://www.museum.unl.edu/research/entomology/endanger.htm.

2. M. Farhadinia, "The last stronghold: cheetah in Iran," *Cat News* 40(2004):11–14.

3. BirdLife International, "Species factsheet: *Leucopsar rothschildi*," http://www.birdlife.org/datazone/search/species_search.html?action=SpcHTMDetails.asp&sid=6822&m=0.

4. Florida Museum of Natural History, "*Alligator sinensis*," http://www.flmnh.ufl.edu/natsci/herpetology/brittoncrocs/csp_asin.htm.

5. UNEP Great Ape Survival Project, "Collaborative Programme for the Conservation of Cross River Gorillas," http://www.unep.org/grasp/supportcrossrivergorilla.asp.

6. Primate Info Net, "Delacour's Langur *Trachypithecus delacouri* Vietnam," http://pin.primate.wisc.edu/news/peril14.html.

7. IUCN/SSC Canid Specialist Group, "Ethiopian Wolf *(Canis simensis),*" http://canids.org/SPPACCTS/ethiopn.htm.

8. IUCN/SSC Iguana Specialist Group, "West Indian iguanas: status survey and conservation action plan," http://www.iucn-isg.org/actionplan/ch2/grandcayman.php.

9. Cetacea, "*Eschrichtius robustus*: Gray whale," http://cetacea.org/gray.htm.

10. World Wildlife Fund U.K., "Iberian lynx," http://wwf.org.uk/core/wildlife/fs_0000000022.asp.

11. International Rhino Foundation, "Javan rhino," http://www.rhinos-irf.org/rhinoinformation/javanrhino/.

12. K. Zippel, "The Kihansi spray toad: African maid of the mist," Detroit Zoological Society, http://detroitzoo.org/dzs/2004/mar2004/kihansi_toad.html; S. Lee, Wildlife Conservation Society, pers. comm., 2004.

13. National Marine Fisheries Service Office of Protected Resources, "Leatherback sea turtle *(Dermochelys coriacea),*" http://www.nmfs.noaa.gov/prot_res/species/turtles/leatherback.html.

14. Monachus.org, "Mediterranean monk seal *(Monachus monachus),*" http://www.monachus.org/profiles/mediseal.htm.

15. S. Wright, "Big fish," *U.C. Davis Magazine Online,* 21(4)(2004), http://www.ucdmag.ucdavis.edu/su04/feature_3.html.

16. Animal Info, "Northern hairy-nosed wombat," http://www.animalinfo.org/species/lasikref.htm.

17. Essig Museum of Entomology, "Palos Verdes blue butterfly (Lepidoptera: Lycaenidae)," http://essig.berkeley.edu/endins/paloverd.htm.

18. Animal Info, "Saola," http://www.animalinfo.org/species/artiperi/pseunghe.htm.

19. Animal Info, "Seychelles sheath-tailed bat," http://animalinfo.org/species/bat/coleseyc.htm.

20. J. Thorbjarnarson, Wildlife Conservation Society, pers. comm., 2004.

21. Commonwealth Scientific and Industrial Research Organisation, "Australia's first endangered marine fish," http://www.csiro.au/index.asp?type=faq&id=Spotted Handfish&stylesheet=divisionFaq.

22. BirdLife International, "Species factsheet: Sulu hornbill," http://www.birdlife.net/datazone/search/species_search.html?action=SpcHTMDetails.asp&sid=950&m=0.

23. D. Janz et al., *National Recovery Plan for the Vancouver Island Marmot* (Marmota vancouverensis), *2000 Update.* RENEW report, no. 19 (Ottawa: Canadian Wildlife Service, 2000).

24. Cetacea, "*Lipotes vexillifer*: Baiji or Chinese river dolphin," http://cetacea.org/baiji.htm.

25. Animal Info, "Yellow-tailed woolly monkey," http://www.animalinfo.org/species/primate/lagoflav.htm#status.

III: Hunting and the Wildlife Trade

A Short History of Hunting in North America

1. P. Matthiessen, *Wildlife in America* (New York: Viking, 1987), pp. 19–21, 26–28.

2. D. Quinn and A. Quinn, *The First Colonists: Documents on the Planting of the First English Settlements in North America, 1584–1590* (Raleigh: North Carolina Division of Archives and History, 1982), pp. 2–3.

3. For a description of southeastern US wildlife in the early 1700s, see J. Lawson, *A New Voyage to Carolina* (London: 1709), pp. 9, 115–126.

4. J. Trefethen, *An American Crusade for Wildlife* (Alexandria, VA: The Boone and Crockett Club, 1975), p. 39.

5. R. McCabe and T. McCabe, "Of slings and arrows: an historical retrospection," in L. K. Halls, *White-Tailed Deer: Ecology and Management* (Harrisburg, PA: Stackpole Books, 1984), p. 63.

6. Trefethen, *An American Crusade,* pp. 32, 38–39.

7. *Rousseau County Times,* April 10, 1896, quoted in R. McCabe and T. McCabe.

8. R. McCabe and T. McCabe, "Of slings and arrows," pp. 29–30, 72.

9. The Watchbison Committee, http://www.bwfly.com/watchbison/.

10. D. Hurteau, "Elk then and now," *Field and Stream* 109(2004/2005):66.

11. J. Yoakum, "Pronghorn," in J. Schmidt and D. Gilbert, *Big Game of North America: Ecology and Management* (Harrisburg, PA: Stackpole Books, 1978), p. 113.

12. W. Banko, *The Trumpeter Swan: Its History, Habits, and Population in the United States* (Lincoln: University of Nebraska Press, 1960), p. 13.

13. F. Graham Jr., *The Audubon Ark: A History of the National Audubon Society* (New York: Alfred A. Knopf, 1990), pp. 24–26. It was Madame de Pompadour, the mistress of Louis XV, who began adorning her hair with exotic bird feathers in the 1740s, setting a standard for women's fashions for the next 160 years.

14. McCabe and McCabe, "Of slings and arrows," p. 66.

15. Trefethen, *An American Crusade,* p. 62.

16. G. Perkins Marsh, *Man and Nature* (Cambridge, MA: Harvard University Press, 2000 reprint of 1864 edition), p. 3.

17. John F. Reiger, *American Sportsmen and the Origins of Conservation* (Norman: University of Oklahoma Press, 1986), pp. 26, 31, 29.

18. Reiger, *American Sportsmen,* pp. 67–69.

19. G. Grinnell and T. Roosevelt, *Trail and Camp-Fire: The Book of the Boone and Crockett Club* (New York: Forest and Stream Publishing Co., 1897), p. 343.

20. Grinnell and Roosevelt, *Trail and Camp-Fire,* pp. 350–355. The Boone and Crockett Club roster included John Jay Pierrepont, Rutherford Stuyvesant, Secretary of the Interior Carl Schurz, US Senator George G. Vest, the US Geological Survey's Arnold Hague, and Supreme Court lawyer William Hallett.

21. T. Lund, *American Wildlife Law* (Berkeley: University of California Press, 1980), p. 61.

22. Aldo Leopold, *A Sand County Almanac* (London: Oxford University Press, 1975), pp. 224–225.

23. Personal communication: Ducks Unlimited has spent $1.4 billion to protect 10 million acres (4 million ha), the Rocky Mountain Elk Foundation, $154 million to buy/enhance 3 million acres (1.2 million ha), the National Wild Turkey Federation, $120 million for 2.2 million acres (890,000 ha), Pheasants Forever, $70 million for 2 million acres (809,000 ha), the Ruffed Grouse Society, $7.2 million for 450,000 acres (182,000 ha), and Quail Unlimited, $6 million for 400,000 acres (162,000 ha).

24. Rocky Mountain Game and Fish, http://www.rmgameandfish.com/rm_aa074503a/.

25. Oakland Zoo, http://www.oaklandzoo.org/atoz/azbison.html.

26. National Bison Association, http://www.bisoncentral.com/history/history.asp.

27. Figures are from Rocky Mountain Elk Foundation, National Wild Turkey Federation, Foundation for North American Wild Sheep, and Buckmasters America Deer Foundation.

28. S. Mahoney, "The seven sisters: pillars of the North American wildlife conservation model," *Bugle: The Journal of the Rocky Mountain Elk Foundation,* September/October 2004, p. 144.

29. T. Roosevelt, *The Wilderness Hunter* (New York: G.P. Putnam's Sons, 1900), p. 255.

30. R. Harris, W. Wall, and F. Allendorf, "Genetic consequences of hunting: what do we know and what should we do?" *Wildlife Society Bulletin* 30(2002):634–643.

31. J. Ray et al., *Carnivores and Biodiversity: Does Saving One Conserve the Other?* (Washington, DC: Island Press, 2005).

Consuming Wildlife in the Tropics, by Elizabeth L. Bennett

1. J. Robinson, "Calculating maximum sustainable harvests and percentage offtakes," in J. Robinson and E. Bennett, eds., *Hunting for Sustainability in Tropical Forests* (New York: Columbia University Press, 2000), pp. 521–524.

2. In parts of Africa, wild meat is called "bushmeat." In this paper, the term "wild meat" is used to reflect the global nature of the issue.

3. That is, the total weight of animals or plants in a defined area.

4. J. Robinson and E. Bennett, "Carrying capacity limits to sustainable hunting in tropical forests," in Robinson and Bennett, *Hunting for Sustainability,* pp. 13–30.

5. J. Robinson and E. Bennett, "Having your wildlife and eating it too: an analysis of hunting sustainability across tropical ecosystems," *Animal Conservation* 7(2004):1–12.

6. E. Bennett, A. Nyaoi, and J. Sompud, "Saving Borneo's bacon: the sustainability of hunting in Sarawak and Sabah," in Robinson and Bennett, *Hunting for Sustainability*, pp. 305–324.

7. R. Bailey and N. Peacoc, "Efe pygmies of northeast Zaire: subsistence strategies in the Ituri Forest," in I. de Garine and G. Harrison, *Uncertainty in the Food Supply* (Cambridge, UK: Cambridge University Press, 1988), pp. 88–117.

8. W. Townsend, "The sustainability of hunting by the Sirionó Indians of Boliva," in Robinson and Bennett, *Hunting for Sustainability*, pp. 267–281.

9. N. Chagnon and R. Hames, "Protein deficiency and tribal warfare in Amazonia: new data," *Science* 203(1979):910–913.

10. P. Chardonnet et al., "Current importance of traditional hunting and major contrasts in wild meat consumption in Sub-Saharan Africa," in J. Bisonette and P. Krausman, eds., *Integrating People and Wildlife for a Sustainable Future* (Bethesda, MD: The Wildlife Society, 1995), pp. 304–307.

11. P. Auzel and D. Wilkie, "Wildlife use in northern Congo: hunting in a commercial logging concession," in Robinson and Bennett, *Hunting for Sustainability*, pp. 413–426.

12. All figures in this paper refer to dressed weight of meat, i.e., the weight of the carcass minus the bones and intestines. The conversion rate used from whole animal to dressed weight is 60 percent.

13. E. Bennett and M. Gumal, "The inter-relationships of commercial logging, hunting, and wildlife in Sarawak, and recommendations for forest management," in R. Fimbel, A. Grajal, and J. Robinson, eds., *The Cutting Edge: Conserving Wildlife in Managed Tropical Forests* (New York: Columbia University Press, 2001), pp. 359–374.

14. L. Clayton and E. Milner-Gulland, "The trade in wildlife in North Sulawesi, Indonesia," in Robinson and Bennett, *Hunting for Sustainability*, pp. 473–496.

15. D. Wilkie et al., "If trade in bushmeat is legalized, can the laws be enforced and wildlife survive in Central Africa: evidence from Gabon," *Journal of International Wildlife Law and Policy*, in press.

16. R. Bodmer, this volume.

17. C. Shepherd, "Export of live freshwater turtles and tortoises from North Sumatra and Riau, Indonesia: a case study," in P. van Dijk, B. Stuart, and A. Rhodin, eds., *Asian Turtle Trade: Proceedings of a Workshop on Conservation and Trade of Freshwater Turtles and Tortoises in Asia* (Lunenberg, MA: Chelonian Research Foundation, 2000), pp. 112–119.

18. S. Roberton et al., *The Illegal Wildlife Trade in Quang Nam Province: Covert Investigations by Specially Trained Forest Rangers,* Wildlife Law Enforcement Strengthening: Report No. 5 (Hanoi, Vietnam: The Quang Nam Forest Protection Department and WWF Indochina, 2004).

19. T. O'Brien and M. Kinnaird, "Changing populations of birds and mammals in North Sulawesi," *Oryx* 30(1996):150–156.

20. J. Fa, "Hunted animals in Bioko Island, West Africa: sustainability and future," in Robinson and Bennett, *Hunting for Sustainability*, pp. 168–198.

21. C. Peres, "Evaluating the impact and sustainability of subsistence hunting at multiple Amazonian forest sites," in Robinson and Bennett, *Hunting for Sustainability*, pp. 31–56.

22. E. Bennett and M. Rao, *Hunting and Wildlife Trade in Tropical and Subtropical Asia: Identifying Gaps and Developing Strategies* (Bangkok, Wildlife Conservation Society, 2002).

23. P. Griffin and M. Griffin, "Agta hunting and the sustainability of resource use in

northeastern Luzon, Philippines," in Robinson and Bennett, *Hunting for Sustainability,* pp. 325–335.

24. A. Stearman, "A pound of flesh: social change and modernization as factors in hunting sustainability among Neotropical indigenous societies," in Robinson and Bennett, *Hunting for Sustainability,* pp. 233–250.

Wildlife Trade within East Asia: Supply and Demand for Traditional Oriental Medicine, by James Compton and Samuel K. H. Lee

1. S. Lee, TRAFFIC Southeast Asia, pers. comm., 2004.

2. *Guidelines on the Conservation of Medicinal Plants* (Switzerland: IUCN, WHO and WWF, 1993), p. 1.

3. C. Shepherd and N. Magnus, *Nowhere to Hide: The Trade in Sumatran Tiger* (TRAFFIC Southeast Asia, 2004), p. 54; income figures based on World Bank calculations of gross national income.

4. Shepherd and Magnus, *Nowhere to Hide,* p. 12.

5. Shepherd and Magnus, *Nowhere to Hide,* p. 68.

6. J. Seidensticker, S. Christie, and P. Jackson, eds., *Riding the Tiger: Tiger Conservation in Human-Dominated Landscapes* (Cambridge, UK: Cambridge University Press, 1999), p. xvii.

7. Z. Shi, *The History of Chinese Medicine* (Taipei: Cheng Chung Book Co., Ltd., 1984).

8. D. Reid, *Chinese Herbal Medicine* (Brookline, MA: CFW Publications, 1993).

9. S. Lee, *Attitudes of Hong Kong Chinese towards Wildlife Conservation and the Use of Wildlife as Medicine and Food* (Hong Kong: TRAFFIC East Asia, 1995).

10. J. Mills, *Rhinoceros Horn and Tiger Bone: An Investigation of Trade since the 1993 Ban* (Cambridge, U.K.: TRAFFIC International, 1997), p. 49.

11. K. Baik, "New developments in the use of synthesized bear bile in medicine," in *Proceedings of the Third International Symposium on the Trade in Bear Parts* (Hong Kong: TRAFFIC East Asia, 2001).

12. H. H. C. Chu, and P. H. But, "Progress in the research of tiger bone substitutes," *Proceedings of the First International Symposium on Endangered Species Used in Traditional East Asian Medicine: Substitutes for Tiger Bone and Musk* (Hong Kong: TRAFFIC East Asia, 2001) [in Chinese].

13. P. H. But, L. V. C. Lung, and Y. Tam, "Profiles of Chinese medicines 4, rhinoceros horn," *Abstracts of Chinese Medicines* 2(1988):351–360.

14. R. Parry-Jones and J. Wu, *Musk Deer Farming as a Conservation Tool in China* (Hong Kong: TRAFFIC East Asia, 2001), pp. 7, 26–27.

Twine and the Ancient Mariners: Albatrosses, Sea Turtles, and Fishing Gear Encounters, by Carl Safina, Eric Gilman, and Wallace J. Nichols.

1. Food and Agriculture Organization of the United Nations, "A global assessment of fisheries bycatch and discards," Fisheries Technical Paper 339, http://www.fao.org/DOCREP/003/T4890E/T4890E00.htm.

2. R. Myers and B. Worm, "Rapid world-wide depletion of predatory fish communities." *Nature* 423(2003):280–283.

3. A. Bjordal and S. Løkkeborg, *Longlining* (Oxford, UK: Fishing News Books, 1996).

4. R. Lewison, S. Freeman, and L. Crowder, "Quantifying the effects of fisheries on threatened species: the impact of pelagic longlines on loggerhead and leatherback sea turtles," *Ecology Letters* 7(2004):221–231.

5. N. Brothers, J. Cooper, and S. Løkkeborg, *The Incidental Catch of Seabirds by Long-line Fisheries: Worldwide Review and Technical Guidelines for Mitigation,* FAO Fisheries Circular No. 937 (Rome: Food and Agriculture Organization of the United Nations, 1999).

6. Brothers et al., *Incidental Catch of Seabirds.*

7. K. Cousins and J. Cooper, eds., *The Population Biology of the Black-Footed Albatross in Relation to Mortality Caused by Longline Fishing* (Honolulu: US Western Pacific Regional Fishery Management Council, 2000).

8. R. Lewison and L. Crowder, "Estimating fishery bycatch and effects on a vulnerable seabird population," *Ecological Applications* 13(2003):743–753.

9. Committee of the Commission for the Conservation of Antarctic Marine Living Resources, "Incidental mortality arising from longline fishing," *Report of the Twenty-first Meeting of the Scientific Committee of the Commission for the Conservation of Antarctic Marine Living Resources* (Hobart, Australia, 2002), pp. 288–331.

10. J. Spotila et al., "Pacific Leatherback Turtles Face Extinction," *Nature* 405 (2000):529–530.

11. M. Sarti et al., "Decline of the world's largest nesting assemblage of leatherback turtles," *Marine Turtle Newsletter* 74(1996):2–5.

12. J. Frazier and J. Montero, "Incidental capture of marine turtles by the swordfish fishery at San Antonio, Chile," *Marine Turtle Newsletter* 49(1990):8–13.

13. S. Gardner and W. Nichols, "Assessment of sea turtle mortality rates in the Bahía Magdalena Region, B.C.S., Mexico," *Chelonian Conservation and Biology* 4(2001):197–199; W. Nichols, "Biology and Conservation of Sea Turtles in Baja California, Mexico" (Ph.D. diss., University of Arizona, Tucson, Wildlife & Fisheries Sciences, School of Renewable Natural Resources, 1999).

14. N. Kamezaki et al., "Loggerhead turtles nesting in Japan," in A. Bolten and B. Witherington, eds., *Loggerhead Sea Turtles* (Washington, DC: Smithsonian Institution Press, 2003), pp. 210–217.

15. Nichols, *Sea Turtles in Baja California;* W. Nichols and S. Peckham, unpublished data.

16. K. Murray, "Bycatch of sea turtles in the Mid-Atlantic sea scallop *(Placopecten magellanicus)* dredge fishery during 2003," US Department of Commerce Commercial Northeast Fisheries Science Center Reference Document 04-11(2004).

17. C. Oravetz, "Reducing incidental catch in fisheries," in K. Eckert et al., eds., *Research and Management Techniques for the Conservation of Sea Turtles,* IUCN/SSC Marine Turtle Specialist Group Publication No. 4, 1999, pp. 189–196.

18. B. Pandav and B. Choudhury, "An update on the mortality of the olive ridley sea turtles in Orissa, India," *Marine Turtle Newsletter* 83(1999):10–12.

19. E. Gilman, Review of the State of Knowledge for Reducing Marine Turtle and Seabird Bycatch in Longline Gear, *Proceedings of the Workshop to Plan a Joint Japan–Hawaii Sea Turtle and Seabird Experiment to Reduce Bycatch and Injury in Pelagic Longline Fisheries,* Japan Fisheries Research Agency (Honolulu: NOAA Fisheries, and Western Pacific Regional Fishery Management Council, 2004).

20. E. Gilman, C. Boggs, and N. Brothers, "Performance assessment of an underwater setting chute to mitigate seabird bycatch in the Hawaii pelagic longline tuna fishery," *Ocean and Coastal Management* 46(2003):985–1010.

21. Reviewed in E. Gilman and H. Freifeld, "Seabird mortality in North Pacific longline fisheries," *Endangered Species Update* 20(2003):35–46.

22. FAO, "Implementation of the NPOA-Seabirds," *Committee on Fisheries Progress*

Report from 24th Session on Implementation of the International Plan of Action for Reducing Incidental Catch of Seabirds in Longline Fisheries (Rome: Food and Agriculture Organization of the United Nations, Committee on Fisheries, 2003).

23. E. Melvin, J. Parrish, and L. Conquest, "Novel tools to reduce seabird bycatch in coastal gillnet fisheries," in E. Melvin, J. Parrish, eds., *Seabird Bycatch: Trends, Roadblocks and Solutions* (Fairbanks: University of Alaska Sea Grant, 2001), pp. 161–184.

24. E. Gilman, "Integrated management approach to address incidental mortality of seabirds in longline fisheries," *Aquatic Conservation: Marine and Freshwater Ecosystems* 11(2001):391–414.

25. C. Safina, "Launching a sea ethic, *Wild Earth* 12(2003):2–5.

Ebola, SARS, and Other Diseases That Imperil People and Animals, by Robert A. Cook and William B. Karesh

1. M. Smolinski, M. Hamburg, and J. Lederberg, eds., *Microbial Threats to Health: Emergence, Detection, and Response* (Washington, DC: National Academies Press, 2003).

2. M. Enserink, "Malaysian researchers trace nipah virus to bats," *Science* 289(2000):518–519.

3. T. Geisbert et al., "Evaluation in nonhuman primates of vaccines against Ebola virus," *Emerging Infectious Diseases* 8(2002):503–507.

4. J. Breman et al., "A search for Ebola virus in animals in the Democratic Republic of the Congo and Cameroon: ecologic, virologic, and serologic surveys, 1979–1980," *Journal of Infectious Diseases* 179(1999):S139–S147.

5. N. Jaax et al., "Transmission of Ebola virus (Zaire strain) to uninfected control monkeys in a biocontainment laboratory," *Lancet* 346(1995):1669–1671.

6. P. Walsh et al., "Catastrophic ape decline in western equatorial Africa," *Nature* 422(2003):611–614.

7. E. Leroy et al., "Multiple Ebola virus transmission events and rapid decline of Central African wildlife," *Science* 303(2004):387–390.

8. Asia Animals Foundation, "List of animals seen in the markets by AAF investigators," http://www.animalsasia.org/index.php?module=6&menupos=2&submenupos=5&lg=en.

9. J. Peiris and Y. Guan, "Confronting SARS: a view from Hong Kong," *Philosophical Transactions of the Royal Society of London Series B, Biological Sciences* 359(2004):1075–1079.

10. World Health Organization Communicable Disease Surveillance & Response, "Cumulative number of reported probabl cases of SARS," www.who.int/csr/sars/country/2003_07_11/_en/.

11. R. Walgate, "WHO says coronavirus causes SARS," *Scientist,* April 16, 2003, http://www.biomedcentral.com/news/20030416/04/.

12. Y. Guan et al., "Isolation and characterization of viruses related to the SARS coronavirus from animals in southern China," *Science* 302(2003):276–278.

13. R. Walgate, "Human SARS virus not identical to civet virus," *Scientist,* May 27, 2003, http://www.biomedcentral.com/news/20030527/03.

14. World Health Organization, *Consensus Document on the Epidemiology of Severe Acute Respiratory Syndrome (SARS)* (Geneva, Switzerland: WHO, 2003).

15. A. Wagener, "Endangered species: traded to death," *Earth Trends,* August 2001, http://earthtrends.wri.org/features/view_feature.cfm?theme=7&fid=25.

16. D. Roe et al., *Making a Killing or Making a Living?* Biodiversity and Livelihoods Issues No. 6 (Herts, UK: International Institute for Environment and Development and TRAFFIC, 2002).

17. United States Animal Health Association, "Report of the Committee on Public Health and Environmental Quality," *Proceedings of the Ninety-ninth Annual Meeting,* Reno, Nevada, 1995.

18. Y. Hutin et al., "Outbreak of human monkeypox, Democratic Republic of Congo, 1996–1997," *Emerging Infectious Diseases* 7(2001):434–438.

19. J. Guarner et al., "Monkeypox transmission and pathogenesis in prairie dogs," *Emerging Infectious Diseases* 10(2004):426–431.

20. World Health Organization, "Avian influenza fact sheet," January 15, 2002, http://www.who.int/csr/don/2004_01_15/en/.

21. R. Webster, "Influenza: an emerging disease," *Emerging Infectious Diseases* 4(1998):436–441.

22. Food and Agricultural Organization of the United Nations, "FAO/OIE cautious about declaring victory over avian flu in Asia," March 19, 2004, www.fao.org/newsroom/en/news/2004/38927/index.html.

23. Food and Agricultural Organization of the United Nations, "Avian flu: no need to kill wild birds," July 16, 2004, www.fao.org/newsroom/en/news/2004/48287/index.html.

24. Food and Agriculture Organization of the United Nations, *Manual on the Diagnosis of Nipah Virus Infection in Animals,* RAP publication 2002/01 (Bangkok: FAO, 2002).

25. M. Johara et al., "Nipah virus infection in bats (order Chiropter) in peninsular Malaysia," *Emerging Infectious Diseases* 7(2001):439–441.

26. World Health Organization, Nipah Virus Fact Sheet no. 262, 2001, www.who.int/mediacentre/factsheets/fs262/en/.

Hunting for Conservation in the Amazon Rain Forests: Lessons Learned from Peru, by Richard Bodmer

1. J. Robinson and E. Bennett, *Hunting for Sustainability in Tropical Forests* (New York: Columbia University Press, 2000).

2. R. Bodmer, E. Pezo Lozano, and T. Fang, "Economic analysis of wildlife use in the Peruvian Amazon," in K. Silvius, R. Bodmer and J. Fragoso, eds., *People in Nature: Wildlife Conservation in South and Central America* (New York: Columbia University Press, 2004), pp. 191–209.

3. M. Recharte and R. Bodmer, "Status of giant river otter in the Yavari Miri River, Peru," paper presented at the 6th International Conference on Wildlife Management in Amazonia and Latin America, Iquitos, Peru, 2004.

4. R. Bodmer et al., "Hunting and the likelihood of extinction of Amazonian mammals," *Conservation Biology* 11(1997):460–466.

5. Bodmer et al., "Hunting and the likelihood of extinction."

6. R. Bodmer, "Managing Amazonian wildlife: biological correlates of game choice by detribalized hunters," *Ecological Applications* 5(1995): 872–877.

7. P. Puertas and R. Bodmer, "Hunting effort as a tool for community-based wildlife management in Amazonia," in Silvius et al., *People in Nature,* pp. 123–135.

8. R. Bodmer and J. Robinson, "Evaluating the sustainability of hunting in the Neotropics," in Silvius et al., *People in Nature,* pp. 299–323.

9. R. Bodmer et al., "Linking conservation and local people through sustainable use of natural resources: community-based management in the Peruvian Amazon," in C.H. Freese, ed., *Harvesting Wild Species: Implications for Biodiversity Conservation* (Baltimore: John Hopkins University Press, 1997), pp. 315–358.

IV: Conservation Controversies

Let Them Eat Cake? Some Skeptical Thoughts on Conservation Strategies in the Bushmeat Range States, by David Brown

1. E. De Merode, K. Homewood, and G. Cowlishaw, *Wild Resources and the Livelihoods of Poor Households in the Democratic Republic of Congo,* ODI Wildlife Policy Briefing No. 1 (London: ODI, 2003).

Biting the Hand That Feeds You: The Consumption of Nature and Natural Resources in the Tropics, by John Robinson

1. D. Petersen, *Eating Apes* (Berkeley: University of California Press, 2003).

2. D. Brown, "Is the best the enemy of the good? Livelihoods perspectives on bushmeat harvesting and trade—some issues and challenges," paper submitted to the CIFOR-Bonn Conference on Rural Livelihoods, Forests and Biodiversity, May 2003.

3. J. Robinson and E. Bennett, "Carrying capacity limits to sustainable hunting in tropical forests," in J. Robinson and E. Bennett, eds., *Hunting for Sustainability in Tropical Forests* (New York: Columbia University Press, 2000).

4. J. Fa, D. Currie, and J. Meeuwig, "Bushmeat and food security in the Congo Basin: linkages between wildlife and people's future," *Environmental Conservation* 30(2003):71–78.

5. J. Robinson and K. Redford, "Jack of all trades, master of none: inherent contradictions in ICD approaches," in T. McShane and M. Wells, eds., *Getting Biodiversity Projects to Work: Towards More Effective Conservation and Development* (New York: Columbia University Press, 2004).

6. J. Robinson and E. Bennett, "Having your wildlife and eating it too: an analysis of hunting sustainability across tropical ecosystems," *Animal Conservation* 7(2004):1–12.

Point–Counterpoint: Response to John Robinson: Postindustrial Conservation Ideals and Real-World Politics, by David Brown

1. A. Balmford et al., "Conservation conflicts across Africa," *Nature* 291(2001):2616–2619.

2. J. Adams and T. MacShane, *The Myth of Wild Africa: Conservation without Illusion* (Berkeley: University of California Press, 1996).

Through the Looking Glass: The Tragedy of Depleting Wildlife Resources: A Response to John Robinson and David Brown, by Kathy MacKinnon

1. T. McShane and M. Wells, eds., *Getting Biodiversity Projects to Work: Towards More Effective Conservation and Development* (New York: Columbia University Press, 2004).

2. E. Bennett and J. Robinson, "Hunting of wildlife in tropical forests: implications for biodiversity and forest peoples," Environment Department papers No.76, Biodiversity Series, Impact Studies (Washington, DC: World Bank, 2000).

Let Them Eat LSD Bushmeat: Thoughts Arising from Brown vs. Robinson, by Ian Redmond

1. I. Redmond, "The ethics of eating ape," *BBC Wildlife* 13(1995):72–74.

V: Wildlife

Listening to the Birds, by Joseph Tobias, Leon Bennun, and Alison Stattersfield

1. BirdLife International (www.birdlife.org) is a partnership of independent, national NGOs working in over 100 countries to conserve wild birds, their habitats, and global biodiversity.

2. *State of the World's Birds 2004: Indicators for Our Changing World* (Cambridge, UK: BirdLife International, 2004).

3. Unless stated, all figures are from *State of the World's Birds,* except those on extinct and globally threatened birds, which are from *Threatened Birds of the World 2004,* CD-ROM (Cambridge, UK: BirdLife International, 2004).

4. T. Brooks, S. L. Pimm, and J. O. Oyugi, "Time lag between deforestation and bird extinction in tropical forest fragments," *Conservation Biology* 13(1999):1140–1150.

5. S. Butchart et al., "Measuring global trends in the status of biodiversity: Red List Indices for birds," *Public Library of Science, Biology,* 2(2004):383.

6. See http://www.birdlife.net/action/science/indicators/eu_briefing_bird_indicator.pdf.

7. M. Murphy, "Avian population trends within the evolving agricultural landscape of eastern and central United States," *Auk* 120(2003):20–34.

8. Wetlands International, *Waterbird Population Estimates* (Wageningen, Netherlands: Wetlands International, 2002).

9. Data from the British Antarctic Survey, United Kingdom.

10. D. Nel et al., "Foraging interactions of wandering albatrosses *Diomedea exulans* breeding on Marion Island with longline fisheries in the southern Indian Ocean," *Ibis* 44(2002):E141–154.

11. Anon., *Making a Killing or Making a Living? Wildlife Trade, Trade Controls and Rural Livelihoods,* Biodiversity and Livelihoods Issues No. 6 (London and Cambridge, UK: IIED and TRAFFIC, 2002).

12. A. James, K. Gaston, and A. Balmford, "Can we afford to conserve biodiversity?" *BioScience* 51(2001):43–52; A. James, M. Green, and J. R. Paine, *Global Review of Protected Area Budgets and Staff* (Cambridge, UK: World Conservation Monitoring Centre, 2003).

13. Important Bird Areas (IBAs) form a network of critical bird sites, identified according to standard criteria: IBAs sustain threatened species—those with restricted ranges or confined to a particular biome and/or those that congregate in large numbers.

14. A. Balmford et al., "Economic reasons for conserving wild nature," *Science* 297(2002):950–953.

15. In September 2002, world leaders agreed on a Plan of Implementation that states, "achievement by 2010 of a significant reduction in the current rate of loss of biodiversity will require the provision of new and additional financial and technical resources," among other actions.

Species in Focus: Saving Jaguars throughout Their Range: From Theory to Practice, by Alan Rabinowitz

1. N. Saunders, *People of the Jaguar: The Living Spirit of Ancient America* (London: Souvenir Press, 1989).

2. N. Smith, "Spotted cats and the Amazon skin trade," *Oryx* 13(1976):362–271.

3. A. Rabinowitz, *Jaguar: One Man's Struggle to Establish the World's First Jaguar Preserve* (Washington, DC: Island Press, 2000).

4. E. Sanderson et al., "Planning to save a species: the Jaguar as a model," *Conservation Biology* 16(2002):58–72.

5. R. Medellin et al., *El Jaguar en el nuevo milenio* (Mexico City: Fondo de Cultura Económica, 2002) [in Spanish].

6. A. Rabinowitz and B. Nottingham, "Ecology and behavior of the jaguar *(Panthera onca)* in Belize, Central America," *Journal of Zoology London* 210(1986):149–159.

7. G. Schaller and P. Crawshaw, "Movement patterns of jaguar," *Biotrópica* 12(1980):161–168.

8. S. Silver et al., "The use of camera traps for estimating jaguar *(Panthera onca)* abundance and density using capture/recapture analysis," *Oryx* 38(2004):148–154.

9. A. Rabinowitz, "Jaguar predation on domestic livestock in Belize," *Wildlife Society Bulletin* 14(1986):170–174.

10. R. Hoogesteijn, A. Hoogesteijn, and E. Mondolfi, "Jaguar predation and conservation: cattle mortality caused by felines on three ranches in the Venezuelan llanos," in N. Dunstone and M. L. Gorman, eds., *Mammals as Predators* (London: London Zoological Society, 1993).

11. G. Schaller, "Mammals and their biomass on a Brazilian ranch," *Arquivos de Zool., S. Paulo* 31(1983):1–36.

Climate Change and the Wild: Into the Great Unknown, by Glenn Scherer

1. Intergovernmental Panel on Climate Change, *IPCC Third Assessment Report—Climate Change 2001,* http://www.ipcc.ch/.

2. W. Stevens, *The Change in the Weather: People, Weather, and the Science of Climate* (New York: Random House, 1999), p. 287.

3. T. Root et al., "Fingerprints of global warming on wild animals and plants," *Nature* 421(2003):57–60.

4. C. Parmesan and G. Yohe, "A globally coherent fingerprint of climate change impacts across natural systems," *Nature* 421(2003):37–42.

5. C. Thomas et al., "Extinction risk from climate change," *Nature* 427(2004):107–109.

6. M. Edwards and A. Richardson, "Marine pelagic phenology and trophic mismatch," *Nature* 430(2004):881–884

7. A. Prasad and L. Iverson, *A Climate Atlas for 80 Forest Tree Species of the Eastern United States,* US Department of Agriculture, www.fs.fed.us/ne/delaware/atlas/.

8. C. O'Reilly et al., "Climate change decreases aquatic ecosystem productivity of Lake Tanganyika, Africa," *Nature* 424(2003):766–768.

9. C. Lewis and M. A. Coffroth, "The acquisition of exogenous algal symbionts by an octocoral after bleaching," *Science* 304(2004):1490–1492.

10. Root, "Fingerprints," pp. 57–60.

11. Parmesan, "A globally coherent fingerprint," pp. 37–42.

12. M. Visser and L. Holleman, "Warmer springs disrupt the synchrony of oak and winter moth phenology," *Biological Science 2001* 268(1464):289–94.

13. IPCC Assessment Report 2001.

14. National Oceanic and Atmospheric Administration, http://hurricanes.noaa.gov/.

15. D. Grossman, "Spring forward," *Scientific American* (Jan. 2004) 85–91.

16. D. Harvell et al., "Climate warming and disease risks for terrestrial and marine biota," *Science* 296(2002):2158–2162.

17. R. Gelbspan, *Boiling Point* (New York: Basic Books, 2004), p. 173.

18. W. Laurance et al., "Pervasive alteration of tree communities in undisturbed Amazonian Forests," *Nature* 428(2004):171–175.

19. L. Ziska, "Evaluation of the growth response of six invasive species to past, present and future atmospheric carbon dioxide," *Journal of Experimental Botany* 54(2003):381, 395–404.

20. I. Loladze, "Rising atmospheric CO_2 and human nutrition: toward globally imbalanced plant stoichiometry?" *Trends in Ecology & Evolution* 17(2002):457–461.

21. P. Stiling et al., "Decreased leaf-miner abundance in elevated CO_2: reduced leaf quality and increased parasitoid attack," *Ecological Applications* 9(1999):240–244.

22. C. Sabine and R. Feely, "The Fate of Industrial Carbon Dioxide," *Science* 305(2004):352–353.

23. H. Neufeld et al., "Ozone in Great Smoky Mountains National Park: dynamics and effects on plants," *Tropospheric Ozone and the Environment II* (Pittsburgh, PA: Air & Waste Management Association, 1992), pp. 594–617.

The Gathering Wave of Ocean Extinctions, by Ellen K. Pikitch

1. R. Myers and B. Worm, "Rapid worldwide depletion of predatory fish communities," *Nature* 423(2003):280–283.

2. N. Dulvy, Y. Sadovy, and J. Reynolds, "Extinction vulnerability in marine populations," *Fish and Fisheries* 4(2003):25–64.

3. Of the 21 worldwide marine population extinctions reported by Dulvy et al., three were fishes, whose range was limited geographically and were specialized in their ecological habits; none were attributed to fishing.

4. S. Garcia and C. Newton, "Current situation, trends, and prospects in world capture fisheries," in Pikitch et al., eds., *Global Trends: Fisheries Management,* American Fisheries Society Symposium 20 (Bethesda, MD: American Fisheries Society, 1997), p. 328.

5. L. Morgan and R. Cheungpadee, *Shifting Gears: Addressing the Collateral Impacts of Fishing Methods in U.S. Waters* (Washington, DC: Island Press, 2003).

6. L. Watling and E. Norse, "Disturbance of the seabed by mobile fishing gear: a comparison to forest clearcutting," *Conservation Biology* 12(1998):1180–1197.

7. P. Dayton et al., "Environmental effects of marine fishing," *Aquatic Conservation: Marine and Freshwater Ecosystems* 5(1995):205–232.

8. J. Hutchings, "Conservation biology of marine fishes: perceptions and caveats regarding assignment of extinction risk," *Canadian Journal of Fisheries and Aquatic Sciences* 58(2001):108–121.

9. Guinness book record: http://www.guinnessworldrecords.com/.

10. E. Pikitch et al., "Status, trends, and management of sturgeon and paddlefish nurseries," *Fish and Fisheries,* accepted 2005.

11. T. DeMeulenaer and C. Raymakers, *Sturgeons of the Caspian Sea and Investigation of the International Trade in Caviar* (Cambridge, UK: TRAFFIC International, 1996).

12. A. Vaisman and C. Raymakers, "Legal status of sturgeon fisheries in the Russian Federation," *TRAFFIC Bulletin* 19(2001):33–44.

13. R. Stone, "Caspian ecology teeters on the brink," *Science* 295(2002):430–433.

14. Y. Sadovy and W. Cheung, "Near extinction of a highly fecund fish: the one that nearly got away," *Fish and Fisheries* 4(2003):86–99.

15. K. Brander, "Disappearance of common skate *Raja batis* from Irish Sea," *Nature* 290(1981):48–49.

16. J. Baum and R. Myers, "Shifting baselines and the decline of pelagic sharks in the Gulf of Mexico," *Ecology Letters* 7(2004):135–145.

17. R. Cavanagh et al., eds., *The Conservation Status of Australian Chondrichthyans: Report of the IUCN Shark Specialist Group Australia and Oceania Regional Red List Workshop* (Brisbane: The University of Queensland, School of Biomedical Sciences, 2003).

VI: Wildlands and Oceans

Marine Protected Areas: Can We Rebuild Marine Ecosystems by Closing Areas to Fishing? by Callum M. Roberts

1. C. Roberts et al., "Effects of marine reserves on adjacent fisheries," *Science* 294(2001):1920–1923.

2. F. Gell, C. Roberts, P. Hubert, and A. J. Clarke, unpublished data.

3. J. Esquemeling, *The Buccaneers of America* (New York: Dover Publications Inc., 1967). Originally published in 1678.

4. J. Bohnsack and A. Ault, *Reef Fish Community Dynamics and Linkages with Florida Bay,* Annual Progress Report for South Florida Ecosystem Restoration Program, NOAA/NMFS/SEFSC Protected Resources Division, PRD/01/02-06, 2002.

5. T. Willis, R. Millar, and R. Babcock, "Protection of exploited fish in temperate regions: high density and biomass of snapper *Pagrus auratus* (Sparidae) in northern New Zealand marine reserves," *Journal of Applied Ecology* 40, (2)(2005):212–227.

6. P. Cowley et al., "The role of the Tsitsikamma National Park in the management of four shore-angling fish along the south-eastern cape coast of South Africa," *South African Journal of Marine Science* 24(2002):27–36.

7. F. Gell and C. Roberts, "Benefits beyond boundaries: the fishery effects of marine reserves," *Trends in Ecology and Evolution* 18(2003):148–155; B. Halpern, "The impact of marine reserves: do reserves work and does size matter?" *Ecological Applications* 13(2003):117–137; G. Russ, *Coral Reef Fishes: Dynamics and Diversity in a Complex Ecosystem* (San Diego: Academic Press, 2002), pp. 421–443.

8. Data from the International Council for the Exploration of the Sea, www.ices.dk.

9. National Research Council, *Marine Protected Areas: Tools for Sustaining Ocean Ecosystems* (Washington, DC: National Academies Press, 2002); F. Gell and C. Roberts, "Benefits beyond boundaries," pp. 148–155.

10. A. Balmford et al., "The worldwide costs of marine protected areas," *Proceedings of the National Academy of Sciences* 101(2004):9694–9697.

VIII: The Art and Practice of Conservation

Conservation and Conflict: The Importance of Continuing Conservation Work during Political Upheaval and Armed Conflict, by Peter Zahler

1. Although there is no universal definition of "armed conflict," there were between 21 and 36 major conflicts affecting up to 50 countries in 2003 and the first half of 2004: http://www.infoplease.com/ipa/A0904550.html.

2. For example, see J. Austin and C. Bruch, eds., *The Environmental Consequences of War: Legal, Economic, and Scientific Perspectives* (Cambridge, UK: Cambridge University Press, 2000).

3. J. McNeely, "Conserving forest biodiversity in times of violent conflict," *Oryx* 37(2003):142–152; UNEP, *Afghanistan: Post-Conflict Environmental Assessment* (Geneva:

United Nations Environment Programme, 2002). UNEP estimated the number of land mines in Afghanistan alone at over 10 million, or about six per square mile (15.5/km^2).

4. D. Huynh, "The impact of chemical war on biodiversity in Vietnam," in E. Blom et al., eds., *Nature in War: Biodiversity Conservation during Conflicts* (Amsterdam: Netherlands Commission for International Nature Protection, 2000).

5. C. H. Koerbel, "Environment: a challenge for peace," in Blom et al., eds., *Nature in War: Biodiversity Conservation during Conflicts* (Amsterdam: Netherlands Commission for International Nature Protection, 2000).

6. For example, see R. Harbinson, "Burma's forests fall victim to war," *Ecologist* 22(1992):72–73.

7. UNHCR, *Refugee Operations and Environmental Management: Selected Lessons Learned* (Geneva: The Environmental Unit, UNHCR, 1998).

8. D. Malakoff, "Rebels seize research team in Colombia," *Science* 304(2004):1223; S. Kanyamibwa and O. Chantereau, "Building regional linkages and supporting stakeholders in areas affected by conflicts: experiences from the Albertine Rift region," in Blom et al., eds., *Nature in War*.

9. P. Martin and C. Szuter, "War zones and game sinks in Lewis and Clark's West," *Conservation Biology* 13(2002):36–45; and McNeely, "Conserving forest biodiversity"; see J. Dudley et al., "Effects of war and civil strife on wildlife and wildlife habitats," *Conservation Biology* 16(2002):319–329 for a rebuttal.

10. A. Plumptre, M. Masozera, and A. Vedder, *The Impact of Civil War on the Conservation of Protected Areas in Rwanda* (Washington, DC: Biodiversity Support Program, 2001).

11. J. Shambaugh, J. Oglethorpe, and R. Ham, *The Trampled Grass: Mitigating the Impacts of Armed Conflict on the Environment* (Washington, DC: Biodiversity Support Program, 2001).

12. M. Alvarez, "Illicit crops and bird conservation priorities in Colombia," *Conservation Biology* 16(2002):1086–1096; D. Armenteras et al., "Andean forest fragmentation and the representativeness of protected natural areas in the eastern Andes, Colombia," *Biological Conservation*, 113(2003):245–256.

13. S. Candotti, "The evolving role of an international conservation organization in times of war: WWF in the Democratic Republic of Congo," in Blom et al., eds., *Nature in War*.

14. Potential actors include the United Nations (UNDP, UNEP, UNHCR, OCHA, UNICEF, WFP, and others), IMF, World Bank, Asian Development Bank, European Union, and donor states.

Neither War nor Peace: Protected Areas Still at Risk in DR Congo, 2005, by John Hart

1. J. and T. Hart, "Rules of engagement for conservation: lessons from the Democratic Republic of Congo," *Conservation in Practice* 4(2003):14–22.

2. R. Mwinyihali, T. Hart, and H. P. Eloma, "Why armed conflict persists in the Kivu region of the Congo," *European Tropical Forest Research Network* 43/44, http://www.etfrn.org/etfrn/newsletter/news4344/nl43_oip_2_5.htm.

The Destruction of Iraq's Wetlands and Impacts on Biodiversity, by David Jensen, Hassan Partow, and Chizuru Aoki

1. http://www.grid.unep.ch/activities/sustainable/tigris/mesopotamia.pdf.

2. http://postconflict.unep.ch/iraq_new.htm.

3. Ministry of Environment report presented at United Nations Environment Programme (UNEP) Training Programme on Water Quality Management, Shiga, Japan, December 6, 2004.

4. UNEP, "Project Document for Support for Environmental Management of the Iraqi Marshlands," submitted to UN Iraq Trust Fund, 2004, http://marshlands.unep.or.jp/.

Captive Breeding: Miracle Under Fire, by Dan Wharton

1. J. Lankard, ed., *AZA Annual Report on Conservation and Science 2002–2003,* Conservation Programs Reports, vol. 1 (Silver Spring, MD: American Zoo and Aquarium Association, 2004).

2. G. Meffe, "Crisis in a crisis discipline," *Conservation Biology* 15(2001):303.

3. F. Pitelka, "The condor case: an uphill struggle in a downhill crush," *Auk* 98(1981):634–635.

4. D. Wilcove and R. May, "The fate of the California condor," *Nature* 319(1986):16l.

5. C. Kuehler and P. Witman, "Artificial incubation of the California condor *Gymnogyps californianus* eggs removed the wild," *Zoo Biology* 7(1988):123–132.

6. R. May, "The cautionary tale of the black-footed ferret," *Nature* 320(1989):13–14.

7. Conservation Breeding Specialist Group, *Black-Footed Ferret Population Management Planning Workshop Final Report* (Apple Valley, MN: IUCN/SSC CBSG, 2004), pp. 58–68.

8. IUCN, *IUCN Policy Statement on Captive Breeding* (Gland, Switzerland: IUCN, Species Survival Commission, Captive Breeding Specialist Group, 1987).

9. W. Newmark, "A land-bridge island perspective on mammalian extinctions in western North American parks," *Nature* 325(1987):430–432.

10. R. Frankham et al., "Selection in captive populations," *Zoo Biology* 5(1986):127–138.

11. B. Dresser, "Cryobiology, embryo transfer and artificial insemination in ex situ animal conservation programs," in E. O. Wilson, ed., *Biodiversity* (Washington, DC: National Academy Press, 1988), pp. 296–308.

12. D. Wildt et al., "Genome resource banks: living collections for biodiversity conservation," *Bioscience* 47(1997):689–698.

13. J. Terborgh and B. Winter, "Some causes of extinction," in M. Soule, M. Wilcox, and B. Wilcox, eds., *Conservation Biology* (Sunderland, MA: Sinauer Associates, Inc., 1980), pp. 119–133.

14. M. Soule et al., "The Millennium Ark: how long a voyage, how many staterooms, how many passengers?" *Zoo Biology* 5(1986):101–113.

15. K. Ralls and J. Ballou, "Captive breeding programs for populations with a small number of founders," *Trends in Ecology and Evolution* 1(1986):19–22.

16. B. Beck et al., "Reintroduction of captive born animals," in P. Olney, G. Mace, and A. Feistner, eds., *Creative Conservation: Interactive Management of Wild and Captive Animals* (London: Chapman and Hall, 1994), pp. 265–286.

17. R. A. Meyers et al., "Hatcheries and endangered salmon," *Science* 303(2004):1980.

18. W. Conway et al., eds., *The AZA Field Conservation Resource Guide* (Atlanta: Zoo Atlanta, 2001).

19. CBSG News, *Newsletter of the Conservation Breeding Specialist Group, SSC, IUCN* 15: (2)(2004):6–20.

Can Tropical Forests Be Managed for Timber Production and Wildlife Protection? by Francis E. Putz

1. F. E. Putz, "Are you a logging advocate or a conservationist?" in D. Zarin, F. E. Putz, J. Alavalapati, and M. Schmink, eds., *Working Forests in the Tropics* (New York: Columbia University Press, 2004).

2. M. Berlik et al., "The illusion of preservation: a global environmental argument for the local production of natural resources," *Journal of Biogeography* 29(2002):1557–1568.

3. F. E. Putz et al., "Biodiversity conservation in the context of tropical forest management," *Conservation Biology* 15(2001):7–20.

4. C. Mann, "1491," *Atlantic Monthly* 289(3)(2002):41–53.

5. G. Applegate, F. Putz, and L. Snook, *Who Pays for and Who Benefits from Improved Timber Harvesting Practices in the Tropics?* (Bogor, Indonesia: Center for International Forestry Research, 2004).

6. T. Holmes et al., "Financial and ecological indicators of reduced impact logging performance in the eastern Amazon," *Forest Ecology and Management* 163(2002):93–110.

7. J. G. Robinson and E. L. Bennett, eds., *Hunting for Sustainability in Tropical Forests* (New York: Columbia University Press, 2000).

8. R. Fimbel, R. A. Grajal, and J. Robinson, eds., *The Cutting Edge: Conserving Wildlife in Managed Tropical Forests* (New York: Columbia University Press, 2001).

9. R. Ravenel, I. M. E. Granoff, and C. Magee, eds., *Illegal Logging in the Tropics: Strategies for Cutting Crime* (New York: Haworth Press, 2004).

What Falls through the Cracks in Conservation Strategies?
Interviews with Sylvia Earle and Thomas Lovejoy, by Sharon Guynup

1. L. Glover and S. Earle, eds., *Defying Ocean's End: An Agenda for Action* (Washington, DC: Island Press, 2004).

Contributors

CHIZURU AOKI first joined the United Nations Environment Programme in 1993, where she is currently the Iraq project coordinator. She holds a Ph.D. from Massachusetts Institute of Technology, where she studied the effects of technological change for environmental improvement in developing countries.

RICK BASS is the author of 21 books of fiction and nonfiction, including his most recent novel, *The Diezmo*. He is a board member of the Yaak Valley Forest Council, the Montana Wilderness Association, Cabinet Resource Group, and Round River Conservation Studies.

ELIZABETH L. BENNETT is director of the Wildlife Conservation Society's Hunting and Wildlife Trade Program. She worked in Sarawak, Malaysia, for 18 years, where she helped plan Sarawak's protected area system and implement controls on hunting and wildlife trade. She has published widely and received many awards, including the Order of the Golden Ark from the Netherlands' Prince Bernhard in 1994.

LEON BENNUN is director of science and policy at the BirdLife International Secretariat. He worked for over a decade as head of the ornithology department at the National Museums of Kenya and as chairman of Nature Kenya. He holds a doctorate in zoology from Oxford University.

MICHAEL BERENS is currently pursuing a J.D. degree at the University of California, Davis, where he is an assistant editor at the *Journal of International Law and Policy*.

RICHARD BODMER has worked on Amazon rainforest conservation for 20 years, studying the relationships between human uses of natural ecosystems and sustainability. He works with the Durrell Institute of Conservation and Ecology at the University of Kent and heads the Wildlife Conservation Society's Peruvian Amazon projects.

DAVID BROWN is a research fellow and program coordinator at the Overseas Development Institute, specializing in tropical forest policy. He has worked on the bushmeat issue since the 1970s and coauthored the UK submission to CITES on bushmeat as a trade and wildlife management issue, which helped create the CITES Bushmeat Working Group. He also directs a MacArthur Foundation–funded research and dissemination project on wild meat, livelihoods security, and conservation in the tropics.

JESSE CHAPMAN-BRUSCHINI is senior editor of *State of the Wild* and has been with the Wildlife Conservation Society since 2001. She holds an M.A. in Spanish linguistics from the University of Illinois and has worked extensively in communications and public relations. She has served as a translator, interpreter, writer, and editor for environmental organizations since 1988.

JAMES COMPTON is the regional director for TRAFFIC Southeast Asia, based in Kuala Lumpur. He was trained as a teacher and journalist before he began researching wildlife trade in Vietnam in 1997, where he helped establish an office for TRAFFIC Southeast Asia in 1999.

WILLIAM CONWAY is a senior conservationist with the Wildlife Conservation Society and was previously the society's president and general director. He is the father of both the American Zoo Association's Species Survival Plan and the Accreditation and Field Conservation Program. Bill is the recipient of many honors and awards, including the IUCN Peter Scott Medal, the National Audubon Society Medal, the Order of the Golden Ark from the Netherlands' Prince Bernhard, and the Distinguished Achievement Award of the Society for Conservation Biology. He has published widely on the preservation of vanishing species.

ROBERT A. COOK is vice president and chief veterinarian of the Wildlife Health Sciences Division at the Wildlife Conservation Society and has spent more than 20 years in zoo and wildlife medicine. He chairs the Animal Health Committee at the American Zoo and Aquarium Association and the Captive Wildlife and Alternative Livestock Committee at the United States Animal Health Association.

GLYN DAVIES has over 25 years of experience as a research scientist, technical consultant, project leader, and policy adviser on forest, wildlife, and biodiversity issues. He has worked in Africa, Asia, Europe, and the United States and has a particular interest in integrating biological, social, and economic information to help direct forest management and conservation.

SYLVIA EARLE has led more than 60 expeditions worldwide and logged more than 7,000 hours underwater. She has received numerous awards and honors, including the 2003 Wings of Trust Award, the 1999 Ding Darling Conservation Medal, and the Order of the Golden Ark from the Netherlands' Prince Bernhard. Sylvia is currently the executive director of Conservation International's Global Marine Program, program director for the Harte Research Institute, and an Explorer-in-Residence at the National Geographic Society. She has authored more than 100 publications concerning marine science and technology.

ERIC GILMAN manages the Blue Ocean Institute's Fisheries Bycatch Program. He founded and manages the Ramsar Support Grant Program, which supports implementation of the Ramsar Convention on Wetlands. He has also served as an environmental adviser to the governor of the Northern Mariana Islands and the Pohnpei Port Authority of the Federated States of Micronesia.

SHARON GUYNUP is editor of *State of the Wild*. She has worked as a science and environmental writer for National Geographic News Service (run in collaboration with the New York Times Syndicate), *Audubon, Popular Science,* and other publications, and has edited for *Scientific American* and others. She is a Fulbright scholar and was awarded a New Jersey State Council on the Arts Fellowship, among other awards. She worked as a professional photographer for 20 years and has traveled extensively on assignment.

JOHN HART is a senior scientist at the Wildlife Conservation Society and has worked in the Democratic Republic of Congo since 1973. His fieldwork, along with that of his wife, Terese, was instrumental in the 1992 formation of the Okapi Wildlife Reserve and its declaration as a World Heritage Site in 1996. He has studied the economic and ecological impact of hunting by the Mbuti Pygmies and inventoried some of Congo's last remaining forest wilderness.

DAVID JENSEN has been with the United Nations Environment Programme (UNEP) Post-Conflict Assessment Unit since 2000 and has conducted post-conflict environmental assessments in Serbia-Montenegro, Macedonia, Albania, Liberia, and Iraq. Since 2002, he has been project coordinator for UNEP's activities in Afghanistan.

WILLIAM B. KARESH began caring for orphan wild animals at age seven. He now directs the Wildlife Conservation Society's International Field Veterinary Program and is chairman of the IUCN's Veterinary Specialist Group. During his career he has published over 100 scientific articles on wildlife health and conservation issues.

TED KERASOTE has been published in over 50 periodicals and a dozen anthologies, including *Audubon, National Geographic Traveler, The Best American Science,* and *Nature Writing 2001.* He has authored four books—*Navigations, Bloodties, Heart of Home,* and *Out There: In The Wild in a Wired Age*—and edited *Return of the Wild: The Future of Our Natural Lands.*

KEN KOSTEL was *State of the Wild's* associate editor and is currently senior science writer with the Earth Institute at Columbia University. He holds an M.A. in environmental science and an M.S. in journalism from Columbia University and is also a freelance writer specializing in science and the environment. His work has appeared in *Discover, Wildlife Conservation, OnEarth, The Scientist,* and *Audubon,* among others.

SAMUEL K. H. LEE joined the regional office of TRAFFIC East Asia in Hong Kong in 1996, focusing on the use of threatened species in traditional medicine. He does outreach work with traditional medicine practitioners and is a representative of Project Seahorse's Marine Medicinal Conservation Program in Hong Kong.

THOMAS LOVEJOY is president of the H. John Heinz III Center for Science Economics and the Environment. He has served as executive vice president of World Wildlife Fund–U.S., president of the American Institute of Biological Sciences, and president of the Society for Conservation Biology. A tropical and conservation biologist, he originated the concept of international debt-for-nature swaps and coined the term "biological diversity." His honors include the Order of Rio Branco, the Grand Cross of the Order of Scientific Merit, the Tyler Prize for Environmental Achievement, and the 2002 Lindbergh Award. He has authored or edited numerous articles and five books.

KATHY MACKINNON has more than 30 years' experience planning, implementing, and supervising biodiversity conservation and sustainable use projects around the globe. She has extensive field experience, especially in Asia, where she has worked on primate research, protected area planning, natural resource management, and national biodiversity strategies. She has authored several texts, including *Managing Protected Areas in the Tropics.* She is currently a biodiversity specialist at the Environment Department of the World Bank.

BILL MCKIBBEN is the author of nine books. His first, *The End of Nature,* was the first book about global warming for a general audience. A former staff writer for *The New Yorker,* his work appears in *Harpers, The Atlantic,* the *New York Review of Books,* and other national publications. A scholar-in-residence at Middlebury College, he is the recipient of Guggenheim and Lyndhurst fellowships and the Lannan Prize in Nonfiction Writing.

WALLACE J. NICHOLS is a scientist, educator, ocean activist, and author. He is the director of the Pacific Ocean region at the Blue Ocean Institute and a research associate at the California Academy of Sciences. In 1999 he cofounded and directed the WILDCOAST international conservation team to protect coastal, wildland and ocean resources by building alliances with fishermen and ranchers.

HASSAN PARTOW authored a report in 2001 that helped place the plight of Iraq's Mesopotamian marshlands in the public spotlight. He is an environment officer with the United Nations Environment Programme Post-Conflict Assessment Unit and previously worked with various environmental nongovernmental organizations and UN projects in East and Southern Africa, the Middle East, and Europe.

ELLEN K. PIKITCH is executive director of the Pew Institute for Ocean Science and a professor of marine biology at the University of Miami. She founded and directed the Wildlife Conservation Society's Marine Conservation and Ocean Strategy programs, is vice chair of the IUCN's Sturgeon Specialist Group, and is a member of the Environmental Sustainability Task Force. Ellen has authored and edited over 100 articles and books on fisheries science and management.

FRANCIS E. PUTZ is a conservation biologist and professor of botany at the University of Florida and the Prince Bernhard Professor of International Conservation at Utrecht University in the Netherlands. His research focuses on forests that are managed for timber, promote forest conservation, and use economic mechanisms that pay for good management.

ALAN RABINOWITZ is director of Science and Exploration at the Wildlife Conservation Society. His fieldwork helped create the world's first jaguar sanctuary in Belize, Taiwan's largest nature reserve, and five new protected areas in Myanmar—including the world's largest tiger reserve. He has published more than 50 scientific and popular articles and four books. Currently, he is working to establish and secure a contiguous wild jaguar corridor from Mexico to Argentina.

KENT H. REDFORD is director of the Wildlife Conservation Society Institute and vice president for conservation strategy at WCS, where he has worked for seven years. He previously worked at The Nature Conservancy and the University of Florida. His areas of interest include biodiversity conservation, sustainable use, the politics of conservation, and the mammals of South America.

IAN REDMOND is a tropical field biologist known for his work with apes and elephants. He is chief consultant with the Great Apes Survival Project (GRASP) of the United Nations Environment Programme / United Nations Educational, Scientific, and Cultural Organization. He has worked with the Born Free Foundation, the Dian Fossey Gorilla Fund, and the International Fund for Animal Welfare. Ian established and chairs the Ape Alliance, the African Ele-Fund, and the UK Rhino Group.

CALLUM M. ROBERTS is a professor of marine conservation at the University of York and a Pew Fellow in Marine Conservation. His research focuses on ways to protect marine ecosystems and species and the threats they face.

JOHN ROBINSON is senior vice president and director of International Conservation at the Wildlife Conservation Society, where he oversees more than 300 projects in 51 countries. In 1980, he established the Program for Studies in Tropical Conservation at the University of Florida, providing conservation training to students from tropical countries. In 2003, Prince Bernhard of the Netherlands awarded him the Order of the Golden Ark. He has published widely on wildlife management and sustainability in tropical forests.

CARL SAFINA is president of the Blue Ocean Institute, a nonprofit he cofounded in 2003, to inspire the formation of a "sea ethic." He is author of more than a hundred publications, including the books *Song for the Blue Ocean* and *Eye of the Albatross*. He is a recipient of the Pew Scholar's Award in Conservation and the Environment, a World Wildlife Fund Senior Fellowship, the Lannan Literary Award for nonfiction, the John Burroughs Writer's Medal, and a MacArthur Prize.

ERIC W. SANDERSON is the associate director of the Landscape Ecology and Geographic Analysis Program at the Wildlife Conservation Society. He received his Ph.D. in ecology from the University of California, Davis, in 1998. His research includes the application of landscape ecology and geospatial techniques to conservation.

GEORGE B. SCHALLER is vice president of the Science and Exploration Program and holds the Ella Millbank Foshay Chair in Wildlife Conservation at the Wildlife Conservation Society. Over the past 50 years in the wilds of Asia, Africa, and South America, he has studied and helped protect animals as diverse as mountain gorillas, giant pandas, lions, and the wild sheep of the Himalayas. He is the author of numerous scientific and popular writings and 15 books, including *The Year of the Gorilla, The Last Panda,* and *The Serengeti Lion,* which received the National Book Award. His other awards include the International Cosmos Prize and the Tyler Prize for Environmental Achievement.

GLENN SCHERER is a science writer whose work has appeared in magazines, books, and on websites for more than a decade. He has written on the environment for Salon.com, Grist.org, *E the Environmental Magazine,* and other national publications, and is the former editor of Blue Ridge Press.

ALISON STATTERSFIELD is head of science at BirdLife International's Secretariat Office in Cambridge. After receiving a degree in zoology with a postgraduate certificate in education from Cambridge University, she taught in schools and in The Broads, Britain's largest protected wetland. In 1986 she joined the International Council for Bird Preservation.

JOSEPH TOBIAS is a freelance writer and photographer who holds a doctorate in zoology from Cambridge University. He has worked for the Wildlife Conservation Society, IUCN, and BirdLife International.

BIJAL TRIVEDI is a freelance science writer. She was an editor for the National Geographic News Service, which she launched in collaboration with the New York Times Syndicate. Her work has appeared in *National Geographic, Science, Wired, Air&Space, The Economist, Popular Science,* and *New Scientist.* She holds an M.S. in biology from UCLA and an MA in science journalism from New York University.

BILL WEBER has worked for 30 years in international conservation. He lived in Africa for nine years, cofounded the Mountain Gorilla Project in Rwanda, and helped design forest protection initiatives across the Congo Basin. For the past decade, he has directed North America Programs for the Wildlife Conservation Society. Bill has authored dozens of articles, edited *African Rain Forest Ecology and Conservation,* and coauthored *In the Kingdom of Gorillas* with Amy Vedder.

DAN WHARTON is director of the Central Park Zoo in New York City and has worked for the Wildlife Conservation Society since 1979. As a Fulbright Scholar to Germany, he studied population genetics and management of German zoos and has worked in South America and East Africa. He is executive editor of *Zoo Biology* and is the chairman of American Zoo and Aquarium Association Species Survival Plans for the western lowland gorilla and the snow leopard.

PETER ZAHLER is the assistant director of the Asia Program for the Wildlife Conservation Society. He has over 20 years of experience in conservation biology, working primarily in Western and Central Asia and Latin America. In 2002, he coordinated and led the United Nations Environment Programme Post-Conflict Environmental Assessment of Afghanistan.

Index

4998